The Experience of Work

ORGANIZATIONAL AND OCCUPATIONAL PSYCHOLOGY

Series Editor: PETER WARR
MRC/SSRC Social and Applied Psychology Unit, Department of Psychology, The University, Sheffield, England

In preparation

The Experience of Work

A Compendium and Review of 249 Measures and their Use

JOHN D. COOK, SUSAN J. HEPWORTH,
TOBY D. WALL and PETER B. WARR

*MRC/SSRC Social and Applied Psychology Unit
University of Sheffield, England*

1981

ACADEMIC PRESS
A Subsidiary of Harcourt Brace Jovanovich, Publishers
LONDON   NEW YORK   TORONTO   SYDNEY   SAN FRANCISCO

ACADEMIC PRESS INC. (LONDON) LTD
24/28 Oval Road,
London NW1

United States Edition published by
ACADEMIC PRESS INC.
111 Fifth Avenue,
New York, New York 10003

British Library Cataloguing in Publication Data

The Experience of Work
 1. Work — Social aspects   2. Public opinion
 — Research
 I. Cook, J.D.
 305.3   HD6955   81-66680

ISBN 0-12-187050-2

Phototypeset by Oxford Publishing Services, Oxford
Printed by T. J. Press (Padstow) Ltd., Padstow

Preface

This book draws upon more than 4000 research reports to bring together and examine nearly two hundred and fifty scales for measuring work attitudes, values and perceptions. It is one outcome of a research project designed to identify, assess and develop measures of work experience relevant to the quality of working life. As such it attempts to be comprehensive in its coverage of scales both with respect to content and subsequent published use.

The research was made possible by a fruitful collaboration between the Medical Research Council and the Department of Employment. Both these institutions have a long and continuing interest in occupational well-being, its measurement and its enhancement. We are very grateful to them for institutional and financial support.

During the book's preparation we have spent substantial amounts of time examining and cross-checking many topical and important journals from the library of the Social and Applied Psychology Unit (since October 1980 a joint Unit of the Medical Research Council and the Social Science Research Council). The tolerance and support of our thus deprived colleagues is much appreciated. We are also grateful for heroic feats of typing and retyping by Elisabeth Chadwick, Jennifer Cox, Judith Hallam, Lynne Jarvis, June Staniland and Karen Thompson. The quality of their working life will undoubtedly be improved by the book's completion, and we hope that its publication will have a wider ranging impact of the same kind.

Finally, a comment on the respective roles of the authors. We have all been involved in every aspect of the work, but in practice differential emphases in contributions emerged. Thus John Cook and Sue Hepworth carried the bulk of the load of the literature searches to 1978 and set up the initial presentational format. Toby Wall and Peter Warr carried out the subsequent searches and had principal responsibility for presentation of material from all years in its final form.

Sheffield
June 1981

J.D.C., S.J.H, T.D.W., P.B.W.

Acknowledgements

We are grateful to the following for permission to reprint scale items. In the case of previously published scales, copyright is retained by the copyright holder from the date of initial publication.

Previously Published Scales

Academic Press, 4.5, 4.9, 4.12, 7.11, 9.7. Associated permission granted by M. London, 4.9; L.W. Porter, 4.5; H.P. Sims, 9.7; R.M. Steers, 7.11.

Academy of Management Journal, 8.3, 8.26, 8.27. Associated permission granted by H.P. Sims, 8.3, 8.26; R.M. Steers, 8.27.

Administrative Science Quarterly, 4.6, 8.7, 8.8, 8.15, 8.16.

American Psychological Association and J.R. Hackman, 8.1.

American Sociological Review, 4.1, 4.2, 4.3, 8.25. Associated permission granted by J. Hage, 4.1, 8.25; G.A. Miller, 4.2; M. Seeman, 4.3.

Bowling Green State University, 3.3, 7.1.

British Psychological Society and S. Fineman, 7.12.

R.V. Dawis and L.H. Lofquist, 2.4.

R. Hoppock, 2.1.

Institute for Social Research, 2.5, 6.8, 9.6, 9.10
Any material used from the copyrighted Survey of Organizations (2.5, 9.6, 9.10) may not be reproduced in any form without permission from Dr. D.G. Bowers, author.

Macmillan Publishing Company, 4.11.

McGraw-Hill Book Company, 9.4, 9.9.

Ohio State University, 2.3, 9.1, 9.3.

Prentice-Hall, 2.10, 5.3, 8.24.

Psychological Corporation, 7.13 (part).

Riverside Publishing Company, 7.9 (part).

F.J. Smith, 3.1.

Sociological Quarterly, 4.4

John Wiley and Sons, 5.1, 5.2.

Previously Unpublished Scales

B. Buchanan, 4.7

R.A. Bucholz, 7.2

R.D. Caplan, 8.17, 8.18, 8.19, 8.20

R. Dubin, 7.10

J.L. Franklin, 4.8

R.J. House, 5.4.

E.E. Lawler, 2.9, 3.8, 3.9, 3.10, 4.13, 6.2, 6.6, 8.6, 9.5, 9.11.

M. London, 9.8.

P. Spector, 4.14.

E.F. Stone, 8.4.

Contents

1 Introduction and Overview

Organizational learning can be accelerated by systematic examination of the current situation: first gather and organize information and then feed it back for members' consideration and action. In the same way the development of a profession or discipline can be assisted through the publication of comprehensive and structured accounts of the status quo. This book is an attempt to increase understanding and to improve research practice through a detailed review of one area of organizational and occupational psychology.

The area in question covers the measurement of occupational experiences. Many thousands of investigations have been carried out in this field but it is our belief that investigators have not in general learned from their endeavours as successfully as they might. Specifically, there has often been insufficient attention paid to issues of conceptualization and measurement, so that cumulative development of the area has been retarded. By presenting this account of the current position we hope to encourage examination of strengths and weaknesses and to provide a spur to more effective research and practice.

The book contains information about 249 measures of work attitudes, values and perceptions employed in all articles in 15 principal international journals from 1974 to mid-1980. For each measure all published uses in these journals are cited, and principal scale characteristics are described. The measures' original dates range from 1935 to 1980, with sources in books, journals and unpublished reports. Popular instruments are of course included, with detailed information about their applications, but so too are less well known measures which might otherwise escape notice.

We have aimed to meet the needs of three principal types of reader. First, we have supplied a comprehensive account of the current situation and a review of many substantive research findings. Readers seeking an overview of the field, an understanding of current biases and preoccupations, or a summary of empirical relationships should therefore find much which is of value. For example, the material contained in the book and its overall structure are likely to be useful at several levels to teachers of industrial and organizational psychology, organizational behaviour, management science, industrial relations and several other subjects. However, in presenting this report we are also writing for future as well as contemporary readers, and have kept in mind the need for a historical record against which the position in 1990 or 2000 may be compared.

Second, we have provided a source for researchers and practitioners who wish to locate a specific measure appropriate to their needs. Such users may range from undergraduate and graduate students initiating course projects to senior researchers, practitioners and all those with a suitable background in applied behavioural science, who wish to deploy tools to study well-being and effectiveness at work, to investigate the impact of paid employment, or to evaluate a change programme in an occupational setting. From the evidence set out here it is possible to make an initial judgement on the existence and appropriateness of alternative instruments. Having thus narrowed the field, further detail may be obtained by following up references to the source publication and subsequent uses which are given for each scale.

Our third target group (naturally overlapping with the others) contains readers who wish to interpret published data more fully than is often possible from a journal article. Because of space limitations authors frequently provide but scant detail of their instruments, merely referring to a scale's title or citing one or two illustrative items. Yet proper interpretation of findings in this area requires relatively detailed knowledge of item content. A construct's label (Alienation, Commitment, Job-related Tension, or Routinization, for example) often describes only loosely the feature which is measured through items in a scale with that label. Without an appreciation of the nature of a scale's items and their conceptual and statistical properties, readers of research reports may often be misled.

Several scales with the same title may in practice vary substantially at the operational level. Conversely, measures intended to tap different constructs and having different titles are sometimes very similar to each other in terms of item content. (Satisfaction with the Supervisor and Leader's Consideration come to mind here, as do several measures of perceived Job Characteristics and Organizational Climate.) However, researchers and journal editors have become excessively concerned with the structure of empirical data (their interrelationships and patterns) to the detriment of observed content: structure has driven out content in much psychological research. Those who seek structural knowledge which is informed by a sound understanding of content are our third target group.

Criteria for Scale Inclusion

The 249 entries which follow are of two principal kinds, with 100 and 149 instances respectively. In the case of "major entries", we have provided an account of construct definition, scale development, item content, scoring procedures, and, subject to copyright permission where required, we have also presented the items in full. Illustrative means, standard deviations, reliability coefficients and validity findings are cited, and all applications in the 15 specified journals during our search period are recorded. For "minor entries" we have provided an outline description of a scale and summary details of research applications.

In both cases three main criteria have guided the choice of scales for inclusion. These concern content, response mode, and length.

1 *Content*. Scales were included if they operationalize a construct reflecting individuals' experience of paid employment. Within this general domain we have separated three main types of measure. First are scales of affective response to one's work content and setting. Measures of this kind are described in Chapters 2 to 5 and cover such constructs as Overall Job Satisfaction, Specific Satisfactions, Alienation, Commitment, Job-related Tension and Psychological Symptoms of Stress. The second group of measures tap those work-related beliefs, values and needs which may affect or reflect the quality of individuals' experience of work. Examples (in Chapters 6 and 7) are Work Motivation and Involvement, the Protestant Work Ethic, Higher Order Need Strength and Need for Achievement. The final group comprises scales designed to quantify individuals' perceptions of their work experience (see Chapters 8 and 9). These are essentially descriptive measures, in contrast with affective reactions in the first group and enduring dispositions in the second set. Included in this third category are measures of perceived Job Characteristics, Role Ambiguity and Conflict, Responsibility, Participation, Organizational Climate, Leadership Practices and Work Group Properties.

Consideration of measures which have been excluded serves further to identify the content of our domain. We have omitted instruments which, although applicable to employees or self-employed workers, are not in themselves focussed on work. Measures of social attitudes or political beliefs, personality inventories, and intelligence, aptitude and attainment tests are in this category. Also excluded are general vocational interest measures, scales for training assessment or for identifying training needs, and ratings of skill and performance. We have also omitted scales capable of application only to extremely restricted samples of employees.

2 *Response mode*. We have included within our review only those scales which are appropriate for self-completion or interview administration and which have specified response alternatives each carrying a numerical weight. This criterion leads to the exclusion of observational measures, behavioural rating scales, and open-ended questions.

3 *Scale length*. To be included as a scale, a measure has to comprise a minimum of three relatively homogeneous items. These must represent different indices of the focal construct and be used in combination as a measure of that construct. Thus excluded from consideration are all single and two-item measures, and all longer instruments whose items are not combined to produce one or more scores based on three or more items. Exceptions to this are a very limited number of two-item indices which appear within the compendium as part of longer instruments, within which the majority of component scales contain three or more items.

These three criteria were applied to all the articles published in the following 15 journals in the six-and-a-half years between the beginning of 1974 and the middle of 1980: *Academy of Management Journal, Administrative Science Quarterly, British Journal of Industrial Relations, Human Relations, Industrial Relations, International Review of Applied Psychology, Journal of Applied Psychology, Journal of Applied Social Psychology, Journal of Management Studies, Journal of Occupational Behaviour, Journal of Occupational Psychology, Journal of Vocational Behavior, Organizational Behavior and Human Performance, Personnel Psychology*, and *Personnel Review*.

Approximately 4000 articles were studied in this way, and in addition we have traced and summarized source publications for measures used during our search period but initially presented before 1974. For example, Hoppock's measure of Overall Job Satisfaction (entry 2.1) was published in 1935, and the Minnesota Satisfaction Questionnaire (entry 2.4) appeared in 1967; material from these source publications is included as central to our account of the development and characteristics of those scales. However, intervening reports have not been searched, so that, for example, uses of the Minnesota Satisfaction Questionnaire between 1968 and 1973 are not covered, although they can easily be traced through the references we provide. Applications of a measure during 1974 to 1980 but outside the 15 journals are not routinely described, although we have in practice included a number of these.

We are confident that our sample of journals comes close to containing all relevant scales used during the period described, and that the chapters which follow contain all but very few of the scales which meet the three criteria set out above. However, a number of measures were excluded because of their extremely sketchy presentation. A small number of authors have limited their account to expressions like "a measure of X was administered" or "a three-item composite was used as an index of X". We have not thought it appropriate to include these ephemeral creations.

The Major Entries

The 100 major entries are set out in a broadly standard manner. In each case we cover the following features.

1 *Description and background.* Each entry opens with the scale title and source reference. This is followed by a description covering the construct(s) the scale is designed to measure, developmental, theoretical and other background information, and characteristics of the scale itself, in terms of sub-scales, number of items, response format and scoring.

2 *Descriptive statistics.* Next are presented available means and standard deviations, first from the source publication and then from subsequent applications. In the vast majority of cases, norms in the full sense of descriptive statistics based on probability samples from specified populations are not available. Nor are breakdowns of scale scores according to percentiles or deciles. The information provided is therefore necessarily restricted to means and standard deviations reported in particular studies, and is thus based on what Quinn and Gonzales (1979) describe as "samples of convenience". Wherever possible we identify the characteristics of the particular samples according to job level, sex and other relevant properties detailed by authors. Unless otherwise stated, respondents are from the United States.

3 *Scale reliability.* Major entries also contain information about the reliability of scores obtained with an instrument, and since the reliability measure used is identified only briefly in each case we should here introduce the principal features and indices. Fuller accounts and detailed references are provided by Anastasi (1976), Campbell (1976), Guilford (1954), Guilford and Fruchter (1973), Lord and Novick (1968), Nunnally (1967), Zeller and Carmines (1980) and others.

Statements about reliability are statements about the repeatability of measurement results, assessed through types of self-correlation where scores from a measure are correlated with other scores from the same measure. This is sometimes a question of *test–retest reliability*, or stability across time, where values from the same respondents on two separate occasions are examined. For scales designed to quantify relatively permanent characteristics, where no relevant changes have intervened, similarity between repeated measurements is of course desirable. A product–moment correlation coefficient is usually calculated as an index of this form of reliability.

However, self-correlation may also be assessed in terms of *internal consistency reliability*: on a single measurement occasion how strongly associated are scores from different parts of the same measure? Several techniques have been developed to quantify the homogeneity of scale items in this sense, all yielding values between 0 and 1. The earliest assessments were in terms of "split-half" reliability, where scores from two halves of the test were examined for intercorrelation. This procedure yields a value which strictly speaking reflects the reliability of only half the full scale, and a correction factor is typically introduced to estimate from a split-half value the reliability of the full measure. The correction factor is based upon the Spearman-Brown formula, which is a general proposition for estimating the reliability of a test of any length extrapolated from the one for which a self-correlation is known. The Spearman-Brown formula is also widely applied to other types of self-correlation, for example the median inter-item correlation, and in the entries which follow we will refer to all these applications as instances of Spearman-Brown internal reliability.

Other coefficients are based upon Kuder-Richardson formulae, of which formulae 20 and 21 are notable for their applicability to dichotomously scored items. A general estimate of reliability which incorporates information about covariance between all the items in a measure is coefficient alpha (Cronbach, 1951; Novick and Lewis, 1967). Other less common estimates of internal reliability include the Kuder-Richardson formula 8 and the Hoyt coefficient.

It should be noted that internal reliability is a feature of a set of measurements rather than of a scale itself. For this reason it is necessary to accumulate reliability data from a range of samples, although it naturally becomes convenient after numerous illustrations of acceptable reliability to assume that the measure itself has this property to a satisfactory degree. Note also that internal reliability is influenced by the variance of item scores (high variance encouraging high reliability), so that very skewed item responses yield lower coefficients of reliability; and that scale length is also important, in that given similar inter-item correlations longer scales will yield higher reliability estimates than shorter ones. Care must therefore be taken in comparing reliability coefficients across scales of widely differing lengths.

4 *Scale validity*. Major entries also contain selected evidence of validity. This concept is sometimes defined in terms of the extent to which a scale operationalizes the construct it is intended to represent, but in practice direct assessments are often not practicable with self-report measures. Several estimates are however possible, usually described in terms of face validity, content validity, criterion validity, and construct validity.

Face validity reflects the degree to which an instrument appears on inspection to resemble the intended construct and is thus deemed acceptable by respondents and users. *Content validity* is a question of how far scale items adequately represent the universe of elements of the focal construct. In both cases conclusions about validity are based upon subjective interpretation, perhaps in the light of expert judgments on item appropriateness or evaluations of homogeneity in terms of internal consistency coefficients or factor analytic data. *Criterion validity* refers to the relationship between scale scores and an independent and relatively objective measure of the focal construct; for example, a scale to assess Intention to Leave might be validated in terms of actual turnover data. Where the independent criterion is measured before, at the same time, or after the scale itself is administered, the index is said to be one of postdictive, concurrent and predictive criterion validity respectively.

Construct validity is particularly important where the construct operationalized by a scale has no corresponding simple or single external referent against which the measure may be evaluated. This is of course typical of most measures in this book. The determination of construct validity is a combination of logical and empirical processes. From a conceptual specification of the focal construct, one draws out likely relationships with other variables, and then examines evidence to determine the extent to which these are in fact observed. The presence or absence of group differences, intercorrelations between variables, a known factor structure, and changes in scores with respect to known manipulations are all important sources of information relevant to construct validity, as is evidence bearing on content and criterion validity. Where, across a range of circumstances, the measure behaves as predicted, then its construct validity is enhanced. If, however, it fails to be associated with expected correlates, is indistinguishable from proven measures of different constructs, or in other ways does not run true to form, its construct validity is brought into question.

Discussions of validity are sometimes aided by reference to "convergent" and "discriminant" validity, a categorization which cuts across the conventional framework we have described. Convergent validity is a question of how far a measure yields empirical similarities with other comparable measures; thus two scales of Overall Job Satisfaction are expected to be intercorrelated, and observed close associations between them are evidence of convergent validity. Conversely, low correlations between measures whose constructs are conceptually distinct provide evidence of discriminant validity. Discussions of both of these will be found throughout the book.

5 *Scale usage.* Each major entry also contains reference to every application of a scale which we have identified. In many cases these applica-

tions are referenced in the course of a description of relevant findings, but additional published uses from which we have not summarized results are listed towards the end of each entry.

6 *Scale items and response format.* Each major entry ends by specifying scale items and response format(s). Reverse-scored items are denoted by (R) which appears immediately after the item. In a few instances, where copyright regulations apply and permission to reproduce the items was not forthcoming, several illustrative items are instead presented.

In general, the absence in major entries of information as specified under 1 to 6 above signifies that none was located in our searches. Thus, for example, an absence of mean values indicates that we have failed to locate any within the publications cited, except perhaps some based upon very small or idiosyncratic samples. To avoid constant repetition throughout the entries, we have refrained from explicitly noting such omissions.

Both major and minor entries are identified numerically in terms of a chapter number and the scale's sequential location within that chapter (2.1, 2.2, 2.3, etc.). The text contains many cross-references, and these are also given in numerical terms, usually with an indication of authorship.

The State of the Art

It is clear that the area covered by this book is a lively and developing one. Theoretical and practical advances have been substantial, and will continue to be so. However, there is undoubtedly room for improvement, at both a conceptual and an empirical level.

There is a clear need for more careful and subtle conceptual analysis. Occupational experience is in content and structure as difficult to characterize as are other forms of everyday experience, and organizational and occupational psychologists have made as much progress as their colleagues in other areas. However, they have often been reluctant to attempt enquiries into the meaning and boundaries of their concepts. Traditional constructs of Overall and Specific Job Satisfactions are fairly well mapped out, but the essence of, for example, Alienation, Job Involvement or Role Overload is much more problematic than many researchers admit.

Problems of conceptual opaqueness and overlap are increased by empirical research indicating moderate correlations between work experience variables of many different kinds. In part this is due to consistency of response style in terms of evaluative tone, a "halo effect" in the perception of jobs. Employees tend to respond partly in terms of whether a job or job feature is personally attractive, irrespective of the conceptual category into which it happens that an investigator has chosen to place his question. In effect, the principal conceptual issue is one of discriminant validity: concepts need to be more carefully defined so that their differences are made clear, and measures need to be constructed to reflect empirically these separated constructs.

Contemporary conventions of empirical research and publication also warrant comment. It is clear from the entries in this compendium that very few scales are supported by the range and amount of evidence which measurement theory would indicate as desirable. This is not to say that the scales are inadequate for the purpose to which they have been put, but in general their adequacy has not been properly demonstrated.

A major contributory factor to this state of affairs lies in publication policy and practice. With professional interest focussed upon substantive findings and being under pressure to keep journal articles as brief as possible, an author tends to devote only a minimum of space to an account of the instruments used. Typically this account is restricted to an assertion of face and content validity, usually without presentation of more than a few items, and some evidence that the measure shows internal consistency. Satisfactory levels of the latter property are often introduced from an earlier study or are obtained by selecting items from a larger pool, so that replication or cross-standardization across samples remains unattempted. Other researchers seeking to measure the same variable either adopt or adapt this scantily supported scale or develop one of their own, and so the process continues with only incidental attention being paid to the properties of the instrument itself. These problems may be illustrated in terms of the following five deficiencies, which have some overlap with the issues identified by Dunnette (1966) and Flanagan and Robinson (1978).

Scale characteristics. Authors are often notably reticent about the characteristics of their measure. Items are rarely cited in full, and response dimensions and verbal labels are usually inadequately described. This is despite the fact that the meaning of an individual or average scale score cannot be determined without a clear specification of the response continuum. Information about numerical response weights is of course also required, but is not always included. These points gain additional force from researchers' tendency idiosyncratically to vary items and response alternatives without adequately specifying their amendments.

Descriptive statistics. The publication of means and standard deviations is quite essential. However, many reports contain no such information, so that assessment of overall levels of a variable is not possible. For instance, was that sample really "alienated", or is the author's account of the correlates of "alienation" misleadingly based upon a low average score? By the same token, comparisons between groups and studies cannot be undertaken in the absence of published descriptive statistics. Means and standard deviations are necessary for adequate interpretation of both cross-sectional correlational studies and change investigations. For example, if a sample yields an extreme or restricted range of scores, then associations with other variables or patterns of change need special interpretation; however, readers are usually unable to make this assessment since the information is lacking.

Sample characteristics. Many journal articles contain only a brief and indeterminate account of research participants, so that age, sex, job level, job type, length of service, or organizational context cannot be discerned. Yet these features are often crucial in the interpretation of results, and are vital for assessing the extent to which results are replicated or otherwise across samples of different types.

Reliability. Authors tend to be more consistent in their presentation of reliability data, although there remains a willingness to cite previous investigators' values, sometimes in language which hints that these were observed in the present study.

Validity. In so far as most research reports are geared to particular questions or hypotheses, they necessarily contain information relevant to criterion or construct validity. However, published information is often far from complete. A full correlation matrix is for example necessary for assessment of discriminant validity and for the computation of partial or multiple correlations. Similarly, details of factor structure are often very helpful in the assessment of convergent and discriminant validity.

But are we asking too much? Can journals reasonably be expected to contain so much material? A compromise might serve well the interests of authors, publishers and future investigators. Journals might require inclusion of material essential for another investigator's replication of a study, but accept that very bulky information may be retained in an unpublished appendix available on request from an author. Lengthy scales or large correlation matrices might be in the latter category, but information about samples and basic descriptive statistics would be required within the text before a paper is accepted for publication.

In summary, we are impressed by the ingenuity and enthusiasm of researchers in this field. Progress has been substantial, but reporting has been inadequate. Much information has been collected which would permit stronger assessments of measures than is at present possible from published accounts. Encouragement of better professional practices in this regard should be accompanied by stronger conceptual thrusts and greater adherence to the precepts of measurement theory. For the present, 249 measuring instruments await examination and further use.

2 Overall Job Satisfaction

The extent to which people are satisfied with their jobs has been of enduring research interest. A number of studies have used single question measures such as "All in all, how satisfied would you say you are with your job?", but as indicated in Chapter 1 we will not be examining those here. Interested readers might wish to consult McGehee and Tullar (1979), Quinn, Staines and McCullough (1974), and Weaver (1980).

Our concern is with multiple-item measures, and we will review 46 of these in Chapters 2 and 3. We have distinguished between measures of Overall Job Satisfaction and those which assess Specific Satisfactions, treating these two categories separately in the two chapters. The distinction is based upon the reasoning that all attitudes can be viewed at several levels of abstractness, ranging from an overall evaluation of the attitude object to very specific reactions to limited features of that object. The measures of Specific Satisfactions reviewed in Chapter 3 typically focus upon discriminable features of a job, such as pay, working conditions, or the supervisor, yielding separate scores for satisfaction with each feature. Ten principal scales of Specific Satisfactions are examined in Chapter 3, and at the end of that chapter we also provide briefer descriptions of a further 19 measures.

The present chapter contains 13 major and four minor entries of scales to assess Overall Job Satisfaction. This overarching attitude, which is sometimes referred to as General Job Satisfaction, may be measured in three different ways:

1. One can obtain separate reactions of specific features of a job, summing or averaging across these to obtain an overall score. This procedure is widely used in social psychological investigations of many kinds, and is the sole basis of measurement in four of the principal scales described in this chapter (2.4, 2.5, 2.11 and 2.12).

2. One can obtain a number of general evaluative reactions to a job without citing specific features. In this case questions are variants of the central theme "how much do you like your job?", being phrased in terms of interest, attraction, satisfaction, boredom etc. Scales 2.1, 2.2, 2.6, 2.7 and 2.9 are of this kind.

3. Some investigators have combined the previous approaches, introducing both specific and general evaluations into their scales. Measures 2.3, 2.8, 2.10 and 2.13 contain both types of question.

The scales set out in this chapter span 45 years of research. The earlier measures (2.1, 2.2 and 2.3) are mainly of the second type, obtaining a general evaluation of a job. There is naturally a limit to the number of different ways a general evaluation can be worded, so that the type-2 scales appearing later in the chapter are quite similar in content to the earlier ones. The type-1 scales vary in the comprehensiveness of their coverage of job features, and prospective users should ensure that coverage is appropriate for their needs.

Although the measures described in Chapter 3 are discriminable from Overall Job Satisfaction scales (treated in the present chapter) because of their focus upon Specific Satisfactions, it should be noted that the two forms of measure are not absolutely contrasting. Some scales in the following chapter yield a wide range of scores (satisfaction with different job features) and were initially designed with a view to keeping separate these sub-scale values. However, investigators have sometimes aggregated across sub-scales to yield a measure of Overall Job Satisfaction. For example, the Job Descriptive Index (Smith, Kendall and Hulin, 1969) (scale 3.3) has five sub-scales, each tapping a different feature of work, but these are sometimes combined into a total satisfaction score. (This is a variant of type-1 measurement of Overall Job Satisfaction, described above.) Conversely, some of the Overall Job Satisfaction scales described in the present chapter may be scored in sub-scale terms. For example, the overall scale of Warr, Cook and Wall (1979) (2.11) contains within it measures of Intrinsic Job Satisfaction and Extrinsic Job Satisfaction.

Which is more useful: a measure of Overall Job Satisfaction or one of Specific Satisfactions? This partly depends upon the number of questions which seem appropriate and upon the goals of a project. For example, if data are being gathered in order to identify and remedy organizational deficiencies, then more focussed scales have greater informational potential. A good solution in many cases is to include measures of both Overall Job Satisfaction and Specific Satisfactions. Note that the correlations between these are usually statistically significant but vary according to the specific feature in question. On the whole, it is intrinsic rather than extrinsic satisfactions which are more strongly associated with Overall Job Satisfaction; see the evidence presented in this chapter and in Chapter 3.

Another introductory issue concerns the weighting of individual items within a scale. Each job satisfaction measure cited here yields a score in terms of an unweighted total or average: all items are treated as making an equal contribution to the final value. One might expect that some questions tap issues of particularly great personal importance, thus contributing more substantially to the attitude in question. However, methodological inquiries have consistently indicated that attempts to weight specific attitudes by importance ratings do not significantly increase the reliability or validity of measurement (e.g. Blood, 1971; Mikes and Hulin, 1968; Quinn and Mangione, 1973). This could be because the specific job attitudes studied are all of approximately equal and high importance, or it may be that attitude responses already contain some built-in assessment of personal importance.

Conceptual and methodological discussions of job satisfaction have been contributed, among others, by Aldag and Brief (1978), Barth (1976), Evans (1969), Locke (1976), Nord (1977), Quinn and Gonzales (1979), Salancik and Pfeffer (1977), Wanous and Lawler (1972) and Warr (1978a).

Before reviewing the instruments which form the body of this chapter, we should introduce the "Faces Scale", since that has been used as a validating criterion in a number of studies. The Faces Scale was devised by Kunin (1955) to provide an overall attitude index which did not depend upon verbal responses. It consists of 11 male faces with expressions ranging from a broad smile to a deep scowl, and respondents are asked to identify the face which best describes how they feel about their job in general. Since it contains but a single item, the scale does not warrant a full entry in this compendium, but we refer to it on several occasions. Dunham and Herman (1975) have published a Female Faces Scale which yields very similar results to Kunin's version. They conclude that "either the male or the female Faces Scale may be used to measure the job satisfaction of male or female employees" (p. 631).

2.1 Overall Job Satisfaction

Source: Hoppock, 1935

The first published measure of Overall Job Satisfaction arose from a study of 500 teachers and administrators, followed by research into approximately 90% of the employed population of a small Pennsylvania town (N=309). A battery of questions included four which were combined into a single Satisfaction scale. Responses are in terms of seven-point dimensions (see below), and recent users have summed these to yield a possible range of Overall Job Satisfaction scores between 4 and 28. The source publication reports a Spearman-Brown reliability coefficient of 0.93.

McNichols, Stahl and Manley (1978) have described four studies to assess the value of the measure. With a total sample of almost 30,000 employees they report that coefficient alpha ranged from 0.76 to 0.89. Mean values were 21.25 (s.d. 2.73) for 360 managers, 19.31 (s.d. 4.07) for 17,110 civil servants, 17.69 (s.d. 4.98) for 10,996 military personnel, and 15.87 (s.d. 5.08) for a second military group (N=628). In each case employees of higher status scored more highly than their lower-status counterparts, a finding also reported by Hoppock (1935). Using data from the fourth sample (N=628), correlations with the five sub-scales of the Job Descriptive Index (Smith, Kendall and Hulin, 1969) (3.3) ranged from 0.73 for Work Satisfaction to 0.16 for Pay Satisfaction, and a correlation of 0.40 was found between reported intention to remain in military service and Overall Job Satisfaction.

In an associated study of project managers and other personnel, Dunne, Stahl and Melhart (1978) cite a mean of 20.4 (s.d. 2.9) and a coefficient alpha of 0.81. Stahl, Manley and McNichols (1978) examined associations between Overall Job Satisfaction and the type of work orientation ("institutional" and "occupational") reported by 49 US Air Force personnel, finding for example that involvement in the USAF as an institution was correlated 0.24 with Overall Job Satisfaction. In a study of 103 clerical and technical employees (54% female)

Dunham and Herman (1975) observed a correlation of 0.75 between the Hoppock measure and Overall Job Satisfaction on male and female Faces Scales (see p. 14). Wiggins (1976) investigated 110 female teachers of mentally handicapped children, recording systematic links with vocational interest measures (Holland, 1956). Other studies using the Hoppock scale include those by Cashman, Dansereau, Graen and Haga (1976), Dansereau, Graen and Haga (1975), Graen, Orris and Johnson (1973), Graen, Cashman, Ginsburg and Schieman (1977), Kesselman, Hagen and Wherry (1974), and Perone, DeWaard and Baron (1979).

Items and Responses

1. Choose the one of the following statements which best tells how well you like your job. Place a check mark against that statement:
I hate it; I dislike it; I don't like it; I am indifferent to it; I like it; I am enthusiastic about it; I love it; scored 1 to 7 respectively.

2. Check one of the following to show how much of the time you feel satisfied with your job:
All of the time; Most of the time; A good deal of the time; About half of the time; Occasionally; Seldom; Never; scored 7 to 1 respectively.

3. Check the one of the following which best tells how you feel about changing your job:
I would quit this job at once if I could get anything else to do; I would take almost any other job in which I could earn as much as I am earning now; I would like to change both my job and my occupation; I would like to exchange my present job for another job in the same line of work; I am not eager to change my job but I would do so if I could get a better job; I cannot think of any jobs for which I would exchange mine; I would not exchange my job for any other; scored 1 to 7 respectively.

4. Check one of the following to show how you think you compare with other people:
No-one likes his job better than I like mine; I like my job much better than most people like theirs; I like my job better than most people like theirs; I like my job about as well as most people like theirs; I dislike my job more than most people dislike theirs; I dislike my job much more than most people dislike theirs; No-one dislikes his job more than I dislike mine; scored 7 to 1 respectively.

2.2   Overall Job Satisfaction

Source: Brayfield and Rothe, 1951

This scale has 18 items, with five-point agree–disagree responses which are scored 1 to 5 and summed; the possible range of scores is thus between 18 and 90. Half the items (marked "R" below) are reverse-scored. The authors intend the measure to be applicable to a wide variety of jobs.

The items cover a range of evaluative reactions, and were chosen through statistical and other examinations from a pool of over 1000 statements. The first respondents to complete the final set of items were 231 young female office workers. Their mean score was 63.8 (s.d. 9.4), and the Spearman-Brown coefficient of internal reliability was 0.87. A second sample, of 91 night-school students in various jobs, yielded a mean of 70.4 (s.d. 13.2), and Overall Job Satisfaction scores were correlated 0.92 with those from the Hoppock measure (2.1).

Brayfield, Wells and Strate (1957), in a study of civil service office employees, report means of 60.54 (s.d. 14.98) and 63.81 (s.d. 8.62) for 41 men and 52 women respectively. Spearman-Brown internal reliability coefficients were 0.90 and 0.78. Orpen (1974a) cites means for 62 coloured and 72 white South African clerical workers of 76.51 and 65.42 respectively. Average scores ranging from 56.79 (for 332 taxi drivers) to 66.02 (for 195 nurses' aides) are reported by Baker and Hansen (1975). Ninety part-time Master's degree students produced a mean of 63.78 and a Kuder-Richardson internal reliability of 0.99 in research described by Johnson and Stinson (1975) and Stinson and Johnson (1975).

Three studies have used the Brayfield-Rothe index with a narrower focus to assess Satisfaction with the Work Itself. Respondents are asked to "think only about the work that you do", not about other factors such as pay or colleagues. In research embracing many types of job in a single company, Stone, Mowday and Porter (1977) found this type of satisfaction to be significantly associated ($r=0.38$, $N=335$) with Job Scope (perceived Variety, Autonomy, Task Identity and Feedback) (Stone, 1974) (8.4). A comparable value of 0.43 was recorded by Stone (1976) ($N=594$ varied employees), and in a similar enquiry with 149 enlisted naval personnel (Stone, 1975) the correlation between Brayfield-Rothe Satisfaction with the Work Itself and Job Scope was found to be 0.50. The association with a Protestant Ethic score derived from the Survey of Work Values (Wollack, Goodale, Wijting and Smith, 1971) (7.1) was 0.43, and this latter measure did not moderate the relationship between Job Scope and Satisfaction. Using a modified version of the Job Diagnostic Survey (8.2) to measure perceived Job Characteristics, Rousseau (1977) found a consistent pattern of significant positive correlations with Overall Job Satisfaction. She quotes mean scores on the Brayfield-Rothe measure between 61.59 and 71.08 for differing work technologies. Further analyses are described by Rousseau (1978a).

Ronen (1977) used Hebrew translations to examine the relationship between Specific Satisfactions measured through the Job Descriptive Index (3.3) and Overall Job Satisfaction in two samples of Israeli workers. The strongest association was with Satisfaction with the Work Itself ($r=0.73$, N=135) and the weakest with Pay Satisfaction ($r=0.18$, N=187), a pattern very similar to that observed for the Hoppock measure (2.1) by McNichols, Stahl and Manley (1978). Relationships between Overall Job Satisfaction and age, occupational level and job tenure were examined by Ronen (1978b), and associations with a range of personal values by Ronen (1978a). The latter paper presents mean Overall Job Satisfaction values of 65.29 (s.d. 9.92) and 61.13 (s.d. 11.91) for 135 kibbutz and 187 private sector employees respectively (the difference is significant at the 0.01 level).

A mean of 62.3 (s.d. 10.4) and an internal reliability (type unspecified) of 0.87 are reported by Lopez and Greenhaus (1978) in their study of 523 academic and support staff in a school system. Overall Job Satisfaction was correlated 0.27 with Self-esteem (Rosenberg, 1965) (5.25), and black employees were more satisfied than whites. Nursing, clerical and support staff of a single hospital were studied by Mobley, Horner and Hollingsworth (1978). Mean Overall Job Satisfaction was 66.0 (s.d. 8.9, N=203), and the correlation with personal turnover in the subsequent 47 weeks was -0.21. Particularly strong was the association (-0.54) with reported thinking of quitting, and this latter index emerged from multiple regression analysis as the most likely outcome of dissatisfaction, feeding subsequently into job search behaviour and actual turnover. Orpen (1978a) has described a two-phase study of 73 white South African managers; the test–retest correlation between Overall Job Satisfaction scores across 12 months was 0.27.

Other investigations using the Brayfield-Rothe measure include those by Carrell and Elbert (1974), Evans (1974), Feild and Ridenhour (1975), Kavanagh and Halpern (1977), Martin (1979), O'Reilly and Caldwell (1979), Orpen (1974a, b; 1978b) and Stinson and Johnson (1977).

Items

1. My job is like a hobby to me
2. My job is usually interesting enough to keep me from getting bored
3. It seems that my friends are more interested in their jobs (R)
4. I consider my job rather unpleasant (R)
5. I enjoy my work more than my leisure time
6. I am often bored with my job (R)
7. I feel fairly well satisfied with my present job
8. Most of the time I have to force myself to go to work (R)
9. I am satisfied with my job for the time being

10. I feel that my job is no more interesting than others I could get (R)
11. I definitely dislike my work (R)
12. I feel that I am happier in my work than most other people
13. Most days I am enthusiastic about my work
14. Each day of work seems like it will never end (R)
15. I like my job better than the average worker does
16. My job is pretty uninteresting (R)
17. I find real enjoyment in my work
18. I am disappointed that I ever took this job (R)

Responses

Strongly agree; Agree; Undecided; Disagree; Strongly disagree; scored 5 to 1 respectively.

2.3 Overall Job Satisfaction

Source: Bullock, 1952

This scale was devised within the framework of humans relations research, seeking to identify social factors associated with job satisfaction. The author provides an explicit definition: "job satisfaction is considered to be an attitude which results from a balancing and summation of many specific likes and dislikes experienced in connection with the job. This attitude manifests itself in evaluation of the job and of the employing organization . . . as contributing suitably to the attainment of one's personal objectives" (Bullock, 1952, p. 7).

The scale has ten items with five-point responses scored from 1 to 5 and thus a possible range of scores between 10 and 50. The evaluative direction of response presentation varies (five in each direction). Reliability and validity data were originally derived from 100 employees within a single organization; the sample is described as predominantly young, female, of rural background, and of limited education and work experience. The mean score was 39.10 with a range between 22 and 50, and the Spearman-Brown reliability coefficient was 0.90. A test–retest correlation across six weeks of 0.94 was obtained in a separate study of 53 students, although responses appear to have been in terms of jobs which had been held previously. A comparison group of respondents who had left the target organization revealed a significantly lower mean satisfaction score (34.31), although retrospective distortion cannot be ruled out when interpreting that finding.

Miles and his colleagues have employed the scale in research with 152 managers, scientists and engineers. Despite the difference from Bullock's sample their mean score per item was very similar (3.85; s.d.

nternal reliability remained high (a Spearman-Brown
0.91) (Miles and Petty, 1975). Correlations with measures
iguity and Role Conflict (Rizzo, House and Lirtzman,
and 8.16) are reported by Miles (1976a) as −0.49 and
−0.25. Miles (1975) reports a test–retest reliability coefficient over four months of 0.80; other analyses are described by Miles and Perreault (1976).

Item and Responses

1. Place a check mark in front of the statement which best tells how good a job you have:
The job is an excellent one, very much above the average; The job is a fairly good one; The job is only average; The job is not as good as average in this kind of work; The job is a very poor one, very much below the average; scored 5 to 1 respectively.

2. Place a check mark in front of the statement which best describes your feelings about your job:
I am very satisfied and happy on this job; I am fairly well satisfied on this job; I am neither satisfied nor dissatisfied — it is just average; I am a little dissatisfied on this job; I am very dissatisfied and unhappy on this job; scored 5 to 1 respectively.

3. Check one of the following statements to show how much of the time you are satisfied with your job:
Most of the time; A good deal of the time; About half of the time; Occasionally; Seldom; scored 5 to 1 respectively.

4. Place a check mark in front of the statement which best tells what kind of an organization it is to work for:
It is an excellent organization to work for — one of the best organizations I know of; It is a good organization to work for, but not one of the best; It is only an average organization to work for — many others are just as good; It is below average as an organization to work for — many others are better; It is probably one of the poorest organizations to work for that I know of; scored 5 to 1 respectively.

5. Place a check mark in front of the statement which best tells how your feelings compare with those of other people you know:
I dislike my job much more than most people dislike theirs; I dislike my job more than most people dislike theirs; I like my job about as well as most people like theirs; I like my job better than most people like theirs; I like my job much better than most people like theirs; scored 1 to 5 respectively.

6. Place a check mark in front of the statement which best tells how you feel about the work you do on your job:
The work I do is very unpleasant — I dislike it; The work I do is not pleasant; The work is just about average — I don't have any feelings about whether it is pleasant or not; The work is pleasant and enjoyable; The work is very enjoyable — I very much like to do the work called for on this job; scored 1 to 5 respectively.

7. Check one of the following statements which best describes any general conditions which affect your work or comfort on this job:
General working conditions are very bad; General working conditions are poor — not so good as the average for this kind of job; General conditions are about average, neither good nor bad; In general, working conditions are good, better than average; General working conditions are very good, much better than average for this kind of job; scored 1 to 5 respectively.

8. Check one of the following statements which best tells how you feel about changing your job:
I would quit this job at once if I had anything else to do; I would take almost any other job in which I could earn as much as I am earning here; This job is as good as the average and I would just as soon have it as any other; I am not eager to change jobs but would do so if I could make more money; I do not want to change jobs even for more money because this is a good one; scored 1 to 5 respectively.

9. Suppose you had a very good friend who is looking for a job in your line of work and you knew of a vacancy in this organization which your friend is well qualified to fill. Would you:
Recommend this job as a good one to apply for? Recommend this job but caution your friend about its shortcomings? Tell your friend about the vacancy but not anything else, then let him or her decide whether to apply or not? Tell your friend about the vacancy but suggest that he or she look for other vacancies elsewhere before applying? Try to discourage your friend from applying by telling the bad things about the job? Scored 5 to 1 respectively.

10. On the line below, place a check mark to show how well satisfied you are with this job.

| Completely dissatisfied | More dissatisfied than satisfied | About half and half | More satisfied than dissatisfied | Completely satisfied |

Scored 1 to 5 respectively, in terms of the nearest response.

2.4   Minnesota Satisfaction Questionnaire

Source: Weiss, Dawis, England and Lofquist, 1967

This is one of several measures associated with a comprehensive theory of work adjustment presented by Lofquist and Dawis (1969). The theory is constructed around the assumption that each person seeks to achieve and maintain correspondence with his or her environment. Correspondence with the environment at work can be described in terms of the individual fulfilling the requirements of this environment (satisfactoriness), and the work environment fulfilling the requirements of the individual (satisfaction).

Drawing upon previously published scales and upon their own

theorizing, the authors first carried out preliminary studies with a pool of 80 satisfaction items. These items were subsequently amended and augmented to yield a 100-item scale, with five items tapping each of 20 sub-scales. This scale was administered to 1793 employed individuals and extensive statistical analyses were carried out (see Weiss, Dawis, England and Lofquist, 1967). These included the calculation of item-total correlations for each sub-scale, and the 20 items most strongly associated with their respective sub-scale totals were brought together into a short form of the questionnaire.

The present account deals only with this 20-item short form. Studies using the long form (100 items) or a modification of it include those by Ilgen and Hollenback (1977), Katz (1978a), Katz and Van Maanen (1977), Pritchard and Peters (1974), Schriesheim (1978a), Schwab and Wallace (1974), and Van Maanen and Katz (1976). A matrix of inter-correlations between the 20 sub-scales and with Job Descriptive Index (3.3) scores for 273 production workers is provided by Gillet and Schwab (1975), and similar information for six of the sub-scales with the Job Descriptive Index and the Index of Organizational Reactions (3.1) for 622 varied employees is provided by Dunham, Smith and Blackburn (1977).

Items in the Minnesota Satisfaction Questionnaire were worded in order to enhance readability. Against each item below is the long-form sub-scale label offered by the authors. It can be seen that the measure taps a wide range of features, and the total of the 20 items (five response alternatives in each case) is taken as an index of General Satisfaction. Factor analysis of responses from 1460 employed men suggested the presence of two main components, representing Intrinsic and Extrinsic Satisfaction. Separate scores may be computed for these two components (12 and six items respectively, omitting items 17 and 18), in addition to the General Satisfaction score; items to be included are identified below by "I" or "E" respectively. The possible range of scores is between 20 and 100 for General Satisfaction, 12 and 60 for Intrinsic Satisfaction, and 6 and 30 for Extrinsic Satisfaction. Weiss, Dawis, England and Lofquist (1967) present mean scores from 1723 employees of various kinds as 74.85 (s.d. 11.92), 47.14 (s.d. 7.42) and 19.98 (s.d. 4.78) for the three measures. The source publication also presents normative data for a range of different occupational groups.

The authors report Hoyt internal reliability coefficients for the sub-scales and overall scale for a number of samples, as follows: Intrinsic Satisfaction, median 0.86, range 0.84 to 0.91; Extrinsic Satisfaction, median 0.80, range 0.77 to 0.82; General Satisfaction, median 0.90, range 0.87 to 0.92. The correlations between Intrinsic and Extrinsic

Satisfaction ranged in the initial research from 0.52 to 0.68, with an overall value of 0.60. Test–retest reliability was reported as 0.89 across one week (for 75 employees attending night school) and 0.70 across one year (for 115 varied employees).

Several authors have reported mean values for General Satisfaction, including: Arvey and Dewhirst (1976), with 271 scientists and engineers, 79.5 (s.d. 10.7); Enderlein (1975), with 208 young workers, 72.10 (s.d. 13.68); Jermier and Berkes (1979), with 158 police officers, 68.9 (s.d. 12.8), Schriesheim and Murphy (1976), with 54 social service counsellors, 83.22 (s.d. 6.76).

Wanous (1974a) observed a correlation for "about 80" newly hired female telephone operators of 0.71 between General Satisfaction scores and the sum of the five Job Descriptive Index sub-scales (3.3). In their study of 271 scientists and engineers Arvey, Dewhirst and Boling (1976) reported General Satisfaction differences associated with, for example, perceived participation in goal setting: means of 82.9, 81.0 and 74.0 for high, medium and low participation respectively. (The individual respondent values yielded a correlation between participation and General Satisfaction of 0.37; see Arvey and Dewhirst, 1976. A similar result is reported by Jermier and Berkes, 1979.) With 54 social service counsellors from 19 organizations, Schriesheim and Murphy (1976) recorded a correlation between General Satisfaction and unit size of -0.25; the Satisfaction scale itself had a Kuder-Richardson internal reliability coefficient of 0.74. Ivancevich (1978) reported coefficients alpha of 0.80 and 0.84 for the Intrinsic and Extrinsic Satisfaction sub-scales in a study of 170 machinists and technicians. The Kuder-Richardson coefficient of internal reliability for General Satisfaction was 0.92 in the study by Jermier and Berkes (1979) of 158 police officers. Motowidlo and Borman (1978) studied 614 soldiers in 47 army platoons; mean platoon General Satisfaction was correlated 0.24 with officers' ratings of platoon morale. Perceived equity of Pay Rules and Work Pace (8.45) were significantly associated with General Satisfaction in Dittrich and Carrell's (1979) study of 126 clerical employees.

In research with 194 varied employees (46% female), Wexley, Alexander, Greenawalt and Couch (1980) reported a correlation between Intrinsic and Extrinsic Satisfaction scores of 0.63. Schmitt, Coyle, White and Rauschenberger (1978) reported an equivalent correlation of 0.83 (N=411 young employees), with internal reliabilities (type unspecified) of 0.81 and 0.78 respectively. Corresponding values from 772 civil service retirees and non-retirees were 0.64, 0.90 and 0.85 respectively (Schmitt, Coyle, Rauschenberger and White, 1979). Ivancevich (1979a), with 184 project engineers, reported an intercorrelation between the sub-scales of 0.15 and alpha coefficients above 0.80. With 398 office employees, Pierce, Dunham and Blackburn (1979) recorded an intercorrelation of 0.67, alpha coefficients of 0.88 and 0.84 for Intrinsic and Extrinsic Satisfaction respectively, and test–retest correlations across one month (N=30) of 0.50 and 0.63. The latter authors cite item means of 3.66 (s.d. 0.69) and 2.89 (s.d. 0.93) for Intrinsic and Extrinsic Satisfaction. Test–retest correlations across one year averaged 0.56 and 0.59 for Intrinsic and Extrinsic Satisfaction respectively in Schmitt and Mellon's (1980) study of 254 varied employees.

Other investigators using the short form or a modification of it include Berger and Schwab (1980), Culha (1977), Desmond and Weiss (1975), Dipboye, Zultowski, Dewhirst and Arvey (1978, 1979), Elizur and Tziner (1977), Fisher (1978), Ilgen and Fujii (1976), Ivancevich (1980), Kazanas (1978), Schwab and Heneman (1977), and Wanous (1974a, b; 1976).

The Minnesota Satisfaction Questionnaire appears to yield a sound measure of Overall Job Satisfaction, although some items may not represent universally valued features ("Being able to keep busy all the time", for example); this is a problem which faces many scales requiring responses to specific job features. Note also that "men" in item 5 will sometimes need amendment.

We have some reservations about the assignment of items to the Intrinsic and Extrinsic Satisfaction sub-scales. The factor analytic basis for this yields some curious allocations (e.g. "steady employment" emerges as an intrinsic feature) and it omits "working conditions". The disparity in the number of items (12 and 6) in the two sub-scales is also troublesome. Arvey and Dewhirst (1979), Arvey, Dewhirst and Brown (1978) and Zultowski, Arvey and Dewhirst (1978) have devised their own allocation of items to these two sub-scales. However, many users have scored the items only for General Satisfaction, bypassing this type of criticism.

Items

On my present job, this is how I feel about:
1. Being able to keep busy all the time (Activity, I)
2. The chance to work alone on the job (Independence, I)
3. The chance to do different things from time to time (Variety, I)
4. The chance to be "somebody" in the community (Social status, I)
5. The way my boss handles his men (Supervision—human relations, E)
6. The competence of my supervisor in making decisions (Supervision —technical, E)
7. Being able to do things that don't go against my conscience (Moral values, I)

8. The way my job provides for steady employment (Security, I)
9. The chance to do things for other people (Social service, I)
10. The chance to tell people what to do (Authority, I)
11. The chance to do something that makes use of my abilities (Ability utilization, I)
12. The way company policies are put into practice (Company policies and practices, E)
13. My pay and the amount of work I do (Compensation, E)
14. The chances for advancement on this job (Advancement, E)
15. The freedom to use my own judgment (Responsibility, I)
16. The chance to try my own methods of doing the job (Creativity, I)
17. The working conditions (Working conditions)
18. The way my co-workers get along with each other (Co-workers)
19. The praise I get for doing a good job (Recognition, E)
20. The feeling of accomplishment I get from the job (Achievement, I)

Responses

Very dissatisfied; Dissatisfied; I can't decide whether I am satisfied or not; Satisfied; Very satisfied; scored 1 to 5 respectively.

2.5   General Satisfaction

Source: Taylor and Bowers, 1972

Within the Survey of Organizations questionnaire, developed by the Institute for Social Research at the University of Michigan, are seven items designed to tap General Satisfaction. The questionnaire as a whole was developed through several revisions over a number of years in order to operationalize constructs central to the "metatheory of organizational functioning" described by Likert (1961, 1967) and Bowers (1972).

The initial version was constructed in 1967 from items previously employed in the Institute, and subsequent versions were adjusted for machine-scoring: respondents blot out one of the circles representing response alternatives, and these responses are read by machine for computer analysis. The Survey of Organizations is designed for application at all levels of an organization, and has been widely used in survey-feedback organization development projects. In many cases, therefore, data have been presented and analysed in terms of work-group averages. Work-group membership is in these cases determined by having individuals indicate their supervisor on the survey form.

Scales within the Survey of Organizations are said to be made up of "only the most valid, reliable and efficient single items" from previous studies (Taylor and Bowers, 1972, p. 2), but no further details are given.

The General Satisfaction items were selected to cover six principal components identified in earlier research: satisfaction with pay, supervision, the firm as a whole, the job itself, fellow employees, and prospects of advancement. One item taps each of the first five of these components and two items the sixth feature. Responses are on a five-point scale, and the average of the seven responses is calculated.

In earlier studies the seven items were scored and presented separately, but following cluster analysis of data from 749 work groups it was concluded that they could be treated as a single scale. Coefficient alpha is cited as 0.87 for these data; but note that group averages rather than individual responses appear to have been used to generate this coefficient. Means and standard deviations are not given in the source publication, but a test–retest correlation value of 0.55 is cited for 284 work groups; the time intervals are not specified and presumably vary.

The General Satisfaction scale has been used by Bowers and Hausser (1977), Drenth, Koopman, Rus, Odar, Heller and Brown (1979), Koch (1978, 1979) and Motowidlo and Borman (1978), but little psychometric evidence is presented in those papers. The latter authors report a correlation of 0.34 between average General Satisfaction scores of 47 army platoons and officers' ratings of platoon morale. Armenakis and Smith (1978) describe the use of 80 modified items from the Survey of Organizations, but information on the General Satisfaction scale is not presented.

The scale covers conventional features of satisfaction, but the double weighting for personal advancement may be queried. Very little evidence of validity and reliability is available in the open literature, despite the scale's extensive use by its originators.

Items

1. All in all, how satisfied are you with the persons in your work group?
2. All in all, how satisfied are you with your supervisor?
3. All in all, how satisfied are you with your job?
4. All in all, how satisfied are you with this organization, compared to most others?
5. Considering your skills and the effort you put into the work, how satisfied are you with your pay?
6. How satisfied do you feel with the progress you have made in this organization up to now?
7. How satisfied do you feel with your chances for getting ahead in this organization in the future?

Responses

Very dissatisfied; Somewhat dissatisfied; Neither satisfied nor dissatisfied; Fairly satisfied; Very satisfied; scored 1 to 5 respectively.

2.6 General Job Satisfaction

Source: Hackman and Oldham, 1975

Hackman and Oldham (1975) describe "an overall measure of the degree to which the employee is satisfied and happy with the job" (p. 162) within their broad-ranging Job Diagnostic Survey (see also 3.6, 6.3, 7.7, 8.2, 8.28). The measure comprises five items inserted in two different sections of the questionnaire, with seven-point responses from strongly disagree to strongly agree in each case. Two items are reverse scored. Hackman and Lawler (1971) previously employed the first three items only, and these are described by Hackman and Oldham (1974) as a short form of the measure. A mean response is taken in both cases.

In a study of 208 telephone company employees Hackman and Lawler (1971) observed a mean of 4.97 (s.d. 1.26) for the short form, with an internal consistency reliability (type unspecified) of 0.76. Using the long form these values were 4.62 (s.d. 1.18) and 0.76 in a study of 658 employees in varied jobs in seven organizations (Hackman and Oldham, 1975, 1976). In this case reliabilities were computed by applying the Spearman-Brown formula to the median inter-item correlation.

The same calculation was used in the report by Oldham, Hackman and Stepina (1978), who summarize results from 6930 employees working on 876 jobs in 56 organizations. They report an overall internal reliability coefficient of 0.77, a mean of 4.65 and a standard deviation of 1.27. General Job Satisfaction was shown to be significantly associated with perceived Job Characteristics (8.2) and Specific Satisfactions (3.6). The authors also categorize their results by organization size (observing a significant negative association), by geographical location (significantly higher scores in rural locations), and by job level (a significant positive association).

In a British replication of the Hackman and Oldham (1975) study, Wall, Clegg and Jackson (1978) observed for 47 shop-floor employees a mean General Job Satisfaction score of 4.23 (s.d. 1.31) and a coefficient alpha of 0.74. Katz (1978a) described a study of 2094 government employees, whose mean short-form score was 4.80 (s.d. 1.22) with an internal consistency reliability (type unspecified) of 0.74. Relationships between perceived Job Characteristics (8.2) and General Job Satisfaction were strongest for employees with job tenure between four and 36 months; see also Katz (1978b). Steers (1975b) observed a correlation between General Job Satisfaction (short form) and rated performance of 133 female clerical supervisors of 0.26.

Mean long-form scores for 94 clerical workers of 4.52 (s.d. 1.17) and

3.90 (s.d. 1.23) before and after an organizational change are reported
by Hackman, Pearce and Wolfe (1978). In a study using the long form
with 118 nursing and technical staff in a single hospital, Feldman
(1976) observed a mean score of 5.21 (s.d. 1.14) and a Spearman-Brown
reliability of 0.80. General Job Satisfaction was strongly associated with
the motivational fit between individuals and their work; see also
Feldman (1977). Other studies using the measure include Aldag and
Brief (1975, 1978), Arnold and House (1980), Bhagat and Chassie
(1980), Brief and Aldag (1975), Champoux (1978), Dailey (1979),
Evans, Kiggundu and House (1979), Gilmore, Beehr and Richter
(1979), Peters, O'Connor and Rudolf (1980), White and Mitchell
(1979), and White, Mitchell and Bell (1977). A description of the
instrument is also presented in Hackman and Oldham (1980).

Items

1. Generally speaking, I am very satisfied with this job
2. I frequently think of quitting this job (R)
3. I am generally satisfied with the kind of work I do in this job
4. Most people on this job are very satisfied with the job
5. People on this job often think of quitting (R)

Responses

Disagree strongly; Disagree; Disagree slightly; Neutral; Agree slightly; Agree;
Agree strongly; scored 1 to 7 respectively.

2.7   Facet-free Job Satisfaction

Source: Quinn and Staines, 1979

As part of a national "quality of employment survey" carried out in
1977, the authors used five items to tap "a worker's general affective
reaction to the job without reference to any specific job facet" (p. 205).
The questions were previously used in 1969 and 1973 surveys, and
comparisons between the three years are possible from data in the
source publication (see also Quinn *et al.*, 1971; Quinn and Shepard,
1974).

The items were drawn from earlier research in order to yield a simple
instrument which was easy to administer. Applicability to all levels and
types of employee was a primary criterion for item selection. The 1977
sample contained 1515 respondents representative of all employed
adults, all industries, and all occupations in the United States.

The items have three or four response alternatives, but are scored from one to five in each case. Values are given against each response below: note the asymmetric weighting for items 1 and 2. The mean score is calculated, with a higher value indicating higher Satisfaction. Quinn and Staines (1979) cite an overall mean of 3.66 (s.d. 1.02) for their 1977 national sample (N=1515, 36% female), with an alpha coefficient of 0.77. Readers may wish to examine the source publication for percentages of the sample giving each response.

A correlation of 0.55 is reported with the authors' measure of Facet-specific Job Satisfaction (3.7). Two short forms of the Facet-free Satisfaction scale are described, containing either three or two items (numbers 1, 2, and 3; or 1 and 2, below) with reported alpha coefficients (N=740) of 0.56 and 0.65 respectively, and correlations with the full scale of 0.93 and 0.84. Means of the short forms were 3.56 (s.d. 1.14) and 3.24 (s.d. 1.35) respectively.

Beehr (1976) used items 1, 3, 4 and 5 in a study of 651 employees from five organizations (49% female), reporting a mean of 3.94 (s.d. 0.97) and a Spearman-Brown coefficient of 0.80. Facet-free Job Satisfaction correlated −0.22 with a measure of role ambiguity and 0.43 with Quinn and Shepard's (1974) index of Depressed Mood at Work (5.5). Beehr, Walsh and Taber (1976) employed items 1 and 3, using a four-point scale; and Eden (1975) has combined items 1, 3, 4 and 5 with other questions in a secondary analysis of some of the 1969 data (Quinn *et al.*, 1971).

Items and Responses

1. All in all, how satisfied would you say you are with your job?
Very satisfied; Somewhat satisfied; Not too satisfied; Not at all satisfied; scored 5, 3, 1 and 1 respectively.

2. If you were free to go into any type of job you wanted, what would your choice be?
Would want the job you have now; Would want to retire and not work at all; Would prefer some other job to the job you have now; scored 5, 1 and 1 respectively.

3. Knowing what you know now, if you had to decide all over again whether to take the job you now have, what would you decide?
Decide without hesitation to take the same job; Have some second thoughts; Decide definitely not to take the same job; scored 5, 3 and 1 respectively.

4. In general how well would you say that your job measures up to the sort of job you wanted when you took it?
Very much like the job you wanted; Somewhat like the job you wanted; Not very much like the job you wanted; scored 5, 3 and 1 respectively.

5. If a good friend of yours told you he or she was interested in working in a job like yours for your employer (*omit the last three words for self-employed*

respondents), what would you tell him or her?
Would strongly recommend it; Would have doubts about recommending it;
Would advise the friend against it; scored 5, 3 and 1 respectively.

2.8   Overall Job Satisfaction

Source: Quinn and Staines, 1979

This measure is derived by combining the authors' measures of Facet-specific Job Satisfaction (3.7) and Facet-free Job Satisfaction (2.7). The former scale is scored in terms of the mean of 33 responses to individual job features, each with a range from 1 to 4; and the latter yields a mean from five general items on a scale from 1 to 5. Overall Job Satisfaction scores are created by transforming the distributions of raw scores for Facet-specific and Facet-free Job Satisfaction into z scores and taking a mean of the two resulting z scores for each respondent. These scores are then multiplied by 100 to remove decimal points, and the resulting values are positive or negative numbers which can be interpreted as deviations from the national sample's mean of zero.

The source publication describes findings from national surveys carried out in 1973 and 1977 (see also Quinn and Shepard, 1974). Overall Job Satisfaction scores are presented in terms of the 1973 mean, which is zero by definition (s.d. 88, N=1455); levels of satisfaction are reported to have declined by 1977, yielding a mean of −21 (s.d. 89, N=1515). Quinn and Staines (1979) also publish mean values for several groups, for example in terms of sex, age, race, education, geographical region, and occupation. Two examples from the 1977 data may be cited (recall that the national mean value is −21):

Size of place of employment
1 to 9 workers (N=370): +2
10 to 99 workers (N=546): −20
100 to 999 workers (N=365): −37
1000 or more workers (N=200): −36

Collar colour
White-collar workers (N=769): −8
Service workers (N=184): −22
Farm workers (N=42): +19
Other blue-collar workers (N=520): −44

Coefficient alpha is cited as 0.85 for the 1977 sample, and the inter-correlation between the two component measures is 0.55. The items are well tested and validity evidence is encouraging. However, the equal weighting of two components of very unequal length and the complicated procedure for deriving overall scores might persuade some potential users to use the Facet-specific and Facet-free measures separately.

Items

See entries 2.7 and 3.7.

2.9 Overall Job Satisfaction

Source: Cammann, Fichman, Jenkins and Klesh, 1979; Seashore,
Lawler, Mirvis and Cammann, 1982

The Michigan Organizational Assessment Questionnaire contains a number of scales to measure work attitudes and perceptions; see also 3.8, 3.9, 3.10, 4.13, 6.2, 6.6, 8.6, 9.5 and 9.11. Items and scales have been developed through a series of substantial empirical analyses, and the Questionnaire has been administered to several thousand employees from many organizations.

A three-item scale of Overall Job Satisfaction is included, in order to assess "organization members' overall affective responses to their jobs". Responses are on a seven-point dimension, and the mean value across the items (with one reverse-scored) constitutes the scale score. Means are not cited in the source publication, but coefficient alpha is given as 0.77 (N>400). Correlations of 0.35 and −0.58 are reported with the authors' measures of Job Involvement (6.2) and Intention to Turn Over (4.13). Moch (1980a) has recorded an average intercorrelation between the three scale items of 0.50 (N=466 packaging and assembly workers).

Items

1. All in all, I am satisfied with my job
2. In general, I don't like my job (R)
3. In general, I like working here

Responses

Strongly disagree; Disagree; Slightly disagree; Neither agree nor disagree; Slightly agree; Agree; Strongly agree; scored 1 to 7 respectively.

2.10 Attitude Toward the Job

Source: Vroom, 1960

This three-item measure was designed for research into supervisory staff in a single company. A total of three five-point responses serves as the attitude score, with five as the most positive reaction in each case. Vroom (1960) reports a test–retest reliability coefficient over six months of 0.75, but inter-item correlations were low (0.21, 0.07 and 0.25). Hollon and

Chesser (1976) used the scale as a measure of Overall Job Satisfaction in a study of 321 college faculty members (altering "supervisory work" in question 1 to "your current job situation"), and reported an internal reliability coefficient (type unspecified) of 0.71, a mean of 11.8, and a standard deviation of 2.3. They report that Overall Satisfaction correlated −0.43 with desired increase in personal influence, −0.49 with Job-related Tension (Kahn, Wolfe, Quinn and Snoek, 1964) (5.1), and 0.32 with the six-item Job Involvement scale of Lodahl and Kejner (1965) (6.1).

Items and Responses

1. How much do you like supervisory work?
I like it very much; I like it pretty well; I like it in some ways but not in others; I don't like it very much; I don't like it at all; scored 5 to 1 respectively.

2. How much chance does your job give you to do the things you are best at?
A very good chance to do the things I am best at; A fairly good chance; Some chance; Very little chance; No chance to do the things I am best at; scored 5 to 1 respectively.

3. How good is your immediate superior in dealing with people?
He does an excellent job in dealing with people; A very good job; A fairly good job; A fairly poor job; A poor job in dealing with people; scored 5 to 1 respectively.

2.11   Overall Job Satisfaction

Source: Warr, Cook and Wall, 1979

The authors note the need for short, robust scales which are easily completed by blue-collar workers of modest educational attainment. From a literature review, a pilot study, and two investigations with samples of 200 and 390 male blue-collar employees in United Kingdom manufacturing industry, a 15-item Job Satisfaction scale was created. Respondents indicate upon a seven-point dimension their satisfaction or dissatisfaction with each of 15 features of their job. A total score (ranging from 15 to 105) is taken, with a higher score representing higher Overall Satisfaction.

The principal samples were drawn from ten widely dispersed locations according to a predetermined frame which approximately matched national demographic characteristics. Coefficient alpha was observed to be 0.85 and 0.88 for the two samples (N=200 and 390 respectively) and the combined mean value (N=590) was 70.53 (s.d. 15.42); decile scores are also presented in the source publication. A test–retest correlation of 0.63 was observed across six months (N=60).

The scale was designed to cover both extrinsic and intrinsic job features, and cluster analyses using the furthest neighbour method separated these two sets of items. The use of separate sub-scales of Extrinsic and Intrinsic Job Satisfaction is thus advocated in certain cases. The Extrinsic Satisfaction sub-scale contains eight items (1, 3, 5, 7, 9, 11, 13 and 15), with coefficients alpha of 0.74 and 0.78 for the two principal samples. The remaining seven items (2, 4, 6, 8, 10, 12, 14) comprise the Intrinsic Satisfaction sub-scale, with coefficients alpha of 0.79 and 0.85 for the two samples. Means from the second study (N=390) were 38.22 (s.d. 7.81) and 32.74 (s.d. 7.69) for the Extrinsic and Intrinsic Satisfaction sub-scales respectively. The sub-scales were found to be inter-correlated 0.72, a figure similar to that reported in entry 2.4 for the Minnesota Satisfaction Questionnaire.

The authors examined the associations between their measures of Job Satisfaction and other newly-created scales. Correlations with Work Involvement (7.5) were 0.30, 0.30 and 0.27 for Overall Job Satisfaction, Extrinsic Job Satisfaction and Intrinsic Job Satisfaction respectively. Comparable correlations with Intrinsic Job Motivation (6.7) were 0.35, 0.30 and 0.36; and with Overall Life Satisfaction (5.30) they were 0.42, 0.38 and 0.39. Confirmatory factor analyses were conducted to examine the factorial independence of Overall Job Satisfaction and five other measures; items in each scale all loaded highly on a separate factor, and the loadings were extremely similar in the two principal studies.

In a separate study of 574 varied employees in an engineering company (Clegg and Wall, 1981), the mean Overall Job Satisfaction score was 71.90 (s.d. 13.58) and coefficient alpha was 0.92. Overall Job Satisfaction was correlated 0.58 with Organizational Commitment (Cook and Wall, 1980) (4.10) and −0.29 with the General Health Questionnaire (5.21). One-way analysis of variance revealed a highly significant positive association between Overall Job Satisfaction and job level.

Items

1. The physical work conditions
2. The freedom to choose your own method of working
3. Your fellow workers
4. The recognition you get for good work
5. Your immediate boss
6. The amount of responsibility you are given
7. Your rate of pay
8. Your opportunity to use your abilities
9. Industrial relations between management and workers in your firm
10. Your chance of promotion
11. The way your firm is managed

12. The attention paid to suggestions you make
13. Your hours of work
14. The amount of variety in your job
15. Your job security

Responses

I'm extremely dissatisfied; I'm very dissatisfied; I'm moderately dissatisfied; I'm not sure; I'm moderately satisfied; I'm very satisfied; I'm extremely satisfied; scored 1 to 7 respectively.

2.12 and 2.13   Home and Employment Role Scales

Source: Parry and Warr, 1980

The authors point out that many measures of occupational experience are less than adequate for employed mothers with young children. They set out to devise robust and simple measures of mothers' attitudes to paid employment and to employment in the home, and also an index of Interaction Strain experienced by employed mothers in coping with both domestic and paid work (5.7). The constructs tapped by the Home and Employment Role Scales are defined as a mother's overall attitude to her present domestic and childcare work (Home Role Attitude, 2.12) and a mother's overall attitude to her present paid employment (Employment Role Attitude, 2.13).

An initial pool of items was derived from the literature and from two phases of pilot interviews. A sample of 185 mothers with children under 14 was drawn from ten widely dispersed areas in the United Kingdom; 125 were in paid employment and 60 were not. Respondents were all identified as "working class" and were contacted at home. Analyses of self-completion questionnaire responses from this sample yielded two 12-item scales with seven and six items reverse-scored in measures 2.12 and 2.13 respectively. A three-point response scale is used, and scores are summed across items.

The mean Home Role Attitude score (N=185) was 26.69 (s.d. 5.46), and no significant difference between employed and unemployed mothers was found. The mean Employment Role Attitude score (N=125) was 29.13 (s.d. 5.32), and the two scales were intercorrelated 0.29; this latter value dropped to 0.16 when reported Life Satisfaction (a two-item measure) was partialled out. Alpha coefficients were 0.71 and 0.78 respectively. A cross-over pattern of relationships with Positive and Negative Affect (Bradburn, 1969) (5.20) was observed: Employment Role Attitude was more closely associated with Positive than with Negative Affect (0.53 and -0.23), whereas Home Role Attitude was more highly correlated with Negative than with Positive Affect (-0.45 and 0.35).

Items

Home Role Attitude (2.12)

1. My family really shows that they appreciate all I do for them
2. I get a lot of help from my husband with routine tasks in the home
3. Being a mother leaves me enough time to spend on myself
4. I would like more adult conversation and company than I get at home with the children (R)
5. One of the good things about being a housewife is that I can plan my own day in the way I want
6. I feel my family takes me too much for granted (R)
7. On the whole I have enough free time to do the things I want to do
8. Life at home is too much the same routine day after day (R)
9. I wish my children showed their love for me more (R)
10. My family lives in accommodation that is too small (R)
11. One of the bad things about being a mother is that I often have to put my family first and go without things myself (R)
12. I sometimes get in a panic about the problems of running a home (R)

Employment Role Attitude (2.13)

1. People where I work are very friendly
2. My job is very boring (R)
3. I get a feeling of achieving something worthwhile in my job
4. I only do my job because I need the money (R)
5. My boss is always ready to discuss people's problems
6. My boss takes the work I do too much for granted (R)
7. I wish I had more security in my job (R)
8. There is a happy atmosphere in the place I work
9. I really dislike my job (R)
10. My boss is fair to everyone
11. Where I work, management asks workers first about changing anything that affects them
12. I am unhappy with my working conditions (R)

Responses

Yes, true; No, untrue; and Don't know; scored 3, 1 and 2 respectively.

2.14 to 2.17   Other Measures of Overall Job Satisfaction

2.14 Kornhauser (1965) describes 11 items from his interview schedule for manual workers which are intended to tap Job Satisfaction. Several questions are open-ended, with limited indication of coding procedures, and a number make no direct mention of employment-related topics. Seven (unspecified) items from the schedule were employed with 54 female teachers in written questionnaire form by Gechman and Wiener (1975).

2.15 Koch (1977) describes a five-item Overall Satisfaction scale and cites means for 501 technicians. Items are presented in full.

2.16 McDonald and Gunderson (1974) describe the Navy Job Satisfaction Scale. This is a three-item measure (How satisfied are you with your present job? Do your present duties employ your abilities in the best possible way? Are you often bored?), which the authors examine in relation to demographic and occupational variables in a study of 1021 naval enlisted personnel. Responses were found to correlate 0.61 with total Satisfaction scores from the Job Descriptive Index (3.3)

2.17 In a study of 1383 Australian workers, O'Brien and Dowling (1980) report the use of an 18-item Job Satisfaction measure. Respondents indicate their degree of satisfaction (five-point scale) with each feature and a total score is taken. Coefficient alpha is reported as 0.91.

3 Specific Satisfactions

In this chapter we review 29 instruments which have been designed to assess satisfaction with specific features of paid employment. Some of these (e.g. 3.1, 3.3 to 3.6) set out to measure a range of different attitudes, whereas others focus only upon a single feature, for example pay (3.10), social relationships (3.9), or one's trade union (3.26, 3.27). Ten scales of Specific Satisfactions will be described in detail, with minor entries provided for a further 19.

The topics covered by each measure are summarized in Table 1. In practice, the concepts and language used by different authors diverge considerably, so that the pattern of contents is less consistent than suggested in the table; further details are available in the text which follows. Note also that it is not necessarily desirable that a scale should cover a very wide range of job features. Some research projects are purposely directed at detailed examination of only a limited set of issues; space restrictions in a questionnaire may be severe; and separate sub-scales tend in practice to be factorially overlapping so that extensive differentiation through verbal labelling can give a misleading picture of fragmented reactions.

Table 1   Job features covered by measures of Specific Satisfactions

		Number of items	Supervision	The company	Co-workers	Working conditions	Career progress	Promotion prospects	Pay	Subordinates	Job security	General extrinsic	Kind of work	Amount of work	Personal growth	General intrinsic	Other
3.1	Index of Organizational Reactions	42	×	×	×	×	×	×					×	×			
3.2	Need Satisfaction Questionnaire	13		×							×				×		×
3.3	Job Descriptive Index	72	×		×				×	×			×				
3.4	Managerial Opinion Scale	77	×	×	×				×	×	×		×				
3.5	Worker Opinion Survey	92	×	×	×				×	×			×				
3.6	Specific Satisfactions	14	×		×				×	×				×			
3.7	Facet-specific Satisfaction	33	×		×	×			×	×				×	×		
3.8	Intrinsic and Extrinsic Rewards	7										×			×		
3.9	Social Rewards Satisfaction	3			×												
3.10	Pay Satisfaction	3							×								
3.11	Job Expectations	28							×	×		×	×		×		×
3.12	Company Satisfaction	12		×													
3.13	Company Satisfaction	20		×													
3.14	Triple Audit	112	×	×	×				×	×	×	×	×		×		×
3.15	Achievement Satisfaction	4					×										
3.16	Career Dissatisfaction	35					×										
3.17	Content and Context Satisfaction	36										×			×		
3.18	Motivator-Hygiene Attribution	12										×			×		
3.19	Role Orientation Index	25	×		×					×					×		
3.20	Attitude toward Flexitime	18															×
3.21	Job Satisfaction Questionnaire	33	×		×				×	×			×				
3.22	Job Satisfaction Scale	25	×		×					×	×		×	×	×		
3.23	Satisfaction with Rewards	19			×					×	×			×	×		
3.24	Subordinate Evaluation Questionnaire	20									×						
3.25	Morale Scales	299	×		×	×				×			×		×		×
3.26	Union Satisfaction	6															×
3.27	Union Attitude Questionnaire	77															×
3.28	ERG Satisfaction	35	×		×	×				×					×		×
3.29	Information System Satisfaction	57															×
2.4	Minnesota Satisfaction Questionnaire	20										×			×		
2.11	Overall Job Satisfaction	15										×			×		

Since some investigators seek information about general Intrinsic and Extrinsic Satisfaction scores, we have included within Table 1 scales 2.4 and 2.11, which although primarily measures of Overall Job Satisfaction also contain sub-scales for those separate attitudes. Reactions to the physical conditions of work (lighting, noise, environmental appearance, etc.) are subsumed within Extrinsic Satisfaction, but as Table 1 makes clear, scale designers have tended to neglect measures which provide detailed assessments of working conditions. That is regrettable.

3.1 Index of Organizational Reactions

Source: Smith, 1962, 1976

This 42-item scale taps eight Specific Satisfactions. It was designed for use at all levels in an organization and constructed to reduce the positive skewing of responses which sometimes occurs. Each item has its own five-alternative response, scored from 1 to 5 and averaged within a sub-scale. The items of each sub-scale are presented together in blocks, as follows: Supervision, six items; Company Identification, five items; Kind of Work, six items; Amount of Work, four items; Co-workers, five items; Physical Work Conditions, six items; Financial Rewards, five items; Career Future, five items. Item content extends beyond merely affective reactions to cover the perceived relationship between job features and work performance. For example, item 36 asks whether payment practices encourage or discourage hard work.

The Index of Organizational Reactions (IOR) has been used extensively within Sears, Roebuck and Company, a large merchandise distribution organization. Mean scores for a large number of samples are published by Smith, Roberts and Hulin (1976), and interested readers should consult that article for further information. One illustrative set of mean values for seven of the sub-scales may be presented here (N=40,340 blue- and white-collar employees): Supervision 3.19, Kind of Work 3.36, Amount of Work 3.06, Co-workers 3.41, Physical Work Conditions 3.10, Financial Rewards 2.77, Career Future 3.09.

Dunham, Smith and Blackburn (1977) have provided reliability and validity data for the eight sub-scales. Kuder-Richardson internal reliability estimates are summarized in the top line of Table 2; the five samples referred to there contain a total of 12,971 respondents. These reliability values are higher than many in the literature, and the test–retest coefficients are similarly satisfactory. (The latter results are discussed more fully by Katerberg, Smith and Hoy (1977) in an exami-

Table 2   Illustrative reliability and validity evidence for the Index of Organizational Reactions

	Supervision	Company Identification	Index of Organizational Reactions Sub-scale						Number of cases
			Kind of Work	Amount of Work	Co-workers	Physical Conditions	Financial Rewards	Career Future	
Median internal reliability across 5 samples	0.90	0.82	0.89	0.77	0.77	0.90	0.85	0.83	
Test–retest reliability across 6 weeks	0.69	0.71	0.74	0.62	0.65	0.64	0.72	0.76	128
Correlation with corresponding Faces Scale	0.65	0.62	0.58	0.53	0.51	0.55	0.64	0.67	622
Correlation with corresponding JDI sub-scale	0.44		0.51		0.50		0.45	0.39	622
Correlation with corresponding MSQ sub-scale	0.71	0.70			0.61	0.64	0.70	0.68	622

Source: Dunham, Smith and Blackburn (1977)

nation of a Spanish translation of the Index.) Table 2 also sets out evidence for convergent validity in terms of three other Job Satisfaction measures. Responses on the Faces Scale (Kunin, 1955, see p. 14) were obtained for each of the eight areas covered by the Index, and results from relevant Job Descriptive Index (JDI) (3.3) and Minnesota Satisfaction Questionnaire (MSQ) (2.4) sub-scales were also entered in the analysis. These results are in the lower three lines of the table.

The same article examines the discriminant validity of the IOR with that of the JDI and MSQ, concluding that the Index of Organizational Reactions is the most successful in that respect. Shortage of space precludes a detailed account here, but we may note that the inter-correlations between IOR sub-scales in the data presented (N=622) were relatively high, ranging from 0.32 to 0.77 with a median of 0.49. However, factor analyses to confirm the intended structure of the scale were encouraging, with clearly identifiable factors for each of the sub-scales; the Company Identification items were least satisfactory in this respect.

Dunham (1976) recorded correlations between the Kind of Work sub-scale and five perceived Job Characteristics tapped by the Job Diagnostic Survey (8.2) of between 0.29 and 0.37 (median 0.36; N=784 employees from several levels). A matrix of correlations for six of the sub-scales (using data from the same sample) is given by Dunham (1977b). Alpha coefficients (from a validation sample of 3610) were cited as: Supervision 0.88, Company Identification 0.79, Kind of Work 0.71, Amount of Work 0.72, Financial Rewards 0.77, Career Future 0.78.

Validation evidence in terms of managers' attendance at work on the day after a severe snowstorm has been presented by Smith (1977). Correlations between workgroup scores and attendance levels for 27 workgroups were: Supervision 0.54, Company Identification 0.42, Kind of Work 0.37, Amount of Work 0.36, Financial Rewards 0.46, Career Future 0.60. Similar associations in another city on the same day (with no weather and travel difficulties) were all around zero, indicating that attitudes and behaviour are likely to be linked only in conditions where a person's freedom of choice is salient.

Other studies using some items from the Index of Organizational Reactions include those by Hamner and Smith (1978), Hom (1979), Katerberg, Hom and Hulin (1979), Motowidlo and Borman (1978), and Pierce, Dunham and Blackburn (1979).

Items and Responses

Supervision

1. Do you ever have the feeling you would be better off working under different supervision? (*Rate overall supervision*)
I almost always feel this way; I frequently feel this way; I occasionally feel this way: I seldom feel this way; I never feel this way; scored 1 to 5 respectively.

2. How do you feel about the supervision you receive? (*Rate overall supervision*)
I am extremely satisfied; I am well satisfied; I am only moderately satisfied; I am somewhat dissatisfied; I am very dissatisfied; scored 5 to 1 respectively.

3. How does the way you are treated by those who supervise you influence your overall attitude toward your job? (*Rate overall supervision*)
It has a very unfavourable influence; It has a slightly unfavourable influence; It has no real effect; It has a favourable influence; It has a very favourable influence; scored 1 to 5 respectively.

4. How much do the efforts of those who supervise you add to the success of your organization? (*Rate overall supervision*)
A very great deal; Quite a bit; Only a little; Very little; Almost nothing; scored 5 to 1 respectively.

5. The people who supervise me have: (*Rate overall supervision*)
Many more good traits than bad ones; More good traits than bad ones; About the same number of good traits as bad ones; More bad traits than good ones; Many more bad traits than good ones; scored 5 to 1 respectively.

6. The supervision I receive is the kind that: (*Rate overall supervision*)
Greatly *discourages* me from giving extra effort; Tends to *discourage* me from giving extra effort; Has little influence on me; *Encourages* me to give extra effort; Greatly *encourages* me to give extra effort; scored 1 to 5 respectively.

Company Identification

7. There is something about working for this organization that:
Greatly *encourages* me to do my best: Definitely *encourages* me to do my best; Only slightly *encourages* me to do my best; Tends to *discourage* me from doing my best; Definitely *discourages* me from doing my best; scored 5 to 1 respectively.

8. From my experience, I feel this organization probably treats its employees:
Poorly; Somewhat poorly; Fairly well; Quite well; Extremely well; scored 1 to 5 respectively.

9. How does working for this organization influence your overall attitude toward your job?
It has a very unfavourable influence; It has an unfavourable influence; It has no influence one way or the other; It has a favourable influence; It has a very favourable influence; scored 1 to 5 respectively.

10. How do you describe this organization as a company to work for?
Couldn't be much better; Very good; Fairly good; Just another place to work; Poor; scored 5 to 1 respectively.

11. I think this organization, as a company, considers employee welfare:
Much less important than sales and profits; Less important than sales and

profits; About as important as sales and profits; More important than sales and profits; Much more important than sales and profits; scored 1 to 5 respectively.

Kind of Work

12. Work like mine:
Discourages me from doing my best; Tends to *discourage* me from doing my best; Makes little difference; Slightly *encourages* me to do my best; Greatly *encourages* me to do my best; scored 1 to 5 respectively.

13. How often when you finish a day's work do you feel you've accomplished something really worthwhile?
All of the time; Most of the time; About half of the time; Less than half of the time; Rarely; scored 5 to 1 respectively.

14. How does the kind of work you do influence your overall attitude toward your job?
It has a very unfavourable influence; It has a slightly unfavourable influence; It has no influence one way or the other; It has a fairly favourable influence; It has a very favourable influence; scored 1 to 5 respectively.

15. How many of the things you do on your job do you enjoy?
Nearly all; More than half; About half; Less than half; Almost none; scored 5 to 1 respectively.

16. How much of the work you do stirs up real enthusiasm on your part?
Nearly all of it; More than half of it; About half of it; Less than half of it; Almost none of it; scored 5 to 1 respectively.

17. How do you feel about the kind of work you do?
Don't like it, would prefer some other kind of work; It's OK, there's other work I like better; I like it, but there is other work I like as much; I like it very much; It's exactly the kind of work I like best; scored 1 to 5 respectively.

Amount of Work

18. I feel my workload is:
Never too heavy; Seldom too heavy; Sometimes too heavy; Often too heavy; Almost always too heavy; scored 5 to 1 respectively.

19. How does the amount of work you're expected to do influence the way you do your job?
It never allows me to do a good job; It seldom allows me to do a good job; It has no effect on how I do my job; It usually allows me to do a good job; It always allows me to do a good job; scored 1 to 5 respectively.

20. How does the amount of work you're expected to do influence your overall attitude toward your job?
It has a very favourable influence; It has a favourable influence; It has no influence one way or the other; It has an unfavourable influence; It has a very unfavourable influence; scored 5 to 1 respectively.

21. How do you feel about the amount of work you're expected to do?
Very dissatisfied; Somewhat dissatisfied; Neither satisfied nor dissatisfied; Somewhat satisfied; Very satisfied; scored 1 to 5 respectively.

Co-Workers

22. How do you generally feel about the employees you work with?
They are the best group I could ask for; I like them a great deal; I like them fairly well; I have no feeling one way or the other; I don't particularly care for them; scored 5 to 1 respectively.

23. How is your overall attitude toward your job influenced by the people you work with?
It is very favourably influenced; It is favourably influenced; It is not influenced one way or the other; It is unfavourably influenced; It is very unfavourably influenced; scored 5 to 1 respectively.

24. The example my fellow employees set:
Greatly *discourages* me from working hard; Somewhat *discourages* me from working hard; Has little effect on me; Somewhat *encourages* me to work hard; Greatly *encourages* me to work hard; scored 1 to 5 respectively.

25. How much does the way co-workers handle their jobs add to the success of your organization?
It adds almost nothing; It adds very little; It adds only a little; It adds quite a bit; It adds a very great deal; scored 1 to 5 respectively.

26. In this organization, there is:
A very great deal of friction; Quite a bit of friction; Some friction; Little friction; Almost no friction; scored 1 to 5 respectively.

Physical Work Conditions

27. How much pride can you take in the appearance of your work place?
A very great deal; Quite a bit; Some; Little; Very little; scored 5 to 1 respectively.

28. How do you feel about your physical working conditions?
Extremely satisfied; Well satisfied; Only moderately satisfied; Somewhat dissatisfied; Very dissatisfied; scored 5 to 1 respectively.

29. How do your physical working conditions influence your overall attitude toward your job?
They have a very unfavourable influence; They have a slightly unfavourable influence; They have no influence one way or the other; They have a favourable influence; They have a very favourable influence; scored 1 to 5 respectively.

30. The physical working conditions make working here:
Very unpleasant; Unpleasant; Neither pleasant nor unpleasant; Pleasant; Very pleasant; scored 1 to 5 respectively.

31. For the work I do, my physical working conditions are:
Very poor; Relatively poor; Neither good nor poor; Reasonably good; Very good; scored 1 to 5 respectively.

32. How do your physical working conditions affect the way you do your job?
They help me a great deal; They help me a little; They make little difference; They tend to make it difficult; They make it very difficult; scored 5 to 1 respectively.

Financial Rewards

33. For the job I do, I feel the amount of money I make is:
Extremely good; Good; Neither good nor poor; Fairly poor; Very poor; scored
5 to 1 respectively.

34. To what extent are your needs satisfied by the pay and benefits you receive?
Almost none of my needs are satisfied; Very few of my needs are satisfied; A few of my needs are satisfied; Many of my needs are satisfied; Almost all of my needs are satisfied; scored 1 to 5 respectively.

35. Considering what it costs to live in this area, my pay is:
Very inadequate; Inadequate; Barely adequate; Adequate; More than adequate; scored 1 to 5 respectively.

36. Does the way pay is handled around here make it worthwhile for a person to work especially hard?
It definitely *encourages* hard work; It tends to *encourage* hard work; It makes little difference; It tends to *discourage* hard work; It definitely *discourages* hard work; scored 5 to 1 respectively.

37. How does the amount of money you now make influence your overall attitude toward your job?
It has a very favourable influence; It has a fairly favourable influence; It has no influence one way or the other; It has a slightly unfavourable influence; It has a very unfavourable influence; scored 5 to 1 respectively.

Career Future

38. How do you feel about your future with this organization?
I am very worried about it; I am somewhat worried about it; I have mixed feelings about it; I feel good about it; I feel very good about it; scored 1 to 5 respectively.

39. How do your feelings about your future with the company influence your overall attitude toward your job?
They have a very favourable influence; They have a favourable influence; They have no influence one way or the other; They have a slightly unfavourable influence; They have a very unfavourable influence; scored 5 to 1 respectively.

40. The way my future with the company looks to me now:
Hard work seems very worthwhile; Hard work seems fairly worthwhile; Hard work seems worthwhile; Hard work hardly seems worthwhile; Hard work seems almost worthless; scored 5 to 1 respectively.

41. Do you feel you are getting ahead in the company?
I'm making a great deal of progress; I'm making some progress; I'm not sure; I'm making very little progress; I'm making no progress; scored 5 to 1 respectively.

42. How secure are you in your present job?
I feel very uneasy about it; I feel fairly uneasy about it; I feel somewhat uneasy about it; I feel fairly sure of it; I feel very sure of it; scored 1 to 5 respectively.

3.2   Need Satisfaction Questionnaire

Source: Porter, 1961, 1962

Porter's approach differs from most others described in this chapter in that his measure focusses upon a set of personal needs rather than directly upon features of a job. He draws upon Maslow's (e.g. 1943, 1954) theory of motivation in order to measure managers' perceived deficiencies in Security, Social, Esteem, Autonomy and Self-Actualization Needs. The selection of items is not explicitly justified, nor is statistical evidence for the five sub-scales introduced, but the final numbers in each class are one, two, three, four and three respectively. Two responses are obtained for each item, as in this illustration:

The opportunity for independent thought and action in my management position:

(a)   How much is there now?
(minimum)   1   2   3   4   5   6   7   (maximum)

(b)   How much should there be?
(minimum)   1   2   3   4   5   6   7   (maximum)

Need deficiency is calculated by subtracting (a) from (b), on the assumption "that the larger the difference, the larger the degree of dissatisfaction or the smaller the degree of satisfaction" (Porter, 1962, p. 378).

Deficiency scores can be analysed separately for individual items or summed across each need category as a whole. Porter (1961) cites the percentage of managers at bottom and middle organizational levels who report for each item a deficiency (i.e. (a) is less than (b) by any amount), but in his second study (N=1916) he reports 17 mean values for each item (four age groups and five management levels, with three empty cells) (Porter, 1962). The data are too bulky for reproduction here, but we may note that deficiencies were greater for junior managers in comparison with their senior colleagues in the case of the higher-order needs: Esteem, Autonomy and Self-Actualization.

Deficiency scores of these kinds have been used fairly widely, but few studies in the later 1970's have employed Porter's measure without amendment. Using the original measure, Van Maanen (1975) examined the pattern of Need Satisfaction in police recruits across their initial seven months, and Gavin and Maynard (1975) studied correlates of bank employees' responses. However, neither report provides normative or psychometric information. Lefkowitz (1974) cites mean deficiency scores for the five sub-scales in a study of 312 police personnel: Security 1.23 (s.d. 2.68), Social 1.84 (s.d. 3.21), Esteem 6.00

(s.d. 5.41), Autonomy 7.29 (s.d. 6.37), Self-Actualization 6.36 (s.d. 6.09). A large number of scores are brought together by Howell, Strauss and Sorensen (1975), who set their data from a sample of Liberian managers into normative values from 11 other countries published by other investigators.

Hall and Mansfield (1975) present average values for four age groups of non-managerial professionals at two points in time (N=290 and 90) using 12 of the original 13 items. Sheridan and Slocum (1975) used the original items, but summed over the five needs together. They cite test–retest reliability correlations for these total scores across 12 months of around 0.45 for 59 machine operators and around 0.67 for 35 managers.

Other studies employing variants of the measure include Cummings and Bigelow (1976), Frost and Jamal (1979), Helmich (1975), Hunt and Saul (1975), Jamal and Mitchell (1980), La Rocco, Pugh and Gunderson (1977), Lawler, Hall and Oldham (1974), Meadows (1980b), Mitchell and Moudgill (1976), Muczyk (1978), Nystrom (1978), Orpen (1974a), Reif, Newstrom and St Louis (1976), and Wexley, McLaughlin and Sterns (1975).

The value of the instrument lies principally in its focus upon five separate needs drawn from an important theoretical framework. This focus assumes that the separate need measures are internally consistent and are not strongly intercorrelated, but evidence on these points is not encouraging (e.g. Schwab, 1980; Wahba and Bridwell, 1976). The five needs themselves are unequally covered (with Security being tapped by a single item), and the original wording reflects an intention to deal primarily with managers. We are also concerned that the response alternatives are labelled only at the poles.

A more general criticism may be raised, that deficiency scores have important disadvantages in assessing work experiences. Their meaning is unclear, being a function of two separate indices, although the two scores are likely to be linked since particular "should be" responses are typically somewhat higher than corresponding "is now" reactions (Wall and Payne, 1973; Van Maanen, 1975). This is particularly problematic when deficiency scores are used in correlation analyses, since observed correlations may merely reflect the current level of an attribute ("is now") rather than fulfilment of a need itself.

Items

The items are randomly presented in the questionnaire, but are listed below in terms of five separate needs.

Security needs

1. The feeling of security in my management position

Social needs

2. The opportunity, in my management position, to give help to other people
3. The opportunity to develop close friendships in my management position

Esteem needs

4. The feeling of self-esteem a person gets from being in my management position
5. The prestige of my management position inside the company (that is, the regard received from others in the company)
6. The prestige of my management position outside the company (that is, the regard received from others not in the company)

Autonomy needs

7. The authority connected with my management position
8. The opportunity for independent thought and action in my management position
9. The opportunity, in my management position, for participation in the setting of goals
10. The opportunity, in my management position, for participation in the determination of methods and procedures

Self-Actualization needs

11. The opportunity for personal growth and development in my management position
12. The feeling of self-fulfilment a person gets from being in my management position (that is, the feeling of being able to use one's own unique capabilities, realizing one's potentialities)
13. The feeling of worthwhile accomplishment in my management position

Responses

See the text above

3.3   Job Descriptive Index

Source: Smith, Kendall and Hulin, 1969

The authors define job satisfactions (in the plural) as "the feelings a worker has about his job", noting that "there are different feelings corresponding to differentiable aspects of the job" (p. 12). Their expressed goal was to measure the principal features of satisfaction, recognizing that not all components can be examined within a brief questionnaire.

The Job Descriptive Index (JDI) asks respondents to describe their work rather than their feelings about that work. Part of the description sought is in terms of explicitly evaluative words (e.g. satisfying, good), where the distinction between job-reference and self-reference is small. Other descriptions are in terms of more objective features which are either clearly factual (e.g. on my feet) or involve evaluative interpretations of facts (e.g. strict supervision).

The Job Descriptive Index was developed through several data-based revisions from an initial pool of more than 100 items. The stages of development are fully described in the source publication; one goal was comprehensibility by workers of low educational level. The final version contains five separately presented sub-scales, covering Satisfaction with Type of Work (18 items), Pay (nine items), Promotion Opportunities (nine items), Supervision (18 items) and Co-workers (18 items). Each of the 72 items is an adjective or phrase, and respondents indicate whether it describes the job aspect in question (pay, co-workers etc.). Approximately half the items in each scale are negatively worded.

Responses are Yes, Uncertain, or No. The authors suggest that Uncertain responses are more indicative of dissatisfaction than satisfaction, so that, instead of a traditional scoring frame of 3, 2 and 1, Yes, Uncertain and No responses receive weights of 3, 1 and 0 respectively; these values are of course reversed for negatively-worded items. A total score is calculated for each of the five sub-scales. The Pay and Promotions sub-scales contain half the number of items of the other sub-scales (nine rather than 18), and the JDI manual indicates that scores on these two sub-scales should be doubled in order to make them comparable with the other values.

It is also possible to sum across the five sub-scales to create an Overall Job Satisfaction score. That procedure is supported by moderate intercorrelations between the sub-scales, although the authors do not favour it. Smith, Kendall and Hulin (1969) reported a median correlation between the sub-scales of 0.39 and 0.32 for men and women respectively, and similar results have been obtained by subsequent investigators. We have brought these together with the original data in Table 3. A related study is that by Hunt, Osborn and Schuler (1978) with 395 white-collar and managerial employees. They calculated an Overall Job Satisfaction score (summing all the 72 items) and obtained an alpha coefficient of internal reliability of 0.93. The same figure was recorded with 308 managerial and clerical employees by Schriesheim (1979) and Schriesheim, Kinicki and Schriesheim (1979).

Smith, Smith and Rollo (1974) describe a principal components

Table 3. Summary of intercorrelations between sub-scales of the Job
Descriptive Index

Author(s)	Sample size	Sample type	Intercorrelations Median	Range
Bigoness (1978)	222	University faculty members	0.37	0.17 to 0.50
Dunham, Smith and Blackburn (1977)	622	Company employees	0.42	0.29 to 0.59
Garrison and Muchinsky (1977)	196	Clerical employees	0.31	0.23 to 0.47
Gillet and Schwab (1975)	273	Production workers (65% female)	0.31	0.14 to 0.44
Herman, Dunham and Hulin (1975)	392	Company employees	0.34	0.16 to 0.44
Jacobs and Solomon (1977)	251	Salesmen and managers	0.30	0.22 to 0.44
MacEachron (1977)	70	Female nurses	0.30	0.15 to 0.45
Newman (1974)	108	Nursing home employees (88% female)	0.23	0.07 to 0.35
Newman (1975)	710	Insurance company employees (72% female)	0.40	0.31 to 0.44
O'Reilly, Bretton and Roberts (1974)	252	Military officers and technicians	0.43	0.31 to 0.55
Penley and Hawkins (1980)	264	Company employees (82% female)	0.79	0.16 to 0.90
Ronen (1977, 1978a)	187	Israeli industrial employees	0.20	0.04 to 0.30
Sauser and York (1978)	480	State employees	0.37	0.18 to 0.50
Schneider and Dachler (1978)	306	Non-management employees	0.28	0.12 to 0.37
Schneider and Dachler (1978)	541	Management employees	0.22	0.14 to 0.40
Smith, Kendall and Hulin (1969)	980	Male employees	0.39	0.28 to 0.42
Smith, Kendall and Hulin (1969)	627	Female employees	0.32	0.16 to 0.52
Stone and Porter (1975)	556	Telephone company employees	0.27	0.02 to 0.38
Waters, Roach and Waters (1976)	152	Female clerical employees	0.22	0.09 to 0.36

analysis of the 72 items. Loadings for items on the Pay, Promotion and
Co-workers sub-scales are reported to be consistent across three
samples, but the Supervision sub-scale split into two factors in each case
(tentatively identified as quality of actions and personal characteristics). The Work sub-scale yielded two factors for one sample, containing descriptive and evaluative items respectively.

Author(s)	Sample size	Sample type	Measure of reliability	Work sub-scale	Pay sub-scale	Promotion sub-scale	Supervision sub-scale	Co-workers sub-scale
Abdel-Halim (1978)	89	Managers	Spearman-Brown	0.69				
Downey, Sheridan and Slocum (1976)	68	Managers	Alpha	0.84		0.86	0.87	
Downey, Sheridan and Slocum (1976)	68	Machine operators	Alpha	0.87		0.84	0.89	
Dunham, Smith and Blackburn (1977)	622	Company employees	Spearman-Brown	0.84	0.70	0.79	0.87	0.88
Hall et al. (1978)	153	Operators and supervisors	Alpha	0.81				
Herman, Dunham and Hulin (1975)	392	Company employees	Kuder-Richardson	0.90	0.82	0.86	0.85	0.89
Ivancevich (1976b)	171	Technicians	Spearman-Brown	0.81	0.84	0.79	0.83	0.80
Ivancevich (1976b)	153	Technicians	Spearman-Brown	0.78	0.79	0.72	0.86	0.81
Ivancevich (1976c)	32	Salespeople	Spearman-Brown	0.80			0.82	
Ivancevich (1977)	54	Technicians	Spearman-Brown	0.75			0.81	
Kim and Hamner (1976)	113	Blue-collar employees	Alpha			0.83	0.61	
Reinharth and Wahba (1976)	215	Salespeople	Spearman-Brown	0.85	0.79	0.90	0.89	0.93
Schriesheim (1979, 1980)	308	White-collar employees	Alpha				0.88	
Schuler (1979)	382	Manufacturing employees (34% female)	Alpha	0.82			0.87	0.83
Schuler (1979)	429	Public utility employees (26% female)	Alpha	0.79			0.86	0.89
Smith, Kendall and Hulin (1969)	80	Male employees	Spearman-Brown	0.84	0.80	0.86	0.87	0.88

The sub-scales' Spearman-Brown coefficients were reported in the source publication to range from 0.80 to 0.88. These values are presented in Table 4 in conjunction with internal reliability data reported by later investigators. The range of alpha coefficient values reported by Johns (1978a, b), without attributing them to sub-scales, was from 0.78 to 0.84.

The source publication also contains information about mean values and standard deviations for samples of men and women. These data are summarized in Table 5, which also brings together relevant material from subsequent studies. Caution should be exercised with the mean values for Pay and Promotion Satisfaction, since not all investigators have doubled the scores in these cases. Sauser and York (1978) point out that their values need to be doubled for external comparability, and this might also be the case for several other low values cited in the table.

A number of investigators have examined the stability of JDI scores across time. Schneider and Dachler (1978) studied 541 managers (30% female) and 306 non-managers (50% female) in a single organization, obtaining data on two occasions separated by 16 months. The test–retest stability co-efficients for the Work, Pay, Promotion, Supervision and Co-workers sub-scales were 0.61, 0.61, 0.64, 0.46, and 0.47 respectively for managers and 0.66, 0.62, 0.56, 0.45, and 0.58 for non-managers. Downey, Sheridan and Slocum (1976) applied the Work, Promotion and Supervision sub-scales to 68 managers and 68 machine operators on two occasions 12 months apart. Test–retest coefficients were 0.70, 0.73 and 0.70 for managers and 0.64, 0.29 and 0.35 for machine operators. Schuler (1979) reports correlations across seven months of 0.82, 0.77 and 0.79 for the Work, Supervision and Co-workers sub-scales respectively (N=224 public utility employees). A Spanish version of the JDI has been constructed by Katerberg, Smith and Hoy (1977). Test–retest correlations over six weeks with a sample of 128 bilingual white-collar employees were all in excess of 0.81 for both the English and the Spanish forms. Other translations include a Hebrew version by Ronen (1977, 1978a, b) and a French version by Johns (1978a, b).

A number of researchers have correlated the JDI sub-scales with measures of Overall Job Satisfaction. Results are summarized in Table 6, from which it can be seen that the Work sub-scale is most closely associated with Overall Job Satisfaction. A study by Seybolt and Gruenfeld (1976) examined the correlation between this sub-scale and the Work Alienation index of Seeman (1967) (4.3). Across six different samples the median correlation was −0.66 (range −0.52 to −0.70).

The total JDI score was used in Wanous's (1974a) study of "about brackets.

Author(s)	Sample size	Sample type	Work (18 items)	Pay (9 items)	Promotion (9 items)	Supervision (18 items)	Co-workers (18 items)
Abdel-Halim (1979a)	87	Male managers	36.62 (10.16)	30.45 (7.00)	31.00 (8.86)	44.14 (9.86)	47.81 (8.07)
Abdel-Halim (1980b)	123	Salespeople (36% female)	40.00 (8.38)	17.00 (6.45)	12.44 (8.59)	44.18 (9.50)	42.57 (11.11)
Bartol (1979a)	159	Computer professionals				41.06 (10.28)	40.93 (10.66)
Bartol and Wortman (1975)	105	Male employees	35.78	18.98	19.99	41.69	24.91
Bernadin (1979)	57	Policemen	25.4 (10.2)			23.5 (11.4)	31.8 (11.1)
Lefkowitz (1974)	312	City policemen	33.71 (11.20)			40.65 (13.68)	41.42 (12.74)
Maccachron (1977)	70	Female nurses	37.96 (8.42)	24.86 (12.69)	18.83 (13.38)	42.02 (9.81)	43.52 (9.18)
Miles and Petty (1977)	235	Social service staff (88% female)	36.10 (4.90)	33.65 (6.27)	24.27 (9.96)	43.88 (6.45)	45.19 (5.62)
Milutinovich (1977)	230	Black employees (26% female)	28.61	13.25	20.49	35.00	36.41
Milutinovich (1977)	230	White employees (26% female)	29.16	13.20	17.85	37.59	39.58
Mobley, Horner and Hollingsworth (1978)	203	Hospital employees	35.9 (10.5)	20.5 (13.8)	17.3 (13.0)	42.2 (10.3)	42.2 (11.1)
Odewahn and Petty (1980)	102	Nursing aides (72% female)	27.76	13.02	17.33	35.17	35.91
Sauser and York (1978)	154	Male employees	33.75 (13.58)	9.47 (7.12)	11.37 (8.40)	42.06 (11.29)	39.49 (12.19)
Sauser and York (1978)	326	Female employees	30.67 (11.41)	9.90 (6.42)	8.90 (7.90)	39.41 (11.88)	37.93 (12.37)
Schuler (1979)	382	Manufacturing employees (34% female)	37.29 (11.20)			40.95 (12.07)	41.76 (10.13)
Schuler (1979)	429	Public utility employees (26% female)	37.57 (10.27)			39.55 (11.97)	39.60 (12.43)
Smith, Kendall and Hulin (1969)	1951	Male employees	36.57 (10.54)	29.90 (14.53)	22.06 (15.77)	41.10 (10.58)	43.49 (10.02)
Smith, Kendall and Hulin (1969)	636	Female employees	35.74 (9.88)	27.90 (13.65)	17.77 (13.38)	41.13 (10.05)	42.09 (10.51)

Table 6   Correlations between JDI sub-scale scores and separate measures of Overall Job Satisfaction

Author(s)	Sample size	Sample type	Measure of Overall Job Satisfaction	Work sub-scale	Pay sub-scale	Promotion sub-scale	Supervision sub-scale	Co-workers sub-scale
Herman, Dunham and Hulin (1975)	392	Company employees	Faces scale	0.66	0.42	0.38	0.44	0.27
McNichols, Stahl and Manley (1978)	628	Military personnel	Hoppock (2.1)	0.73	0.16	0.40	0.46	0.34
Mobley, Horner and Hollingsworth (1978)	203	Hospital employees	Brayfield-Rothe (2.2)	0.53	0.37	0.23	0.29	0.29
Newman (1974)	108	Nursing home staff	Faces scale	0.62	0.26	0.41	0.15	0.36
O'Reilly, Bretton and Roberts (1974)	252	Military officers and technicians	Faces scale	0.74	0.44	0.41	0.46	0.45
O'Reilly and Roberts (1978)	562	Naval aviation personnel	Faces scale	0.59		0.22	0.25	
Ronen (1977, 1978a)	187	Israeli industrial workers	Brayfield-Rothe (2.2)	0.73	0.18	0.34	0.27	0.34
Wexley, Alexander, Greenawalt and Couch (1980)	194	Varied employees (46% female)	MSQ General Satisfaction (2.4)	0.66			0.63	

Note: The Faces scale (Kunin, 1955) is a range of faces representing differing degrees of satisfaction with the job in general; a respondent chooses the face most indicative of his or her own reaction. See p. 14.

80" newly hired female telephone operators. Overall Satisfaction correlated 0.71 with the short-form General Satisfaction score of the Minnesota Satisfaction Questionnaire (2.4). Koch and Steers (1978) reported a correlation of 0.66 between the total JDI score and their measure of Job Attachment (4.11) in a study of 77 non-managerial employees. A full matrix of intercorrelations between the five JDI sub-scales and the 20 sub-scales of the long-form Minnesota Satisfaction Questionnaire (2.4) for 273 production workers is provided by Gillet and Schwab (1975). Correlations with six sub-scales of the long-form Minnesota Satisfaction Questionnaire and with eight sub-scales of the Index of Organizational Reactions (Smith, 1962) (3.1) are reported by Dunham, Smith and Blackburn (1977) in a study of 622 employees in a single company. In both cases the associations between measures of the same satisfaction construct were strong.

The relationships between sub-scale scores and supervisor ratings of the work performance of 76 draftswomen and telephone operators were examined by Kesselman, Wood and Hagen (1974). Correlations were 0.44, 0.46, 0.18, 0.33 and 0.34 for Satisfaction with Work, Pay, Promotion Opportunities, Supervision and Co-workers respectively. Comparable values of 0.19, 0.08, 0.15, 0.32 and 0.11 were reported by Inkson (1978) in a study of 93 New Zealand male manual employees. Correlations (in the same sequence) with the 20-item Job Involvement scale of Lodahl and Kejner (1965) (6.1) were observed by Saal (1978) in a study of 218 non-supervisory employees to be 0.52, 0.33, 0.24, 0.47 and 0.29. Using the six-item form of that Job Involvement scale, Newman (1975) reported correlations for 710 insurance company staff of 0.57, 0.22, 0.24, 0.30 and 0.20 respectively.

O'Reilly, Bretton and Roberts (1974) studied 252 officers and technicians in two military aviation units. Correlations with Organizational Commitment (Porter and Smith, 1970) (4.5) were 0.56, 0.45, 0.34, 0.40 and 0.47 for the Work, Pay, Promotion, Supervision and Co-workers sub-scales respectively. Comparable values in Stone and Porter's (1975) study of 556 telephone company employees were 0.51, 0.29, 0.49, 0.43 and 0.21. Small but generally significant correlations with Lodahl and Kejner's (1965) Job Involvement scale (6.1) and Hrebeniak and Alutto's (1972) measure of Organizational Commitment (4.6) are reported by Wiener and Vardi (1980) (N=85 professional employees and 56 insurance agents). Dubin and Champoux (1977) employed the Central Life Interests questionnaire (Dubin, 1956) (7.10) to yield a measure of the extent to which respondents were oriented towards their job as a central interest in their life. Several analyses with different samples indicated that job orientation and some forms of Job Satisfaction were statistically linked. For example, a group of 430 blue-collar male employees yielded correlations with Work, Pay, Promotion, Supervision and Co-worker Satisfactions of 0.96, 0.00, 0.46, 0.32 and 0.24 respectively.

Perceived Role Conflict and Role Ambiguity (Rizzo, House and Lirtzman, 1970) (8.16, 8.15) were studied by Brief and Aldag (1976). In research with 77 nursing aides, Role Conflict was correlated −0.29 with both the Work and the Supervision sub-scales; for Role Ambiguity these values were −0.09 and −0.16. Schuler's (1975) data from 76 white- and blue-collar non-supervisory employees included correlations of −0.54 and −0.42 between Role Conflict and Ambiguity and the Work sub-scale. Comparable values of −0.19 and −0.54 were observed in Keller's (1975) study of 51 government scientists. Additional data on Conflict and Ambiguity are provided by Abdel-Halim (1978), Schuler (1977 a, b, c), Schuler, Aldag and Brief (1977), Sims and Szilagyi (1975a), Szilagyi (1977), and Szilagyi, Sims and Keller (1976). In very general terms it may be concluded that the perceived role variables are statistically associated with several facets of Job Satisfaction, but values vary somewhat between studies.

Salary level predicted Pay Satisfaction scores ($r=0.46$) in a study of 180 managers by Dyer and Theriault (1976); see also Schwab and Wallace (1974). Perceived Job Characteristics (Hackman and Lawler, 1971) (8.1) were found to be associated with several JDI sub-scale scores in Brief and Aldag's (1975) study of 104 correction staff. For example, perceived Autonomy was correlated 0.51, 0.21, 0.23, 0.38 and 0.37 with the Work, Pay, Promotion, Supervision and Co-workers sub-scales respectively. Similar results, but with slightly lower values, are reported by Evans, Kiggundu and House (1979). Katerberg, Hom and Hulin (1979) studied 395 part-time national Guardsmen, reporting that a measure of Job Complexity correlated 0.59 with the Work sub-scale.

Positive and Punitive Leader Reward Behaviors (9.7) were studied by Keller and Szilagyi (1976). With a sample of 192 managerial, engineering and supervisory employees they reported correlations between Positive Leader Reward Behavior and Satisfaction with Work, Pay, Promotion, Supervision and Co-workers of 0.29, 0.35, 0.31, 0.75 and 0.30 respectively. For Punitive Leader Reward Behavior (a leader's tendency to reprimand for low performance) the correlations were −0.10, −0.02, 0.03, −0.01 and 0.11. (See also Keller and Szilagyi, 1978.) Alutto and Acito (1974) studied "decisional deprivation"—not being permitted to participate in decisions in which participation was desired. Their index of this deprivation correlated −0.27, −0.29, −0.56 and −0.44 with the Work, Pay, Promotion and Supervision sub-scales respectively (N=75 employees, mainly production workers).

Differences in satisfaction levels between white-collar and blue-collar employees were observed by Milutinovich (1977), especially in the case of the Work sub-scale. For example, in a sample of white employees means of 35.05 and 26.46 were recorded for 41 white-collar males and 129 blue-collar males respectively. Ronen (1978b) observed a significant linear effect of occupational level upon Satisfaction with Work, senior employees being more satisfied; a curvilinear relationship was suggested for the other four sub-scales, with medium-level employees most satisfied. Waters, Roach and Waters (1976) studied 152 non-supervisory female clerks and recorded correlations with job grade of 0.49, 0.23, −0.10, 0.17 and 0.15 for the Work, Pay, Promotion, Supervision and Co-workers sub-scales respectively.

A large number of other investigators have employed the Job Descriptive Index during our search period, including the following: Abdel-Halim (1979b, 1980a), Abdel-Halim and Rowland (1976), Adam (1975), Adams (1978), Adams, Laker and Hulin (1977), Aldag and Brief (1978, 1979), Baird (1976, 1977), Bhagat and Chassie (1978), Billings, Klimoski, and Breaugh (1977), Brief, Aldag and Van Sell (1977), Di Marco (1975), Downey, Sheridan and Slocum (1975), Dyer, Schwab, and Theriault (1976), Farr (1976a, b), Farr, Vance and McIntyre (1977), Forbes and Barrett (1978), Futrell (1978), Gavin and Kelley (1978), Golembiewski and Yeager (1978), Gordon and Arvey (1975), Gould (1979b), Gould and Hawkins (1978), Hammer (1978), Hanser and Muchinsky (1978), Hill and Ruhe (1974), Hom, Katerberg and Hulin (1979), Howard, Cunningham and Rechnitzer (1977), Hunt, Osborn and Larson (1975), Ivancevich (1979b), Jacobs and Solomon (1977), Keller, Szilagyi and Holland (1976), Kesselman, Hagen and Wherry (1974), Kim and Schuler (1979), Klein and Wiener (1977), Koch (1979), Lafollette and Sims (1975), Larson, Hunt and Osborn (1976), London and Klimoski (1975a, b), Margerison and Glube (1979), McDonald and Gunderson (1974), Miller, Katerberg and Hulin (1979), Milutinovich and Tsaklanganos (1976), Motowidlo and Borman (1978), Mount and Muchinsky (1978), Mowday, Porter and Dubin (1974), Nicholson, Brown and Chadwick-Jones (1976), O'Reilly (1977, 1978), O'Reilly and Roberts (1975), Orpen (1979a, b), Osborn and Hunt (1975), Osborn and Vicars (1976), Perone, DeWaard and Baron (1979), Peters, O'Connor and Rudolf (1980), Petty and Lee (1975), Petty and Miles (1976), Phillips and Lord (1980), Porter, Steers, Mowday and Boulian (1974), Roberts and O'Reilly (1979), Schmitt and White (1978), Schuler (1976, 1980), Schwab and Heneman (1977), Seybolt (1976), Sims and Szilagyi

(1975b), Szilagyi and Keller (1976), Szilagyi and Sims (1974b), Umstot, Bell and Mitchell (1976), Wexley and Nemeroff (1975), White, Mitchell and Bell (1977), Wiener and Klein (1978), Wimperis and Farr (1979), Yunker and Hunt (1976), and Zemelman, Di Marco and Norton (1979).

The Job Descriptive Index will deservedly find a place in future research, but it is not without limitations. It was devised in the 1960's, before the upsurge of interest in intrinsic job characteristics, and its emphasis is therefore upon Extrinsic Satisfaction. For example, several investigators have examined Extrinsic Satisfaction in terms of the Pay, Promotion, Supervision and Co-workers sub-scales, with the Work sub-scale necessarily serving as the only measure of Intrinsic Satisfaction. There will be cases where a more comprehensive or differentiated intrinsic measure is required.

It may also sometimes be desirable to cover additional facets of Job Satisfaction. For example, studies of managers might wish to examine attitudes towards subordinates; the Managerial Opinion Scale (Warr and Routledge, 1969) (3.4) is a development in that direction. Furthermore, some of the items are unusual in (for example) British contexts, and the Worker Opinion Survey (Cross, 1973) (3.5) may be useful there.

Items

Work on Present Job

Fascinating, routine (R), satisfying, boring (R), good, creative, respected, hot (R), pleasant, useful, tiresome (R), healthful, challenging, on your feet (R), frustrating (R), simple (R), endless (R), gives sense of accomplishment

Present Pay

Income adequate for normal expenses, satisfactory profit sharing, barely live on income (R), bad (R), income provides luxuries, insecure (R), less than I deserve (R), highly paid, underpaid (R)

Opportunities for Promotion

Good opportunity for promotion, opportunity somewhat limited (R), promotion on ability, dead-end job (R), good chance for promotion, unfair promotion policy (R), infrequent promotions (R), regular promotions, fairly good chance for promotion

Supervision on Present Job

Asks my advice, hard to please (R), impolite (R), praises good work, tactful, influential, up-to-date, doesn't supervise enough (R), quick-tempered (R), tells me where I stand, annoying (R), stubborn (R), knows job well, bad (R), intelligent, leaves me on my own, around when needed, lazy (R)

People on your Present Job

Stimulating, boring (R), slow (R), ambitious, stupid (R), responsible, fast, intelligent, easy to make enemies (R), talk too much (R), smart, lazy (R), unpleasant (R), no privacy (R), active, narrow interests (R), loyal, hard to meet (R)

Responses

Respondents are asked to put Y beside each item if it describes the feature in question (Work, Pay, etc.), N if the item does not describe that feature, or ? if they cannot decide.

3.4 Managerial Opinion Scale

Source: Warr and Routledge, 1969

The authors observe that the broad applicability of the Job Descriptive Index (3.3) is often extremely valuable, but argue that there is also a need for similar scales of Job Satisfaction which more adequately cover features of particular relevance to supervisors and managers. Seven such features are identified: the Work Itself, Pay, Prospects of Promotion, Immediate Superior, Managers of Own Level, Subordinates, and the Firm as a Whole. The first four of these are addressed by the JDI, the fifth and sixth are two aspects of "co-workers" relevant to managers, and the seventh feature is a more general one thought to warrant measurement in its own right.

An initial pool of more than 200 items was drawn from the literature to form sub-scales to tap these seven components. This number was reduced to 126 according to criteria specified in the source publication, and responses were obtained from 200 British managers, supervisors and foremen. Analyses of these data led to the establishment of a 77-item measure, with 15, 7, 8, 13, 10, 12 and 12 items representing the seven sub-scales. Additional data were then obtained from a second sample of 63 respondents.

The items themselves refer to features of the job rather than to the respondent, but the large majority are explicitly value-laden, containing terms like "poor", "unfair", "satisfactory" and "worthwhile". Approximately half the items in each sub-scale are reverse-scored. Items are presented in blocks covering each feature, and responses are Y (for yes), ? (for uncertain, if you cannot decide), or N (for no). A traditional scoring frame is used: 3, 2 or 1, with 3 indicating high Satisfaction. A total score is derived for each sub-scale, and as these are of different length the possible range of scores varies among them; it appears preferable to use mean scores in future.

The source publication includes the following sub-scale totals (N=200): Work Itself 39.09 (s.d. 4.68), Pay 15.32 (s.d. 3.44), Prospects of Promotion 18.18 (s.d. 4.40), Immediate Superior 34.33 (s.d. 5.22), Managers of Own Level 26.21 (s.d. 3.92), Subordinates 31.52 (s.d. 4.43), and the Firm as a Whole 29.42 (s.d. 4.92). Spearman-Brown coefficients were 0.81, 0.74, 0.80, 0.86, 0.82, 0.81 and 0.80 respectively, and intercorrelations between the sub-scales ranged from 0.01 to 0.45, with a median of 0.23. Correlations with a ten-point Overall Job Satisfaction rating were 0.61, 0.21, 0.23, 0.22, 0.10, 0.17 and 0.31 respectively. The sub-scales have been employed during our search period in a study of managerial motivation by Evans (1974).

Items

The Work Itself

Frustrating (R), respected, discouraging (R), satisfying, not enough responsibility (R), gives a sense of self-respect, requires quite a lot of skill, the wrong sort of job for me (R), time passes quickly, worthwhile, not enough authority (R), needs a lot of experience, I can learn a lot from this job, challenging, are you uncertain of the limits of your authority and responsibility? (R)

Your Present Pay

Fairly satisfactory, underpaid for what I do (R), is there enough difference between your income and that of your immediate subordinates? Is your income as good as that of similar managers your own age? poor (R), quite highly paid, is your income as good as that of the friends you mix with socially?

Your Prospects of Promotion

Good opportunities, prospects as good as with any other firm, my experience increases my prospects, do you feel you've stayed at your present level for too long? (R), I expect to get quite a lot higher, unfair promotion policy in this firm (R), dead-end job (R), my educational qualifications and training increase my prospects.

Your Immediate Superior

Friendly, impolite (R), fair, knows his job, I feel I can discuss problems with him, nagging (R), well organized, snobbish (R), stubborn (R), reliable, accepts my advice, interferes in my work too much (R), I can feel confident of his support when I make a decision.

Managers of your Own Level

Friendly, intelligent, very much like myself, not enough experience (R), too old-fashioned (R), most of them should not have got where they are (R), unwilling to try out new ideas (R), snobbish (R), boring (R), some of them think they own the place (R).

Your Subordinates

Unintelligent (R), lazy (R), rather have older workers (R), work well as a group, distrustful (R), poorly trained (R), would you replace many of your subordinates if possible? (R), good fun, reliable, need too much supervision (R), know their jobs, hardworking

Your Firm

Too big (R), feel you belong, has a good reputation, go-ahead, needs some fresh people at the top (R), higher management keep us in the dark about things we ought to know (R), efficient, too much class distinction (R), looks after employees well, too many rules and regulations (R), insufficient co-ordination between departments (R), a good firm to work for

Responses

As 3.3

3.5 Worker Opinion Survey

Source: Cross, 1973

This measure employs the format of the Job Descriptive Index (3.3), but differs from the JDI in three principal ways. It is aimed only at shop-floor workers (thus complementing the Managerial Opinion Scale (3.4)), it avoids terms familiar only within the USA, and it contains one extra sub-scale.

An initial pool of almost 300 items was reduced to 92 terms covering six occupational features: the Work Itself, Pay, Opportunities for Promotion, Immediate Superior, Co-workers and the Firm as a Whole. (The author points out that the words "company", "organization" etc. may be substituted for "firm" when appropriate.) Responses were obtained from 431 British shop-floor manual workers (210 men, 221 women), and item analyses resulted in the establishment of a 48-item measure, with eight items in each sub-scale. Additional data were then obtained from a second sample of 114 male workers.

Half the items in each sub-scale are reverse-scored. Items are presented in blocks covering each feature, and responses (Y, N or ?) and scoring weights (3, 1 or 0) are as for the Job Descriptive Index (3.3).

The source publication includes the following information, where "r with OJS" is the correlation with a single-item rating of Overall Job Satisfaction:

	Work	Pay	Promotion	Superior	Co-workers	Firm
Mean (210 men)	13.13	11.84	9.19	15.81	18.68	13.54
s.d. (210 men)	6.63	7.79	7.00	6.61	5.41	7.41
Mean (221 women)	14.11	14.17	9.33	15.68	17.58	16.04
s.d. (221 women)	5.48	7.08	5.94	6.50	4.84	5.69
Kuder-Richardson (210 men)	0.76	0.86	0.82	0.80	0.74	0.84
Kuder-Richardson (221 women)	0.68	0.84	0.73	0.78	0.70	0.69
r with OJS (172 men)	0.69	0.42	0.41	0.21	0.18	0.51
r with OJS (221 women)	0.63	0.37	0.44	0.28	0.15	0.46

Intercorrelations between the sub-scales ranged from 0.03 to 0.62 (median 0.35) for 210 men, and from 0.12 to 0.52 (median 0.32) for 221 women. Data from the full sample (N=431) were submitted to factor analysis to test the assumed six-factor model. The first five sub-scales emerged very clearly from this analysis, but items tapping Satisfaction with the Firm were more widely dispersed, in keeping with the general nature of that sub-scale.

Lischeron and Wall (1975a, b) have employed the Worker Opinion Survey in an experimental field study of employee participation (see also Wall and Lischeron, 1977), and Nicholson, Wall and Lischeron (1977) have used the measure in the prediction of casual absence and propensity to leave.

Items

The Work Itself

It's the same day after day (R), the wrong sort of job for me (R), worthwhile, routine (R), time passes quickly, satisfying, better than other jobs I've had, endless (R)

Your Present Pay

Underpaid for what I do (R), adequate for my needs, far too low (R), quite highly paid, fairly satisfactory, poor (R), well paid, less than I deserve (R)

Opportunities for Promotion

The system for promotion is fair, prospects very limited (R), easy to get on, too much favouritism (R), good opportunities, my experience increases my prospects, dead-end job (R), the good jobs are usually taken before you hear of them (R)

Your Immediate Superior

Lets you know where you stand, does a good job, interferes too much (R), always too busy to see you (R), stands up for you, quick tempered (R), can discuss problems with him, hard to please (R)

The People you Work With

Easy to make enemies (R), hard working, some of them think they run the place (R), know their jobs, work well as a group, stupid (R), unpleasant (R), do their share of the work

The Firm as a Whole

Looks after its employees, a poor firm to work for (R), they treat you like a number (R), has a good reputation, too much class distinction (R), feel you belong, needs some fresh people at the top (R), the best firm I have worked for

Responses

As 3.3

3.6 Specific Satisfactions

Source: Hackman and Oldham, 1975

Within their broad-ranging Job Diagnostic Survey (see also 2.6, 6.3, 7.7, 8.2, 8.28), the authors include a 14-item measure to tap five Specific Satisfactions: Pay (two items), Job Security (two items), Social (three items), Supervisory (three items) and Growth Satisfaction (four items). The first four of these are referred to as Work Context Satisfaction. Growth Satisfaction is concerned with intrinsic features of the job, being the degree to which an employee is satisfied with opportunities for personal growth and development on the job. A seven-point response dimension is used, and scores are averaged (from 1 to 7) within each sub-scale.

Descriptive statistics and psychometric data have been published by Hackman and Oldham (1974, 1975, 1980), Hackman, Pearce and Wolfe (1978), Oldham (1976) and Oldham, Hackman and Pearce (1976). However, a comprehensive summary of data from 6930 employees working on 876 jobs in 56 organizations is provided by Oldham, Hackman and Stepina (1978), and from this we have drawn the material in Table 7.

Oldham, Hackman and Stepina (1978) also report intercorrelations between sub-scales, which are generally rather high. Within the four Context Satisfactions the median intercorrelation is 0.42 (range 0.28 to 0.47); however, the Growth Satisfaction sub-scale is correlated still more highly with the others: 0.43, 0.51, 0.57 and 0.55 with Pay, Security, Social and Supervisory Satisfaction respectively. The data are also tabulated according to organization size and type, geographical location, job level and type etc.

Social and Supervisory Satisfaction items have been combined into "Interpersonal Satisfaction" by Oldham and Brass (1979). Data from the Growth Satisfaction measure have been presented by Arnold and House (1980), Bhagat and Chassie (1980), Champoux (1978), Oldham and Brass (1979), Staw and Oldham (1978), and Wall, Clegg and Jackson (1978). Other uses of one or more of the indices include those by Gilmore, Beehr and Richter (1979), Oldham and Miller (1979), and O'Reilly and Caldwell (1979).

Table 7   Normative and psychometric information for Specific Satisfactions (N=6930)

	Specific Satisfactions				
	Pay	Security	Social	Supervisory	Growth
Number of items	2	2	3	3	4
Mean	4.16	4.76	5.31	4.79	4.74
Standard deviation	1.66	1.48	1.02	1.57	1.33
Spearman-Brown reliability	0.86	0.73	0.64	0.87	0.84
r with General Satisfaction (2.6)	0.42	0.48	0.47	0.50	0.69

Items

Sub-scales are made up of items as follows: Pay, 2,9; Security, 1,11; Social, 4, 7, 12; Supervisory, 5, 8, 14; Growth, 3, 6, 10, 13.

How satisfied are you with this aspect of your job?
  1. The amount of job security I have
  2. The amount of pay and fringe benefits I receive
  3. The amount of personal growth and development I get in doing my job
  4. The people I talk to and work with on my job
  5. The degree of respect and fair treatment I receive from my boss
  6. The feeling of worthwhile accomplishment I get from doing my job
  7. The chance to get to know other people while on the job
  8. The amount of support and guidance I receive from my supervisor
  9. The degree to which I am fairly paid for what I contribute to this organization

10. The amount of independent thought and action I can exercise in my job
11. How secure things look for me in the future in this organization
12. The chance to help other people while at work
13. The amount of challenge in my job
14. The overall quality of the supervision I receive in my work

Responses

Extremely dissatisfied; Dissatisfied; Slightly dissatisfied; Neutral; Slightly satisfied; Satisfied; Extremely satisfied; scored 1 to 7 respectively.

3.7 Facet-specific Job Satisfaction

Source: Quinn and Staines, 1979

As part of a national "quality of employment survey" carried out in 1977, the authors used 33 items to tap a worker's evaluation of six features of the job. The items (each tapping a "facet", as indicated in the scale's title) were previously used in a 1973 survey, and a similar measure was employed in 1969. Comparisons between the three years are possible from data in the source publication (see also Quinn *et al.*, 1971; Quinn and Shepard, 1974).

The items were drawn from earlier research in order to yield a simple instrument which was easy to administer. Applicability to all levels and types of employee was a primary criterion for item selection. The 1977 sample contained 1515 respondents (36% female) representative of all employed adults, all industries, and all occupations in the United States.

Responses to each item are scored from 1 to 4, and mean values are calculated for each sub-scale and the overall scale. Characteristics of the measure and some results from the 1977 survey are set out in Table 8. This table also indicates that two short forms are offered, of 18 and seven items. These items were selected because of their close associations with the overall 33-item measure, and the authors report that the short forms correlate 0.97 and 0.91 respectively with the full scale. Items in the short forms are indicated below as (A) (18-item form) or (B) (seven-item form).

The six factors were derived through factor analysis, although no details of factor loadings or intercorrelations are given. (Note incidentally that items about supervision fall within the "resource adequacy" factor.) The high alpha coefficient (0.92) for the complete scale suggests (as with other measures in this area) that the sub-scales are not independent. The total score is reported to correlate 0.55 with Facet-free

Table 8   Facet-specific Job Satisfaction: data from the 1977 Quality of Employment Survey

			Sub-scales				
	Comfort	Challenge	Financial Rewards	Relations with Co-workers	Resource Adequacy	Promotions	Complete scale
Complete scale							
Number of items	7	6	3	3	11	3	33
Mean value (N=1515)	2.87	3.00	2.89	3.26	3.19	2.46	3.02
Standard deviation	0.57	0.68	0.81	0.61	0.57	0.86	0.49
Coefficient alpha	0.69	0.88	0.66	0.61	0.88	0.76	0.92
Short form A							
Number of items	5	3	2	2	4	2	18
Mean value (N=740)							2.96
Standard deviation							0.52
Coefficient alpha	0.61	0.67	0.64	0.48	0.71	0.66	0.85
Short form B							
Number of items	2	1	1	1	1	1	7
Mean value (N=740)							2.75
Standard deviation							0.64
Coefficient alpha							0.75

Job Satisfaction (2.7), and the authors tend to imply a preference for a single Satisfaction score rather than six sub-scale scores, especially in the case of the short forms. However, they also provide response distributions for each of the 33 facets separately.

Elements from the 1969 version of the scale have been employed by Mitchell, Smyser and Weed (1975). Gupta and Beehr (1979) have reported relationships between the Resource Adequacy sub-scale, Role Ambiguity (8.37) and absenteeism.

Items

Comfort

1. I have enough time to get the job done (A)
2. The hours are good (A)
3. Travel to and from work is convenient (A)
4. The physical surroundings are pleasant (A, B)
5. I can forget about my personal problems
6. I am free from the conflicting demands that other people make of me (A, B)
7. I am not asked to do excessive amounts of work

Challenge

8. The work is interesting
9. I have an opportunity to develop my own special abilities (A)
10. I can see the results of my work
11. I am given the chance to do the things I do best (A, B)
12. I am given a lot of freedom to decide how I do my own work
13. The problems I am expected to solve are hard enough (A)

Financial Rewards

14. The pay is good
15. The job security is good (A)
16. My fringe benefits are good (A, B)

Relations with Co-workers

17. The people I work with are friendly
18. I am given a lot of chances to make friends (A)
19. The people I work with take a personal interest in me (A, B)

Resource Adequacy

20. I have enough information to get the job done
21. I receive enough help and equipment to get the job done (A)
22. I have enough authority to do my job (A)
23. My supervisor is competent in doing his or her job
24. My responsibilities are clearly defined
25. The people I work with are competent in doing their jobs
26. My supervisor is very concerned about the welfare of those under him or her

27. My supervisor is successful in getting people to work together (A, B)
28. My supervisor is helpful to me in getting my job done (A)
29. The people I work with are helpful to me in getting my job done
30. My supervisor is friendly

Promotions

31. Promotions are handled fairly (A, B)
32. The chances for promotion are good (A)
33. My employer is concerned about giving everyone a chance to get ahead

Responses

Very true; Somewhat true; A little true; Not at all true; scored 4, 3, 2 and 1 respectively.

3.8   Intrinsic and Extrinsic Rewards Satisfaction

Source: Cammann, Fichman, Jenkins and Klesh, 1979; Seashore, Lawler, Mirvis and Cammann, 1982

The Michigan Organizational Assessment Questionnaire contains a number of scales to measure work attitudes and perceptions; see also 2.9, 3.9, 3.10, 4.13, 6.2, 6.6, 8.6, 9.5 and 9.11. Items and scales have been developed through a series of substantial empirical analyses, and the Questionnaire has been administered to several thousand employees from many organizations.

Two scales are included to tap employees' Satisfaction with certain Intrinsic and Extrinsic Rewards. They contain four and three items respectively, with seven response alternatives. The mean value across items constitutes the scale score in each case. Items are interspersed in presentation, also with those from the Social Rewards Satisfaction scale (3.9).

Means are not cited in the source publication, but coefficient alpha is given as 0.87 and 0.63 for Intrinsic Rewards Satisfaction and Extrinsic Rewards Satisfaction respectively (N>400). The two scales are associated 0.62 and 0.33 respectively with the authors' measure of Overall Job Satisfaction (2.9) and are themselves intercorrelated 0.36. Correlations with the authors' scales of Job Involvement (6.2) and Intention to Turn Over (4.13) are reported as 0.38 and −0.45 for Intrinsic Rewards Satisfaction and 0.14 and −0.28 for Extrinsic Rewards Satisfaction.

Mirvis and Lawler (1977) employed an expanded (six-item) version of the Intrinsic Rewards Satisfaction scale in a study of 160 bank tellers. They reported a correlation with number of absence incidents three months later of −0.81.

Items

Intrinsic Rewards Satisfaction

1. How satisfied are you with the chances you have to learn new things?
2. How satisfied are you with the chances you have to accomplish something worthwhile?
3. How satisfied are you with the chances you have to do something that makes you feel good about yourself as a person?

Extrinsic Rewards Satisfaction

1. How satisfied are you with the amount of pay you get?
2. How satisfied are you with the fringe benefits you receive?
3. How satisfied are you with the amount of job security you have?

Responses

Very dissatisfied; Dissatisfied; Slightly dissatisfied; Neither satisfied nor dissatisfied; Slightly satisfied; Satisfied; Very satisfied; scored 1 to 7 respectively.

3.9 Social Rewards Satisfaction

Source: Cammann, Fichman, Jenkins and Klesh, 1979; Seashore, Lawler, Mirvis and Cammann, 1982

Although some authors include social relationships among the extrinsic features of work, Social Rewards Satisfaction is in the Michigan Organizational Assessment Questionnaire a scale separate from the measure of Extrinsic Rewards Satisfaction. It contains three items, which are presented among those from scale 3.8, and which are responded to and scored in the same way.

Coefficient alpha is given as 0.87 (N>400), and Social Rewards Satisfaction is reported to correlate 0.40, 0.41 and 0.30 with the authors' measures of Overall Job Satisfaction (2.9), Intrinsic Rewards Satisfaction (3.8), and Extrinsic Rewards Satisfaction (3.8) respectively.

Items

1. How satisfied are you with the way you are treated by the people you work with?
2. How satisfied are you with the respect you receive from the people you work with?
3. How satisfied are you with the friendliness of the people you work with?

Responses

As 3.8

3.10   Pay Satisfaction

Source: Cammann, Fichman, Jenkins and Klesh, 1979; Seashore, Lawler, Mirvis and Cammann, 1982

Pay is often viewed as a major contributor to extrinsic job satisfaction, and within the Michigan Organizational Assessment Questionnaire the scale to measure Extrinsic Rewards Satisfaction contains two items dealing with pay and fringe benefits. However, the questionnaire also contains a separate three-item Pay Satisfaction scale.

Responses are upon one of two seven-point dimensions, and the mean value across the items constitutes the scale score. Means are not cited in the source publications, but coefficient alpha is reported as 0.89 (N>400). Correlations of 0.38, 0.38 and 0.72 were observed with the authors' measures of Overall Job Satisfaction (2.9), Intrinsic Rewards Satisfaction (3.8) and Extrinsic Rewards Satisfaction (3.8) respectively. The latter value is partly due to the fact that some items are extremely similar across the two scales. Pay Satisfaction was also found to correlate −0.35 with Intention to Turn Over (Seashore, Lawler, Mirvis and Cammann, 1982) (4.13).

Items

1. I am very happy with the amount of money I make
2. Considering my skills and the effort I put into my work, I am very satisfied with my pay
3. How satisfied are you with the amount of pay you get?

Responses

Items 1 and 2: Strongly disagree; Disagree; Slightly disagree; Neither agree nor disagree; Slightly agree; Agree; Strongly agree; scored 1 to 7 respectively. Item 3: As 3.8.

3.11 to 3.29   Other Measures of Specific Satisfactions

3.11 Stogdill (1965) has developed a 28-item Job Expectations Questionnaire which contains seven four-item sub-scales: Work, Advancement, Friends' Attitudes, Pay, Freedom on the Job, Family Attitudes, and Job Security. Responses to each item (e.g. Satisfaction with my present job) are in terms of a five-point dimension from Much better than expected to Much poorer than expected. The author cites Kuder-Richardson reliability coefficients for the sub-scales between 0.54 (N=59) and 0.87 (N=63), and presents means and standard deviations from varied samples in five organizations. Greene (1975, 1979) and Organ and Greene (1974a, b) have examined a range of correlates of the Work sub-scale.

3.12 A related measure is Stogdill's (1965) 12-item Job Description Questionnaire which taps Satisfaction with the Company and its Management. Responses against each feature (e.g. This company's reputation in the community) are in terms of very good, good, fair, poor, or very poor, scored 5 to 1 respectively and summed. From studies with varied samples in several organizations, the author cites Kuder-Richardson reliability coefficients between 0.85 (N=63) and 0.92 (N=157). Schriesheim and Von Glinow (1977) report a comparable coefficient of 0.95 (N=242). See also Schriesheim, House and Kerr (1976).

3.13 King (1960) also sets out to measure Company Satisfaction, developing a 20-item measure which has a split-half reliability coefficient of 0.92. Responses are Yes or No to questions like: Is your company a good one for a person trying to get ahead? Six items are reverse-scored, and the full measure is set out in the source publication. Alutto and Acito (1974) studied "decisional deprivation" (not being permitted to participate in decisions in which participation is desired), reporting a correlation of −0.50 with Company Satisfaction (N=75 mainly production workers). Ivancevich (1979b), with a ten-item version and 154 project engineers, found that this relationship was insignificant when age and job tenure were partialled out.

3.14 Within a wide-ranging Triple Audit Opinion Survey, Dawis, Pinto, Weitzel and Nezzer (1974) describe a 112-item Job Satisfaction measure, in which four items comprise each of 28 scales. Twenty-seven of the scales cover specific features of work, and one scale taps Overall Satisfaction; responses are on a five-point dimension from not satisfied to extremely satisfied. In a study of 1088 managers, Hoyt internal reliability coefficients for the Specific Satisfaction scales ranged from 0.55 to 0.95. Correlations between Overall Satisfaction and the 27 Specific Satisfaction scales are also reported, the strongest associations being with Ability Utilization (r=0.78), Work Challenge (r=0.74), Progress of Career (r=0.74), and Choice of Career (r=0.74).

Scale intercorrelations from the original study were submitted to hierarchical factor analysis by Weitzel, Pinto, Dawis and Jury (1973). Correlations between Specific Satisfactions and Overall Job Satisfaction for employees with differing needs have been examined by Pinto and Davis (1974), and the scales have been used in studies of pay attitudes by Weitzel, Harpaz and Weiner (1977) and Mahoney and Weitzel (1978).

3.15 Achievement Satisfaction is measured by Kopelman's (1976) four-item scale. Respondents indicate how often they are bothered (from Never to Nearly all the time) by, for example, "feeling like you are in a rut and that you are not getting anywhere".

3.16 Alutto and Vredenburgh (1977) describe a 35-item Career Dissatisfaction scale, which "measures a respondent's displeasure with the organization's promotional rewards policy by comparing the actual importance of 35 characteristics for organizational advancement with the pattern of preferred importance" (p. 342). The authors analyse data from 197 nurses.

3.17 Murphy and Fraser (1978) describe an instrument designed to yield independent measures of Content Satisfaction (with those "elements of the work situation related to the opportunities for self-actualization") and Context Satisfaction (with those "elements revolving around the social and technical environment of the job"). The measure is intended for use with professional employees, and respondents check Satisfied, Not sure, or Dissatisfied against each of 36 features of their job.

3.18 Szura and Vermillion (1975) have described a Motivator–Hygiene Attribution Scale, which combines elicitation of exceptionally good and bad job incidents with four-point ratings of the extent to which those incidents contributed to each of six motivator and six hygiene outcomes, as conceptualized by Herzberg, Mausner and Snyderman (1959).

3.19 A 25-item Role Orientation Index has been used by Graen, Dansereau and Minami (1972) to measure five Specific Satisfactions: the Intrinsic Value of Work, Interpersonal Relations with Superior, Technical Competence of Superior, Fellow Participants, and Psychological Value of Job Performance Rewards. It has been used in a programme of leadership research by Cashman, Dansereau, Graen and Haga (1976), Dansereau, Graen and Haga (1975), and Graen and Ginsburgh (1977); and also by Johnson and Stinson (1975), Stinson and Johnson (1975), and Dansereau, Cashman and Graen (1974).

3.20 Attitudes towards Flexitime have been assessed by Golembiewski, Yeager and Hilles (1975). An 18-item scale is described in terms of seven factors, labelled as: Participative worksite with good communication (two items), Positive impact of work hours on person/productivity (three items), Flexibility, personal and work-related (four items), Reinforced motivation to contribute beyond standard (two items), Unconflictful worksite (four items), Worksite attractiveness/availability of human resources (two items), and Ease of scheduling work (one item).

3.21 Katzell, Ewen and Korman (1974) describe a 33-item Job Satisfaction Questionnaire, simply worded for respondents of modest education, which yields scores for five intercorrelated sub-scales: Advancement (four items), Job Content (three items), Supervision (12 items), Co-workers (four items), Pay (three items), together with a miscellaneous category (seven items).

3.22 A 25-item Job Satisfaction scale with seven sub-scales (Advancement Opportunity, Autonomy, Intrinsic Job Satisfaction, Job Security, Pay Recognition, Personal Recognition, Social Pleasantness) is outlined by Rizzo, House and Lirtzman (1970), who cite means and other features. The scale was employed in research by Dessler and Valenzi (1977) and Valenzi and Dessler (1978).

3.23 Ivancevich (1974) has described a 19-item measure to assess Satisfaction with Rewards in six areas: Self-Actualization, Autonomy, Personal Worth, Social Affiliation, Job Security, and Pay. The scale was initially used in a study of the introduction of a four-day 40-hour week (see also Ivancevich and Lyon, 1977), but has also been applied in research into organizational climate (Lyon and Ivancevich, 1974) and group training (Ivancevich and McMahon, 1976).

3.24 A 20-item Subordinate Evaluation Questionnaire is presented in full by McFillen (1978) and used in laboratory research. It contains items for recording opinions about individual subordinates, for example: I believe this subordinate is a reliable, dependable worker. See also McFillen and New (1979).

3.25 From the standpoint that Morale is multidimensional, Scott (1967) presents 299 bipolar rating scales in seven-point semantic differential form. Respondents rate nine concepts on the number of scales cited in brackets: Me at Work (75), My Opportunities for Growth (27), My Job (25), My Supervisor (35), Top Management (31), Company Benefits (26), My Fellow Workers (30), My Pay (25), and My Working Conditions (25). Factor analyses are reported by Scott (1967) and checked for generality by Scott and Rowland (1970). The scale has been used in full by Forbes and Barrett (1978) and in part by Cherrington and England (1980), Greene and Schriesheim (1980), Phillips and Lord (1980), Scott and Erskine (1980), and Sims, Szilagyi and Keller (1976). The source publication lists the items in full.

3.26 Members' attitudes to their trade union have been tapped by Glick, Mirvis and Harder (1977). They describe a six-item measure of

Overall Union Satisfaction (alpha 0.85) and separate indices of willingness to attend union meetings and to represent the union.

3.27 The Union Attitude Questionnaire (Uphoff and Dunnette, 1956) consists of 77 items designed to obtain union members' evaluations with respect to: Unionism in General (20 items); Local Union in General (seven items); Local Union Policies and Practices (nine items); Local Union Officers (12 items); Local Union Administration (eight items); National Union (eight items). A further 13 items are of a general (mixed) nature. Split-half reliability for the six sub-scales ranged from 0.71 to 0.90, and was 0.96 for all combined, on a sample of 1251 union members. Schriesheim (1978a) used two of the sub-scales with a sample of 59 production workers.

3.28 Alderfer (1972) has presented an Existence, Relatedness and Growth theory of motivation and satisfaction. This builds upon the hierarchical model of Maslow (e.g. 1943, 1954) and is accompanied by measures of satisfactions and desires. The Existence, Relatedness and Growth Satisfaction Scale contains 35 items in seven sub-scales: Pay (six items), Fringe Benefits (four items), Physical Danger (two items), Respect from Superiors (eight items), Respect from Peers (five items), Respect from Customers (four items), and Growth (six items). Existence Need Satisfaction is tapped by the first three sub-scales, Relatedness Satisfaction by the three Respect sub-scales, and Growth Satisfaction by the final sub-scale. Responses are upon a six-point agree–disagree continuum, and 18 items are reverse-scored. An illustrative item from the Growth sub-scale is "I have an opportunity to use many of my skills at work".

The source publication includes results of a factor analysis with orthogonal rotation, demonstrating the independence of the seven sub-scales. The items and some validation evidence are also presented. Wilcove (1978) has adapted the measure for use with naval personnel, and selected items have been used by Szilagyi (1980) and Szilagyi and Holland (1980). The author's Need measure which parallels this Satisfaction Scale is described in entry 7.25.

3.29 Schultz and Slevin (1975) have described a 57-item questionnaire to assess users' attitudes to their Computer Information System. The measure contains seven sub-scales to measure respondents' evaluations of Performance, Interpersonal Aspects, Organizational Changes, Goals, Support, Client Relations, and Urgency. Robey (1979), in a study of 66 sales employees, observed significant correlations (median 0.69, range 0.42 to 0.79) between attitudes and actual use of a system.

4 Alienation and Commitment

In this chapter we examine scales to measure Work Alienation, Organizational Commitment and related constructs. These have often been distinguished from the General and Specific Satisfactions described in Chapters 2 and 3, but conceptual separation has not always been matched by differentiation at the empirical level. We will here present four measures of Alienation, six scales of Commitment, and six associated indices.

Kanungo (1979) has described how the notion of Alienation has long been of interest. For example, theologians have viewed the meaninglessness of human existence in terms of spiritual alienation or separation from God and moral principles. Sociologists such as Marx, Weber and Durkheim gave the concept comprehensive treatment, with Marx in particular addressing himself to Alienation from Work. His view was that working on a job should be a voluntary, conscious activity which contributed to the development of mental and physical powers and which thus had its own intrinsic value. When employees were denied such freedom and personal development, then Marx spoke of Alienation, in two senses:

(a) separation of workers from the products of their labour, when producers feel that they cannot influence what is produced and how it is made; and

(b) separation of workers from the means of production, when producers have no ownership or control of factories and equipment.

Seeman (1959) attempted to specify the distinctive core of Alienation by proposing five different types of separation. These may be summarized in terms of separation from control, prediction, moral values, other people, and oneself, as follows:

Powerlessness: an inability to influence the course of events in one's lifespace.

Meaninglessness: an inability to predict events and the outcomes of one's own and others' behaviour.

Normlessness: a belief that morally undesirable means are often the only way to achieve desired ends.

Isolation: a feeling that one is not a member of any important social network.

Self-estrangement: a feeling that one's activities are undertaken for extrinsic reasons (for example, to provide the basis for mere survival) rather than for their intrinsic meaning and personal value.

Several of these components in the work setting are tapped by Shepard's (1972) scale (4.4), but other measures of Work Alienation have more in common with indices of Overall Job Satisfaction or Intrinsic Satisfaction. This point is documented in the entries which follow, and has been substantiated by Lefkowitz and Brigando (1980), who examined the relationships within and between the dimensions of Work Alienation and of Job Satisfaction. In a study of 268 computer engineers, they observed that the average correlation between measures of Alienation and Satisfaction was as high as the average correlation within Alienation and within Satisfaction measures themselves (around 0.30). Work Involvement (see Chapter 6) also has some overlap with features of Alienation (see Kanungo, 1979, for a discussion of this point), and elements of both Satisfaction and Involvement are reflected in several items of scales 4.1 to 4.4.

Organizational Commitment also has some affinity with these other concepts. It is generally viewed as a broad attitude towards one's employing organization, with components in terms of loyalty, acceptance of organizational goals and a desire to remain as a member; expanded definitions are given in the entries for scales 4.5 to 4.10 and in

Salancik's (1977) discussion of the concept. Commitment items are sometimes similar to those included in scales of Job Satisfaction, and the empirical correlation between the two variables is moderately high; see the entries which follow.

Job Attachment (4.11) is a slightly more focussed concept than Organizational Commitment, being an attitude to one's job rather than towards the organization as a whole. However, it too is significantly associated with Satisfaction and contains similar items; for example two items from scale 4.11 also appear in 2.7, Facet-free Job Satisfaction. Scales 4.12 and 4.13 tap specific intentions to leave one's current employer, and entry 4.14 describes a measure of Organizational Frustration, a generalized negative reaction which covers a range of features subsumed in earlier measures. The chapter closes with two briefer entries, covering Organizational Identification and Organizational Loyalty.

4.1 Organizational Alienation

Source: Aiken and Hage, 1966

In order to examine the correlates of two organizational features—Centralization and Formalization—the authors devised two measures of alienation for use with professional employees. Alienation from Work reflects a feeling of disappointment with career and professional development, as well as disappointment over the inability to fulfil professional norms. Alienation from Expressive Relations reflects dissatisfaction in social relations with supervisors and fellow workers. These concepts were measured through scales of six and two items respectively, the items having been drawn from a Work Satisfaction scale of Gross, Mason and McEachern (1958). The response alternatives and scoring procedures are not described, nor are means or reliability estimates provided.

In a sample of 314 psychiatrists, social workers and rehabilitation counsellors from 16 social welfare organizations, Aiken and Hage (1966) found that Alienation from Work was positively correlated (median $r=0.53$; $N=16$ organizations) with measures of Centralization (8.25) and Formalization (8.46); this may be partly due to overlap between items, since items one and four have some similarity with items used to tap the organizational variables. Associations between the latter measures and Alienation from Expressive Relations ranged from 0.17 to 0.65. The two forms of Alienation were themselves intercorrelated 0.75. Note that the authors analysed data by agency scores (averaging the values for each organizational level) rather than in terms of individual respondents; such a grouping of data tends to enhance observed associations between variables. Allen and Lafollette (1977) examined similar data from 86 managers in a single company, using individuals as the unit of analysis. Correlations between Alienation from Work and perceived organizational Centralization and Formalization were statistically significant (median $r=0.37$), but correlations with Alienation from Expressive Relations were not significant. Information about means and reliabilities is again lacking, but correlations between alienation and age and job tenure are reported as around zero.

The scales' label, "alienation", appears to be misleading, and it is preferable to think in terms of two highly intercorrelated features of Job Satisfaction. The two-item Alienation from Expressive Relations scale is unsatisfactory, especially as the item content suggests a low item–item correlation and differing associations with other variables (see Aiken and Hage, 1966, n. 25). The failure to publish information about score distributions is particularly disturbing, since there is a tendency to assume high levels of whatever is measured; Aiken and Hage's (1966, p. 506) assertion that "this study indicates that the problem of alienation also occurs in welfare agencies, schools and hospitals" is not supported by the published evidence.

Items

Alienation from Work

1. How satisfied are you that you have been given enough authority by your board of directors to do your job well?
2. How satisfied are you with your present job when you compare it to similar positions in the state?
3. How satisfied are you with the progress you are making towards the goals which you set for yourself in your present position?
4. On the whole, how satisfied are you that (your superior) accepts you as a professional expert to the degree to which you are entitled by reason of position, training and experience?
5. On the whole, how satisfied are you with your present job when you consider the expectations you had when you took the job?
6. How satisfied are you with your present job in light of career expectations?

Alienation from Expressive Relations

7. How satisfied are you with your supervisor?
8. How satisfied are you with your fellow workers?

4.2 Work Alienation

Source: Miller, 1967

The author examines potential conflicts between individual professional autonomy and organizational constraints in terms of Seeman's
(1959) account of "self-estrangement". Occupational self-estrangement is said to be exhibited by employees who do not experience pride
or meaning in their work, by those who work solely for money, or those
who find no reward in work activities themselves. Miller argues that
self-estrangement in this sense is not the same as dissatisfaction with
one's job.

Drawing upon Morse's (1953) scale of intrinsic pride in work and
introducing three new items, a five-item instrument was constructed,
initial data being gathered from 419 scientists and engineers within a
single company. One item is reverse-scored. Responses are on a four-
point scale, subsequently reduced to either agree (0) or disagree (1); the
total number of items disagreed with constitutes the Work Alienation
score. Using this dichotomous scoring procedure, the items yielded a
Guttman scale with a coefficient of reproducibility of 0.91. Thirty
percent of respondents disagreed with none of the items, 40% disagreed
with one or two items, and 30% disagreed with three, four or five items.
These respondent groups were described as low, medium and high
Work Alienation respectively.

Miller (1967) identified several factors significantly correlated with
Work Alienation, for example working for a directive supervisor.
Rousseau (1977) studied 201 production workers and reported strong
associations (ranging from -0.25 to -0.68, median -0.45) between
Work Alienation and perceived Job Characteristics measured by a
modified version of the Job Diagnostic Survey (8.2). Work Alienation
was also found to correlate -0.72 with the Brayfield-Rothe measure of
Overall Job Satisfaction (2.2) and -0.43 with Index B of Patchen's
measure of Job Involvement (6.8). Rousseau quotes means for employees in three different technologies (Long-linked, Mediating, and
Intensive; see Thompson, 1967) of 1.92 (s.d. 1.54), 0.69 (s.d. 1.02) and
0.75 (s.d. 1.08). Being the number of items receiving "disagree" responses, these values indicate rather low levels of Alienation. Further
analyses of the data are reported in Rousseau (1978a). In research with
163 varied employees from a single company, Hammer and Stern
(1980) report a Spearman-Brown internal reliability coefficient of 0.82.
Greene (1978) with 247 senior scientists and engineers found that the
relationship between Work Alienation and Organizational Formaliza-

tion (House and Rizzo 1972a) (8.57) was significant for two out of four groups.

As with other measures of Alienation, it is unclear what concept is being operationalized. Despite Miller's (1967) argument (above), Rousseau (1977) included the questionnaire as "a measure of intrinsic satisfaction in that it deals with the extent to which the employee experiences pride and the use of valued skills while doing his or her job" (p. 28), and the observed scores were indeed closely associated with Overall Job Satisfaction. Mean values appear to be typically low, so that care is needed in talking of "alienated workers", and the items have some similarity with those used to tap Job Involvement and Intrinsic Motivation (see Chapter 6).

Items

1. I really don't feel a sense of pride or accomplishment as a result of the type of work that I do (R)
2. My work gives me a feeling of pride in having done the job well
3. I very much like the type of work that I am doing
4. My job gives me a chance to do the things that I do best
5. My work is my most rewarding experience

Responses

Strongly agree; Agree; Disagree; Strongly disagree; scored 0, 0, 1 and 1 respectively.

4.3 Work Alienation

Source: Seeman, 1967

The author examines the possibility that the consequences of Alienation from Work generalize out of the work sphere into other areas of social life. Drawing from questions used by Blauner (1964), he constructs an index of Work Alienation, containing seven items asking "essentially whether the respondent finds his work engaging and rewarding in itself".

Seeman examined the correlations between Work Alienation and a range of social processes, such as generalized powerlessness, intergroup hostility and social mobility orientation. There was no firm evidence in favour of the generalization hypothesis, although the other variables were intercorrelated in consistent patterns.

Seybolt and Gruenfeld (1976) note how "alienation" is a widely used term of uncertain meaning. They quote Lee's (1972) belief that the term has "died of overweening claims and overwork", and suggest that in practice Seeman's (1976) measure has substantial overlap with measures of Job Satisfaction. Taking the Work sub-scale of the Job Descriptive Index (3.3) as an example, they report correlations with a slightly revised Alienation scale (allowing three-point responses) of -0.68, -0.70, -0.60, -0.67, -0.52 and -0.65 for six different employee samples, identified by sex and job level. Patterns of association with other variables such as pay and age also pointed to substantial redundancy between the two concepts. No means or standard deviations were reported, but coefficient alpha for the Work Alienation index was found to be 0.59.

Items

1. Is your job too simple to bring out your best abilities, or not?
2. Can you do the work on the job and keep your mind on other things most of the time or not?
3. Which one of the following statements comes closest to describing how you feel about your present job? (Four statements, uncited, from "interesting nearly all the time" to "completely dull and monotonous").
4. Does your job make you work too fast most of the time, or not?
5. Does your job really give you a chance to try out ideas of your own, or not? (R).
6. If you had the opportunity to retire right now, would you prefer to do that, or would you prefer to go on working at your present job?
7. On an ordinary workday, do you have the opportunity to make independent decisions when you are carrying out your tasks, or is it rather routine work? (R).

Responses

Not described

4.4   Alienation from Work

Source: Shepard, 1972

Drawing upon Marx's concept of alienation, the author views this as "social psychological separation from some social referent". He points out that people may be differentially alienated from different aspects of their social life, and takes the work setting as one illustrative social referent. Using Seeman's (1959) analysis, he sets out to operationalize five uses of the term in respect to work:

Powerlessness refers to perceived lack of freedom and personal control on the job, where the worker feels that he or she is dominated by other people or a technological system.

Meaninglessness refers to an inability to understand the events in which one is engaged, for example how one's work activities relate to other jobs and the larger organization.

Normlessness is the expectation that culturally accepted goals (such as upward mobility in a company) can only be achieved through illegitimate means.

Instrumental Work Orientation is a specific case of "self-estrangement", when activities are undertaken solely for anticipated future rewards and not for any intrinsic value. Working merely for money is cited as an example from the occupational setting.

Self-evaluative Involvement refers to the degree to which a person tests his or her self-esteem through involvement in a particular role, for example as a worker. In this specific sense it has similarities with the concept of Work Involvement (7.5).

The full scale has 30 items, with 8, 8, 5, 4 and 5 tapping the five separate constructs. Sub-scale scores are obtained by summing responses across items, with a high score indicating low Alienation. The Powerlessness, Meaninglessness and Normlessness items each refer to a characteristic of work, and responses are in terms of the extent to which that feature exists in the respondent's job, from minimum (scored 1) to maximum (scored 7). Instrumental Work Orientation and Self-evaluative Involvement are measured through statements open to agreement or disagreement, scored from 1 to 5.

With a sample of 305 male production workers, corrected item–whole reliabilities were within the following ranges for items from the five sub-scales respectively: 0.49 to 0.63, 0.35 to 0.70, 0.50 to 0.65, 0.38 to 0.48, 0.29 to 0.49. Means and standard deviations are not given, but the author describes how the five sub-scales were all significantly inter-correlated. Values ranged from 0.52 between Powerlessness and Meaninglessness to 0.15 between Meaninglessness and Instrumental Work Orientation. Self-evaluative Involvement was correlated negatively with the other measures, between -0.17 and -0.25 (Shepard, 1972).

Cummings and Manring (1977) employed (with some very small amendments) 20 of Shepard's items in order to extract sub-scales which were factorially independent. They achieved this through ten items (3, 2, 2, 2 and 1 for each component respectively). Their sample comprised 96 male blue-collar forging employees, and the measures of Powerlessness, Normlessness and Meaninglessness were found to be significantly associated with employee lateness but not with absenteeism. Significant relationships were also observed with supervisors' ratings of effort for the first two sub-scales ($r=0.20$ in each case) but not with supervisors' ratings of performance.

Items

Powerlessness: To what extent can you vary the steps involved in doing your job? To what extent can you move from your immediate work area during working hours? To what extent can you control how much work you produce? To what extent can you help decide on the methods and procedures used in your job? To what extent do you have influence over what happens to you at work? To what extent can you work ahead and take short rest breaks during work hours? To what extent are you free from close supervision while doing your job? To what extent can you increase or decrease the speed at which you work?

Meaninglessness: To what extent do you know how your job fits into the total work organization? To what extent do you know how your work contributes to company products? To what extent does management give workers enough information about what is going on in the company? To what extent do you know how your job fits into the work of other departments? To what extent do you know how your work affects the jobs of others you work with? To what extent do you know how your job fits in with other jobs in the company? To what extent are you learning a great deal about the company while doing your job? To what extent does management give workers enough information about what is going on in your department?

Normlessness: To what extent do you feel that people who get ahead in the company deserve it? To what extent do you feel that pull and connection get a person ahead in the company? (R). To what extent do you feel that to get ahead in the company you would have to become a good "politician"? (R). To what extent do you feel that getting ahead in the company is based on ability? To what extent do you feel that people who get ahead in the company are usually just lucky? (R).

Instrumental Work Orientation: Your job is something you have to do to earn a living—most of your real interests are centred outside your job. Money is the most rewarding reason for working. Working is a necessary evil to provide things your family and you want. You are living for the day when you can collect your retirement and do the things that are important to you.

Self-evaluative Involvement: You would like people to judge you for the most part by what you spend your money on, rather than by how you make your money. Success in the things you do away from the job is more important to your opinion of yourself than success in your work career. To you your work is only a small part of who you are. If you had to choose, you would much prefer that others not judge you by the kind of job you hold, but rather by your off-the-job accomplishments. The best description of who you are would not be based on the kind of job you hold.

Responses

Powerlessness, Meaninglessness and Normlessness: Minimum to maximum, intermediate labels not cited; scored from 1 to 7 respectively.

Instrumental Work Orientation and Self-evaluative Involvement: Strongly agree; Agree; Undecided; Disagree; Strongly disagree; scored from 1 to 5 respectively.

4.5   Organizational Commitment Questionnaire

Source: Porter and Smith, 1970

The authors distinguish between treatments of Organizational Commitment as an attitude and as a behaviour, and take the former
approach. However, they view it as more than a passive loyalty,
committed individuals being willing to give something of themselves in
order to contribute to the organization. The construct is thought to be
more global than Job Satisfaction, being a generally affective reaction to
the organization rather than specifically to the work. Organizational
Commitment is also held to differ from Job Satisfaction in that it is likely
to be less subject to transitory changes associated with day-to-day
events. It is defined as the strength of an individual's identification with
and involvement in a particular organization, and is said to be characterized by three factors: a strong belief in, and acceptance of, the
organization's goals and values; a readiness to exert considerable effort
on behalf of the organization; and a strong desire to remain a member of
the organization.

The Organizational Commitment Questionnaire has 15 items, six of
which are negatively phrased and reverse scored. There is a seven-point
response dimension. The authors point out that responses to the scale
can easily be faked, so that researchers should be aware of the possibility of distorted responses in situations threatening to employees. A
short form is also available, in which the negatively phrased items (3, 7,
9, 11, 12, 15) are omitted. Item scores are summed and the mean is
taken. Thus there is a possible range of scores from one to seven, and the
higher the score the more organizationally committed an individual is
judged to be.

Reliability and validity evidence has been provided by Dubin,
Champoux and Porter (1975), Mowday, Porter and Dubin (1974),
Porter, Crampon and Smith (1976), Porter, Steers, Mowday and
Boulian (1974), Steers (1977), Steers and Spencer (1977) and Stone and
Porter (1975). These studies, together with a number of unpublished
investigations, have been reviewed by Mowday, Steers and Porter
(1979), and we will summarize their general conclusions, supplement-
ing them with data from research not covered in their review.

Coefficient alpha is consistently high in the studies they describe,
ranging from 0.82 to 0.93 with a median of 0.90. Additional evidence
about internal reliability comes from Kerr and Jermier (1978) whose
investigation of 113 police officers yielded a Kuder-Richardson coefficient of 0.86; with 158 police officers Jermier and Berkes (1979) obtained a comparable figure of 0.91; and in Ivancevich's (1979b) study of

154 project engineers the value was 0.84. O'Reilly and Roberts (1978), with 562 members of a high-technology naval aviation unit, recorded a coefficient alpha of 0.54. Scale means reported by Mowday, Steers and Porter (1979) range from 4.0 to 6.1 with a median of 4.5. Standard deviations range from 0.64 to 1.30 around a median of 1.06. Aldag and Brief (1977) in a study of 75 police employees report a mean of 5.46 (s.d. 1.04). Van Maanen (1975) recorded means from 5.1 (s.d. 1.2) to 6.3 (s.d. 0.6) with 136 male police recruits and 5.7 (s.d. 0.6) with 58 experienced police officers. Bartol (1979b) obtained a mean of 4.78 with 159 computer professionals. Illustrative test–retest reliability coefficients from Mowday and colleagues' review are 0.72 across two months and 0.62 across three months.

Evidence for the convergent validity of the Organizational Commitment Questionnaire comes from significant negative correlations with stated intention to leave the organization and positive associations with work-oriented interests, using Dubin's (1956) measure of Central Life Interests (7.10) (see also Van Maanen, 1975). Mowday, Steers and Porter (1979) also summarize longitudinal studies indicating that Organizational Commitment scores significantly predict leaving behaviour in a range of samples; their conclusion is supported by additional data from Hom, Katerberg and Hulin (1979) and Kerr and Jermier (1978).

Mowday and colleagues also review evidence for discriminant validity: how far the measure yields information different from that yielded by other measures. Correlations across four samples with Job Involvement (Lodahl and Kejner, 1965) (6.1) were high (median 0.55, range 0.30 to 0.56). So, too, were associations with indices of specific Job Satisfaction. Median correlations with the Job Descriptive Index subscales (3.3) are reported as 0.61 for Satisfaction with Work (range 0.37 to 0.64), 0.29 for Pay (range 0.01 to 0.68), 0.39 for Promotion Prospects (range 0.14 to 0.51), 0.41 for Supervision (range 0.22 to 0.68) and 0.36 for Co-workers (range 0.20 to 0.55). In research with 395 part-time National Guardsmen, Katerberg, Hom and Hulin (1979) observed a correlation of 0.59 with the Work sub-scale; and O'Reilly and Roberts (1978) report correlations of 0.40, 0.20 and 0.18 with the Work, Promotion and Supervision sub-scales in a study of 562 naval aviation personnel. Jermier and Berkes (1979) report a correlation of 0.68 between Organizational Commitment and General Job Satisfaction, measured by the short form of the Minnesota Satisfaction Questionnaire (2.4). Steers and Braunstein (1976) describe correlations with personality variables measured through their Manifest Needs Questionnaire (7.11); in a study of 115 white-collar employees Organizational Commitment was correlated 0.25 with Need for Achievement and −0.25 with Need for Autonomy.

Other studies employing the questionnaire during our search period include Ivancevich (1980), Morris and Koch (1979), Morris and Snyder (1979), O'Reilly (1977), O'Reilly, Bretton and Roberts (1974), and Roberts and O'Reilly (1979).

Items

1. I am willing to put in a great deal of effort beyond that normally expected in order to help this organization be successful
2. I talk up this organization to my friends as a great organization to work for
3. I feel very little loyalty to this organization (R)
4. I would accept almost any type of job assignment in order to keep working for this organization
5. I find that my values and the organization's values are very similar
6. I am proud to tell others that I am part of this organization
7. I could just as well be working for a different organization as long as the type of work were similar (R)
8. This organization really inspires the very best in me in the way of job performance
9. It would take very little change in my present circumstances to cause me to leave this organization (R)
10. I am extremely glad that I chose this organization to work for, over others I was considering at the time I joined
11. There's not too much to be gained by sticking with this organization indefinitely (R)
12. Often, I find it difficult to agree with this organization's policies on important matters relating to its employees (R)
13. I really care about the fate of this organization
14. For me this is the best of all possible organizations for which to work
15. Deciding to work for this organization was a definite mistake on my part (R)

Responses

Strongly disagree; Moderately disagree; Slightly disagree; Neither disagree nor agree; Slightly agree; Moderately agree; Strongly agree; scored 1 to 7 respectively.

4.6   Organizational Commitment

Source: Hrebeniak and Alutto, 1972

The authors view commitment to an organization in terms of the perceived utility of continued participation ("calculative involvement in the utilitarian employing system", p. 560), so that strong commitment is reflected in an unwillingness to change organizations for moderate personal advantage. In a study of 318 teachers and 395 nurses they operationalized this idea in terms of respondents' reported willingness to move for a variety of different benefits, finally choosing the four most reliable items: slight increases in pay, professional freedom, status, and friendliness of co-workers. Responses are on a three-point dimension, scored 1, 2 and 3 and totalled, so that the potential range is from 4 to 12 with a high value representing strong Commitment.

Spearman-Brown reliability of this four-item scale on the initial sample was 0.79, with means of 10.33 and 10.36 for teachers and nurses respectively. In the source publication the authors report significant associations with a number of variables (see also Alutto, Hrebeniak and Alonso, 1973). For example, Organizational Commitment varied with years in current job: one to four years 9.88 (N=227); five to 12 years 10.29 (N=261); 13 or more years 10.87 (N=225). Hrebeniak (1974) studied 46 paramedical staff in a general hospital, reporting correlations with job tenure of 0.31, with job level of 0.42, and with role tension of −0.36. In a similar study with 75 employees of a single company (mainly production workers), Alutto and Acito (1974) presented data in terms of respondents' "decisional deprivation"—the number of decisions (out of a set of seven) in which a person wished to participate but did not at present participate. Organizational Commitment scores were 9.5, 7.6, and 6.3 for low deprivation (0 or 1 decisions), medium deprivation (2 or 3 decisions) and high deprivation (4 to 7 decisions) respectively; the correlation between the two variables was −0.49. A mean of 10.09 (s.d. 2.20) is reported by Wiener and Vardi (1980) from a sample of 85 professional employees; low but statistically significant associations were observed with Job Involvement (Lodahl and Kejner, 1965) (6.1) and the Work and Pay Satisfaction sub-scales of the Job Descriptive Index (3.3).

Variants of the measure, using the same items but with reference to job changing ("job commitment") and movement out of one's current profession ("professional commitment") have been described by Alutto and Acito (1974) and Alutto, Hrebeniak and Alonso (1973) respectively.

Items

Assume you were offered a position as a (teacher, nurse, etc.), but with another employing organization. Would you leave your present organization under any of the following conditions?
1. With a slight increase in pay

2. With slightly more freedom to be professionally creative
3. With slightly more status
4. To work with people who are a little friendlier

Responses

Yes definitely; Uncertain; No definitely not; scored 1 to 3 respectively.

4.7   Organizational Commitment

Source: Buchanan, 1974

Buchanan views commitment as "a partisan, affective attachment to the goals and values of an organization, to one's role in relation to goals and values, and to the organization for its own sake, apart from its purely instrumental worth" (p. 533). The concept is therefore measured through three components:

Identification is viewed as "adopting as one's own the goals and values of the organization". It is tapped through six items, which are said to be drawn from Hall, Schneider and Nygren (1970) but in practice are not the ones cited in that publication.

Job Involvement is measured through four items drawn from Lodahl and Kejner's (1965) (6.1) scale, together with two other items. These are intended to measure "psychological immersion or absorption in the activities of one's work role".

Loyalty. The author introduces a new 11-item sub-scale to tap the "feeling of affection for and attachment to the organization".

The 23-item scale contains seven reverse-scored items. Buchanan (1974) obtained responses from 279 managers from eight organizations, and coefficients alpha of 0.86, 0.84, 0.92 and 0.94 were recorded for the three sub-scales and the total scale respectively. The sub-scales were found to be intercorrelated as follows: Identification and Involvement 0.65, Identification and Loyalty 0.74, Involvement and Loyalty 0.58. A number of perceived organizational characteristics were observed to be significantly associated with individual managers' Commitment scores, for example the extent to which one's work was thought to be generally accepted as important to the company.

Items

Identification

1. This organization has a fine tradition of public service
2. If I had my life to live over again, I would still choose to work for this organization

3. I really feel as if this organization's problems are my problems
4. I feel a sense of pride in working for this organization
5. The record of this organization is an example of what dedicated people can achieve
6. I would advise a young college graduate to choose a management career in this organization

Job Involvement

7. The major satisfaction in my life comes from my job
8. I do what my job description requires; this organization does not have the right to expect more (R)
9. I don't mind spending a half-hour past quitting time if I can finish a task
10. The most important things that happen to me involve my work
11. I live, eat and breathe my job
12. Most things in life are more important than my work (R)

Loyalty

13. As long as I am doing the kind of work I enjoy, it doesn't matter what particular organization I work for (R)
14. I feel a strong sense of loyalty toward this organization
15. If another organization offered me more money for the same kind of work, I would almost certainly accept (R)
16. I have always felt that this organization was a cold, unfriendly place to work (R)
17. Over the years I have grown fond of this organization as a place to live and work
18. Generally speaking, my career in this organization has been satisfactory
19. I have warm feelings toward this organization as a place to live and work
20. I have no particular feelings or sentiments toward this organization at all (R)
21. My loyalty is to my work, not to any particular organization (R)
22. Few organizations can match this one as a good place to live and work
23. Based on what I know now and what I believe I can expect, I would be quite willing to spend the rest of my career with this organization

Responses

A seven-point dimension is used, from Strongly disagree to Strongly agree, scored 1 to 7 respectively. Intermediate labels are not provided.

4.8 Commitment to the Formal Organization

Source: Franklin, 1975c

The author views employees' Commitment to the Formal Organization in terms of two kinds of orientation: willingness to uphold norms and rules, and willingness to remain with the organization. These are measured by 11-item and five-item sub-scales respectively, each with

five-point response continua ranging from 0 to 4 such that high Commitment is reflected in high scores. Ten items are reverse-scored.

Little information about the sub-scales is provided in the source
publication but an unpublished report by the author indicates that
coefficients alpha were 0.83 and 0.62 respectively with a sample of 265
white- and blue-collar non-supervisory employees from six organizations. Mean scores from this sample were 29.92 (s.d. 8.94) and 12.51
(s.d. 4.44) for the two measures.

Items

Willingness to Uphold Norms and Rules

1. This organization has a poor way of handling employee complaints (R)
2. The organizational rules operative in this company are made so that
   everyone gets a fair break on the job
3. Most of the time the organization tries to be honest and fair in dealing
   with its employees
4. I don't really feel a part of this organization (R)
5. I feel that promotions are not handled fairly (R)
6. Many of the rules here are annoying (R)
7. The longer you work here the more you feel you belong
8. I seldom feel I am really part of what goes on around here (R)
9. Management here is interested in the welfare of its people
10. Management fails to take action on our complaints (R)
11. There are good opportunities here for those who want to get ahead

Continuance Commitment

1. If another organization offered you the same sort of job you have now and
   you were able to keep all of the benefits you now have, would you accept the
   offer? (R)
2. Suppose the same sort of offer was made except you were offered an additional $20.00 a week, would you accept the offer? (R)
3. I feel that my job is no more interesting than others I could get (R)
4. I plan to continue to work here until I retire
5. If I had a chance I would change to some other organization (R)

Responses

Norms Commitment sub-scale: Strongly disagree; Mildly disagree; Neutral (both
agree and disagree); Mildly agree; Strongly agree; scored 0 to 4 respectively.
Continuance Commitment sub-scale: Items 3 to 5 are as above. Items 1 and 2:
Absolutely would not; Would not; Neutral; Would; Absolutely would; scored
0 to 4, but in practice the scoring is reversed.

4.9   Commitment to the Organization

Source: London and Howat, 1978

To study the bond between an individual and his or her organization, the authors created a five-item scale with a seven-point response continuum. Two items are reversed-scored, and the mean is calculated. A sample of 98 professional employees (15% female) yielded a mean of 4.71 (s.d. 1.03) and a Spearman-Brown coefficient of internal reliability of 0.52. Commitment to the Organization was significantly related to age ($r=0.34$) but not to job tenure (correlation value not cited).

Items

1. I would leave this agency if offered the same job with another agency (R)
2. Barring unforeseen circumstances, I would remain in this agency indefinitely
3. It is important that we all pull together for the good of our agency because if our agency is successful then we will be successful
4. Although there are probably reasons for this, it is too bad salaries at our agency are so low (R)
5. Suppose a young friend of yours has completed his or her training in your field. Even though he or she has also been offered positions of equal rank and salary with several other agencies, I would still advise him or her to consider our agency

Responses

A seven-point dimension is used from Strongly disagree, through Neither agree or disagree, to Strongly agree, with the remaining alternatives unlabelled. Scoring is from 1 to 7 respectively.

4.10   Organizational Commitment

Source: Cook and Wall, 1980

The authors note the need for short, robust scales which are easily completed by blue-collar respondents of modest educational attainment. Drawing upon work by Buchanan (1974) and Porter, Steers, Mowday and Boulian (1974) (see 4.7 and 4.5) they view Organizational Commitment in terms of three interrelated components: *Identification*: pride in the organization, internalization of the organization's goals. *Involvement*: willingness to invest personal effort as a member of the organization, for the sake of the organization. *Loyalty*: affection for and attachment to the organization, a wish to remain a member of the organization.

A nine-item commitment scale was constructed, with three items tapping each of the components; numbers 1, 5 and 8 cover Organizational Identification, 3, 6 and 9 cover Organizational Involvement, and 2, 4 and 7 cover Organizational Loyalty. Separate sub-scale scores are cited in addition to an overall Commitment score. Responses are on a seven-point dimension, scored 1 to 7 respectively and totalled across the items, so that the possible range of scores for the full scale is from 9 to 63 with a high score indicating high Commitment; three items are reverse-scored.

The instrument was developed through application of a larger item pool to two samples (N=390 and 260), with the least effective items being removed after the first investigation. Respondents were male, full-time employees in British manufacturing industry and were selected in order to represent national demographic characteristics. Mean Organizational Commitment scores from the two samples were 44.64 (s.d. 11.45) and 45.37 (s.d. 9.55) with coefficients alpha of 0.87 and 0.80 respectively. A test–retest correlation across six months of 0.50 (N=63) was also observed.

Correlations between the three subscales were 0.54, 0.57 and 0.43, being lower then those reported by Buchanan (1974) with different items (4.7). Coefficients alpha from the two studies were 0.74 and 0.71, 0.87 and 0.71, and 0.82 and 0.60 for Identification, Involvement and Loyalty respectively. Test–retest correlations across six months (N=63) were 0.60, 0.53 and 0.35 for the three sub-scales in that sequence; the authors point out that the last of these is not really adequate. Mean values in the two studies for Identification were 15.04 (s.d. 4.38) and 15.77 (s.d. 4.00), for Involvement 16.99 (s.d. 3.11) and 16.58 (s.d. 3.08), and for Loyalty 12.63 (s.d. 5.51) and 12.99 (s.d. 4.47). Decile scores for the Organizational Commitment scale and for the three sub-scales are also provided in the source publication.

The authors examined correlations (N=260) between Organizational Commitment and 14 other variables. The full Commitment scale was associated 0.28 with age and 0.22 with current job tenure, 0.56 with a new measure of Interpersonal Trust at Work (9.12), and 0.62 with Overall Job Satisfaction (2.11). Correlations with Intrinsic Job Motivation (6.7) and Work Involvement (7.5) of 0.45 and 0.39 were also reported. Clegg and Wall (1981) describe results based on a six-item version of the scale.

Items

1. I am quite proud to be able to tell people who it is I work for
2. I sometimes feel like leaving this employment for good (R)

3. I'm not willing to put myself out just to help the organization (R)
4. Even if the firm were not doing too well financially, I would be reluctant to change to another employer
5. I feel myself to be part of the organization
6. In my work I like to feel I am making some effort, not just for myself but for the organization as well
7. The offer of a bit more money with another employer would not seriously make me think of changing my job
8. I would not recommend a close friend to join our staff (R)
9. To know that my own work had made a contribution to the good of the organization would please me

Responses

No, I strongly disagree; No, I disagree quite a lot; No, I disagree just a little; I'm not sure; Yes, I agree just a little; Yes, I agree quite a lot; Yes, I strongly agree; scored 1 to 7 respectively.

4.11 Job Attachment

Source: Koch and Steers, 1978

The authors view Job Attachment as similar to Organizational Commitment but with a more specific focus. Attachment is said to be characterized by a congruence between one's actual and ideal jobs, an identification with one's chosen occupation, and a reluctance to seek different employment. In that latter respect it is seen as a behavioural intention.

Koch and Steers created a Job Attachment scale from four items used by Sheppard and Herrick (1972, pp. 204–205). Each item is scored from 1 to 5, although the number of response alternatives varies between questions. Scores are summed, so that the range of possible values is between 4 and 20. In a study of 77 unskilled public service employees (60% female) coefficient alpha was found to be 0.71. The mean score for 66 employees remaining with their organization in the subsequent eight months was 10.44 (s.d. 2.80), and for 11 voluntary leavers it was 7.18 (s.d. 2.64). Job Attachment was correlated 0.59 with age and 0.39 with length of tenure in the organization. Attachment was found to correlate 0.61 with Job Satisfaction (an overall score derived from the Job Descriptive Index (3.3)), but these two variables were differently associated with job and personal characteristics.

Note that item 1 may not represent a directional continuum as indicated by the scoring.

Items and Responses

1. If you were completely free to go into any type of job you wanted, what would your choice be?
Want the same type of job you now hold; Want to retire, not work at all; Prefer some other job to the kind you have; scored 5, 3 and 1 respectively

2. How often have you thought very seriously about making a real effort to enter a new and different type of occupation?
Very often; Once in a while; Hardly ever; Never; scored 1, 2, 4 and 5 respectively.

3. Check one of the following statements which best tells how you feel about changing your job.
I would quit my job now if I had anything else to do; I would take almost any other job in which I could earn as much as I am earning now; My job is as good as the average and I would just as soon have it as any other job, but would change jobs if I could make more money; I am not eager to change jobs, but would do so if I could make more money; I do not want to change jobs even for more money, because the one I have now is a good one; scored 1 to 5 respectively.

4. How well would you say your job measures up to the kind you wanted when you first took it? Is it very much like the kind of job you wanted? Somewhat like the job you wanted? Not very much like the kind you wanted?
Very much; Somewhat; Not very much; scored 5, 3 and 1 respectively.

4.12   Propensity to Leave

Source: Lyons, 1971

The author describes a three-item measure which taps respondents' reported tendency to leave their employing organization. Five-point response dimensions are used for each item but these are not described, nor are mean values cited. We have calculated from the source publication that the Spearman-Brown internal reliability coefficient was 0.81 for a sample of 156 female nurses, and the author reports a correlation for this sample of −0.27 with his index of Role Clarity (8.38).

In Rousseau's (1978b) study of 271 employees from several levels of two organizations (65% female) the scale was used as "a measure of an employee's affective response to work" (p. 527); the item wording was presumably modified to avoid reference to "this hospital". Coefficient alpha was found to be 0.71 and the test–retest reliability coefficient over three months was 0.63. Length of job tenure correlated −0.19 with Propensity to Leave, and several statistically significant associations with perceived task and role characteristics were observed. Scores for eight different departments are cited, ranging from 3.0 to 4.4, with a median of 3.9. The Propensity to Leave measure has also been used by

Sutton and Rousseau (1979); and Brief and Aldag (1976) record correlations with Role Ambiguity and Role Conflict (8.15 and 8.16) of 0.25 and 0.23 respectively (N=77 nursing aides and assistants).

Items

1. If you were completely free to choose, would you prefer to continue working in this hospital or would you prefer not to?
2. How long would you like to stay in this hospital?
3. If you had to quit work for a while (for example because of pregnancy), would you return to this hospital?

Responses

Not described

4.13 Intention to Turn Over

Source: Cammann, Fichman, Jenkins and Klesh, 1979; Seashore, Lawler, Mirvis and Cammann, 1982

The Michigan Organizational Assessment Questionnaire contains a number of scales to measure work attitudes and perceptions; see also 2.9, 3.8, 3.9, 3.10, 6.2, 6.6, 8.6, 9.5 and 9.11. These include a three-item index of employees' intention to leave their job. Responses are on one of two seven-point dimensions, and the mean value across the items constitutes the scale score. Means are not cited in the source publication, but coefficient alpha is given as 0.83 (N>400). Correlations of −0.58 and −0.27 are reported with the authors' measures of Overall Job Satisfaction (2.9) and Job Involvement (6.2) respectively.

Items

1. How likely is it that you will actively look for a new job in the next year?
2. I often think about quitting
3. I will probably look for a new job in the next year

Responses

Item 1: A range of numbers, 1 to 7, with 1, 3, 5 and 7 labelled as follows: Not at all likely; Somewhat likely; Quite likely; Extremely likely. Items 2 and 3: Strongly disagree; Disagree; Slightly disagree; Neither agree nor disagree; Slightly agree; Agree; Strongly agree; scored 1 to 7 respectively.

4.14   Organizational Frustration

Source: Spector, 1975

The author sets out to measure personal frustration in an organizational setting and to examine possible correlates of this frustration in terms of reported aggression against others, sabotage of equipment, time-wasting and other activities. He prepared an item pool from answers to open-ended questions about frustrations at work, and through examination of item–whole correlations reduced an initial set of 37 to a scale of 29 items. Responses are on a six-point dimension, scored from 6 to 1 and totalled, so that the possible range of scores is from 174 to 29 with a high score representing high Frustration. Five items are reverse-scored. Coefficient alpha with a sample of 50 employees in service (mainly medical) organizations was 0.88.

The source paper describes how 19 out of 35 correlations between Organizational Frustration scores and possible reactions to frustration were significant beyond the 0.05 level. For example, Organizational Frustration was associated 0.42 with the item "purposely littered or dirtied your place of work or your employer's property" and 0.59 with "said something derogatory about your boss to other people". As the author points out, common method variance is likely to have inflated these values.

Spector (personal communication) has provided the following descriptive statistics from varied samples: a psychiatric hospital, N=31, mean 80.1, s.d. 25.0; a general hospital, N=120, mean 69.9, s.d. 22.8; a county engineering department, N=50, mean 60.5, s.d. 19.7; a general hospital, N=140, mean 73.2, s.d. 16.5.

The items themselves cover topics often presented in scales of Satisfaction and Alienation, and validity evidence is currently very limited. However, the instrument is notable for its somewhat unusual orientation.

Items

1. People act nasty toward me at work
2. I find that every time I try to do something at work I run into obstacles
3. There are a lot of petty and arbitrary rules at work
4. I feel thwarted in my efforts to be creative
5. My supervisor is always chewing me out
6. My supervisor feels my performance is worse than it is
7. I find it easy to talk to my supervisor (R)
8. I feel that I am accomplishing something worthwhile at work (R)
9. I enjoy my job (R)
10. The demands made of me at work are reasonable (R)

11. Policies at work are not fair
12. My work area is a pleasant place to be (R)
13. I often feel that I am being run ragged
14. I am given entirely too much work to do
15. I find that some of the people I have to deal with are not competent
16. I often have problems doing my job because of the incompetence of others
17. My supervisor always seems to be looking over my shoulder
18. My supervisor does not trust me
19. I feel trapped in my job
20. My job is not at all fulfilling
21. I dread having to interact with my supervisor
22. I do not like many of the tasks I have to do
23. My job is boring and monotonous
24. I get blamed for things that are not my fault
25. I don't have the authority to do what I am supposed to do at work
26. It seems that one person tells me to do one thing and another person tells me to do something else at work
27. I am told to do things I don't think I should do at work
28. I often have to waste time doing administrative tasks at work
29. I often feel frustrated at work

Responses

Agree completely; Agree pretty much; Agree slightly; Disagree slightly; Disagree pretty much; Disagree completely; scored 6 to 1 respectively.

4.15 and 4.16   Other measures of Alienation and Commitment

4.15 Rotondi (1975) has described a five-item measure of Organizational Identification. This taps support for management, pride in organizational membership, support for policies, and desire to remain with the organization. With a sample of 107 nonmanagerial scientists and engineers a Spearman-Brown internal reliability coefficient of 0.80 was obtained.

4.16 Jauch, Glueck and Osborn (1978) studied Organizational Loyalty in a sample of 84 university researchers. Five items (of the kind: There are few people here at the university with whom I can share my professional interests) yielded a Spearman-Brown internal reliability coefficient of 0.73.

5 Occupational Mental Health and Ill-health

Growing interest in the quality of working life has been accompanied by increased research into those negative aspects of psychological well-being which may be characterized as mental ill-health. The development of instruments is here less advanced than in the case of, for example, Job Satisfaction. This is partly attributable to conceptual difficulties in unravelling the separate components of ill-health; authors vary in their conceptual frameworks and their use of terms such as stress, strain, anxiety, depression, psychosomatic symptoms, tension, and low self-esteem, sometimes employing several of these interchangeably. There is undoubtedly much overlap between several of these states and processes, and it would not be surprising to find empirical associations between them, but there also remains scope for more careful conceptualization before investigators set out to create additional instruments.

A second difficulty in the scaling of mental ill-health arises from the wide range of particular features which might be included in a single measure and the fact that aggregation across this range may not adequately measure person-specific strains. For example, several of the instruments described in this chapter yield total scores across a number of widely disparate symptoms. Such aggregate scales are often internally reliable and have proved their worth. However, it is possible for some respondents to be overwhelmed by a small set of issues, conflicts between employment and home for example, but to be relatively free of other problems. In such cases the simple aggregation of frequency of negative experiences of all kinds would generate a low score, which would be quite misleading.

Research into Job Satisfaction measures has indicated that weighting individual items by their personal importance has little material effect upon the pattern of overall scores (see p. 14). However, there may be greater need in the area covered by this chapter to introduce severity weightings, since the breadth of topics covered by many scales is such that measurement of any one issue is rather superficial. The present generation of scales tends to summate across a broad range of possible features of psychological ill-health without comprehending differences in intensity of particular experiences.

A third problem in the study of occupational mental health is that psychological well-being is strongly influenced by non-work factors as well as those located in the workplace. For example, anxiety may be a product of both employment and family experiences, and is also mediated by personal vulnerability. It is very difficult to separate these several sources, and some measures of job-related experiences therefore also include psychological processes more generally.

Other organizational researchers have met this difficulty by using within work settings measures which are of completely general focus, with no specific reference to occupational features. In the final part of this chapter (entries 5.13 to 5.34) we summarize the use of these general measures in employment research during our period, covering such states as Anxiety, Depression, indices of Physical Stress Symptoms, Positive and Negative Affect, Self-esteem and measures of Mental Health. We also describe some indices of Life Satisfaction which have been employed in occupational studies. The chapter opens with fuller descriptions of seven measures of Tension, Strain, Depression and Self-esteem at work, followed by brief entries for five other measures of work-related ill-health.

Care must be taken in the interpretation of results in this area, as many investigators fail to report or to take notice of mean values. There is a tendency to describe associations between job variables and (for example) employee Anxiety, as though the presence of those variables accompanied or caused high levels of Anxiety. In practice the average level of Anxiety in a sample is often quite low, so that statistical associations with job factors warrant a quite different presentation. A similar point has been made elsewhere in the book, for example in terms of Alienation, where mean scores are also typically fairly low.

5.1   Job-related Tension

Source: Kahn, Wolfe, Quinn and Snoek, 1964

The authors set out to examine the nature, causes and consequences of two kinds of organizational stress: role conflict and role ambiguity. Their inquiry was in two parts, an intensive study of 53 foremen and managers (with 381 colleagues in these persons' "role sets") and a national survey of 725 paid employees and self-employed people at all organizational levels. Among the measures constructed was a scale of Job-related Tension, based upon items used by Gurin, Veroff and Feld (1960). Fourteen items were employed in the intensive study, but changes were made before the national survey when a 15-item scale was used, with 11 items common to the two investigations.

Respondents indicate how frequently they feel bothered about named features of work, with answers scored from 1 to 5. A total or a mean score is calculated, with a high value indicating high Tension. The source publication cites an overall mean from the national survey of 1.7. Sheridan and Vredenburgh (1978a) record a mean of 2.35 (s.d. 0.60) from 216 nurses (nearly all female) and a coefficient alpha of 0.87. The correlation between Job-related Tension and rated performance was 0.01; other analyses are reported by Sheridan and Vredenburgh (1978b, 1979). Ivancevich (1980) obtained a correlation of -0.39 with the short form of Hackman and Oldham's (1975) Internal Work Motivation scale (6.3) in a study of 249 engineers. Seventeen (unspecified) items from the original measure were used by Alutto and Acito (1974) in their study of 75 employees (mainly production workers) in a single company. Job-related Tension was correlated 0.35 with "decisional deprivation"—not being permitted to participate in decisions as desired. Hrebeniak (1974), also using 17 items, recorded a comparable value of 0.17 with 46 paramedical hospital staff. In a similar study of 321 teachers, Hollon and Chesser (1976) reported a correlation of 0.30 between scores on the 15-item scale and "influence dissonance", the absolute difference between actual and preferred influence. The correlation with Attitude toward the Job (Vroom, 1960) (2.10) was -0.49.

The 14-item version of the Job-related Tension index yielded a coefficient alpha of 0.84 with 179 senior Israeli managers (Eden and Jacobson, 1976). Research with a five-item version has been described by Eden (1975) and with a nine-item version by Ivancevich (1974, 1979b) and Ivancevich and Lyon (1977). Odewahn and Petty (1980) used a 13-item form. Mackinnon (1978) has reviewed the factor structure of Kahn *et al.*'s (1964) results from 596 employed respondents and of new data from 267 unemployed trainees in an adult education centre. The structure was consistent across the samples, with four principal components reflecting features of ambiguity and conflict.

Items

How frequently are you bothered at work by:
1. Feeling that you have too little authority to carry out the responsibilities assigned to you
2. Being unclear on just what the scope and responsibilities of your job are
3. Not knowing what opportunities for advancement or promotion exist for you ˙
4. Feeling that you have too heavy a work load, one that you can't possibly finish during an ordinary workday
5. Thinking that you'll not be able to satisfy the conflicting demands of various people over you
6. Feeling that you're not fully qualified to handle your job
7. Not knowing what your immediate supervisor thinks of you, how he or she evaluates your performance
8. The fact that you can't get information needed to carry out your job
9. Having to decide things that affect the lives of individuals, people that you know
10. Feeling that you may not be liked and accepted by the people you work with
11. Feeling unable to influence your immediate supervisor's decisions and actions that affect you
12. Not knowing just what the people you work with expect of you
13. Thinking that the *amount* of work you have to do may interfere with how *well* it gets done
14. Feeling that you have to do things on the job that are against your better judgment
15. Feeling that your job tends to interfere with your family life

Responses

Never; Rarely; Sometimes; Rather often; Nearly all the time; scored 1 to 5 respectively.

5.2 Tension Index

Source: Lyons, 1971

This is a nine-item measure drawn from the scale of Job-related Tension devised by Kahn, Wolfe, Quinn and Snoek (1964) (5.1). Respondents indicate on a five-point continuum how frequently they are bothered by certain features of their work, and responses are summed, yielding a possible range of scores from 9 to 45.

In a study of 156 nurses the author reports a mean of 22.0 (range 10 to

38) and a Spearman-Brown internal reliability coefficient of 0.70. Tension Index scores were correlated −0.59 with scores from the author's measure of perceived Role Clarity (8.38) and −0.09 with respondents' Need for Clarity (7.22). In a study of 77 nursing aides and assistants, Brief and Aldag (1976) recorded a coefficient alpha of 0.77 and correlations of 0.30 and 0.48 with Role Ambiguity (8.15) and Role Conflict (8.16) respectively (Rizzo, House and Lirtzman, 1970); see also Schuler, Aldag and Brief (1977).

Items

Numbers 2, 3, 4, 5, 7, 8, 12, 13 and 14 from 5.1.

Responses

As 5.1

5.3   Psychological Symptoms of Stress

Source: Patchen, 1970

The author describes a wide-ranging study of 834 non-supervisory employees in a single organization. As part of this enquiry he devised a three-item measure to assess how often employees experience during the day three "psychological" symptoms of stress—feeling depressed, tired and tense. Five alternative frequencies are provided for two items and six frequencies for item three. A mean score is taken so that the possible range is between 1 and 5.33. The Psychological Symptoms of Stress scale is accompanied by an index of four Physical Symptoms; these are less clearly work-related, and are described later in the chapter (5.16).

An overall mean score for Psychological Symptoms is not cited. However, 16 sub-group means are provided, and the median value of these is 2.17. The correlations with Physical Symptoms of Stress (5.16) and with the author's measure of Job Motivation (6.8) were 0.51 and −0.56 respectively (N=90 work groups). Associations with items to tap the chance to use abilities, the chance to learn new things, and work overload were −0.26, −0.43 and 0.28 respectively (N=90 work groups).

Rousseau (1978b, c) employed the scale with employees from an electronics firm and a radio station. The correlations (N=139) between Psychological Symptoms and Physical Symptoms, Overall Job Satisfaction (Faces Scale, see p. 14), and Non-work Life Satisfaction (Faces Scale) were 0.50, −0.35, and −0.53 respectively. An additional use is by Sutton and Rousseau (1979).

Items and Responses

1. Most people have days when they feel pretty "blue" or depressed during most of the day. How often does this happen to you?
Two or three times a week; About once a week; Once or twice a month; About once a month; Less than once a month; scored 5 to 1 respectively.

2. Most people have days when they feel tired or worn out during a good part of the day. How often does this happen to you? (Responses as for item 1.)

3. How often do you feel nervous, tense, or edgy while on the job?
More than 50% of the time; About 50% of the time; About 25% of the time; About 10% of the time; About 5% of the time; Very rarely or never; scored 6 to 1 respectively.

5.4 Anxiety-Stress Questionnaire

Source: House and Rizzo, 1972b

As part of a wider study of organizational variables, the authors describe a scale "to measure the existence of tensions and pressures growing out of job requirements, including the possible outcomes in terms of feelings or physical symptoms" (p. 481). An initial set of 26 items, including some from the Taylor Manifest Anxiety Scale (Taylor, 1953), was administered to 200 managerial, professional and technical employees in a single organization, and factor analysis and item analyses were employed to reduce these to 17 statements falling into three sub-scales: Job-induced Tension (seven items), Somatic Tension (five items) and General Fatigue and Uneasiness (five items). Responses are true or false, scored 2 or 1 respectively and averaged. Note that less than half the items refer directly to work.

The source publication reports means from the initial sample of 1.24 (s.d. 0.28), 1.33 (s.d. 0.23), and 1.25 (s.d. 0.31) for the three sub-scales, with Kuder-Richardson internal reliability coefficients of 0.83, 0.76 and 0.72 respectively. Associations with the authors' measures of Role Ambiguity (8.15) and Role Conflict (8.16) were 0.12, 0.07 and 0.22, and 0.20, 0.14 and 0.24 respectively. Rizzo, House and Lirtzman (1970) have published data from a second sample from the same organization; internal reliability coefficients were lower (0.73, 0.60 and 0.42 respectively), as were the correlations with Role Ambiguity and Role Conflict.

Miles and Perreault (1976) describe the use of a 13-item version with 195 managers, scientists and engineers, obtaining responses on a five-point dimension; they cite a mean of 2.21 (s.d. 0.72) and a Spearman-Brown internal reliability coefficient of 0.89. With 148 respondents from this sample, Miles (1975) reported a test–retest correlation over four months of 0.79, and median correlations between overall Anxiety-

Stress scores and Role Ambiguity (8.15) and Role Conflict (8.16) (Rizzo, House and Lirtzman, 1970) of 0.22 and 0.31 respectively. Other analyses of these data are described by Miles (1976a) and Miles and Petty (1975). The 13-item version and five-point scoring were employed in a study of 235 social service staff (88% female) by Miles and Petty (1977). The mean score was 2.16 (s.d. 0.43), and correlations with Supervisory Behavior Description Questionnaire (9.2) measures of leaders' Initiating Structure and Consideration were 0.36 and −0.26 respectively (N=51 organizations).

Brief and Aldag (1976) derived a total score from an 18-item version, and reported correlations with Role Ambiguity and Conflict (Rizzo, House and Lirtzman, 1970) (8.15 and 8.16) of 0.20 and 0.41 in a sample of 77 nursing aides and assistants. The coefficient alpha was 0.70, and the correlation with Lyons' (1971) Tension Index (5.2) was 0.44; see also Schuler, Aldag and Brief (1977).

Items

Job-induced Tension

8. My job tends to directly affect my health
9. I work under a great deal of tension
10. I have felt fidgety or nervous as a result of my job
12. If I had a different job, my health would probably improve
14. Problems associated with my job have kept me awake at night
16. I have felt nervous before attending meetings in the company
17. I often "take my job home with me" in the sense that I think about it when doing other things

Somatic Tension

4. I am often bothered by acid indigestion or heartburn
5. I sometimes feel weak all over
7. I have had trouble getting to sleep or staying asleep
11. I get irritated or annoyed over the way things are going
15. I may now have an ulcer but I am not sure of it

General Fatigue and Uneasiness

1. I would consider myself in good or excellent health (R)
2. I would consider myself in fair health (R)
3. I do not have very good health
6. I wake up with stiffness or aching in joints or muscles
13. I seem to tire quickly

Responses

True or false; scored 2 or 1 respectively.

5.5 Depressed Mood at Work

Source: Quinn and Shepard, 1974

As part of a national "quality of employment survey" carried out in 1972 and 1973, the authors used ten items to measure Depressed Mood in a job-related context. Responses are on a four-point dimension from Often to Never, scored from 4 to 1 respectively with four items reverse-scored. A mean value is taken; note that a numerically high score indicates little depression. The average score for the national sample (N = 1496; 38% female) was 3.32 (s.d. 0.44), with a coefficient alpha of 0.77. Depressed Mood at Work was correlated 0.49 and 0.43 with Life Satisfaction (5.29) and Overall Job Satisfaction (2.8) respectively.

Beehr (1976) used the measure in a study of 651 varied employees from five organizations (49% female), and reported a Spearman-Brown internal reliability coefficient of 0.71. Depressed Mood at Work (reverse-scored compared to the original) correlated −0.43 with a four-item version of the Facet-free Job Satisfaction scale (2.7) and −0.39 with a nine-item variant of Quinn and Shepard's (1974) measure of Life Satisfaction (5.29).

Items

Check how you feel when you think about yourself and your job:
1. I feel downhearted and blue (R)
2. I get tired for no reason (R)
3. I find myself restless and can't keep still (R)
4. My mind is as clear as it used to be
5. I find it easy to do the things I used to do
6. I feel hopeful about the future
7. I find it easy to make decisions
8. I am more irritable than usual (R)
9. I still enjoy the things I used to
10. I feel that I am useful and needed

Responses

Often; Sometimes; Rarely; Never; scored 4 to 1 respectively.

5.6 Self-esteem at Work

Source: Quinn and Shepard, 1974

In their study described under 5.5, Quinn and Shepard employed four items to measure Self-esteem in a job-related context. The items are bipolar adjectival descriptors separated by a seven-point continuum, and respondents indicate how they see themselves in their work. Scoring is from 1 to 7, with a high score representing high Self-esteem at Work, and an average value is taken. In the initial study (N=1496; 38% female) a mean score of 6.01 (s.d. 0.96) was recorded, with a coefficient alpha of 0.70. Self-esteem at Work was correlated 0.44, 0.48 and 0.50 with Depressed Mood at Work (5.5), Life Satisfaction (5.29) and Overall Job Satisfaction (2.8) respectively.

The first three items were used by Beehr (1976) in a study of 651 varied employees from five organizations (49% female). Associations with Depressed Mood at Work (5.5) (reverse-scored compared to the original) and a four-item version of the Facet-free Job Satisfaction scale (2.7) were −0.31 and 0.25 respectively. The Spearman-Brown internal reliability coefficient of this three-item scale was 0.68.

Items

Successful – Not successful; Important – Not important; Doing my best – Not doing my best; Happy – Sad.

Responses

Seven unlabelled boxes separate the two poles of each item, with instructions as follows: Here are some words and phrases which ask you how you see yourself in your work. For example, if you think that you are very "successful" in your work, put a mark in the box right next to the word "successful". If you think that you are not at all successful in your work, put a mark in the box right next to the words "not successful". If you think you are somewhere in between, put a mark where you think it belongs.

5.7   Interaction Strain

Source: Parry and Warr, 1980

The authors point out that many measures of occupational experience are less than adequate for employed mothers with dependent children. They set out to devise robust and simple measures of mothers' attitudes to paid employment and to employment in the home (the Home and Employment Role Scales, 2.12 and 2.13) and also an index of the strain experienced by an employed mother in coping with both domestic and paid work; the latter is referred to as Interaction Strain.

An initial pool of items was derived from the literature and from two phases of pilot interviews. A sample of 125 employed mothers with children under 14 was drawn from ten widely dispersed areas in the United Kingdom; respondents were all identified as "working class" and were contacted at home. Analyses of self-completion questionnaire responses from this sample yielded a 12-item scale, with five items reverse-scored. A three-point response dimension is used, and scores are summed across items, with a high score indicating high Interaction Strain.

Mean scores from the initial sample were 13.90 (s.d. 3.43) and 16.31 (s.d. 5.17) for 65 part-time and 60 full-time employees respectively, the difference between sub-samples being statistically significant. For the full sample, Interaction Strain was correlated -0.38 with both Home and Employment Role Scales (2.12 and 2.13), and -0.38 and 0.36 with Positive and Negative Affect respectively (Bradburn, 1969) (5.20). Coefficient alpha was recorded as 0.75. A measure of social supports available to the employed mother was significantly associated with Interaction Strain, especially for full-time employees ($r = -0.36$).

The authors note that Interaction Strain values from the initial sample (contacted at home and volunteering for the study) are likely to be lower than from samples drawn from within organizations, since volunteers at home will tend to be those who have spare time and energy.

Items

1. The hours I work make it very difficult to look after the children
2. My job leaves me enough time to spend with my family and friends (R)
3. My husband listens to me if I want to talk about what's been happening at work (R)
4. I feel guilty about leaving my children when I go out to work
5. When I am at work, I often worry about things to do with my home or children
6. I get so involved with my job that I feel a conflict of loyalty between my home and work responsibilities
7. I find it hard to get my children looked after when I am at work
8. My job gives me a welcome break from housework and children (R)
9. My husband thinks it's a good idea for me to go out to work (R)
10. My working hours fit in well with those of my husband, and this makes it easier to arrange for the children to be looked after (R)
11. Going to work makes me too tired to enjoy family life properly
12. The amount of travel needed to go to work interferes with family life

Responses

Yes, true; No, untrue; Don't know; scored 3, 1 and 2 respectively.

5.8 to 5.12   Other Measures of Work-related Ill-health

5.8 Indik, Seashore and Slesinger (1964) have described a measure of Job-related Strain. This contains 15 items, 13 of which are similar to those used by Kahn, Wolfe, Quinn and Snoek (1964) (5.1), but which are here accompanied by a three-point response dimension. The items are presented in full in the source paper. Ivancevich and Donnelly (1975) used nine items from the scale, reporting coefficient alphas of 0.80, 0.82 and 0.87 for groups of 118, 77 and 100 salesmen. See also Ivancevich (1974, 1979b) and Ivancevich and Lyon (1977).

5.9 For use in a study of Israeli chief executives Dornstein (1977) developed a ten-item measure of Role Stress. This is partly based upon the research of Kahn, Wolfe, Quinn and Snoek (1964) (5.1) and House and Rizzo (1972b) (5.4), and each item asks "to what extent do you worry in your job about . . . ?" Three sub-scales were identified (Anomie, Self-Role Stress, and Intersender Role Stress), and these are set out in full.

5.10 Schriesheim and Murphy (1976) modified the instructions to the State Anxiety Inventory (Spielberger, Gorsuch and Lushene, 1968, 1970) to request that respondents describe "how you usually feel on your present job". State Anxiety is "conceptualized as consisting of unpleasant, consciously-perceived feelings of tension and apprehension" (Spielberger, 1972, p. 29), and is tapped in the Inventory through items like "I feel nervous" (from Not at all to Very much). A similar amendment to cover feelings at work was made by Abdel-Halim (1978) James, Gent, Hater and Coray (1979), Keenan (1979), Schriesheim (1979) and Schriesheim, Kinicki and Schriesheim (1979).

5.11 Tosi (1971) has described a four-item Job Threat and Anxiety scale, "intended to measure the manager's concern about his job as it may be affected by conditions in the future over which he may have little or no control" (p. 14). An illustrative question is "How likely is it that a major problem, which you cannot now foresee, will affect your job in the next year or so?" The items are presented in full in the source paper, and the scale has also been used by Hamner and Tosi (1974).

5.12 Sutton and Rousseau (1979) describe a four-item scale of perceived Job Pressure. Items are given in full, together with correlations with other variables, but psychometric properties are not examined. An illustrative question is "How often do you feel overcome by pressures from this job?".

5.13 to 5.34 Measures of Other Affective Reactions

Research into the quality of working life is increasingly making use of measures whose focus is not restricted to occupational experience. Broad affective reactions include mental health, generalized anxiety and depression, and life satisfaction. In view of their growing importance, a summary is provided here of employment-related applications of these measures during our search period. Other similar scales have been developed, for example by clinical\psychologists and those concerned with "social indicators" research; interested readers should turn to the wider literature for further information.

5.13 A measure of generalized State Anxiety has been employed by Caplan and Jones (1975) in a study of 122 computer users; scores were associated 0.42 with Role Ambiguity (Caplan, 1971) (8.17).

5.14 Turney (1974) has employed a short form of the Taylor Manifest Anxiety Scale (Taylor, 1953) in research with 106 technical-professional employees.

5.15 Warr, Cook and Wall (1979) describe the development of a six-item measure of Self-rated Anxiety and its use with two samples of British male manual workers ($N=200$ and 390). Respondents indicate their level of worry in recent weeks about, for example, not having enough money for day-to-day living. Items and descriptive statistics are presented in the source paper. A similar instrument with ten items was employed in a study of 1655 redundant British steelworkers by Warr (1978b).

5.16 Patchen (1970) has examined four Physical Symptoms of Stress (headaches, upset stomach, gas or bloated feeling, trouble getting to sleep), enquiring how often each is experienced (from Almost never to Several times a week). Scores on this measure were correlated 0.51 with Psychological Symptoms of Stress (5.3). The Physical Symptoms measure has also been used by Ivancevich (1979b), Rousseau (1978b, c) and Sutton and Rousseau (1979).

5.17 Alexander and Husek's (1962) Anxiety Differential has been employed by Hunt, Osborn and Larson (1975) in a study of organizational leadership. The instrument obtains self-reports in terms of bipolar dimensions such as calm–jittery and fearless–frightened.

5.18 A 19-item Anxiety-Depression-Irritation scale was devised by Gavin and Axelrod (1977) for their study of mining managers. Items were drawn from Caplan, Cobb, French, Van Harrison and Pinneau (1975), Gurin, Veroff and Feld (1960), and Zung (1965). See also

Burke, Weir and Du Wors (1980a).

5.19 Gavin and Axelrod (1977) also used a ten-item Psychosomatic Symptoms Scale based upon that of Gurin, Veroff and Feld (1960). Modified items from the original scale are published by Indik, Seashore and Slesinger (1964).

5.20 Positive and Negative Affect have been tapped in a ten-item measure by Bradburn (1969). Respondents indicate (Yes or No) whether in the past few weeks they have felt, for example, pleased about having accomplished something, or very lonely and remote from other people. In occupational research with British samples, Warr (1978b) has used the measure with 1655 redundant steelworkers and Parry and Warr (1980) with 125 employed mothers of young children. Ouchi and Johnson (1978) have obtained Positive and Negative Affect data in a comparative study of two companies.

5.21 The General Health Questionnaire (Goldberg, 1972) is a self-administered screening test for detecting minor psychiatric disorders in the general population. It covers recent levels of self-confidence, depression, sleep-loss, problem-solving and similar features, and is available in 60, 30, 20 and 12 item versions. The 20-item scale was employed by Wall, Clegg and Jackson (1978) and Wall and Clegg (1981) in research with British shop-floor workers, and the 30-item version by Fineman (1979) in a study of British managers. Banks, Clegg, Jackson, Kemp, Stafford and Wall (1980) have described studies of three British samples (N=659, 512 and 92), also examining the questionnaire's psychometric properties when used in occupational research; see also Hepworth (1980).

5.22 Kornhauser (1965) has described a 57-item interview measure of Mental Health, which taps Anxiety, Self-esteem, Hostility, Sociability, Life Satisfaction and Personal Morale. The measure has been used in questionnaire form in Gechman and Wiener's (1975) study of 54 school-teachers. See also Frost and Jamal (1979), Jamal and Mitchell (1980) and Ronan, Cobb, Garrett, Lazari, Mosser and Racine (1974).

5.23 A 21-item scale of Mental Health was used by Eden (1975) in his secondary analysis of data collected by Quinn, Seashore, Kahn, Mangione, Campbell, Staines and McCullough (1971). The Mental Health scale covers Somatic Complaints, Depression and Performance Debilitation. See also Jamal and Mitchell (1980).

5.24 A general measure of Mental Strain by Karasek (1979) covers Exhaustion, Depression, Nervousness, and Job and Life Satisfaction. This draws partly upon items used by Quinn and Shepard (1974).

5.25 Rosenberg's (1965) Self-esteem Scale requires respondents to indicate agreement or disagreement with ten statements about their perceived worth and confidence. It has been used in occupational settings by Burke, Weir and Du Wors (1979, 1980a, b), Fannin (1979), Gould (1979a), Ivancevich (1979b), Keller and Holland (1978), Lopez and Greenhaus (1978), Schmitt, Coyle, Rauschenberger and White (1979), Schmitt, White, Coyle and Rauschenberger (1979), Weiss (1977, 1978), and Weiss and Knight (1980).

5.26 Variants of Coopersmith's (1967) Self-esteem Inventory have been used in occupational research by Adler (1980), Baird (1977), Dossett, Latham and Mitchell (1979), Latham and Yukl (1976), Lefkowitz and Brigando (1980), Orpen and Nkohande (1977), Weiss and Shaw (1979), and Yukl and Latham (1978). Respondents indicate whether each statement (e.g. I often wish I were someone else) is "like me" or "unlike me".

5.27 Jacobs and Solomon (1977) have measured Self-esteem among 251 managers and salesmen through the Texas Social Behavior Inventory (Helmich and Stapp, 1974).

5.28 An 11-item Depression Inventory from Hunt, Singer and Cobb (1967) has been used by Inkson (1978) in a study of 93 New Zealand manual employees. Respondents record their self-perceptions on a five-point response dimension.

5.29 Quinn and Staines (1979) have described the use in a national survey of a ten-item Life Satisfaction measure. Eight items are bipolar adjectival scales applied to one's present life (e.g. enjoyable–miserable) and two items obtain overall ratings of happiness and life satisfaction. Burke, Weir and Du Wors (1979, 1980a, b) have used these items, and extended versions of the measure have been used by Quinn and Shepard (1974) and Beehr (1976). Several of the items were employed by Warr (1978b) in a study of 1655 redundant British steelworkers.

5.30 Life Satisfaction has been measured by Warr, Cook and Wall (1979) in terms of satisfaction ratings of 15 salient features of respondents' life and life space (e.g. present state of health, social life, education). Items and descriptive statistics from two samples of British blue-collar workers are presented in the source paper.

5.31 Versions of Kornhauser's (1965) interview questions about Life Satisfaction have been used by Bhagat and Chassie (1978) and Orpen (1978a). See also Vredenburgh and Sheridan (1979).

5.32 Wexley, McLaughlin and Sterns (1975) obtained responses from 155 senior and retired employees of a single company on the Life Satisfaction Index of Neugarten, Havighurst and Tobin (1961).

5.33 In a study of the relationship between Life and Job Satisfaction, Kavanagh and Halpern (1977) have employed Weitz's (1952) Test of General Satisfaction, a summation of responses to specific Life Satisfaction items.

5.34 Anomie has been assessed by Ouchi and Johnson (1978) through a variant of Srole's (1956) five-item scale. This contains items of the kind: In spite of what some people say, the condition of the average man is getting worse, not better.

6 Job Involvement and Job Motivation

Job Involvement and Job Motivation are constructs which refer to a person's orientation towards a particular job. They may be distinguished from more general perspectives on work as a whole, such as the Protestant Work Ethic and related entries in Chapter 7. As a variable of interest within occupational and organizational psychology Job Involvement is of relatively recent origin, whereas the study of motivation has a much longer history, as it has in other branches of psychology. The scales available reflect this disparity, and thus the majority of entries in this chapter concern Job Motivation.

Under certain circumstances motivation can of course be inferred from behaviour. It is evident that in most jobs effective performance depends in part on a person's willingness to work hard. However, levels of recorded performance will also be influenced by a range of other factors, such as personal ability, machine capacity and breakdowns, availability of raw materials, and so on. In most cases inferences about personal motivation from observed work behaviour are not easily made, and researchers have therefore turned their attention to the development of more direct indices.

Direct measurement of Job Motivation has followed two distinct paths. The first, which also encompasses Job Involvement, provides the main focus for this chapter, since it has given rise to the most widely used scales. We shall call this the "conventional" approach, as the resulting measures are based on relatively orthodox psychometric reasoning. The basic rationale, as for other measures described in this compendium, is to obtain a number of items each of which is a partial index of the focal construct. Since on conceptual grounds there exists commonality across the items, the empirical justification for combining them into a single index rests on observed interrelationships as evidenced for example by internal reliability coefficients or other psychometric criteria.

Eleven measures of this type are described here. The most frequently used is Lodahl and Kejner's (1965) Job Involvement Scale (6.1). Next most popular are three measures of Job Motivation (6.3 to 6.5) which show considerable overlap with respect to their authorship, theoretical bases and item content, namely those offered by Hackman and Oldham (1975), Hackman and Lawler (1971) and Lawler and Hall (1970). The remaining measures have been used less frequently.

Generally speaking, these conventional measures are short, easily completed and have reasonable face validity. It is difficult to reach more specific conclusions on the acceptability of any one, not so much because of conflicting evidence, but more because of the absence of necessary detail. Nevertheless, three main features may be discerned in the literature. First, there exists a certain ambiguity with respect to the logical status of constructs in this area. The same characteristic is used by some as an individual difference variable (reflecting personal values) and by others as situationally determined outcome variable (reflecting affect). Secondly, there are few multivariate analyses which examine the dimensionality of the measures, or the extent to which they are empirically distinguishable from other related but conceptually distinct scales (e.g. personal values or Job Satisfaction). Finally, and nowhere is this more evident than in relation to Lodahl and Kejner's (1965) measure (6.1), the instruments have rarely been employed in their original form. Researchers have idiosyncratically changed the wording of items, selected different subsets of items, or, most commonly, changed the response format. These modifications were no doubt made for good practical reasons, and arguably have had no deleterious effect on the scaling properties obtained, but the lack of standardization has prevented the accumulation of normative data for use in comparative and diagnostic work.

The second path followed in the measurement of Job Motivation is embedded within expectancy theory in one or other of its several versions (see, for example, Campbell, Dunnette, Lawler and Weick, 1970; Graen, 1969; House, 1970; Leon, 1979; Mitchell, 1974; Porter and Lawler, 1968; Vroom, 1964). This has not given rise to instruments which can be regarded as scales in the conventional sense. The reasons for this lie within the nature of expectancy theory itself, which will therefore be outlined here.

In its simplest form the rationale common to expectancy theories holds that the decision to work hard on a particular task (motivation) is a function of: (a) the individual's estimate that expending effort in achieving the task goal will be followed by certain outcomes (Expectancy, E); and (b) the desirability to the individual of those outcomes (Valence, V). To derive a measure of Job Motivation, given this assumption, a number of salient outcomes are selected, each is rated by the respondent with respect to both Expectancy and Valence, and the cross-product of these ratings is summed across all the outcomes to produce a single score. Symbolically, this may be expressed as follows:

$$\text{Motivation} = \sum_{1}^{n} (E_1 \times V_1)$$

In practice this rationale has given rise to study-specific measures, and this is so for two main reasons. First, expectancy theory is essentially content-free. Whilst it specifies how variables will be combined to produce a single index, the focus of the study and the sample involved determine the particular objectives selected for rating with respect to Expectancy and Valence. This is of course a strength of the approach since it allows population- and problem-specific measurement, but it inhibits the development of standardized and generally applicable measures. Secondly, there are in existence several variations of expectancy theory, each of which involves different ways of combining ratings. Campbell, Dunnette, Lawler and Weick (1970), for example, distinguish between Expectancy 1 (E1), which is the belief that effort will lead to performance, and Expectancy 2 (E2) that performance will lead to outcomes. Hence the index of motivation is represented by:

$$\text{Motivation} = E1 \times \sum_{1}^{n} (E2_1 \times V_1)$$

Several other variations exist.

Equally important to our present aims is the fact that expectancy theory approaches have not generated scales in the conventional sense. The reason for this resides in the internal logic of the theory. This involves the selection of objectives which are not necessarily related one to another except in so far as they are deemed to be representative of the range of objectives which are achievable, and which are of theoretical importance. Moreover, these are rated for both Expectancy and Valence, ratings which themselves are assumed to be independent. In other words, the index obtained cannot be regarded as a scale in the usual sense, since there is no a priori reason to expect the different ratings to correlate with each other. Conventional psychometric techniques for assessing internal consistency are consequently not entirely appropriate. The legitimacy of expectancy theory formulation depends instead on the axioms of the theory itself.

Since, for these reasons, measures of Job Motivation based on expectancy theory cannot be meaningfully evaluated either outside their particular context or by recourse to conventional psychometric criteria, they are not presented in detail in this chapter. However, because of the importance of this approach to motivation, illustrative studies are cited under entry 6.12.

These allow two general comments concerning expectancy theory approaches to the measurement of Job Motivation. First an important weakness evident in the literature concerns measurement reliability. The extensive manipulation of raw scores required by the theory is likely to compound any unreliability existing in the ratings from which they derive, ratings which themselves are typically single items. The general finding that expectancy indices of motivation are rarely better predictors of relevant self-report or behavioural measures than are their constituent ratings is informative. Whilst this may reflect the inadequacies of expectancy theory itself, it is also consistent with the presence of greater measurement error in the index than in its constituent variables. In the absence of evidence to the contrary the empirical adequacy of such indices must be suspect. Lawler and Suttle's (1973) conclusion remains valid: "it seems that the theory has become so complex that it has exceeded the measures which exist to test it" (p. 502). The second observation concerns the popularity of the approach. This was at its height in the late 1960's and early 1970's but has dropped more recently. No doubt measurement problems have played their part in this decline.

5.1   Job Involvement

Source: Lodahl and Kejner, 1965

The authors define Job Involvement in terms of the extent to which a person's work performance affects his self-esteem. The Job-involved person is one for whom paid employment plays a central part in life and who is affected personally by his or her employment circumstances. Job Involvement is seen as conceptually independent from Job Satisfaction, both in terms of its content and because it is relatively resistant to change, having its base in personal value systems. However, the concept is ambiguously defined. On the one hand the authors are interested in an individual's values towards work in general (work involvement rather than involvement in a particular job), and on the other hand they are concerned with the extent to which the person wants to perform well in a particular job (job motivation). Given the predominance in the scale of items concerned with a person's present job, the measure is included in this chapter rather than in Chapter 7 which deals with values, including measures of commitment to work in general.

The measure has 20 items, seven of which are negatively phrased. There is a four-point response dimension running from Strongly agree to Strongly disagree, scored from 1 to 4 respectively and summed. Total scores thus range from 20 to 80, but note that a high score indicates low Job Involvement. A short version of the scale comprises six items, numbers 3, 6, 8, 11, 15 and 18.

Through various judgmental procedures an initial pool of 110 items was reduced to 40, administered to a sample of 137 nursing personnel, and the results factor analysed. The final 20 items were selected by considering item–whole correlations and factorial clarity of the items. These were then re-ordered and administered to 70 development engineers. The factorial structure of the scale was found to be similar but not identical across the two samples. Using varimax rotation three interpretable factors emerged for nurses and four for engineers. The authors conclude that Job Involvement as measured by the 20-item version is multidimensional and probably has at least three dimensions. Nevertheless, they do not provide further suggestions about possible subscales, limiting attention instead to their objective of producing a single index. The 20 items showed low inter-item correlations (an average of 0.17), but relatively high item–whole correlations.

For the 137 nurses the mean score was 43.37 (s.d. 6.52), and the Spearman-Brown internal reliability coefficient was 0.72. For the 70 engineers the figures were 42.62 (s.d. 7.83) and 0.80 respectively, and for a group of 46 students 48.06 (s.d. 9.56) and 0.89. Means and standard deviations for the six-item version are not reported in the source publication, though the Spearman-Brown coefficient was recorded as 0.73, and the correlation (including auto-correlation) with the 20-item version was 0.87. Correlates of the 20-item version included age ($r=0.26$ for the 137 nurses) and four sub-scales of the Job Descriptive Index (3.3) measuring Satisfaction with Work Itself, Promotion, Supervision and Co-workers ($r=0.29$, 0.38, 0.38 and 0.37 for the 70 engineers).

Subsequent researchers have varied widely in their choice of scale items and response format. One of the few instances of the administration of the full 20-item Job Involvement scale is provided by Gechman and Wiener (1975) and Wiener and Gechman (1977). With a sample of 54 female elementary school teachers they obtained a mean of 56.70. However, this appears to be based upon reverse-scoring compared with the original and converts to 43.30 (s.d. 6.70). Job Involvement was significantly correlated with a measure (based on Kornhauser, 1965) (2.14) of Job Satisfaction (0.51) and with personal time devoted to work (0.37), but not to an index of Mental Health (adapted from Kornhauser, 1965) (5.22). A second application of the full instrument is by Wiener and Vardi (1980), who reported a mean of 55.23 (s.d. 6.20) with 85 professional employees; this reverses to 44.77.

The six-item version has been used more frequently, although response dimensions differing from the original have been the rule rather than the exception. Jones, James and Bruni (1975) adopted a five-point response scale reverse-scored compared with the original. With a sample of 112 service and military engineering employees they obtained a mean of 17.56 (s.d. 3.55) and an alpha coefficient of 0.62. Cummings and Bigelow (1976) used a seven-point response dimension in a study of 96 blue-collar employees. A principal components analysis with varimax rotation, including with the items a further six to measure aspects of Job Satisfaction (Porter, 1962) (3.2) and four to measure Intrinsic Motivation (from Lawler and Hall, 1970) (6.5), yielded a three-factor solution. The Job Satisfaction and Intrinsic motivation items comprised distinct factors, but no separate Job Involvement factor was identifiable. Also using a seven-point response continuum, Morris and Snyder (1979) obtained a Spearman-Brown internal reliability coefficient of 0.77 with 262 non-academic university employees. Hollon and Chesser (1976) with a sample of 321 public community college teachers used a five-point response dimension. Reverse-scoring compared with the original, they recorded a mean of 20.2 (s.d. 3.8) and an internal reliability coefficient (type unspecified) of 0.93. Job Involvement was positively related (0.32) to Vroom's (1960) index of

Overall Job Satisfaction (2.10).

Also using a reverse-scored five-point response dimension, Jones, James, Bruni and Sells (1977) with 1451 white and 166 black Navy personnel obtained means of 15.4 and 17.1 respectively, and an overall alpha coefficient of 0.73. Bigoness (1978) reported a Spearman-Brown coefficient of 0.75 from a sample of 222 university faculty members.

Other versions of the Job Involvement scale have been used in research by Herman, Dunham and Hulin (1975) (three items); Rabinowitz, Hall and Goodale (1977), Hall, Goodale, Rabinowitz and Morgan (1978), Schmitt, Coyle, Rauschenberger and White (1979), and Schmitt, White, Coyle and Rauschenberger (1979) (four items); James, Gent, Hater and Coray (1979) and Pierce, Dunham and Blackburn (1979) (five items); White (1978) (seven items); and Ruh, White and Wood (1975) and Schuler (1976) (nine items). A study by Schuler, Aldag and Brief (1977) provides more evidence than most on the internal reliability of such instruments. Using a nine-item version with a sample of 362 manufacturing employees and two samples of 399 and 272 employees from a public utility company, and a three-item version with samples of 374 nursing personnel and 99 food, service and janitorial hospital employees, they obtained alpha coefficients of 0.87, 0.89, 0.83, 0.68 and 0.80 respectively. Job Involvement was also found to correlate negatively with Role Ambiguity (8.15) (range -0.12 to -0.41, median -0.35) and with Role Conflict (8.16) (range -0.12 to -0.28, median -0.18).

Other studies using versions of the Job Involvement scale include those by Abdel-Halim (1978, 1979a), Aldag and Brief (1975, 1979), Brief and Aldag (1975), Feldman (1976, 1977), Hall and Foster (1977), Hall and Mansfield (1975), Kanungo, Misra and Dayal (1975), Katerberg, Hom and Hulin (1979), La Rocco, Pugh and Gunderson (1977), Lefkowitz (1974), Moore and Rickel (1980), Morris and Koch (1979), Newman (1975), Orpen (1979b), Pinder (1977), Saal (1978), Saleh and Hosek (1976), Steers (1975b, 1976) and Wood (1974).

There remains a problem over what the scale actually measures. The conceptual ambiguity evident in the original article, where Job Involvement spanned a relatively stable personal value orientation on the one hand and job-specific motivation on the other, has been confirmed rather than resolved by subsequent uses of the measure. Factor-analytic studies, for example by Lawler and Hall (1970) and Cummings and Bigelow (1976), have shown that, whilst some items load on their own factor and are separate from a factor representing Job Satisfaction, others show loadings at least as strong on a factor representing Intrinsic Motivation. Saleh and Hosek (1976) found that the items were divided between two factors, some loading on a Central Life Interests dimension (along with items from Dubin's (7.10) measure) and others in terms of Importance of Performance with Valued Self. It seems reasonable to conclude with Rabinowitz and Hall (1977) that part of Job Involvement as measured by the present scale reflects a stable value orientation, and another part, like job attitudes, is more situationally determined.

Items

1. I'll stay overtime to finish a job, even if I'm not paid for it
2. You can measure a person pretty well by how good a job he does
3. The major satisfaction in my life comes from my job
4. For me, mornings at work really fly by
5. I usually show up for work a little early, to get things ready
6. The most important things that happen to me involve my work
7. Sometimes I lie awake at night thinking ahead to the next day's work
8. I'm really a perfectionist about my work
9. I feel depressed when I fail at something connected with my job
10. I have other activities more important than my work (R)
11. I live, eat and breathe my job
12. I would probably keep working even if I didn't need the money
13. Quite often I feel like staying home from work instead of coming in (R)
14. To me, my work is only a small part of who I am (R)
15. I am very much involved personally in my work
16. I avoid taking on extra duties and responsibilities in my work (R)
17. I used to be more ambitious about my work than I am now (R)
18. Most things in life are more important than work (R)
19. I used to care more about my work, but now other things are more important to me (R)
20. Sometimes I'd like to kick myself for the mistakes I make in my work

Responses

Strongly agree; Agree; Disagree; Strongly disagree; scored 1 to 4 respectively.

6.2   Job Involvement

Source: Cammann, Fichman, Jenkins and Klesh, 1979; Seashore, Lawler, Mirvis and Cammann, 1982

The Michigan Organizational Assessment Questionnaire contains a number of scales to measure work attitudes and perceptions; see also 2.9, 3.8, 3.9, 3.10, 4.13, 6,6, 8.6, 9.5 and 9.11. A three-item index of Job Involvement is included, drawing items from Lodahl and Kejner's (1965) measure (6.1), in order to assess "the extent to which individuals personally identify with their work". Responses are on a seven-point dimension, and the mean value across the items constitutes the scale score. Means are not cited in the source publication, but coefficient alpha is given as 0.62 (N>400). Factor analysis showed that all items loaded onto a discrete factor. Correlations of 0.35 and −0.27 are reported with the authors' measures of Overall Job Satisfaction (2.9) and Intention to Turn Over (4.13) respectively. An average inter-item correlation of 0.51 is reported by Moch (1980b) in a study of 379 packaging employees.

Items

1. I am very much personally involved in my work
2. I live, eat, and breathe my job
3. The most important things which happen to me involve my job

Responses

Strongly disagree; Disagree; Slightly disagree; Neither agree nor disagree; Slightly agree; Agree; Strongly agree; scored 1 to 7 respectively.

6.3   Internal Work Motivation

Source: Hackman and Oldham, 1975

The authors describe Internal Work Motivation in terms of the degree to which an employee is self-motivated to perform effectively. It refers to the extent to which he or she experiences positive feelings when doing well and negative reactions when working poorly. Their instrument to measure this construct is part of the Job Diagnostic Survey (see also 2.6, 3.6, 7.7, 8.2, 8.28), and has its immediate theoretical basis in the Job Characteristics Model (Hackman and Oldham, 1976, 1980). It is a development from Hackman and Lawler's (1971) measure of Intrinsic Motivation, which in turn is a variant of Lawler and Hall's (1970) scale of the same name. These two measures (6.4 and 6.5) are presented immediately after the present one, and they have much in common.

The Internal Work Motivation scale contains six items, which are embedded within two sections of the Job Diagnostic Survey together with items from other scales. There is a seven-point response dimension, and a mean score is taken. One item is reverse-scored. A short version consists of the first four items.

The authors report that the Job Diagnostic Survey as a whole was developed over a two-year period, during which it was administered to some 1500 individuals in more than 100 jobs in 15 different organizations. It underwent three major revisions aimed at maximizing scale reliabilities and empirical discrimination among scales. The empirical evidence presented in the source publication (and subsequently by Hackman and Oldham, 1976) is based on the final version of the measure administered to 658 employees (41% female) in seven organizations. Their jobs (N=62) spanned blue-collar, white-collar and professional work in both industrial and service organizations. The overall mean score was 5.39 (s.d. 0.96), and a Spearman-Brown internal reliability coefficient of 0.75 was obtained.

With this initial sample, the Internal Work Motivation scale was found to discriminate between holders of different jobs, and to be correlated with General Job Satisfaction (2.6) 0.51, Growth Satisfaction (3.6) 0.56, Experienced Meaningfulness of the Work (8.28) 0.66, Skill Variety 0.42, Task Identity 0.22, Task Significance 0.32, Autonomy 0.33, and Feedback from the Job Itself 0.36 (the latter five indices cover the core Job Characteristics identified in entry 8.2). Hackman and Oldham (1974) also report mean scores obtained by Van Maanen and Katz (1974) from over 3000 respondents. For the total sample the mean was 5.64, and values are given separately for eight different job categories.

Oldham (1976), with 60 employees in a manufacturing company, used the full Job Diagnostic Survey, which encompasses the six-item version. Internal Work Motivation scores were found to correlate with supervisory ratings of work quality 0.25, work quantity 0.22, and work effort 0.22. Wall, Clegg and Jackson (1978) also administered the full Job Diagnostic Survey, in a study of 47 British blue-collar employees. For Internal Work Motivation the mean was 4.78 (s.d. 0.81) and the alpha coefficient of internal reliability was 0.58. Significant correlates of the measure included the perceived Job Characteristics (8.2) of Skill Variety (0.37), Task Significance (0.51), Autonomy (0.40), and Feedback from the Job Itself (0.38), General Job Satisfaction (2.6) (0.46) and Growth Satisfaction (3.6) (0.46). With a sample of 272 public utility employees (20% female) Kim and Schuler (1979) report a coefficient alpha of 0.79 for the six-item version. With the four-item version, coefficient alpha was 0.73 in a study of 398 office employees (Pierce, Dunham and Blackburn, 1979); the mean value in that study was 4.20 (s.d. 0.61).

Champoux (1978) describes a "serendipitous field experiment" involving 71 federal agency employees in the experimental group, and 173 as a comparison group. Repeated measures of Internal Work Motivation were taken, using the full six-item version with the experimental subjects (means varied between 4.6 and 6.1) and the short form with the comparison group subjects (means from 5.5 to 6.1). Little systematic change was found. For comparison group subjects, correlations between Internal Work Motivation at adjacent time periods were reported to range from 0.59 to 0.84, showing that there was considerable stability of individual scores.

Hackman, Pearce and Wolfe (1978) describe a "naturally-occurring quasi-experiment" involving clerical jobs in a bank. The design involved 136 employees providing pre-test data and 201 generating post-test data. Three groups of subjects were identified: those whose jobs were enriched; those who experienced no change; and those whose jobs were impoverished (the majority). Pre-test scores on the six-item measure of Internal Work Motivation yielded a mean of 5.51 (s.d. 0.87) and an internal reliability coefficient (type unspecified) of 0.71. The corresponding post-test figures were 5.18 (s.d. 1.02) and 0.71. Sub-analyses for subjects in "enriched", "no-change" and "de-enriched" jobs showed an increase, no change and a decrease in Internal Work Motivation scores respectively. Another change study is described by Oldham and Brass (1979), where a small decline in Internal Work Motivation was associated with the introduction of open-plan office working. A similar overall decline followed organizational changes in the study by Bhagat and Chassie (1980). White and Mitchell (1979) have used the four-item version in a laboratory study of job enrichment.

Oldham, Hackman and Stepina (1978) have brought together results from several investigations, with an overall sample size of 6930 (46% female). Spearman-Brown internal reliability was 0.69, and the overall mean and standard deviation were 5.50 and 0.89 respectively. Internal Work Motivation was positively correlated with seven measures of perceived Job Characteristics (8.2), from 0.16 for Task Identity to 0.34 for Skill Variety. The association with General Job Satisfaction (2.6) was 0.43, and Internal Work Motivation varied significantly and linearly with job level, from a mean of 5.47 for non-managers to 6.07 for upper-level managers.

Other investigators using the scale include Aldag and Brief (1975, 1979), Arnold and House (1980), Brief and Aldag (1975), Dailey (1979), Feldman (1976, 1977), Ivancevich (1979b, 1980), Mobley, Hand, Baker and Meglino (1979), and Orpen (1979b).

Items

1. My opinion of myself goes up when I do this job well
2. I feel a great sense of personal satisfaction when I do this job well
3. I feel bad and unhappy when I discover that I have performed poorly on this job

4. My own feelings generally are *not* affected much one way or the other by how well I do on this job (R)
5. Most people on this job feel a great sense of personal satisfaction when they do the job well
6. Most people on this job feel bad or unhappy when they find they have performed the work poorly

Responses

Disagree strongly; Disagree; Disagree slightly; Neutral; Agree slightly; Agree; Agree strongly; scored 1 to 7 respectively.

6.4   Intrinsic Motivation

Source: Hackman and Lawler, 1971

This is an earlier version of the Internal Work Motivation scale (6.3). In the source publication the terms "internal (work) motivation" and "intrinsic motivation" appear to be used interchangeably, but since the latter is used when the scale itself is described, it is retained here. Intrinsic Motivation is viewed as the degree to which an individual experiences positive feelings when he or she performs well and negative feelings when performing poorly. This is also the definition given for Internal Work Motivation (Hackman and Oldham, 1975) (6.3).

The measure contains three items (two of which are part of Lawler and Hall's (1970) measure) (6.5), each with a seven-point response dimension. A mean score is taken.

The Intrinsic Motivation scale was first administered to a sample of 208 telephone company non-supervisory employees, both male and female. The mean was 5.96 (s.d. 0.87) and internal reliability (type unspecified) was 0.71. Correlates included General Job Satisfaction (0.39) (Hackman and Lawler, 1971), Job Involvement (0.39) (an abbreviated form of the Lodahl and Kejner (1965) scale) (6.1), and the Job Dimensions of Variety (0.32) and Autonomy (0.30) (Hackman and Lawler, 1971) (8.1).

Subsequent uses of the scale include those by Herman, Dunham and Hulin (1975), Katerberg, Hom and Hulin (1979) and Jones, James, Bruni and Sells (1977). Given the similarity between this measure and that of Internal Work Motivation (6.3), uses referenced in the previous entry are also of relevance here.

Items

1. I feel a great sense of personal satisfaction when I do my job well

2. Doing my job well increases my feeling of self-esteem
3. I feel bad when I do my job poorly

Responses

From Strongly disagree to Strongly agree, with intermediate points not identified in the source publication; scored 1 to 7 respectively.

6.5 Intrinsic Motivation

Source: Lawler and Hall, 1970

Lawler (1969) defines intrinsic motivation in terms of the extent to which an employee is motivated to perform because of subjective rewards or feelings he or she expects as a result of performing well. Lawler and Hall (1970) take this as a working definition in order to explore the empirical relationships between a measure of this construct and those of Job Involvement and Satisfaction.

Their measure of Intrinsic Motivation contains four items each with a seven-point scale. In the initial study (with 291 engineers and scientists) they showed the scale to be factorially independent from items measuring Need Satisfaction (through deficiency scores) and items from Lodahl and Kejner's (1965) Job Involvement scale (6.1). Cummings and Bigelow (1967) describe a similar study with 96 male blue-collar employees, which also supported the factorial independence of the measure from Satisfaction and Involvement items.

The scale has been superseded by measures 6.3 and 6.4, so further details of research results will not be presented here. Interested readers may wish to consult Hall and Mansfield (1975), La Rocco, Pugh and Gunderson (1977), Orpen (1978b), and Waters, Roach and Batlis (1974).

Items

1. When I do my work well, it gives me a feeling of accomplishment
2. When I perform my job well, it contributes to my personal growth and development
3. I feel a great sense of personal satisfaction when I do my job well
4. Doing my job well increases my feeling of self-esteem

Responses

As 6.4

6.6   Internal Work Motivation

Source: Cammann, Fichman, Jenkins and Klesh, 1979; Seashore, Lawler, Mirvis and Cammann, 1982

The Michigan Organizational Assessment Questionnaire contains a number of scales to measure work attitudes and perceptions; see also 2.9, 3.8, 3.9, 3.10, 4.13, 6.2, 8.6, 9.5 and 9.11. A three-item measure of Internal Work Motivation is included to tap "the extent to which doing the job itself is rewarding". Responses are on a seven-point dimension, and the mean value across the items constitutes the scale score. Means are not cited in the source publication, but coefficient alpha is given as 0.60 (N>400). Factor analysis revealed that all three items loaded onto a discrete factor. Correlations of 0.32 and 0.21 are reported with the authors' measures of Overall Job Satisfaction (2.9) and Job Involvement (6.2) respectively.

Mirvis and Lawler (1977) used the scale in a study of 160 bank tellers. The mean score was 6.11 (s.d. 0.96), and individual scores were correlated -0.26 with number of absence incidents three months later. Moch (1980b) presents intercorrelations observed with a sample of 379 packaging employees; for example the association with Job Involvement (6.2) was 0.01.

Items

1. I feel bad when I do a poor job
2. I get a feeling of personal satisfaction from doing my job well
3. Doing my job well gives me a good feeling

Responses

As 6.2

6.7   Intrinsic Job Motivation

Source: Warr, Cook and Wall, 1979

The authors note the need for short, robust scales which are easily completed by employees of modest educational attainment. From a literature review, a pilot study and two investigations with samples of 200 and 390 male blue-collar employees (drawn according to a pre-determined sampling frame designed to match British demographic characteristics) a six-item Intrinsic Job Motivation scale was developed. The construct is defined as "the degree to which a person wants to work well in his or her job in order to achieve intrinsic satisfaction" (p. 135). Responses are upon a seven-point dimension and are summed to yield a possible range of scores between 6 and 42.

In the two samples described above the means were 35.13 (s.d. 5.46) and 36.82 (s.d. 5.45) respectively, with a coefficient alpha of 0.82 in both instances. Decile scores are also presented in the source publication. the test–retest correlation across six months for a sub-sample of 60 respondents was 0.65. Principal components analysis with varimax rotation showed that all scale items loaded on a single factor (loadings from 0.42 to 0.69 in sample 1, and from 0.48 to 0.76 in sample 2) and were factorially independent from other measures employed in the research.

Correlates of Intrinsic Job Motivation in the initial study included Work Involvement (7.5), Perceived Intrinsic Job Characteristics (8.5) and Overall Job Satisfaction (2.11), with values of 0.37, 0.36 and 0.35 respectively. In a subsequent study with a further sample of 260 blue-collar employees (Cook and Wall, 1980) Intrinsic Job Motivation was found to be correlated 0.30 with Interpersonal Trust at Work (9.12) and 0.45 with Organizational Commitment (4.10).

Items

1. I feel a sense of personal satisfaction when I do this job well
2. My opinion of myself goes down when I do this job badly
3. I take pride in doing my job as well as I can
4. I feel unhappy when my work is not up to my usual standard
5. I like to look back on the day's work with a sense of a job well done
6. I try to think of ways of doing my job effectively

Responses

No, I strongly disagree; No, I disagree quite a lot; No, I disagree just a little; I'm not sure about this; Yes, I agree just a little; Yes, I agree quite a lot; Yes, I strongly agree; scored 1 to 7 respectively.

6.8   Job Motivation Indices

Source: Patchen, Pelz and Allen, 1965

The authors describe a measure which has four items each with a different five-point response scale. Three different combinations of these items are offered: Index A comprises items 1 and 2, Index B items 1 to 4, and Index C items 1 to 3. Total scores are calculated in each case.

For groups of 20 salesmen, 106 engineers and 64 production employees, the means for Index B were 17.3, 14.8 and 13.7 respectively.

For Index A the means were 9.1, 7.8 and 6.8; and for Index C they were 13.6, 10.9 and 10.4. Test–retest reliability on a sample of 46 employees (time-lapse and sample type unspecified) was 0.80. For Index A on a sample of 834 respondents the inter-item correlation was 0.32; and for Index B, on a sample of 223, inter-item correlations ranged from 0.05 to 0.38. Associations between the indices and selected correlates across a variety of samples were generally low, but in the predicted direction. Significant correlates included supervisory ratings of individuals' "concern for doing a good job", absence, and ratings of production efficiency.

Patchen (1970) used Index A in a study of 834 non-supervisory employees in a single organization. An overall mean score is not cited, but 27 sub-group means are listed, the median value of which is 6.80. Job Motivation was associated -0.56 with Psychological Symptoms of Stress (5.3) and 0.38 with a measure of pride in work (N=90 work-groups). Index B was used by Rousseau (1977) with 201 non-supervisory employees. She reports means for respondents from three separate technologies (Long-Linked, Mediating and Intensive; see Thompson, 1967) of 13.15 (s.d. 2.82), 16.13 (s.d. 2.02) and 14.76 (s.d. 2.41) respectively. A slightly modified version of Index B was used by Thamhain and Gemmill (1974) with 66 project personnel, yielding a mean of 14.8 (s.d. 2.2).

McKelvey and Sekaran (1977) obtained a coefficient alpha of 0.57 for Index A with a sample of 441 scientists and engineers. Several significant correlates were reported, for example, Satisfaction with Opportunities to Use Knowledge and Skills (0.33), Satisfaction with the Opportunity to Work on Difficult Problems (0.35), Centralization (0.26) and Technical Orientation (-0.29).

Schriesheim (1979), with 308 managerial and clerical employees, reported an alpha coefficient for Index B of 0.57. Other researchers using Index B include Motowidlo and Borman (1977, 1978), Reinharth and Wahba (1975, 1976), and Rousseau (1978a).

Items and Responses

1. On most days on your job, how often does time seem to drag for you?
About half the day or more; About one-third of the day; About one-quarter of the day; About one-eighth of the day; Time never seems to drag; scored 1 to 5 respectively.

2. Some people are completely involved in their job—they are absorbed in it night and day. For other people their job is simply one of several interests. How involved do you feel in your job?
Very little involved—my other interests are more absorbing; Slightly in-

volved; Moderately involved—my job and my other interests are equally absorbing to me; Strongly involved; Very strongly involved—my work is the most absorbing interest in my life; scored 1 to 5 respectively.

3. How often do you do some extra work for your job which isn't really required of you?
Almost every day; Several times a week; About once a week; Once every few weeks; About once a month or less; scored 5 to 1 respectively.

4. Would you say you work harder, less hard, or about the same as other people doing your type of work at (name of organization)?
Much harder than most others; A little harder than most others; About the same as most others; A little less hard than most others; Much less hard than most others; scored 5 to 1 respectively.

6.9 to 6.11   Other Measures of Job Motivation

6.9 Borgatta (1967) has described a Work Components Study to measure Job Motivation. This contains 70 items of the general form "How desirable would you consider a job where . . .?" and is framed within the theory of work motivation set out by Herzberg, Mausner and Snyderman (1959). Further details are provided by Borgatta, Ford and Bohrnstedt (1968), Ford, Borgatta and Bohrnstedt (1969), Miskel (1974), and Miskel and Heller (1973).

6.10 Wherry and South (1977) have developed a 66-item Worker Motivation Scale, the rationale for which stems from earlier studies by Wherry and Waters (1968) and South and Wherry (1975). Two factors are identified, covering Self-Improvement, High Production, and Deadline Attainment (factor A) and Status and Recognition-Seeking (factor B).

6.11 The Desire to Work Scale (Eyde, 1962) was constructed for use with women. It treats work motivation as a function of marital status, presence and age of children, number of children and level of husband's salary. Subjects rate their desire to work for each of 17 situations that combine these four features. Orcutt and Walsh (1979) have used an extended version of this instrument in a study examining traditional and non-traditional career aspirations.

6.12   Expectancy Theory Indices of Motivation

As discussed in the introduction to this chapter, measures of Job Motivation based on expectancy theory have been study-specific and are not scales in the conventional sense. They are consequently not described in full. Instead we cite illustrative studies using indices based on two or more of the following variables, E, E1, E2 and V as defined earlier.

Arvey and Mussio (1973) used two indices of motivation: namely

$$\sum_{1}^{n} (E2_1 \times V_1) \quad \text{and} \quad E1 \times \sum_{1}^{n} (E2_1 \times V_1)$$

E1 was measured by a single item with a five-point response dimension. E2 scores were obtained for each of ten specified outcomes (e.g. making use of abilities, advancement, high salary and praise) also with a five-point response continuum. V was measured by requiring respondents to distribute 100 points among the ten outcomes with respect to their desirability. Findings from 226 female clerical employees showed both indices to be positively but weakly correlated with supervisory ratings of individual performance (0.12 and 0.11 respectively). Miles and Petty (1977) used the same two indices of motivation derived from a modified version of Arvey and Mussio's instrument.

Lawler and Suttle (1973) used three indices of motivation, namely

$$\sum_{1}^{n}(E2_1 \times V_1), \quad E1 \times \sum_{1}^{n} (E2_1 \times V_1) \quad \text{and} \quad E1 \times \sum_{1}^{n} E2_1$$

E1 was measured by two items and E2 and V with respect to 18 different outcomes. Means and standard deviations of the responses obtained from a sample of 69 managers are reported. All three indices were positively but weakly correlated with rankings of effort obtained from superiors and peers (from 0.15 to 0.29, median 0.19).

Downey, Sheridan and Slocum (1975) used

$$\sum_{1}^{n} (E2_1 \times V_1)$$

as the index of motivation in their study of 125 machine operators and 91 managers. E2 and V were measured in relation to 14 outcomes. The index scores were positively but weakly correlated with leader Initiating Structure and Consideration from the Leader Behavior Description Questionnaire (9.1) (median partial correlation, holding constant the other LBDQ variable, 0.19, range 0.12 to 0.45).

Other studies employing expectancy theory indices of motivation include: Reinharth and Wahba (1975, 1976) using E1, E2 and V measures in 9 different combinations covering additive, multiplicative and combined functions; Kopelman (1979), Kopelman and Thompson

(1976) and Van Maanen (1975) using

$$\sum_{1}^{n} (E_1 \times V_1);$$

Ivancevich (1976a) using both

$$\sum_{1}^{n} (E2_1 \times V_1) \quad \text{and} \quad E1 \times \sum_{1}^{n} (E2_1 \times V_1);$$

and Parker and Dyer (1976) using a modification of the latter index. Other recent applications include those by Arvey and Neel (1974), Erez (1979), Herriot and Ecob (1979), Hom (1980), Jacobson and Eran (1980), Seybolt and Pavett (1979), and Shiflet and Cohen (1980). Sims, Szilagyi and McKemey (1976) have developed scales of nine and 17 items respectively to measure E1 and E2; these are described in entry 8.26.

7 Work Values, Beliefs and Needs

The instruments described in this chapter are designed to measure individual work values, beliefs or needs. As such their focus is on the more enduring aspects of people's orientations towards employment in general rather than on their reactions to particular jobs or occupations. Thirteen scales receive major entries, and in the latter part of the chapter a further 16 are described briefly.

Within the major entries there are two relatively coherent groups. The first comprises five scales (7.1 to 7.5) which tap a person's continuing commitment to paid employment. Three of the measures (7.1, 7.3, 7.4) are explicit attempts to operationalize the notion of the Protestant Work Ethic. Whilst differing in scope and theoretical interpretation these share the same starting point, namely that provided by Weber (1958). The second group (7.6 to 7.8) consists of scales concerned with the measurement of Higher Order Need Strength. This term refers to the value which an individual places on such factors as personal development and self-actualization. The choice of the term reflects a theoretical base in the work of Maslow (1943, 1954) where such needs are described as of a higher order than security and social needs. Subsequent empirical and theoretical work by Turner and Lawrence (1965), Hulin and Blood (1968) and others on the moderating effect of personal values on the relationship between job characteristics and job reactions gave impetus to the development of these measures.

The remaining major entries do not form a clearly identifiable category. Some have a broad-ranging focus, such as Super's (1970) measure (7.9) which offers indices of 15 different value orientations, and Dubin's (1956) scale (7.10) which is concerned with the personal importance of work as opposed to non-work activities. Other scales have more specific referents such as achievement needs (7.11, 7.12) or bureaucratic values (7.13). The final measures (7.14 to 7.29) are spread widely across the field covered by the chapter, dealing with attitudes to women as managers, professionalism, need for role clarity, enduring needs, career motivation, managerial philosophies, and related constructs.

7.1   Survey of Work Values

Source: Wollack, Goodale, Wijting and Smith, 1971

The authors set out to develop a set of measures based on a broad interpretation of the construct of secularized Protestant Ethic, drawing principally from the work of Weber (1958). The resultant Survey of Work Values (SWV) consists of six sub-scales each designed to measure a separate value dimension. The sub-scales are: Pride in Work; Job Involvement; Activity Preference—the desire to keep busy at work; Attitude Toward Earnings—the value placed on earning money; Social Status of the Job; and Upward Striving—the desire to increase one's job level and standard of living. The first three of these dimensions are classified as intrinsic, the next two as extrinsic and the last as a mixture of both.

Each of the sub-scales comprises nine items, of which from two to four are reverse-scored. As originally developed a six-point agree–disagree response dimension was used, but a subsequent (1975) revised version of the scale (Form U) deploys a five-point continuum. Sub-scale scores are obtained by averaging item scores.

The careful development of the measure using several samples is described thoroughly in the source publication. With a group of 495 employees in seven occupational groups, the following sub-scale properties were observed. For Pride in Work the mean (on the original six-point dimension) ranged from 4.86 to 5.72, the s.d. from 0.55 to 1.04, and coefficient alpha for the total sample was 0.63. A test–retest correlation (one-month interval) of 0.69 was obtained on a sample of 66 insurance company employees. The corresponding statistics for Job Involvement were: mean 4.16 to 5.42, s.d. 0.63 to 1.34, alpha 0.53, and test–retest correlation 0.68. For Activity Preference the figures were: mean 3.77 to 5.60, s.d. 0.62 to 1.28, alpha 0.63, and test–retest correlation 0.71. For Attitude Toward Earnings: mean 2.01 to 4.41, s.d. 0.99 to 1.33, alpha 0.63, and test–retest correlation 0.65. For Social Status of the Job: mean 2.32 to 3.88; s.d. 0.95 to 1.64, alpha 0.63, and test–retest correlation 0.71. And for Upward Striving: mean 3.47 to 5.54, s.d. 0.55 to 1.36, alpha 0.59, and test–retest correlation 0.76. Alpha coefficients obtained from a sample of 356 government employees were of very similar magnitude. Intercorrelations between sub-scales (N=495) varied from −0.30 to +0.60, with a median (ignoring the sign) of 0.14. However, factor-analytic procedures did not yield a solution corresponding directly to the six a priori dimensions.

The source publication describes three studies using the Survey of Work Values, by Wollack (1968), Wijting (1969) and Goodale (1969). Each obtained findings generally indicative of construct validity in relating scale scores to a variety of biographical and demographic variables such as sex, race, education, urban–rural background and occupational level.

More recently Stone (1975) explored the role of Protestant Ethic values (measured as the unweighted total of the SWV sub-scales) as a moderator of the relationship between Job Scope (Stone, 1974) (8.4) and Satisfaction with the Work Itself (using modified instructions with the Brayfield-Rothe (1951) measure, 2.2). No moderator effect was observed with a sample of 149 enlisted naval personnel, but the total SWV scores correlated 0.32 and 0.43 with Job Scope and Work Satisfaction respectively. In a subsequent study with the same objective, but on a sample of 594 non-managerial employees, Stone (1976) also failed to obtain moderator effects, whether using a total SWV score or the six sub-scales individually. Wijting, Arnold and Conrad (1978) examined the relationships between the values of 324 school children and those of their parents, as measured by the SWV. Means for students, fathers and mothers for each of the sub-scales, broken down by sex and school grade of the child, are presented. Amongst other results it was found that at earlier ages there was greater similarity in values between children and their same-sexed parent, but that older students were most similar to their fathers.

Stone, Ganster, Woodman and Fusilier (1979), using a sample of 133 students, have recorded alpha coefficients of internal reliability for the six sub-scales ranging from 0.57 to 0.82. Other uses of the SWV or selected items include those by Cherrington, Condie and England (1979), Fottler and Schaller (1975) and Rabinowitz, Hall and Goodale (1977).

Items (Form U)

Pride in Work

12. One who does a sloppy job at work should feel a little ashamed of oneself
13. A worker should feel some responsibility to do a decent job, whether or not the supervisor is around
16. There is nothing wrong with doing a poor job at work if one can get away with it (R)
32. There is nothing as satisfying as doing the best job possible
36. One who feels no sense of pride in one's work is probably unhappy
43. Only a fool worries about doing a job well, since it is important only that you do your job well enough not to get fired (R)
48. One should feel a sense of pride in one's work
52. The most important thing about a job is liking the work
53. Doing a good job should mean as much to a worker as a good paycheck

Job Involvement

6. Most companies have suggestion boxes for their workers, but I doubt that the companies take these suggestions seriously (R)
7. A good worker cares about finding ways to improve the job, and when one has an idea, one should pass it on to the supervisor
14. One who has an idea about how to improve one's own job should drop a note in the company suggestion box
17. A good worker is interested in helping a new worker learn the job
24. If a worker has a choice between going to the company picnic or staying home, the worker would probably be better off at home (R)
25. Even if a worker has a very low-level job in a company, it is still possible for the worker to make suggestions which will affect company policy
33. Once a week, after the work day is over, a company may have their workers get together in groups for the purpose of discussing possible job changes. A good worker should remain after quitting time to participate in these discussions
37. If something is wrong with a job, a smart worker will mind his or her own business and let somebody else complain about it (R)
44. One should do one's own job and forget about such things as company meetings or company activities (R)

Activity Preference

5. A job which requires the employee to be busy during the day is better than a job which allows a lot of loafing

9. If a person can get away with it, that person should try to work just a little slower than the boss expects (R)

20. The best job that a worker can get is one which permits the worker to do almost nothing during the work day (R)

27. When an employee can get away with it, the employee should take it easy (R)

29. A worker who takes long rest pauses is probably a poor worker

39. A person would soon grow tired of loafing on a job and would probably be happier if he or she worked hard

46. If a person is given a choice between jobs which pay the same money, the person should choose the one which requires as little work as possible (R)

50. A person should try to stay busy all day rather than try to find ways to get out of doing work

54. If a worker keeps himself busy on the job, the working day passes more quickly than if the worker were loafing

Attitude Toward Earnings

10. A person should hold a second job to bring in extra money if the person can get it

15. A person should choose the job which pays the most

21. If I were paid by the hour, I would probably turn down most offers to make extra money by working overtime (R)

23. A person should take the job which offers the most overtime if the regular pay on the jobs is about the same

30. A person should choose one job over another mostly because of the higher wages

34. The only good part of most jobs is the paycheck

41. When someone is looking for a job, money should not be the most important consideration (R)

47. A good job is a well paying job

51. A person should take a job that pays more than some other job even if that person cannot stand other workers on the job

Social Status of the Job

1. One of the reasons that I work is to make my family respect me

2. A person does not deserve respect just because the person has a good job (R)

3. A job with prestige is not necessarily a better job than one which does not have prestige (R)

4. My friends would not think much of me if I did not have a good job

18. Prestige should not be a factor in choosing a job (R)

26. The person who holds down a good job is the most respected person in the neighborhood

38. Having a good job makes a person more worthy of praise from friends and family

45. As far as my friends are concerned, it could not make any difference if I worked regularly or only once in a while (R)

49. Even though they make the same amount of money, the person who works in an office has a more impressive job than the person working as a sales clerk

Upward Striving

8. Even if a person has a good job, the person should always be looking for a better job
11. In choosing a job, a person ought to consider chances for advancement as well as other factors
19. One should always be thinking about pulling oneself up in the world and should work hard with the hope of being promoted to a higher-level job
22. If a person likes his job, the person should be satisfied with it and should not push for a promotion to another job (R)
28. The trouble with too many people is that when they find a job in which they are interested, they don't try to get a better job
31. A worker who turns down a promotion is probably making a mistake
35. A promotion to a higher-level job usually means more worries and should be avoided for that reason (R)
40. A well-paying job that offers little opportunity for advancement is not a good job for me
42. One is better off if one is satisfied with one's own job and is not concerned about being promoted to another job (R)

Responses

Strongly disagree; Moderately disagree; Neither agree nor disagree; Moderately agree; Strongly agree; scored 1 to 5 respectively.

7.2 Beliefs About Work

Source: Buchholz, 1977

The first published account of the Beliefs About Work questionnaire is that provided by Buchholz (1976). However, a fuller description is offered in Buchholz (1977), and this will be taken as the primary source. The measure contains five indices, as follows: (1) The Work Ethic—the belief that work is good in itself, offers dignity to a person and that success is a result of personal effort; (2) The Organizational Belief System—the view that work takes on meaning only as it affects the organization and contributes to one's position at work; (3) Marxist-related Beliefs—the opinion that work is fundamental to human fulfilment but as currently organized represents exploitation of the worker and consequent alienation; (4) The Humanistic Belief System—the view that individual growth and development in the job is more important than output; and (5) The Leisure Ethic—which regards work as a means to personal fulfilment through its provision of the means to pursue leisure activities.

The questionnaire devised to measure these belief systems comprises 45 items, each with five response alternatives running from strong disagreement to strong agreement. There are five sub-scales, each corresponding to one of the belief systems, which are composed of seven, nine, eleven, ten and eight items respectively. Sub-scale scores are obtained by averaging scores on component items. Four items are reverse-scored. The final items were selected from an original pool of 159 which was first reduced to 100 by content analysis and subsequently to its final size through factor analysis of responses obtained from 340 mainly non-managerial employees. No descriptive statistics or internal reliabilities are described for this sample. However, sub-scale means and standard deviations obtained from 366 senior managers are given. These are as follows: Work Ethic, mean 2.32, s.d. 0.74; Organizational Belief System, mean 3.05, s.d. 0.67; Marxist-related Beliefs, mean 2.01, s.d. 0.51; Humanistic Belief System, mean 4.49, s.d. 0.43; Leisure Ethic, mean 3.09, s.d. 0.70. It should be noted that these figures are based on a reduced number of items (37) selected on the basis of a sample-specific factor analysis, and it is only these items which are given in full in the source publication. Such selection of items has been the practice in other uses of this instrument, so that detailed comparisons across studies are difficult.

Buchholz (1976) drawing on 35 items with a sample of 79 students obtained the following means: Work Ethic, 2.87; Organizational Belief System, 3.10; Marxist-related Beliefs, 2.95; Humanistic Belief System 4.40; and Leisure Ethic, 3.40. Dickson and Buchholz (1977), using all 45 items with 105 American managers and 130 Scottish managers, report means for each of the five sub-scales broken down according to nationality, age, management level, size of company and education. Overall demographic characteristics were found to be more strongly related to expressed beliefs than was nationality, though the American managers showed stronger agreement with Marxist-related Beliefs (mean 2.98) than did their Scottish counterparts (mean 2.46). Buchholz (1978) presents the results obtained by combining responses from 366 senior managers and 340 mainly non-managerial employees (as described in previous studies) with those from 72 union leaders. These three investigations are reviewed together by Dickson and Buchholz (1979).

Items

Work Ethic

1. By working hard a person can overcome every obstacle that life presents
4. One must avoid dependence on other persons wherever possible
6. A man can learn better on the job by striking out boldly on his own than he can by following the advice of others

7. Only those who depend on themselves get ahead in life
11. One should work like a slave at everything he undertakes until he is satisfied with the results
30. One should live one's own life independent of others as much as possible
39. To be superior a man must stand alone

Organizational Belief System

3. Better decisions are made in a group than by individuals
9. One's contribution to the group is the most important thing about his work
10. One should take an active part in all group affairs
18. It is best to have a job as part of an organization where all work together even if you don't get individual credit
22. Working with a group is better than working alone
25. Survival of the group is very important in an organization
31. The group is the most important entity in any organization
41. Work is a means to foster group interests
42. Conformity is necessary for an organization to survive

Marxist-related Beliefs

2. Management does not understand the needs of the worker
13. Workers should be represented on the board of directors of companies
15. Factories would be run better if workers had more of a say in management
26. The most important work in America is done by the laboring classes
27. The working classes should have more say in running society
28. Wealthy people carry their fair share of the burdens of life in this country (R)
29. The rich do not make much of a contribution to society
34. The work of the laboring classes is exploited by the rich for their own benefit
36. Workers should be more active in making decisions about products, financing, and capital investment
44. The free enterprise system mainly benefits the rich and powerful
45. Workers get their fair share of the economic rewards of society (R)

Humanistic Belief System

8. Work can be made satisfying
14. The work place can be humanized
17. Work can be made interesting rather than boring
19. Work can be a means for self-expression
24. Work can be organized to allow for human fulfilment
32. The job should be a source of new experiences
33. Work should enable one to learn new things
37. Work should allow for the use of human capabilities
38. One's job should give him a chance to try out new ideas
40 Work can be made meaningful

Leisure Ethic

5. Increased leisure time is bad for society (R)

12. The less hours one spends working and the more leisure time available the better
16. Success means having ample time to pursue leisure activities
20. The present trend towards a shorter work week is to be encouraged
21. Leisure time activities are more interesting than work
23. Work takes too much of our time, leaving little time to relax
35. More leisure time is good for people
43. The trend towards more leisure is not a good thing (R)

Responses

Strongly disagree; Mildly disagree; Neither agree nor disagree; Mildly agree; Strongly agree; scored 1 to 5 respectively.

7.3   Protestant Ethic Scale

Source: Mirels and Garrett, 1971

The authors interpret the Protestant Ethic as a dispositional variable characterized by a belief in the importance of hard work and frugality which acts as a defence against sloth, sensuality, sexual temptation and religious doubt. As such they set out to construct an instrument with a relatively broad focus. Their scale has 19 items. Three items are reverse-scored. There is a six-point response dimension, and the scale score is obtained by summing across items; higher scores reflect agreement with Protestant Ethic ideals.

The Protestant Ethic Scale was developed through item and factor analyses of data from three student samples. With one group (N=222) the Kuder-Richardson coefficient was observed to be 0.79, and with another (N=117) Protestant Ethic Scale scores correlated 0.29 and 0.30 with Mosher's (1966) Sex Guilt and Morality Conscience Guilt Scale scores respectively and 0.51 with the California F Scale of Authoritarianism (Adorno, Frenkel-Brunswik, Levinson and Sanford, 1950). No significant association with the Crowne-Marlowe (1960) Social Desirability Scale was recorded. A subsequent administration of the Protestant Ethic Scale to 54 male and 55 female students yielded means of 85.7 (s.d. 15.5) and 85.5 (s.d. 16.2) respectively. For these two samples associations with sub-scales of the Strong Vocational Interest Blank (Strong, 1951) are also described.

Merrens and Garrett (1975) in a laboratory study with 40 students showed that those with high scores on the Protestant Ethic Scale spent significantly more time working on a repetitive task, and produced more output, than those with low scores. Greenberg (1977) obtained a similar result, and also found that, when told they were doing poorly, the performance of those students with high scores improved but that of low scorers declined. Kidron (1978) reports statistics for three groups of employees. For example, 237 clerical and supervisory office employees yielded an item mean of 4.60 (s.d. 0.62) and a Spearman-Brown coefficient of 0.67. Lied and Pritchard (1976) administered the scale with five response alternatives to 146 Air Force trainees. They report an alpha coefficient of 0.70 and a correlation of 0.28 between scale scores and self-ratings of effort but no significant association with instructor ratings of effort. An alpha coefficient of 0.75 is reported by Ganster (1980) in research with 190 undergraduate students; in that case a nine-point response scale was employed.

Items

1. Most people spend too much time in unprofitable amusements
2. Our society would have fewer problems if people had less leisure time
3. Money acquired easily (e.g. through gambling or speculation) is usually spent unwisely
4. There are few satisfactions equal to the realization that one has done his best at a job
5. The most difficult college courses usually turn out to be the most rewarding
6. Most people who don't succeed in life are just plain lazy
7. The self-made man is likely to be more ethical than the man born to wealth
8. I often feel I would be more successful if I sacrificed certain pleasures
9. People should have more leisure time to spend in relaxation (R)
10. Any man who is able and willing to work hard has a good chance of succeeding
11. People who fail at a job have usually not tried hard enough
12. Life would have very little meaning if we never had to suffer
13. Hard work offers little guarantee of success (R)
14. The credit card is a ticket to careless spending
15. Life would be more meaningful if we had more leisure time (R)
16. The man who can approach an unpleasant task with enthusiasm is the man who gets ahead
17. If one works hard enough he is likely to make a good life for himself
18. I feel uneasy when there is little work for me to do
19. A distaste for hard work usually reflects a weakness of character

Responses

I disagree strongly to I agree strongly on a six-point scale with no neutral or undecided point; scored 1, 2, 3, 5, 6 and 7 respectively. Intermediate labels are not cited.

7.4   Protestant Ethic

Source: Blood, 1969

The author describes a person who possesses Protestant Ethic ideals as one who feels that personal worth results from self-sacrificing work or occupational achievement. The Protestant Ethic scale was designed to measure the strength of this orientation along with the extent to which individuals disassociate themselves from such values. It is thus composed of two sub-scales labelled Pro-Protestant Ethic and Non-Protestant Ethic, each consisting of four items. The items from both sub-scales are intermixed in presentation. There is a six-point agree–disagree response dimension, and sub-scale scores are obtained by summing across item scores.

The measure was developed with 114 trainee airmen and 306 aircraft maintenance workers. A principal components analysis of the eight items with a varimax rotation of two components showed that they loaded appropriately on the two work value dimensions. The scales intercorrelated 0.11 for the trainee sample and −0.03 among the permanent workers. In both samples Pro-Protestant Ethic scores were positively but weakly correlated (−0.02 to +0.28, median 0.12) with indices of Specific Job Satisfaction (Job Descriptive Index, 3.3), with which the Non-Protestant Ethic scores were negatively correlated (0.02 to −0.31, median −0.13).

Aldag and Brief (1975) obtained results compatible with the factor structure originally reported, with a sample of 131 manufacturing employees. However, whilst the Non-Protestant Ethic sub-scale scores were negatively correlated with indices of Job Satisfaction, the Pro-Protestant Ethic scores were generally independent of Satisfaction. Wanous (1974b) used only the Pro-Protestant Ethic sub-scale and reported a Spearman-Brown internal reliability coefficient of 0.70 with a sample of "about 80" newly hired female telephone operators.

Greenberg (1978) offers some evidence of the scale's construct validity. With a sample of 273 commuters he found that Pro-Protestant Ethic scores were correlated 0.29 with perceiving the journey as part of the work day, 0.46 with engaging in work-related behaviour whilst in transit, and 0.39 with a stronger preference for working than commuting. Filley and Aldag (1978) obtained a mean for the Pro-Protestant Ethic sub-scale of 20.08 (s.d. 2.75) for 107 chief executives of manufacturing firms and 19.75 (s.d. 3.07) for their counterparts from retailing firms. Other studies using the scale are reported by Aldag and Brief (1979), Armenakis, Feild, Holley, Bedeian and Ledbetter (1977), and Rim (1977); selected items were employed by Cherrington, Condie and England (1979).

Items

Pro-Protestant Ethic

2. Hard work makes a man a better person
4. Wasting time is as bad as wasting money
6. A good indication of a man's worth is how well he does his job
7. If all other things are equal, it is better to have a job with a lot of responsibility than one with little responsibility

Non-Protestant Ethic

1. When the workday is finished, a person should forget his job and enjoy himself
3. The principal purpose of a man's job is to provide him with the means for enjoying his free time
5. Wherever possible a person should relax and accept life as it is, rather than always striving for unreachable goals
8. People who "do things the easy way" are the smart ones

Responses

A six-point scale from Disagree completely to Agree completely; scored 1 to 6 respectively. Intermediate labels are not cited.

7.5   Work Involvement

Source: Warr, Cook and Wall, 1979

The authors note the need for short, robust scales which are easily completed by blue-collar workers of modest educational attainment. Work involvement is defined as "the extent to which a person wants to be engaged in work" (p. 130), that is paid employment in general rather than any particular job.

The scale comprises six items. There is a seven-point agree–disagree response dimension, and the scale score is the sum of item scores. The scale was developed from a literature survey, a pilot study, and two investigations with samples of 200 and 390 male blue-collar employees from manufacturing industry. The samples were drawn according to a frame designed to match United Kingdom demographic characteristics. The selection of items was based on findings from the first sample (Study 1), and the properties of the resultant scale confirmed on the second sample (Study 2). For Study 1 the mean was 31.77 (s.d. 5.98), and the alpha coefficient was 0.63; for Study 2 these values were 33.37, 5.86 and 0.64. A test–retest correlation of 0.56 was recorded for a sample of 60 over a period of six months. Decile scores are also presented in the source publication.

Factor analysis with varimax rotation using items from six separate scales showed for Study 1 that the Work Involvement items loaded on two dimensions, one representing the focal construct, the other being Intrinsic Job Motivation (6.7). Findings from Study 2 using the final version of the scale, however, showed that all six items loaded unambiguously on a single factor, with loadings ranging from 0.44 to 0.66. Work Involvement scores correlated 0.37 with Intrinsic Job Motivation (6.7), 0.28 with Perceived Intrinsic Job Characteristics (8.5), and 0.30 with Overall Job Satisfaction (2.11), and were unrelated to age or skill level.

Items

1. Even if I won a great deal of money on the pools I would continue to work somewhere
2. Having a job is very important to me
3. I should hate to be on the dole
4. I would soon get very bored if I had no work to do
5. The most important things that happen to me involve work
6. If unemployment benefit was really high I would still prefer to work

Responses

No, I strongly disagree; No, I disagree quite a lot; No, I disagree just a little; I'm not sure about this; Yes, I agree just a little; Yes, I agree quite a lot; Yes, I strongly agree; scored 1 to 7 respectively.

7.6   Higher Order Need Strength

Source: Hackman and Lawler, 1971

This scale aims to measure the strength of individuals' desire to obtain higher order need satisfaction from work. The concept of higher order need derives from the work of Maslow (1943, 1954) and Alderfer (1969), referring to needs at upper levels within an assumed hierarchy, such as those of personal growth and development, accomplishment and self-actualization. The impetus to develop the measure came from previous empirical and theoretical work (e.g. Turner and Lawrence, 1965; Hulin and Blood, 1968) suggesting that such needs may moderate the relationship between Job Characteristics and Job Satisfaction. The present measure is best considered in conjunction with Hackman and Oldham's (1975) derivative indices of Growth Need Strength which are the subject of the following entry (7.7). A technical report by Hackman (1973) represents an intermediate stage in the development of these measures.

The Higher Order Need Strength scale comprises 12 items. Responses are on a seven-point dimension, and the mean item score is used as the overall index.

With a sample of 208 telephone operators Hackman and Lawler (1971) recorded a mean of 6.01 and an internal reliability (type unspecified) of 0.89. Using sub-group analysis they obtained evidence compatible with the interpretation that Higher Order Need Strength is a moderator of the relationship between perceived Job Dimensions (using their own measures, see 8.1) and several measures of Specific Job Satisfaction. The moderator effect was most apparent in relation to the characteristics of Skill Variety and Autonomy, but the pattern of results was not totally consistent, and statistical tests for the presence of a moderating variable were not rigorous (c.f. Zedeck, 1971).

Although several authors have used measures based on the Higher Order Need Strength scale, few have used it in its original form. Comparable descriptive statistics are therefore not readily available. Wanous (1974b), using eight "almost exactly parallel" items, recorded a Spearman-Brown internal reliability coefficient of 0.78 with a sample of "about 80" newly hired female telephone operators. He also obtained results broadly compatible with the interpretation that Higher Order Need Strength moderates the association between perceived Job Dimensions and Job Satisfaction, and found that scale scores correlated 0.41 with scores on Blood's (1969) Pro-Protestant Ethic sub-scale (7.4). In a longitudinal study involving an initial sample of 332 varied government employees, Rabinowitz, Hall and Goodale (1977) obtained an alpha coefficient of 0.93 using ten items from the scale. The correlation between scores on this modified instrument and a four-item version of the Job Involvement scale (6.1) was 0.33. Using data from the same sample Hall, Goodale, Rabinowitz and Morgan (1978) report an alpha coefficient of 0.88 for a five-item index. Other studies using the scale or modifications of it include Abdel-Halim (1980b), Aldag and Brief (1975, 1979), Armenakis, Feild, Holley, Bedeian and Ledbetter (1977), Farr (1976b), Giles (1977a, b), Jones, James, Bruni and Sells (1977), Katz (1978a), Orpen (1979a, b), and Saal (1978).

Two features of the Higher Order Need Strength scale should be noted. First, it tends to elicit very high scores (typically around 6 on a range of 1 to 7) and consequently has a small standard deviation. Secondly, the term "personal growth" (item 1) is one which, in our experience, is unfamiliar to many respondents.

Items

1. The opportunity for personal growth and development on my job
2. The opportunity for independent thought and action on my job
3. The opportunity to find out how I am doing
4. The opportunity to complete work I start
5. The opportunity to do challenging work
6. The feeling that I know whether I am performing my job well or poorly
7. The opportunity to do a number of different things
8. The opportunity to do a job from the beginning to the end (that is, the chance to do a whole job)
9. The freedom to do pretty much what I want on my job
10. The amount of variety in my job
11. The feeling of worthwhile accomplishment in my job
12. The opportunity, in my job, for participation in the determination of methods, procedures, and goals

Responses

A seven-point dimension from I would like to have none or a minimum amount to I would like to have a maximum amount; scored 1 to 7 respectively. Intermediate labels are not cited.

7.7   Individual Growth Need Strength

Source: Hackman and Oldham, 1974, 1975

Two alternative indices of Individual Growth Need Strength are included in the wide-ranging Job Diagnostic Survey (see also 2.6, 3.6, 6.3, 8.2, 8.28). The focal construct is described as "a malleable individual difference characteristic" which reflects "the strength of the respondent's desire to obtain 'growth' satisfaction from his or her work" (Hackman and Oldham, 1975, pp. 162–163). The latter is viewed as satisfaction of needs in the upper reaches of Maslow's (1943, 1954) hierarchy, such as autonomy, independence, accomplishment, and self-actualization (see also 7.6). The immediate theoretical base for the measure is provided by Hackman and Oldham's (1976) Job Characteristics Model.

One measure of Individual Growth Need Strength, here called Form A, consists of six items which are intermixed in presentation with five others. Responses are obtained on a seven-point dimension running from Would like having this only a moderate amount (or less) to Would like having this extremely much. In an attempt to reduce extreme responses as typically recorded on Hackman and Lawler's (1971) measure of Higher Order Need Strength (7.6), the response dimension has numerical values attached which run from four to ten. However, for scoring purposes a constant of 3 is subtracted to provide a response range between 1 and 7, and item scores are averaged to provide the scale value. The second measure, here called Form B, comprises 12 items. These are presented in a single section of the questionnaire, and are of a forced-choice nature requiring respondents to indicate on a five-point continuum their relative preference between pairs of hypothetical jobs. Each item contrasts a job with properties relevant to Growth Need Strength with one having the potential for satisfying other needs. Half of the items are reverse-scored, and scale scores are the average of item scores.

With a sample of 658 varied employees (41% female) the following scale properties were recorded. For Form A the mean was 5.62 (s.d. 1.28) and internal reliability 0.88 (Spearman-Brown formula applied to median inter-item correlation). No mean was reported for Form B but the internal reliability (type as above) was 0.71. The two scales inter-correlated 0.50 and were only weakly related to 14 other scores from the Job Diagnostic Survey covering perceived Job Characteristics (8.2), Critical Psychological States (8.28), Job Satisfactions (2.6, 3.6) and Internal Work Motivation (6.3). In further analysis of Form B results in the same study Hackman and Oldham (1976) found correlations of −0.26 with sex (men scoring more highly), 0.46 with education, and 0.16 with rural versus urban place of work.

More extensive statistics are reported by Oldham, Hackman and Stepina (1978). With a heterogeneous sample of 6930 employees (46% female) they obtained, for Form A, a mean of 5.64 (s.d. 1.22) and an internal reliability (type as above) of 0.87. For Form B the respective figures were 4.23, 0.81 and 0.71. Note however that scores on Form B were converted from five-point responses to seven-point responses by the following formula: (1.5 times five-point scale score) minus 0.5 (p. 11). The correlation between the two forms was 0.42 for this sample.

Umstot, Bell and Mitchell (1976) and Hackman, Pearce and Wolfe (1978) have used Form A, in a laboratory study and "a naturally occurring quasi-experiment" respectively, to examine whether Growth Need Strength levels moderate the relationship between perceived Job Characteristics and several attitudes and behaviours. The former found no support for a moderating influence, and the latters' results were more suggestive of support but generally insignificant. Form A was also used by Rousseau (1978b), who recorded an alpha coefficient of 0.85 and a test–retest correlation over three months of 0.76 (N=271 employees from two organizations). With 398 office employees, Pierce, Dunham and Blackburn (1979) recorded a mean of 5.75 (s.d. 1.14), an alpha coefficient of 0.86, and a test–retest correlation across one month

(N=30) of 0.68. Another use of Form A is by Abdel-Halim (1979a) who recorded an average total score for the six items of 34.44 (s.d. 5.74) from 89 managerial and professional employees.

Form B of the Individual Growth Need Strength scale was used by Oldham, Hackman and Pearce (1976) in a study of 201 bank employees. They obtained a mean of 4.24 (s.d. 0.68) and an internal reliability coefficient of 0.64 (median inter-item correlation corrected by Spearman-Brown procedures). Scores were found to be associated with measures of perceived Job Characteristics (8.2), various aspects of satisfaction, Internal Work Motivation (6.3) and work performance. The findings were generally consistent with a view of Growth Need Strength as a moderator of the relationship between perceived Job Characteristics and both job performance and Internal Work Motivation. A similar study by Evans, Kiggundu and House (1979), with 343 supervisors and managers also used Form B, but evidence for a moderating impact of Growth Need Strength was limited. The reported mean was 3.21 (s.d. 0.51) and coefficient alpha was 0.66. With 190 undergraduate students Ganster (1980) recorded an alpha coefficient for Form B of 0.73. A Spearman-Brown coefficient of 0.85 was obtained by Bhagat and Chassie (1980) (N=65 varied employees; seven-point response scale).

Stone, Ganster, Woodman and Fusilier (1979) used both A and B Forms in an investigation with 133 students. The correlation between the two was 0.21 and their internal reliabilities (coefficient alpha) were 0.85 and 0.67 respectively. Form A was found to correlate 0.26, 0.23 and 0.21 with the Pride in Work, Upward Striving and Job Involvement sub-scales of the Survey of Work Values (Wollack, Goodale, Wijting and Smith, 1971) (7.1), and was associated 0.36 with an index of socially desirable responding. Form B was less strongly or not related to each of these variables. Arnold and House (1980) also used both forms of the Growth Need Strength measure, concluding that there was some evidence for the moderating influence of GNS on the relationship between Job Characteristics (8.2) and Critical Psychological States (8.28).

Other researchers using these scales or (typically) modifications of them include Aldag and Brief (1975, 1979), Bassett (1979), Brief and Aldag (1975, 1976), Feldman and Arnold (1978), Filley and Aldag (1978), Katz (1978a) and Mobley, Hand, Baker and Meglino (1979). Descriptions and discussion of the measures are included in Hackman and Oldham (1980).

FORM A

Items

1. Stimulating and challenging work
2. Chances to exercise independent thought and action in my job
3. Opportunities to learn new things from my work
4. Opportunities to be creative and imaginative in my work
5. Opportunities for personal growth and development in my job
6. A sense of worthwhile accomplishment in my work

Responses

Would like having this only a moderate amount (or less); Would like having this very much; Would like having this extremely much; scored 4, 7 and 10 respectively. Intermediate scale points are not labelled. Scores are transformed from the range 4 to 10 to the range 1 to 7.

FORM B

Items

Job A	*Job B*
1. A job where the pay is very good	A job where there is considerable opportunity to be creative and innovative
2. A job where you are often required to make important decisions	A job with many pleasant people to work with (**R**)
3. A job in which greater responsibility is given to those who do the best work	A job in which greater responsibility is given to loyal employees who have the most seniority (**R**)
4. A job in an organization which is in financial trouble and might have to close down within the year	A job in which you are not allowed to have any say whatever in how your work is scheduled, or in the procedures to be used in carrying it out (**R**)
5. A very routine job	A job where your co-workers are not very friendly
6. A job with a supervisor who is often very critical of you and your work in front of other people	A job which prevents you from using a number of skills that you worked hard to develop (**R**)
7. A job with a supervisor who respects you and treats you fairly	A job which provides constant opportunities for you to learn new and interesting things
8. A job where there is a real chance you could be laid off	A job with very little chance to do challenging work (**R**)
9. A job in which there is a real chance for you to develop new	A job which provides lots of vacation time and an excellent fringe benefit

Job A	Job B
skills and advance in the organization	package (R)
10. A job with little freedom and independence to do your work in the way you think best	A job where the working conditions are poor
11. A job with very satisfying team-work	A job which allows you to use your skills and abilities to the fullest extent
12. A job which offers little or no challenge	A job which requires you to be completely isolated from co-workers

Responses

Strongly prefer A; Slightly prefer A; Neutral; Slightly prefer B; Strongly prefer B; scored 1 to 5 respectively.

7.8   Higher Order Need Strength

Source: Warr, Cook and Wall, 1979

The authors note the need for short, robust scales which are easily completed by employees of modest educational attainment. From a literature review, a pilot study and two investigations of 200 and 390 male blue-collar employees (drawn according to a predetermined sampling frame designed to match British demographic characteristics) a six-item Higher Order Need Strength scale was developed. This construct is defined as the "need for satisfaction and achievement through work" and "is viewed as a dispositional characteristic" (p. 131). Responses are obtained on a seven-point scale running from Not at all important to Extremely important and summed to provide a scale score.

In the two samples described above the means were 33.69 (s.d. 6.80) and 36.07 (s.d. 5.03) respectively, with the corresponding alpha coefficients being 0.91 and 0.82. Decile scores are also presented in the source publication. The test–retest correlation across six months for a sub-sample of 60 respondents was 0.26, which as the authors note is undesirably low and calls into question the validity of the measure or the stability of the need it is designed to operationalize. However, principal components analysis with varimax rotation including items from five other scales showed that all Higher Order Need Strength items loaded unambiguously on a single factor (loadings from 0.72 to 0.81 in sample 1, and from 0.54 to 0.78 in sample 2). Correlates of Higher Order Need Strength, based on the combined sample of 590 respondents included Intrinsic Job Motivation (6.7), Perceived Intrinsic Job Characteristics (8.5), Work Involvement (7.5), skill level, Life Satisfaction, and Self-rated Anxiety (5.15) with values of 0.33, 0.28, 0.17, 0.17, 0.20 and 0.20 respectively. A subsequent use is reported by Cook and Wall (1980).

Items

1. Using your skills to the maximum
2. Achieving something that you personally value
3. The opportunity to make your own decisions
4. The opportunity to learn new things
5. Challenging work
6. Extending your range of abilities

Responses

Not at all important; Not particularly important; I'm not sure about its importance; Moderately important; Fairly important; Very important; Extremely important; scored 1 to 7 respectively.

7.9 Work Values Inventory

Source: Super, 1970

The Work Values Inventory (WVI) is an instrument to assess the values which affect motivation to work. It was designed for use with all ages from the beginning of junior high school upwards, and is focussed on "the values which are extrinsic to as well as those which are intrinsic in work, the satisfactions which men and women seek in work and the satisfactions which may be concomitants or outcomes of work" (p. 4).

The inventory covers the following 15 values: Altruism—work which enables one to contribute to others' welfare; Aesthetic—work which permits one to make beautiful things; Creativity—work in which one invents new things or develops new ideas; Intellectual Stimulation—work in which one can exercise one's judgment and learn how and why things work; Achievement—work which gives one a feeling of accomplishment in doing a job well, with the emphasis on tangible results; Independence—work which permits one to undertake tasks in one's own way and at one's own pace; Prestige—work which evokes respect in others' eyes; Management—work which involves directing others; Economic Return—work which pays well; Security—work where a job is always secure; Surroundings—work carried out under pleasant conditions; Supervisory Relations—work where the supervisor is fair and congenial; Associates—work which brings one into contact with fellow workers whom one likes; Way of life—work which allows one to live as one wishes, to be the type of person one wishes to be; and Variety—work which allows one to do different types of jobs.⌋Each of these 15 values is tapped by a separate three-item sub-scale with the resultant 45 items being mixed in order of presentation. Responses are obtained on a five-point response continuum running from Very important to Unimportant and are summed to produce sub-scale scores.

Extensive normative information is offered in the source publication, based on a sample of 10,083 students in grades 7 to 12 selected to be representative of the national (USA) school population. Percentiles, means and standard deviations for each sub-scale are presented according to grade and sex. Conventional estimates of internal reliability are not cited, but limited evidence of high inter-item correlations within sub-scales is described. Test–retest correlations over two weeks using a sample of 99 10th grade school-children ranged from 0.74 to 0.88, with a median of 0.83. The sub-scales themselves were shown to be generally positively intercorrelated. For 12th grade boys in the original sample, for example, sub-scale intercorrelations ranged from −0.07 to 0.66 with a median of 0.29. Factor analytic support for the 15 a priori dimensions is not offered. However, selective evidence of construct validity is reported in the form of moderate correlations between sub-scales from the WVI with relevant indices from alternative instruments.

Thomas (1974), in a study of some 240 students, found differences between black and white children with respect to Altruism, Associates, Variety and Intellectual Stimulation. In all cases the white respondents placed greater importance on these values. Moreover, girls tended to place more importance than boys on Creativity and Altruism. Greenhaus and Simon (1977) with a sample of 153 psychology students found that those who were vocationally undecided placed less importance on intrinsic work values than did those committed to an occupation. Other studies, similarly based on student samples, are by Greenhaus and Simon (1976), Pryor (1980), Richardson (1974) and Dietrich (1977). Generally these give descriptive statistics and provide evidence relevant to construct validity.

⌈The relatively simple items and good face validity of the Survey of Work Values suggest this instrument would be useful for studies concerned with work experience.⌉However, at present it suffers from a lack of supporting evidence in three important respects. First, notably absent in the literature are findings based on samples of full-time employees, and thus the acceptability of the instrument in this context remains to be established. Secondly, little information has been reported on the internal reliabilities of the several sub-scales. And finally, we could locate no multivariate analyses of the instrument as a whole carried out in order to determine the empirical justification for its assumed structure of fifteen separable work values.

Items

It should be noted that, as a result of restrictions imposed by the copyright holders, only one of the three items from each sub-scale of the Work Values Inventory is reproduced below.

Work in which you. . .

Altruism	2 . . . help others
Aesthetic	7 . . . need to have artistic ability
Creativity	15 . . . try out new ideas and suggestions
Intellectual Stimulation	1 . . . have to keep solving new problems
Achievement	13 . . . get the feeling of having done a good day's work
Independence	5 . . . have freedom in your own area
Prestige	6 . . . gain prestige in your field
Management	14 . . . have authority over others
Economic Return	3 . . . can get a raise
Security	9 . . . know your job will last
Surroundings	12 . . . like the setting in which the job is done
Supervisory Relations	11 . . . have a boss who gives you a square deal
Associates	8 . . . are one of the gang
Way of life	10 . . . can be the kind of person you would like to be
Variety	4 . . . look forward to changes in your job

Responses

Very important; Important; Moderately important; Of little importance; Unimportant; scored 5 to 1 respectively.

7.10   Central Life Interests

Source: Dubin, 1956

This instrument was developed to determine whether the job and workplace represent principal interests of the respondent or if his or her main orientation is more towards the world outside work. Central life interest is defined as the expressed preference for a given locale in carrying out an activity.

Unlike other measures described in this section, the Central Life Interests Questionnaire is used to classify individuals into discrete groups, rather than to produce continuous scores representing the degree of interest in paid employment. The items require a respondent to select one of three alternatives for a specified activity: one alternative typically represents a preference for a work setting ("job-oriented"), another a preference for a specific setting outside work ("non-job orien-ted"), and the third indicates indifference as to the location for the activity ("unfocussed"). The original instrument comprised 40 such items but was subsequently reduced to 32 items. It is this latter version which has been most used in recent studies and is given below. The items are designed to cover four areas: membership in formal organizations, technological aspects of the environment, informal personal relations, and general everyday experiences. The eight items representing each of these areas are mixed in order of presentation, and the sequence of response alternatives is similarly varied.

Early research employing the measure used a scoring system to differentiate between job-oriented and non-job-oriented individuals. However the more usual recent practice is to use a threefold descriptive system (see Dubin, Champoux and Porter, 1975). Individuals are classed as *job-oriented* if they choose at least 16 job-oriented responses to the 32 items, or if they select 22 job-oriented and unfocussed alterna-tives with a minimum of 13 of these being in the former category. Respondents are considered *non-job-oriented* if they choose at least 16 non-job-oriented responses, or if they select 22 non-job-oriented and unfocussed alternatives with a minimum of 13 of these being of the former type. Respondents choosing at least 13 unfocussed responses and not falling into either of the above categories are classified as having a *flexible focus*. All other response patterns (typically few) are considered uninterpretable.

Neither the source publication nor subsequent reports present normative or internal consistency data. However, evidence pertaining to test–retest reliability is offered by Dalton (1979) from a study of 173 subjects who responded to the Central Life Interests questionnaire on two occasions two weeks apart. A value of 0.92 for the gamma coefficient of association was obtained, and there were no instances of individuals crossing the boundary between job-oriented and non-job-oriented from the first administration to the second.

Dubin and Champoux (1975, 1977) and Dubin, Champoux and Porter (1975) describe findings based on samples of 405 female clerical bank employees and 605 male and female blue-collar employees of a telephone company. In these two samples respectively 18.5% and 11.9% were classified as non-job-oriented, 62.2% and 72.2% as having a flexible focus, and 15.2% and 15.9% as job-oriented. Those classified as job-oriented were characterized by having higher scores on Organizational Commitment (4.5), greater Job Satisfaction (3.3) and stronger attraction to individual features of their work organizations, than those with either a flexible focus or non-job-orientation. Similarly, Wiener and Gechman (1977) in a study of 54 female elementary school teachers found that the more strongly job-oriented respondents devoted more personal time to their work. Saleh and Hosek (1976), Taveggia and Hedley (1976) and Taveggia and Ziemba (1978) describe the use of modified versions of the measure. Earlier applications are summarized in Table 1 of Chapter 7 of Dubin (1976).

The version set out below is for white-collar employees. Revisions, such as changing "office" to "workplace" or "factory", make the instrument appropriate for blue-collar employees. Response coding is here indicated as J (job-oriented), N (non-job-oriented) and U (unfocussed).

Items and responses

Membership in Formal Organizations

4. I would rather accept a committee chairmanship
    anytime, any place (U)
    of a company operating or advisory committee (J)
    in an organization or club of which I am a member (N)

16. I am happier if I am praised for doing a good job of
       something at work (J)
       something in an organization I belong to (N)
       anything, it doesn't matter very much what (U)

17. If I were sick and had to stay home, I would most hate
       missing a day's work (J)
       missing almost anything I usually do (U)
       missing a meeting of an organization I belong to (N)

21. I sometimes hope that
       I'll get special recognition for doing a good job at work (J)
       I'll get to be a more important member of my club, church or lodge
       (N)
       such things will not bother me (U)

23. It is easier for me to take a chewing out
       from anyone—I listen and forget it (U)
       from a policeman (J)
       from my boss (N)

24. I would donate more money in the case of a collection
       if the solicitor was a friend of mine (U)
       for a charitable organization (N)
       for a wedding present or retirement gift for a colleague
        at the office (J)

30. If a company project I knew about but was not involved in gave everybody
  trouble, and I heard another company had solved this problem
       I have too many problems of my own to get involved (N)
       I would tell my boss or colleagues about it (J)
       I don't worry about such things (U)

32. I would much rather be a leader
       in any organization, just so it's a good one (U)
       in my club or church (N)
       in my work (J)

Technological Aspects of the Environment

1. I enjoy reading technical articles and books to learn more about
       only something very special and important (U)
       my hobby or other interests (N)
       my job (J)

2. Interruptions bother me most
       when working at the office (J)
       when working at home (N)
       hardly ever (U)

5. When I am doing some work, I usually try not to waste time
       I seldom worry about wasting time (U)
       on a project at home or in the community (N)
       on my job (J)

9. I most enjoy keeping
       my things around the house in good shape (N)

       my mind off such things (U)

       my desk and reports in good shape at the office (J)

11. Moving ahead on my job

       is not so important to me that I would give up time to make contacts and get information about my work (N)

       is so important to me that I'm willing to spend extra time to make contacts and pick up information about my work (J)

       is not particularly important to me (U)

20. In my spare time

       I just prefer to relax (U)

       I often think of better ways of doing my work (J)

       I have a thousand things that need doing (N)

25. If I have to work with someone else who is a slow worker

       I am annoyed regardless of where we are working (U)

       I am most annoyed on a job at the office (J)

       I am most annoyed on a volunteer community project (N)

26. In getting a job done, it is most important for me to have adequate freedom to plan it

       at the office (J)

       on a community project (N)

       anytime, any place (U)

Informal Personal Relations

7. In my free time at work, I would rather

       talk about whatever comes up (U)

       talk about things I am working on in the company (J)

       talk about things that are going on in sports or politics (N)

10. I prefer to have as friends

       people I get to know in my work (J)

       people who share my leisure interests (N)

       different people according to what they're like (U)

12. If I received a promotion that meant moving to another city

       my friendships wouldn't make any difference in my moving (U)

       I would most dislike leaving my friends at the office (J)

       I would most dislike leaving my other friends (N)

13. The people I can count on most when I need help are

       the friends I have at work (J)

       the friends I have in the community (N)

       almost any of my friends (U)

15. When I am not with them, the people I miss most are

       just people in general (U)

       my friends around town (N)

       my friends with whom I work (J)

22. If I needed ready cash within a few hours for an emergency on a Sunday and had to borrow it, I would probably turn to

       people I know in the community (N)

       people I know in the company (J)

       anyone who would lend it to me (U)

27. I would rather take my vacation with
       some friends from work (J)
       my family (N)
       by myself (U)

28. I most like
       talking with friends about things that are happening (N)
       talking about whatever my friends want to talk about (U)
       talking with my friends about my work and what is happening in
       the company (J)

General Everyday Experiences

3. I do my best work
      when I am at the office (J)
      when I'm not bothered by people (U)
      when I work around the house or on a community project (N)

6. I believe that
      helping my fellow men is more important than anything else (N)
      my career is more important than anything else (J)
      most things are about equally important (U)

8. I am most interested in
      things about my job (J)
      things I usually do around the house or in the community (N)
      just about everything I do (U)

14. When I am worried, it is usually about
       how well I am doing in my career (J)
       just little things (U)
       things that happen at home (N)

18. The most pleasant things I do are concerned with
       relaxation (N)
       my career (J)
       different things at different times (U)

19. I hope my children can
       work in the same kind of occupation as mine (J)
       work in any occupation, just so they enjoy their work (U)
       work in a different kind of occupation from mine (N)

29. In order to get ahead in the world
       you have to have a lot of luck (U)
       you have to be well liked where you work (J)
       you have to be well liked and known in the community (N)

31. I think that if I were suddenly to get a much better job
       probably my life would not change much except that I'd live a little
       better (J)
       probably my life would change and be better in many ways (N)
       I wouldn't know what would happen to my life (U)

7.11 Manifest Needs Questionnaire

Source: Steers and Braunstein, 1976

This instrument is designed to measure the four needs of Achievement, Affiliation, Autonomy and Dominance, through behaviourally-based items with specific reference to work settings. The authors' objective in developing these measures was to provide for organizational researchers short and yet reliable and valid scales to replace other much longer instruments. The theoretical background to the Manifest Needs Questionnaire is to be found in the work of Murray (1938), as developed by McClelland, Atkinson, Clark and Lowell (1953) and Atkinson (1958).

The Manifest Needs Questionnaire consists of four scales, one to measure each need. Each scale comprises five items, of which one or two are reversed-scored. There is a seven-point response dimension running from Always to Never. Each scale score is the mean of its component item scores.

The development and validation of the instrument involved three empirical studies using samples of 96 management students (employed in a variety of jobs) (Study 1), 115 white-collar employees from a car company (Study 2), and 382 hospital employees (Study 3). In Study 1 the following results were obtained. For n Achievement the mean score was 4.3 (s.d. 0.71), the alpha coefficient of internal reliability was 0.66, and with a sub-sample of 41 the test–retest correlation over two weeks was 0.72. The corresponding statistics for n Affiliation were: 4.1, 0.56, 0.56, and 0.75; for n Autonomy: 3.7, 0.62, 0.61, and 0.77; and for n Dominance: 4.2, 1.09, 0.83, and 0.86. In addition scores on the four scales were shown to correlate (0.61, 0.40, 0.42 and 0.62 respectively) with corresponding measures from Jackson's (1967) Personality Research Form, and with independent ratings of the subjects (0.55, 0.33, 0.54 and 0.74 respectively).

Findings from Study 2 (also reported by Steers and Spencer, 1977) showed weak correlations between the four scales. These ranged from −0.34 to +0.36 with a median (ignoring sign) of 0.17. The two highest correlations (as above) were between n Achievement and n Dominance (0.36) and n Affiliation and n Autonomy (−0.34). Need for Achievement, n Affililation and n Autonomy were also found to correlate 0.25, 0.19 and −0.25 respectively with a measure of Organizational Commitment (4.5).

Study 3 (also described by Steers, 1977, in conjunction with findings from a sample of 119 scientists and engineers) yielded the following means: n Achievement, 4.1 (s.d. 0.81); n Affiliation, 4.1 (s.d. 0.61);

n Autonomy, 3.4 (s.d. 0.89); and n Dominance, 3.8 (s.d. 1.18). Correlations between scale scores and need-related behavioural ratings obtained for 62 individuals were 0.58, 0.46, 0.44 and 0.49 respectively. Need for Achievement was found to correlate 0.31 with Job Involvement (6.1), and 0.32 with Organizational Commitment (4.5).

Other uses of the measure are by Bartol (1979a), Dalton and Todor (1979), Morris and Snyder (1979), Mowday (1979), and O'Reilly and Caldwell (1979).

Items

Need for Achievement

 1. I do my best work when my job assignments are fairly difficult
 5. I try very hard to improve on my past performance at work
 9. I take moderate risks and stick my neck out to get ahead at work
13. I try to avoid any added responsibilities on my job (R)
17. I try to perform better than my co-workers

Need for Affiliation

 2. When I have a choice, I try to work in a group instead of by myself
 6. I pay a good deal of attention to the feelings of others at work
10. I prefer to do my own work and let others do theirs (R)
14. I express my disagreements with others openly (R)
18. I find myself talking to those around me about non-business related matters

Need for Autonomy

 3. In my work assignments, I try to be my own boss
 7. I go my own way at work, regardless of the opinions of others
11. I disregard rules and regulations that hamper my personal freedom
15. I consider myself a "team player" at work (R)
19. I try my best to work alone on a job

Need for Dominance

 4. I seek an active role in the leadership of a group
 8. I avoid trying to influence those around me to see things my way (R)
12. I find myself organizing and directing the activities of others
16. I strive to gain more control over the events around me at work
20. I strive to be "in command" when I am working in a group

Responses

Always; Almost always; Usually; Sometimes; Seldom; Almost never; Never; scored 7 to 1 respectively.

7.12   Work Preference Questionnaire

Source: Fineman, 1975a

The Work Preference Questionnaire (WPQ) was developed as a self-report measure of the Need for Achievement in occupational settings. It is based upon Murray's (1938) definition of n Achievement, namely, "the desire or tendency to do things as rapidly and/or as well as possible. . .To excel one's self. To rival and surpass others. To increase self-regard by the successful exercise of talent" (p. 64). As such the instrument covers nine aspects of Need for Achievement: individual responsibility; risk-taking; achievement satisfaction; task activity, task variety; need for achievement versus need for affiliation; competitiveness; incentive value of free time; and researching the environment and language ability. Each of these is seen as part of the total construct and the 24 forced-choice items of the scale which cover them are combined to provide a single score. Items are scored 1 for endorsement of the statement reflecting Achievement need and 0 for the alternative. Eleven items refer to an "ideal organization" and 13 to an "ideal boss".

The development of the WPQ is described in more than usual detail in the source publication. The attainment of four objectives guided its construction, namely psychometric adequacy, standardization in managerial samples, acceptability to managerial respondents, and controls for social desirability and the faking of responses. The original pool of 400 items was reduced to 24 through successive studies using separate samples of managers. Item analysis based on an initial version of the scale administered to a sample of 112 managers led to the use of the finally selected items with samples of 366 and 197 managers. For the first of these two groups the mean is reported as 14 (s.d. 3.43) and Kuder-Richardson internal reliability as 0.68. The test–retest correlation over a period of one year for 18 managers was 0.58, and using 16 of the items with a sample of 87 managers 0.55. In a study using 119 managers the WPQ scores correlated 0.42 with scores on the Achievement Motive scale from the Self Description Inventory (Ghiselli, 1971). Thematic Apperception Test scores (McClelland, Atkinson, Clark and Lowell, 1953) correlated 0.21 with WPQ scores in a sample of 87 managers. A comparison between 20 managers who completed the WPQ as part of their job selection process and 20 managers matched for age to whom the measure was administered under "normal" circumstances, revealed no significant difference in scale scores. This is cited in support of the scale's success in controlling for social desirability, as is the finding, based on a sample of 58 students, that WPQ scores and Social Desirability Scale scores (Crowne and Marlowe, 1960) were unassociated ($r = -0.01$).

Fineman (1975b) describes further results based on the original samples, and an interchange between Nelson (1975) and Fineman (1975c) provides further discussion of the WPQ scale.

Items

Would your ideal organization be one. . .

1. Where a person's promotion is unpredictable and depends largely on his own good performance   or   Where a person can see exactly how his career will progress after certain periods of time

2. That regards special benefits, such as attractive bonuses, free pension schemes and a company car, as the prime incentives to remain in the job   or   That concentrates on tempting new employees with interesting work, although it is not able to pay as much as other organisations providing less interesting work (R)

3. Where it is emphasized that the 'job comes first,' therefore afterwork pleasures should take secondary importance   or   Where it is very difficult to carry on work over a weekend period should someone so desire

4. Where the few changes in tasks that occur allow people to perform one type of work with considerable care and proficiency   or   Where there is constant pressure to complete a task well in a short period of time and to then become involved with another task (R)

5. Where there is a general attitude that even if the working conditions are very poor, much can be compensated by interesting work   or   Where little that is favourable can be said about the work itself but where the attitude of management towards its employees' welfare is first-class.

6. That gives people jobs that can very likely be done well.   or   That gives people work which is not so difficult that they would have to rely on luck to do a good job nor so easy that they are bound to succeed (R)

7. Where it is expected that leisure time will be sacrificed if work pressure is great   or   Where it is felt that working late is undesirable because eventually strain will be experienced in normal working hours

8. That believes that if a person concentrates primarily on working in a warm, close fashion with his co-workers, good work must follow   or   That regards the successful completion of an employee's assignment as more important than the feelings of that person's co-workers (R)

9. That expects individuals to   or   That expects its employees to
    help the organization by ful-   strongly identify with the
    filling their own personal   organization rather than think of
    goals   themselves as individuals apart

10. Where good working com-   or   Where there is more concern with
    panions and generous holidays   employees' satisfaction with the
    are provided to make up for   actual work that they do than with
    the tedious nature of the work   their general conditions of work
                                                 (R)

11. Where each employee is solely   or   Where several people are always
    responsible for most of the   responsible for, and take the credit
    work that he performs   for, a particular piece of work

Would your ideal boss be someone. . .

12. Who gives his employees work   or   Who gives people work requiring
    that they feel sure of doing   quite a lot of struggling to
    well without too much effort   master (R)

13. Who insists on finding out   or   Who regards the pleasure that his
    how worthwhile his employees   employees get from their work as
    see their work but neglects   more important than the actual
    looking into the enjoyment   worthwhileness of the work
    that they get from their work

14. Who emphasizes the impor-   or   Who relies on a particularly
    tance of the work group's   efficient individual in a work
    responsibility for its decisions   group to control the group's
    rather than particular indivi-   activities (R)
    duals in the group taking the
    responsibility

15. Who expects to be consulted   or   Who encourages employees to
    only for very exceptional work   follow set procedures in their work
    problems

16. Who attempts to provide   or   Who would not give people work
    attractive work for his   that they could view as of little
    employees even if it is not of   value even though it may be highly
    great value to them   attractive to them (R)

17. Who gives his employees   or   Who gives clear, very comprehen-
    general guidelines on which to   sive instructions on how employees
    base their own decisions about   should carry out their work
    how to proceed with their work

18. Who finds that for group   or   Who feels that a certain degree of
    morale it is better to try to   bad feeling amongst employees is
    preserve good co-worker rela-   worth tolerating if they are very
    tionships that may be spoiled   much involved with their work (R)
    by letting people keep working
    at a task to their own satisfac-
    tion

19. Who looks for future employees   or   Who looks for future employees
    who will be able to work inde-   who will primarily be good at
    pendently of others   getting on well with other
                                                employees

20. Who would rather employees   or   Who will not interfere with work
    consulted him with work   for which employees have respon-
    difficulties than struggle with   sibility (R)
    them themselves

21. Who expects an individual's   or   Who relies on the group as a whole
    work rate to remain relatively   to produce a given amount of work,
    uninfluenced by his colleagues   expecting the group to influence
                                                an individual's quantity of work
                                                done

22. Who views good employee   or   Who insists on individuals trying
    relations as being most impor-   to achieve a better performance
    tant and incompatible with   rating than their co-workers (R)
    competitiveness

23. Who gives employees work   or   Who gives employees work that
    where they need to write fairly   involves very little written report-
    detailed arguments about   ing or problem discussions
    problem solutions

24. Who feels that working late   or   Who encourages working late in
    should be avoided   order to meet a deadline (R)

Responses

Preference for the first or second alternative, scored 1 to 0 respectively.

7.13   Work Environment Preference Schedule

Source: Gordon, 1973

The Work Environment Preference Schedule (WEPS) is designed to measure individual bureaucratic orientation, that is the respondent's commitment to the set of attitudes, values and behaviours that are characteristic of bureaucratic organizations. Weber's (1946) "ideal type" of bureaucracy was used to specify the main elements of the construct, though the focus here is on individual rather than organizational characteristics. Four features are covered by the instrument: Self-subordination, a willingness to comply fully with authority; Impersonalization, a preference for impersonalized work relationships; Role conformity, a preference for security deriving from following set rules and procedures; and Traditionalism, a need for the security of organizational identification and in-group conformity. An earlier version of the scale (Gordon, 1970) covered the additional aspect of Compartmentalization.

The instrument consists of 24 items (six for each of the four features). All items are worded so that agreement reflects acceptance of bureaucratic norms. No attempt was made to control for acquiescence response set by item reversal, since acquiescence is assumed to be an associated characteristic of bureaucratic orientation. There is a five-point response dimension, and a total score is taken.

Little information is provided in the source publication or by Gordon (1970) with respect to scale development. However reference is made to analyses which "revealed that a single factor accounted for almost all of the response variance" (Gordon, 1970, p. 3) and accordingly a single scale score is used rather than sub-scales scores corresponding to the four a priori categories. Much greater detail is provided concerning the properties of the final scale. The source publication offers descriptive statistics across some 40 samples of different types, covering several thousand respondents.

The following findings are illustrative. For samples of 149 warehouse and delivery men, 72 foremen, 138 salesmen, 276 army ROTC students and 83 nurses the means were 37.8 (s.d. 5.2), 31.4 (s.d. 4.9), 29.7 (s.d. 5.8), 32.1 (s.d. 6.2) and 25.3 (s.d. 6.1). Percentiles for these and several other samples (e.g. high school students, college students and school superintendents) are also provided. Internal reliability coefficients alpha were found to range from 0.83 to 0.91 across five samples of respondents, and the test–retest correlation across 16 months with 105 ROTC students was 0.65.

Varied information relevant to construct validity is also provided in the source publication. Correlates of WEPS scores include: Authoritarianism (California F scale, Adorno, Frenkel-Brunswik, Levinson and Sanford, 1950), which yielded coefficients of 0.50 and 0.66 respectively in samples of 108 and 81 female and male college students; Dogmatism (Rokeach, 1960), giving coefficients of 0.43 and 0.47 in the same two samples; and educational level, showing correlations ranging from −0.57 to −0.22 across five samples of female mental hospital workers. Subsequent uses of the measure include those by Kavanagh (1975) and Lischeron and Wall (1975a).

Items

As a result of copyright restrictions only the first nine items of the Work Environment Preference Schedule are reproduced here.

1. People at higher levels are in the best position to make important decisions for people below them
2. Relationships within an organization should be based on position or level, not on personal considerations

3. In dealing with others, rules and regulations should be followed exactly
4. A person's expressions of feeling about his organization should conform to those of his fellows
5. A person's first real loyalty within the organization should be to his superior
6. Formality, based on rank or position, should be maintained by members of an organization
7. A person should avoid taking any action that might be subject to criticism
8. Outsiders who complain about an organization are usually either ignorant of the facts or misinformed
9. In a good organization, a person's future career will be pretty well planned out for him

Responses

Strongly Agree; Agree; Undecided; Disagree; Strongly Disagree; scored 2, 2, 1, 1 and 0 respectively.

7.14 to 7.29   Other Measures of Work Values, Beliefs and Needs

7.14 Peters, Terborg and Taynor (1974) have developed a 21-item Women as Managers Scale, to tap respondents' attitudes to women in management. This contains items like "It is acceptable for women to compete with men for top executive positions", and is reported to have a Spearman-Brown internal reliability of 0.91 in the source publication and 0.92 by Terborg, Peters, Ilgen and Smith (1977). The latter authors also present the items in full. The measure has been used by Cohen and Leavengood (1978), Garland and Price (1977), Muchinsky and Harris (1977), Stevens and DeNisi (1980), Terborg and Ilgen (1975) and Terborg, Peters and Ilgen (1974).

7.15 A ten-item measure of Role Orientations has been described by Miller and Wager (1971). This taps Professional Identification and Organizational Identification in scientists and engineers, the former being an orientation to one's wider profession and the latter to one's employing organization. The measure has also been used by Greene (1978).

7.16 Bartol (1979a, b) has described a 20-item scale of Professionalism, with five sub-scales: Autonomy, Collegial Maintenance of Standards, Ethics, Professional Commitment, and Professional Identification. Spearman-Brown internal reliabilities (with 159 computer professionals) were 0.82, 0.82, 0.79, 0.75 and 0.85 respectively, and the median intercorrelation between sub-scales was 0.10.

7.17 Hall's (1968) Professionalism Scale has been adapted by O'Reilly, Parlette and Bloom (1980) and Regoli and Poole (1980) for use with selected samples. The measure contains sub-scales to tap Belief in Public Service, Professional Referents, Autonomy, Belief in Self-Regulation, and Sense of Calling.

7.18 The Minnesota Importance Questionnaire (Gay, Weiss, Hendel, Dawis and Lofquist, 1971) is designed to measure 20 vocationally relevant needs: Ability Utilization, Achievement, Activity, Advancement, Authority, Company Policies and Practices, Compensation, Co-Workers, Creativity, Independence, Moral Values, Recognition, Responsibility, Security, Social Service, Social Status, Supervision—Human Relations, Supervision—Technical, Variety, and Working Conditions. Items are composed of statements representing two of the needs, of which respondents are required to indicate the more important. Complete pair-wise comparison and direct ratings for each of the 20 needs results in a 210-item instrument. A shorter "Ranked Form" presents the need statements in groups of five for respondents to rank. In both cases the focus is on "importance to you in your ideal job". Information on scoring, descriptive statistics, reliability and validity is given in the source publication. An evaluation of the measure is included in Lake, Miles and Earle (1973), and recent uses include Elizur and Tziner (1977), Lofquist and Dawis (1978), and Stulman and Dawis (1976).

7.19 Kazanas, Hannah and Gregor (1975) describe a two-part Meaning and Value of Work scale. Part I is designed to tap the breadth of respondents' conceptualization of work, and comprises 40 items with responses of agreement or disagreement. Part II consists of 42 forced-choice items designed to measure preference for intrinsic or extrinsic values associated with work. The two scales are given in full in the source publication. A subsequent use of a 50-item Part I and 62-item Part II is described by Kazanas (1978).

7.20 Saleh and Pasricha (1975) describe a 12-item Job Orientation Index designed to measure the relative importance which individuals attach to intrinsic versus extrinsic job factors.

7.21 Using 25 job outcomes reported by Manhardt (1972), Bartol and Manhardt (1979) obtained job preference scores from a sample of 648 college graduates in an insurance company. Factor analyses revealed three dimensions of Job Orientation, named Long-term Career Objectives (five items), Working Environment and Interpersonal Relationships (six items), and Intrinsic Job Aspects (eight items).

7.22 Lyons (1971) describes a four-item measure of a person's Need for Clarity. With a sample of 156 nurses he obtained a Spearman-Brown internal reliability coefficient of 0.82. The scale was used by Rousseau (1978b) who found, across four repeated administrations to an original sample of 271 employees, a median alpha coefficient of 0.76, and a test–retest correlation (three-month interval) of 0.65. Other uses are by Ivancevich and Donnelly (1974), Keller and Holland (1978), and Miles and Petty (1975).

7.23 Robey (1974) introduces two three-item scales labelled Concern for Extrinsic Job Aspects and Concern for Intrinsic Job Challenge. These were derived from a factor analysis of data from Friedlander's (1963, 1965) questionnaire. Subsequent uses include Robey (1978) and Robey and Bakr (1978).

7.24 The 35-item Work Values System Questionnaire described by Taylor and Thompson (1976) incorporates material from Graen and Dawes (1971) and Sheppard and Herrick (1972). Factor analyses identified five dimensions based on 23 items: Ecosystem Distrust (six items), Intrinsic Reward (six items), Self-Expression (three items), Pride in Work (four items), and Extrinsic Reward (four items).

7.25 Alderfer and Guzzo (1979) have described a measure of Enduring Needs for Existence, Relatedness, and Growth (see 3.28 for an accompanying Satisfaction measure). Their questionnaire contains 40 items and taps Need for Pay (an Existence need), Need for Group Relatedness, Need for Supervisor Relatedness, and Need for Growth in the Job. Each item contrasts two hypothetical jobs (e.g. "A job requiring work with mechanical equipment most of the day" and "A job requiring work with other people most of the day"), and respondents have to indicate their preference for one of these on a five-point dimension. Alpha coefficients are reported as 0.85, 0.70, 0.65 and 0.81 respectively, and the source publication indicates that items and descriptive statistics may be obtained from the first author.

Earlier versions of the Enduring Needs instrument have been used by Alderfer (1972), Keller and Holland (1978), Schmitt and White (1978), Schmitt, Coyle, Rauschenberger and White (1979), Schmitt, Coyle, White and Rauschenberger (1978), and Schmitt, White, Coyle and Rauschenberger (1979).

7.26 Career Motivation is tapped by four sub-scales in Gould's (1979a) 21-item scale. These cover Career Planning (alpha 0.80), Career Involvement (alpha 0.83), Identity Resolution (alpha 0.66), and Adaptability (alpha 0.57). Items and descriptive statistics are given in full.

7.27 Beehr, Walsh and Taber (1976) describe a seven-item measure of Higher Order Need Strength with a Spearman-Brown internal reliability coefficient of 0.82.

7.28 An index of Attitudes towards Unions in general is used by Anderson (1979) and is composed of ten items drawn from Getman, Goldberg and Herman (1976).

7.29 Jacoby and Terborg (1975a, b) developed the Managerial Philosophies Scale, designed to measure the degree to which managers subscribe to McGregor's (1960) Theory X and Theory Y generalizations about the nature of employees. For the X and Y sub-scales respectively they report internal reliability coefficients of 0.85 and 0.77 and test–retest reliabilities of 0.68 and 0.59. A subsequent use is described by Hall and Donnell (1979), who found that support for Theory X beliefs was inversely related to organizational level in a sample of 676 managers.

8 Perceptions of the Job, Work Role, Job Context, and Organizational Climate

Perceived Job Characteristics

8.1   Job Dimensions (17 items). Hackman and Lawler, 1971

8.2   Job Diagnostic Survey: Job Characteristics (21 items). Hackman and Oldham, 1975

8.3   Job Characteristics Inventory (30 items). Sims, Szilagyi and Keller, 1976

8.4   Job Scope (13 items). Stone, 1974

8.5   Perceived Intrinsic Job Characteristics (10 items). Warr, Cook and Wall, 1979

8.6   Michigan Organizational Assessment Questionnaire: Task, Job and Role Characteristics (46 items). Cammann, Fichman, Jenkins and Klesh, 1979; Seashore, Lawler, Mirvis and Cammann, 1982

8.7   Routinization (5 items). Hage and Aiken, 1969

8.8   Autonomy (4 items). Bacharach and Aiken, 1976

8.9   Autonomy (4 items). Beehr, 1976

8.10 to 8.14   Other measures of perceived Job Characteristics

Work Role and Job Context

8.15 and 8.16   Role Ambiguity and Role Conflict (14 items). Rizzo, House and Lirtzman, 1970

8.17   Role Ambiguity (4 items). Caplan, 1971

8.18   Subjective Quantitative Work Load (9 items). Caplan, 1971

8.19 and 8.20   Responsibility for Things and for Persons (6 items). Caplan, 1971

8.21 to 8.23   Role Ambiguity, Role Overload and Nonparticipation (10 items). Beehr, Walsh and Taber, 1976

8.24   Psychological Participation (4 items). Vroom, 1960

8.25   Centralization (9 items). Aiken and Hage, 1966; Hage and Aiken, 1967

8.26   Work-related expectancies (26 items). Sims, Szilagyi and McKemey, 1976

8.27   Task–Goal Attributes (16 items). Steers, 1973

8.28   Job Diagnostic Survey: Critical Psychological States (14 items). Hackman and Oldham, 1975

The instruments described in this chapter are designed to measure employees' perceptions of their jobs, work roles, and organizational features. They are descriptive in orientation, being concerned with what is the case, not with what is desired nor with affective reactions to current circumstances.

A logically prior requirement for the development of perceptual measures is the identification of major dimensions on which jobs or organizations are thought to vary. A wide range of such dimensions is illustrated in this chapter, and it is worth noting here that overlap between them is to be expected. Some scales turn out to be similar to measures independently developed by other researchers, and we should also expect some form of hierarchical pattern gradually to evolve. As with personality structure or aspects of intelligence, some job or organizational characteristics are likely to be relatively pervasive and general across sub-components, whereas other factors may be more specific and localized. The structure of both general and specific factors in this area is gradually becoming clearer, but it is apparent that conceptual and empirical work towards that objective has some way to go.

The instruments to be described fall into three interdependent categories. The first 14 scales are concerned with the perceived characteristics of jobs themselves, focussing upon job content rather than context. The most widely used instruments of this kind have been those of Hackman and Lawler (1971), Hackman and Oldham (1975) and Sims, Szilagyi and Keller (1976). These measures (8.1, 8.2 and 8.3) overlap considerably, sharing a common background in the work of Turner and Lawrence (1965). Their main thrust is to assess features such as perceived Skill Variety, Autonomy, Task Identity and Feedback. Other scales in the first section of the chapter aim to measure single elements of this kind (e.g. 8.7, 8.8, 8.9) or to provide one summary index of several interrelated characteristics (8.4 and 8.5).

Measures in the second category (8.15 to 8.54) have a broader focus, being concerned with work roles within organizations or other aspects of the immediate context within which tasks are carried out. Measures of Role Ambiguity, Role Conflict, Psychological Participation and Task-goal Attributes are examples of this type. Two particular instruments require comment, since they do not fall easily into either of the first two sections. The Task, Job and Role Characteristics module from the Michigan Organizational Assessment Questionnaire (8.6) spans the first two categories of this chapter, and we have somewhat arbitrarily included it in the Job Characteristics group rather than splitting it between the two sections. The second instrument is Hackman and Oldham's (1975) measure of Critical Psychological States (8.28), which is designed to measure Experienced Meaningfulness, Responsibility, and Knowledge of Results stemming from jobs. By nature and theoretical specification, this falls between descriptive measures, which are the subject of the present chapter, and affective measures as described in earlier chapters. Inclusion of the measure in section two of the present chapter is less than ideal, but is as reasonable as placing it elsewhere.

The final section introduces measures of Organizational Climate. As with earlier entries in the chapter, these measures are based on individual perceptions and are essentially descriptive in nature. But they tend to have a wider focus, being concerned with characteristics of the organization as a whole. Tagiuri's (1968) definition of the concept is useful: "Organizational Climate is a relatively enduring quality of the internal environment of the organization that (a) is experienced by its members, (b) influences their behaviour, and (c) can be described in terms of values of a particular set of characteristics" (p. 27). As is evident from this quotation, Organizational Climate, though measured through individual perceptions, is not appropriately treated as an individual variable. Its referent is an organization and its properties impinge upon all members of that organization. Hence the primary unit of analysis is at the level of the organization or an organizational sub-system, and agreement among respondents becomes an important methodological issue (Guion, 1973; Payne, Fineman and Wall, 1976). Given limitations of space, the fact that this category of measure moves away from the individual level of analysis, and the bulkiness of many such measures, we have restricted our presentation of these instruments to a brief summary. For each of the 26 Organizational Climate scales we provide a brief account of the characteristics they are designed to measure, specify the number of items, and provide details of uses from 1974 to mid-1980 within the population of journals searched.

8.1 to 8.14   Perceived Job Characteristics

Features of perceived job content have during the period been measured by 14 instruments. Nine of these are treated here as major entries, with brief accounts being provided for 8.10 to 8.14.

8.1   Job Dimensions

Source: Hackman and Lawler, 1971

The authors set out to examine the features of job content which are thought to have principal influence upon employee attitudes and behaviour. They present a 17-item measure to tap employees' perceptions of six job dimensions: Skill Variety, Autonomy, Task Identity, Feedback, Dealing with Others, and Friendship Opportunities. Their selection of these properties derives in large part from Turner and Lawrence's (1965) study of "requisite task attributes". The first four characteristics are referred to as "core dimensions" and the others as "interpersonal dimensions".

A three-item sub-scale is provided for five of the dimensions, with two items for Dealing with Others. Items are presented in two sections of a questionnaire, with seven-point response dimensions labelled at the poles and mid-point. A mean score is taken for each sub-scale.

The source publication presents results from a study of 208 employees (42% female) and 62 of their superiors in a telephone company. Thirteen jobs were studied, and mean values for each job are cited; the median of these is given here in Table 9. Also in that table are internal reliability coefficients (type unspecified) for the job-holders' data, and the correlations for the 13 jobs between scores of job-holders and their supervisors (the latter were asked to respond in terms of "the job you supervise"). It can be seen that the reliability of the four core dimensions is acceptable, but that there is inconsistency between job holders' and supervisors' perceptions of Feedback. Reliability and concordance data for the interpersonal dimensions are less adequate.

The six job dimensions from the 208 employees were themselves intercorrelated between −0.05 and 0.67, with a median value of 0.17; the strongest association was between Skill Variety and Autonomy. Correlations from the initial study with employees' Intrinsic Motivation (6.4), the short form of the authors' measure of General Job Satisfaction (2.6), and three items from Lodahl and Kejner's (1965) Job Involvement Scale (6.1) are also given in Table 9.

Several researchers have examined the core and interpersonal dimensions of jobs through this measure. The scale was in 1975 superceded by items within the Job Diagnostic Survey (8.2), so that a brief review of studies with the earlier measure will suffice. Stone and Porter (1975) reported coefficients of concordance between job-holders, supervisors and colleagues across 16 jobs in another telephone company. Coefficients of concordance for the 6 dimensions as sequenced in Table 9 were 0.87, 0.76, 0.64, 0.58, 0.75, and 0.46. Other aspects of that

Table 9.   Initial data on Job Dimensions (Hackman and Lawler, 1971)

	Median job score	Job-holders' internal reliability coefficient	r between job-holders and supervisors	Correlation with:		
				Intrinsic Motivation (6.4)	General Job Satisfaction (2.6)	Job Involvement (6.1)
Skill Variety	4.78	0.90	0.87	0.32	0.38	0.24
Autonomy	4.67	0.77	0.85	0.30	0.39	0.22
Task Identity	5.26	0.77	0.65	0.16	0.20	0.12
Feedback	4.88	0.75	0.09	0.18	0.28	0.24
Dealing with others	5.47	0.47	0.31	0.07	0.17	0.03
Friendship Opportunities	4.67	0.43	0.49	0.09	0.21	0.16

investigation are presented by Dubin, Porter, Stone and Champoux (1974). Saal (1978) has described a study of 218 varied employees in a single company. He reports correlations with the 20-item version of Lodahl and Kejner's (1965) Job Involvement scale (6.1) of 0.24, 0.27, 0.20 and 0.30 for the four core dimensions respectively. The correlation with Dealing with Others was 0.24, but a value is not cited for the non-significant association with Friendship Opportunities.

Other applications of the 1971 Job Dimensions measure or a variant of it include those by Aldag and Brief (1975, 1979), Armenakis, Feild, Holley, Bedeian and Ledbetter (1977), Blumberg (1980), Brief and Aldag (1975), Farr (1976b), Graen and Ginsburgh (1977), Hall, Goodale, Rabinowitz and Morgan (1978), Oldham and Brass (1979), Orpen (1979a) Rabinowitz, Hall and Goodale (1977), Steers (1977), Steers and Spencer (1977), and Wanous (1974b).

Items

Items in each sub-scale are as follows: Skill Variety, 1, 7, 13; Autonomy, 2, 8, 14; Task Identity, 3, 9, 15; Feedback, 4, 10, 16; Dealing with Others, 6, 12; Friendship Opportunities, 5, 11, 17.

1. How much variety is there in your job?
Very little, I do pretty much the same things over and over, and use the same pieces of equipment and procedures almost all the time; Moderate variety; Very much, I do many different things and use a wide variety of equipment and procedures; scored 1, 4, and 7 respectively.

2. How much autonomy do you have on your job: how much are you left on your own to do your own work?
Very little, I have almost no "say" about scheduling my work, the work and procedures are all laid out for me in detail; Moderate autonomy, I make some of the decisions about my work, but many of them are made for me; Very much, I have almost all of the "say" about the scheduling of my own work, I alone decide what procedures will be used; scored 1, 4 and 7 respectively.

3. To what extent do you do a "whole" piece of work (as opposed to doing part of a job which is finished by some other employee)?
I do one small part of a job, there are many others who do other parts of the job, I may not see the final result; I do a moderate size "chunk" of the work, there are others involved too, but my contribution is clear; I do an entire piece of work, I do the job from start to finish, and what is done is clearly 'mine'; scored 1, 4 and 7 respectively.

4. To what extent do you find out how well you are doing on the job as you are working?
Very little, I often work for long stretches without finding out how I am doing; Moderately, I sometimes know how I am doing and other times I do not; Very much, I get almost constant "feedback" on my performance as I work; scored 1, 4 and 7 respectively.

5. To what extent do you have the opportunity to talk informally with other employees while at work? (That is, is your job arranged so that you can chat with other workers while on the job—even though the job does not require you to talk to these people?)

Very little, there is almost no chance to talk to other employees except about "business"; Moderately, there is some chance to talk, but you may have to arrange it ahead of time; Very much, there is almost always on opportunity to talk with other employees about non-business topics; scored 1, 4 and 7 respectively.

6. To what extent is dealing with other people a part of your job?

Very little, working with other people is not a very important part of my job; Moderately, I have to deal with some other people, but this is not a major part of my job; Very much, probably the single most important part of my job is working with other people; scored 1, 4 and 7 respectively.

How much of the following attributes are actually present on your job?

7. The amount of variety in my job
8. The opportunity for independent thought and action
9. The opportunity to do a job from the beginning to end (i.e. the chance to do a whole job)
10. The opportunity to find out how well I am doing in my job
11. The opportunity, in my job, to get to know other people
12. The opportunity, in my job, to give help to other people
13. The opportunity to do a number of different things
14. The freedom to do pretty much what I want on my job
15. The opportunity to complete work I start
16. The feeling that I know whether I am performing my job well or poorly
17. The opportunity to develop close friendships in my job

Responses for items 7 to 17

None, or a minimum amount; A moderate amount; A maximum amount; scored 1, 4 and 7 respectively. Other scale anchors are not provided for respondents, but intermediate numbers (2, 3, 5, 6) are included on the response continuum.

8.2   Job Characteristics

Source: Hackman and Oldham, 1975

Embedded within the authors' Job Diagnostic Survey (see also 2.6, 3.6, 6.3, 7.7, 8.28) is a 21-item measure to tap employees' perceptions of seven principal Job Characteristics. The measure is a development from the Job Dimensions scale (8.1), with which it has much similarity. The Job Diagnostic Survey itself has an immediate theoretical basis in the Job Characteristics Model (Hackman and Oldham, 1976, 1980), which proposes that five core job characteristics influence employees' attitudes and behaviour. These are named and defined as follows:

Skill Variety: the degree to which a job requires a variety of different activities in carrying out the work, which involve the use of a number of different skills and talents of the employee.

Task Identity: the degree to which the job requires completion of a "whole" and identifiable piece of work, i.e. doing a job from beginning to end with a visible outcome.

Task Significance: the degree to which the job has a substantial impact on the lives or work of other people, whether in the immediate organization or in the external environment.

Autonomy: the degree to which the job provides substantial freedom, independence, and discretion to the employee in scheduling the work and in determining the procedures to be used in carrying it out.

Feedback from the Job Itself: the degree to which carrying out the work activities required by the job results in the employee obtaining direct and clear information about the effectiveness of his or her performance.

Two additional job characteristics are also introduced as "helpful in understanding jobs and employee reactions to them". These are:

Feedback from Agents: the degree to which the employee receives clear information about his or her performance from supervisors or from co-workers.

Dealing with Others: the degree to which the job requires the employee to work closely with other people in carrying out the work activities (including dealings with other organization members and with external organizational "clients").

The Job Diagnostic Survey contains seven three-item scales to measure employees' perceptions of each Job Characteristic. Items are split between two sections of the questionnaire. In the first section, respondents indicate directly on a seven point continuum the amount of each job characteristic they perceive to be present in their job, and in the second section responses are in terms of the accuracy of a number of statements about features of their job. A mean score is taken across the three items in each sub-scale, with a possible range of scores from 1 to 7, the latter indicating the substantial presence of a job characteristic. One item in each sub-scale is reverse-scored.

The source publication describes results from 658 employees (41% female) working on 62 jobs in seven organizations. A summary of applications of the JDS to some 6930 employees (46% female) working on 876 jobs in 56 organizations has subsequently been reported by Oldham, Hackman and Stepina (1978). Table 10 contains data from both these publications. Internal reliability coefficients were compiled by obtaining the median interitem correlation for each sub-scale and "adjusting this by Spearman-Brown procedures" (Hackman and Oldham, 1975, p. 163). The correlations between job-holders and supervisors were based upon a restricted sample of jobs, those for which more than one set of supervisory ratings were available; N ranged from 12 to 21 jobs.

The results from the two samples are very similar, with moderate internal reliability for the seven Job Characteristics measures and significant positive associations with Internal Work Motivation (6.3), General Job Satisfaction (2.6) and Growth Satisfaction (3.6). Also in the table are some data about the "Motivating Potential Score" (MPS). The index combines scores from the five core characteristics as follows:

$$MPS = \frac{\text{Skill Variety} + \text{Task Identity} + \text{Task Significance}}{3} \times \text{Autonomy} \times \text{Feedback from Job}$$

This combination rule ensures that an increase in Job Characteristics values will increase Motivating Potential Score, but, because of the multiplicative relationships, MPS will be low if any of the major components is low.

Although several dozen articles have employed this measure of perceived Job Characteristics during our search period, relatively few authors have cited means. Aldag and Brief (1977) present scores on the five core characteristics for 75 policemen and 131 varied manufacturing employees. In the sequence used above, means and standard deviations for the policemen were: 5.95 (0.79), 4.62 (1.08), 6.28 (1.01), 5.68 (0.96), and 5.23 (1.26). Results for the manufacturing employees were: 4.32 (1.56), 4.18 (1.61), 5.33 (1.43), 4.42 (1.36), and 4.81 (1.49). Evans, Kiggundu and House (1979) studied 343 Canadian supervisors and managers, reporting means and standard deviations for the core characteristics as sequenced above, as follows: 4.39 (0.98), 4.40 (1.47), 5.84 (0.98), 4.73 (1.37) and 5.02 (1.12). Oldham and Brass (1979) present data from three occasions associated with the introduction of open-plan office working, and mean values before and after an organizational change are also reported by Bhagat and Chassie (1980). Descriptive statistics from 138 Canadian office employees are given by Kiggundu (1980).

Variations in perceived Job Characteristics across organizational level are clearly demonstrated by Oldham, Hackman and Stepina (1978). Non-management employees yield lower scores than managers on all seven characteristics, and there is a linear increase from lower through middle to higher management on the five core characteristics.

Table 10. Job Characteristics. Data from: 1 Hackman and Oldham (1975); and 2 Oldham, Hackman and Stepina (1978). (N=658 and 6930 respectively)

		Mean and standard deviation	Internal reliability coefficient	r between job-holders and supervisors	Correlation with: Internal Work Motivation (6.3)	General Job Satisfaction (2.6)	Growth Satisfaction (3.6)
Skill Variety	1	4.49 (1.67)	0.71	0.64	0.42	0.42	0.52
	2	4.53 (1.57)	0.68		0.34	0.33	0.48
Task Identity	1	4.87 (1.43)	0.59	0.31	0.22	0.22	0.31
	2	4.65 (1.44)	0.61		0.16	0.20	0.24
Task Significance	1	5.49 (1.29)	0.66	0.48	0.32	0.24	0.33
	2	5.49 (1.25)	0.58		0.33	0.29	0.38
Autonomy	1	4.80 (1.43)	0.66	0.58	0.33	0.43	0.58
	2	4.78 (1.39)	0.64		0.31	0.42	0.54
Feedback from the Job	1	4.98 (1.41)	0.71	0.33	0.36	0.37	0.44
	2	4.81 (1.34)	0.68		0.32	0.35	0.43
Feedback from Agents	1	3.98 (1.65)	0.78	0.07	0.25	0.33	0.39
	2	4.06 (1.58)	0.75		0.25	0.32	0.36
Dealing with Others	1	5.29 (1.34)	0.59	0.55	0.30	0.24	0.28
	2	5.46 (1.31)	0.62		0.22	0.13	0.23
Motivating Potential Score	1	128.31 (72.73)		0.56	0.46	0.49	0.63
	2	122.10 (69.41)			0.40	0.46	0.59

Mean values for 500 non-managers were 4.30, 4.65, 5.39, 4.61, 4.70, 3.97 and 5.23 for the seven characteristics in the sequence given in Table 10. Comparable scores from 11 higher managers were 6.65, 5.07, 6.46, 6.13, 5.61, 4.43 and 6.30. Motivating Potential Scores were 113.38 and 217.30 respectively.

Internal reliability coefficients have been quoted more frequently. Dunham (1976) presents alpha coefficients from 784 white-collar employees and managers of 0.76, 0.72, 0.72, 0.73 and 0.75 for the five core characteristics in the sequence used in Table 10. Comparable values from 5945 varied employees were 0.68, 0.70, 0.68, 0.69 and 0.69 in research by Dunham, Aldag and Brief (1977); and with 65 employees from a single company Bhagat and Chassie (1980) recorded Spearman-Brown coefficients of 0.68, 0.78, 0.72, 0.66 and 0.73. Schuler, Aldag and Brief (1977) examined four of the core characteristics together with Feedback from Agents and Dealing with Others. Across four samples of public and nursing employees (total N=815), the median alpha coefficients for the latter two characteristics were 0.71 (range 0.56 to 0.80) and 0.56 (range 0.40 to 0.88) respectively. Other median values were: Skill Variety 0.68 (range 0.20 to 0.91), Task Identity 0.55 (range 0.31 to 0.96), Autonomy 0.62 (range 0.35 to 0.80) and Feedback from the Job 0.55 (range 0.30 to 0.73). The observed variation in reliability values might be partly attributable to educational differences between samples; for example lower consistency was recorded for janitors and food service workers.

Other researchers citing internal reliability figures include Brief and Aldag (1976) with 77 nursing aides and assistants. They quote reliability values (type unspecified) of 0.47, 0.47, 0.60, 0.55 and 0.30 for the five core characteristics in the previously-used sequence. With 272 public utility employees (20% female), Kim and Schuler (1979) report comparable alpha coefficients of 0.80, 0.69, 0.73, 0.67 and 0.73. Pierce and Dunham (1978a, b) with 155 insurance employees (47% female) obtained alpha coefficients of 0.74, 0.70, 0.79 and 0.69 for the characteristics of Skill Variety, Task Identity, Autonomy and Feedback from the Job. Rather lower values are reported by Evans, Kiggundu and House (1979) with 343 supervisors and managers: 0.53, 0.52, 0.50, 0.53, 0.38, 0.45 and 0.51 for the seven characteristics as sequenced above. Kiggundu's (1980) alpha coefficients were 0.78, 0.62, 0.59, 0.63, 0.70, 0.83 and 0.59 from 138 Canadian office employees (69% female).

Two related issues concern the intercorrelations between Job Characteristic sub-scales and the factor structure of responses to individual items. The source publication (N=658) indicated that the five core sub-scales were moderately intercorrelated (median 0.24, range

0.16 to 0.51). Oldham, Hackman and Stepina (1978), with some 6930 respondents, reported a comparable median intercorrelation of 0.33 (range 0.19 to 0.44). The strongest association in both cases was between Skill Variety and Autonomy. Brief and Aldag (1976), with 77 nursing aides and assistants, observed a median correlation between the core sub-scales of 0.32 (range 0.01 to 0.41). The median value from Abdel-Halim (1978, 1979a), with 89 male managers was 0.25 (range 0.15 to 0.40), from Dunham (1976) with 784 white-collar employees and managers 0.52 (range 0.46 to 0.57), from Evans, Kiggundu and House (1979) with 343 Canadian supervisors and managers 0.22 (range 0.05 to 0.60), and from Wall, Clegg and Jackson (1978) with 47 British shop-floor employees 0.30 (range 0.07 to 0.50).

Dunham (1976) also submitted item responses to factor analysis with oblique rotation, obtaining one large factor accounting for 83% of the explained variance; see also Dunham (1977a, b). Pierce and Dunham (1978a) examined four of the core Job Characteristics with 155 insurance employees (omitting the sub-scale for Task significance). Oblique rotation again suggested the presence of a single major factor. However, in 20 separate analyses (again with oblique rotation) of separate job groups (total N = 5945), Dunham, Aldag and Brief (1977) observed that complex four- or five-factor solutions were typical. They recorded only two oblique factor solutions which perfectly matched the a priori dimensions supposedly represented by the five core Job Characteristics, and in no case did they obtain a single-factor solution.

Other investigations into the factor structure of the 15 core Job Characteristics items include those by Abdel-Halim (1978) and Katz (1978a). With oblique rotation of data from 89 male managers, the former observed a five-factor solution which clearly replicated the a priori dimensions. The latter used an orthogonal rotation, and reported (without details) the same outcome. However, Green, Armenakis, Marbert and Bedeian (1979) obtained a four-factor solution incompatible with the assumed structure. It is difficult to summarize these varied results, but the discrepancies may arise partly from variations in the thresholds set for factor inclusion or from differences in reliability of responses. One could conclude that at a relatively abstract level of analysis, a single general factor of job complexity is being tapped by the five core characteristics, at the same time recognizing that in more specific analyses there exist subgeneral factors as well.

This issue bears upon the validity of the Motivating Potential Score (see above). Despite the initial suggestion of a multiplicative combination rule, many authors have taken an unweighted sum of the five core characteristics, in effect producing a single-factor score. See, for example, Baird (1976), Brief, Wallace and Aldag (1975), Brousseau (1978), Dunham (1977a), Ivancevich (1978, 1979a), Kim and Schuler (1979), Oldham and Miller (1979), Pierce, Dunham and Blackburn (1979), and Schuler (1977c). Arnold and House (1980) have described statistical analyses which were generally nonsupportive of the original MPS formulation.

Five reports are relevant to the sensitivity of the Job Characteristics measure. Both Champoux (1978) and Hackman, Pearce and Wolfe (1978) describe job enrichment projects which were accompanied by shifts in Job Characteristics scores in the expected direction; and O'Reilly and Caldwell (1979), Umstot, Bell and Mitchell (1976) and White and Mitchell (1979) showed similar effects in laboratory research, where the five core sub-scales were used for manipulation checks.

Other applications of the measure or a variant of it include those by Aldag and Brief (1975, 1979), Brief and Aldag (1975), Brief, Aldag and Van Sell (1977), Cornelius and Lyness (1980), Katerberg, Hom and Hulin (1979), Katz (1978b), Katz and Van Maanen (1977), Kim (1980), Mobley, Hand, Baker and Meglino (1979), Oldham, Hackman and Pearce (1976), O'Reilly, Parlette and Bloom (1980), Orpen (1979b), Rousseau (1977, 1978a, b, c), Schmitt and White (1978), Schmitt, Coyle, White and Rauschenberger (1978), Schmitt, Coyle, Rauschenberger and White (1979), and Weiss and Shaw (1979).

The measure of Job Characteristics has by now proved its worth. Items have good face validity, and their inclusion into two separate sections probably helps to break response set. Baird (1976) has reported that scores are not significantly associated with Crowne and Marlowe's (1964) measure of socially desirable responding. The internal reliability of sub-scales has often been found acceptable, but there may be some difficulties with respondents of limited educational attainment; indeed the source publication warns against use of the Job Diagnostic Survey with such respondents. Significant correlations with positive job reactions are well established, although the impact of the core Job Characteristics on employee behaviour is more uncertain.

Our major reservation concerns the discriminant validity of the sub-scales, where evidence for five separate factors corresponding to the core characteristics has not usually been found. The joint use of separate sub-scale scores together with an unweighted MPS score might prove advisable, although the more complex procedure advocated by Dunham, Aldag and Brief (1977) of factor computation in each study may sometimes be practicable; note that this has the disadvantage of reducing comparability of scores across investigations. In this respect it may be fair to point out that discriminant validity is the weakest feature of many measures reported throughout this book. Perhaps researchers have first to resolve issues of internal consistency and convergent validity, and with increasing success in those areas then move on to improve discriminant validation. This applies to perceived Job Characteristics as well as to those affective reactions described in other chapters.

Items

Items in each sub-scale are as follows: Skill Variety, 4, 8, 12; Task Identity, 3, 10, 18; Task Significance, 5, 15, 21; Autonomy, 2, 16, 20; Feedback from the Job, 7, 11, 19; Feedback from Agents, 6, 14, 17; Dealing with Others, 1, 9, 13.

Section 1

1. To what extent does your job require you to work closely with other people (either "clients", or people in related jobs in your own organization)?
Very little, dealing with other people is not at all necessary in doing the job; Moderately, some dealing with others is necessary; Very much, dealing with other people is an absolutely essential and crucial part of doing the job; scored 1, 4 and 7 respectively.

2. How much autonomy is there in your job? That is, to what extent does your job permit you to decide on your own how to go about the work?
Very little, the job gives me almost no personal "say" about how and when the work is done; Moderate autonomy, many things are standardized and not under my control, but I can make some decisions about the work; Very much, the job gives me almost complete responsibility for deciding how and when the work is done; scored 1, 4 and 7 respectively.

3. To what extent does your job involve doing a "whole" and identifiable piece of work? That is, is the job a complete piece of work that has an obvious beginning and end? Or is it only a small part of the overall piece of work, which is finished by other people or by automatic machines?
My job is only a tiny part of the overall piece of work, the results of my activities cannot be seen in the final product or service; My job is a moderate sized "chunk" of the overall piece of work, my own contribution can be seen in the final outcome; My job involves doing the whole piece of work from start to finish, the results of my activities are easily seen in the final product or service; scored 1, 4 and 7 respectively.

4. How much variety is there in your job? That is, to what extent does the job require you to do many different things at work, using a variety of your skills and talents?
Very little, the job requires me to do the same routine things over and over again; Moderate variety; Very much, the job requires me to do many different things, using a number of different skills and talents; scored 1, 4 and 7 respectively.

5. In general, how significant or important is your job? That is, are the results

of your work likely to significantly affect the lives or well-being of other people? Not very significant, the outcomes of my work are not likely to have important effects on other people; Moderately significant; Highly significant, the outcomes of my work can affect other people in very important ways; scored 1, 4 and 7 respectively.

6. To what extent do managers or co-workers let you know how well you are doing on your job?

Very little, people almost never let me know how well I am doing; Moderately, sometimes people may give me "feedback", other times they may not; Very much, managers or co-workers provide me with almost constant "feedback" about how well I am doing; scored 1, 4 and 7 respectively.

7. To what extent does doing the job itself provide you with information about your work performance? That is, does the actual work itself provide clues about how well you are doing—aside from any "feedback" co-workers or supervisors may provide?

Very little, the job itself is set up so I could work forever without finding out how well I am doing; Moderately, sometimes doing the job provides "feedback" to me, sometimes it does not; Very much, the job is set up so that I get almost constant "feedback" as I work about how well I am doing; scored 1, 4 and 7 respectively.

Section 2

8. The job requires me to use a number of complex or high-level skills
9. The job requires a lot of co-operative work with other people
10. The job is arranged so that I do not have the chance to do an entire piece of work from beginning to end (R)
11. Just doing the work required by the job provides many chances for me to figure out how well I am doing
12. The job is quite simple and repetitive (R)
13. The job can be done adequately by a person working alone—without talking or checking with other people (R)
14. The supervisors and co-workers on this job almost never give me any "feedback" about how well I am doing in my job (R)
15. This job is one where a lot of other people can be affected by how well the work gets done
16. The job denies me any chance to use my personal initiative or judgment in carrying out the work (R)
17. Supervisors often let me know how well they think I am performing the job
18. The job provides me the chance to completely finish the pieces of work I begin
19. The job itself provides very few clues about whether or not I am performing well (R)
20. The job gives me considerable opportunity for independence and freedom in how I do the work
21. The job itself is not very significant or important in the broader scheme of things (R)

Responses

Items 1 to 7: As indicated above; other scale anchors are not provided for respondents, but intermediate numbers (2, 3, 5, 6) are included in the response continuum.

Items 8 to 21: Very inaccurate; Mostly inaccurate; Slightly inaccurate; Uncertain; Slightly accurate; Mostly accurate; Very accurate; scored 1 to 7 respectively.

8.3   Job Characteristics Inventory

Source: Sims, Szilagyi and Keller, 1976

The authors set out to develop an improved measure of perceived Job Characteristics from the scale provided by Hackman and Lawler (1971) (8.1). Their development work was undertaken during 1974 and 1975, in parallel with but separate from the work leading to the Job Diagnostic Survey (8.2). However, Sims and colleagues have retained the initial set of four "core" dimensions and the two original "interpersonal" dimensions, defined (after Hackman and Lawler, 1971) as follows:

Core Dimensions
Skill Variety: the degree to which a job requires employees to perform a wide range of operations in their work and/or the degree to which employees must use a variety of equipment and procedures in their work.
Autonomy: the extent to which employees have a major say in scheduling their work, selecting the equipment they will use, and deciding on procedures to be followed.
Task Identity: the extent to which employees do an entire or whole piece of work and can clearly identify the results of their efforts.
Feedback: the degree to which employees receive information as they are working which reveals how well they are performing on the job.

Interpersonal Dimensions
Dealing with Others: the degree to which a job requires employees to deal with other people to complete the work.
Friendship Opportunities: the degree to which a job allows employees to talk with one another on the job and to establish informal relationships with other employees at work.

The Job Characteristics Inventory was developed through applications to employees in a large medical centre (N=1161, 80% female) and to managers and supervisors in a manufacturing firm (N=192, all male). The final version of the Inventory contains 30 items, with 5, 6, 4, 5, 3 and 7 tapping the six characteristics in the sequence given above. Responses are upon two five-point dimensions (see below), with mean scores between 1 and 5 being taken for each sub-scale. Two items are reverse-scored.

The source publication contains results from preliminary versions of the Inventory, so that data in that report do not typically arise from the 30-item scale. However, the following means, standard deviations and alpha coefficients of internal reliability appear to refer to the final version (n=192 manufacturing managers): Skill Variety, 3.46, 0.67, 0.82; Autonomy, 3.76, 0.67, 0.84; Feedback, 3.33, 0.75, 0.86; Task Identity, 3.66, 0.67, 0.83; Dealing with Others, 3.68, 0.51, 0.72; Friendship Opportunities, 3.77, 0.64, 0.84. Pierce and Dunham (1978a, b) examined four of the Job Characteristics in a study of 155 clerical employees (47% female), with coefficients alpha as follows: Skill Variety 0.90, Autonomy 0.85, Task Identity 0.89, Feedback 0.90. Mean values associated with an organizational change are cited by Szilagyi and Holland (1980).

Brief and Aldag (1978) obtained Job Characteristics Inventory responses from 155 nurses and 115 of their superiors. Coefficients alpha were calculated for both samples, the latter providing ratings of subordinates' jobs, and were as follows (using the sequence set out above): for nurses, 0.82, 0.81, 0.80, 0.84, 0.43 and 0.84; for superiors, 0.56, 0.80, 0.80, 0.72, 0.55 and 0.85. The authors report a median intercorrelation between the six sub-scales for the nurses of 0.32 (range 0.11 to 0.55) and for their superiors of 0.24 (range −0.01 to 0.66); the strongest association in both cases was between Autonomy and Task Identity. Correlations between nurses' and superiors' perceptions of the nurses' jobs were relatively low, 0.22, 0.21, 0.11, 0.14, 0.10 and 0.17 for the six characteristics in the sequence used above.

Other correlates reported by Brief and Aldag (1978) include the Social Desirability Scale of Crowne and Marlowe (1964) (median 0.02, range −0.06 to 0.19), Satisfaction with the Work Itself (from the Job Descriptive Index, 3.3) (median 0.20, range 0.01 to 0.49) and the Brayfield-Rothe scale of Overall Job Satisfaction (2.2) (median 0.29, range 0.21 to 0.43). Confirmatory factor analysis with varimax rotation indicated that the six a priori sub-scales were clearly defined, except for an overlap between Dealing with Others and Friendship Opportunities (the former sub-scale also yields a low internal reliability coefficient; see above).

Pierce and Dunham (1978a) examined the factor structure (with oblique rotation) of four of the sub-scales (Skill Variety, Autonomy,

Task Identity and Feedback) in research with 155 clerical employees (47% female). They too confirmed the existence of the a priori dimensions of the Inventory. With the same sample Pierce and Dunham (1978b) demonstrated that Hage and Aiken's (1969) measure of Routinization (8.7) was closely linked with Skill Variety ($r = -0.80$), and that perceived Autonomy was strongly correlated with rated Centralization and Formalization (Aiken and Hage, 1966) (8.25, 8.46) ($r = -0.69$ and -0.57 respectively). Convergent validity correlations with corresponding Job Diagnostic Survey scales (8.2) were high: 0.72, 0.68, 0.74 and 0.65 for Skill Variety, Autonomy, Task Identity and Feedback respectively. Common item content is of course partly responsible for these associations.

Other reports of research with the Job Characteristics Inventory include Ganster (1980), Keller, Szilagyi and Holland (1976), O'Reilly and Caldwell (1979), Sims, Szilagyi and McKemey (1976) and Szilagyi and Keller (1976).

Items

Items in each sub-scale are as follows: Skill Variety, 1, 7, 12, 17, 22; Autonomy, 2, 8, 13, 18, 23, 28; Task Identity, 3, 19, 24, 29; Feedback, 4, 9, 14, 20, 25; Dealing with Others, 6, 11, 30; Friendship Opportunities, 5, 10, 15, 16, 21, 26, 27.

1. How much variety is there in your job?
2. How much are you left on your own to do your own work?
3. How often do you see projects or jobs through to completion?
4. To what extent do you find out how well you are doing on the job as you are working?
5. How much opportunity is there to meet individuals whom you would like to develop friendships with?
6. How much of your job depends upon your ability to work with others?
7. How repetitious are your duties? (R)
8. To what extent are you able to act independently of your supervisor in performing your job function?
9. To what extent do you receive information from your superior on your job performance?
10. To what extent do you have the opportunity to talk informally with other employees while at work?
11. To what extent is dealing with other people a part of your job?
12. How similar are the tasks you perform in a typical working day? (R)
13. To what extent are you able to do your job independently of others?
14. The feedback from my supervisor on how well I'm doing
15. Friendship from my co-workers
16. The opportunity to talk to others on my job
17. The opportunity to do a number of different things
18. The freedom to do pretty much what I want on my job

19. The degree to which the work I'm involved with is handled from beginning to end by myself
20. The opportunity to find out how well I am doing on my job
21. The opportunity in my job to get to know other people
22. The amount of variety in my job
23. The opportunity for independent thought and action
24. The opportunity to complete work I start
25. The feeling that I know whether I am performing my job well or poorly
26. The opportunity to develop close friendships in my job
27 Meeting with others in my work
28. The control I have over the pace of my work
29. The opportunity to do a job from the beginning to end (i.e. the chance to do a whole job)
30. The extent of feedback you receive from individuals other than your supervisor.

Responses

Items 1 to 13: Very little; A moderate amount; Very much; scored 1, 3 and 5 respectively. Intermediate labels are not cited.

Items 14 to 30: A minimum amount; A moderate amount; Very much; scored 1, 3 and 5 respectively. Intermediate labels are not cited.

8.4   Job Scope

Source: Stone, 1974

This instrument has in common with measures 8.2 and 8.3 the fact that it was designed as an improvement upon the earlier scales of Turner and Lawrence (1965) and Hackman and Lawler (1971). It differs from 8.2 and 8.3, both of which contained several sub-scales, in that a single overall index is created. This taps a construct identified as Job Scope.

The author argues that the previous measures can easily confuse respondents, and he aims to reduce this confusion by a uniform response dimension with more specific questions. For example, Skill Variety is covered by four separate items dealing with methods variety, tools variety, pace variety, and location variety. There are also four questions about different types of Autonomy. Other items tap Feedback (two questions), Task Identity (one question) and Interaction (two questions), making a 13-item questionnaire.

Responses are upon a five-point continuum, scored 1 to 5, and combined to yield a weighted measure of Job Scope (JS) as follows:

$$JS = [2 \times Variety] + [2 \times Autonomy] + Task\ Identity + Feedback$$

However, the source publication points out that this weighted index is correlated 0.97 with an unweighted total of item scores. Note that the Interaction items (number 12 and 13) are not included in either index.

Stone (1975) has examined the validity of the Job Scope index in terms of independent ratings by job-holders' superiors. In a study of 12 different jobs held by 149 enlisted naval personnel, he also obtained Job Scope ratings from 77 superior officers (an average of 6.4 independent perceptions per job). The mean Job Scope scores from the two sets of raters (N=12 jobs) were intercorrelated 0.63. In a separate study with 594 varied employees, Stone (1976) reported in comparable correlation with independent raters (details not given) of 0.80 (N=11 jobs).

In several studies Stone and his colleagues have amended instructions to the Brayfield–Rothe (1951) Overall Job Satisfaction scale (2.2), so that respondents "think only about the work that you do", not about other job-related factors such as pay, co-workers, promotions and supervision. This measure of "satisfaction with the work itself" is found to be significantly associated with perceived Job Scope. Using the weighted index with 149 enlisted naval personnel, Stone (1975) reported a correlation of 0.50; with 594 varied employees, Stone (1976) recorded a correlation with the weighted index of 0.43; and with the unweighted total, Stone, Mowday and Porter (1977) reported a correlation of 0.38 (N=335 varied employees, 32% female). Other applications of the measure are by Mowday, Stone and Porter (1979) and Stone (1979).

Items

Items in each component of Job Scope are as follows: Variety, 1, 2, 3, 4; Autonomy, 5, 6, 7, 8; Task Identity, 9; Feedback, 10, 11; Interaction, 12, 13.

1. How often do you use the same methods over and over again in doing your work?
2. How often do you use the same tools, machines, or pieces of equipment over and over again in doing your work?
3. How often do you work at a constant speed in doing your work?
4. How often do you work at a fixed location (for example, at one bench or one machine) during a normal workday?
5. How often are you able to choose the methods you use to do your work?
6. How frequently are you able to choose the order of things you do in doing your work?
7. How often are you able to choose the speed at which you work?
8. How often are you able to choose the tools, machines, or equipment you use in doing your work?
9. How often do you alone do everything that is needed to produce an entire product, or provide an entire service?
10. How frequently are you able to tell from your own observations how well you are doing your work (in terms of quantity and quality)?

11. How often are you given information by others (for example, other workers, supervisors, customers, etc.) about how well you are doing your work (in terms of quantity and quality)?

12. How frequently are you able to talk to others (for example, other workers, supervisors, customers, etc.) about *non-work* matters while working on your job?

13. How often are you required to talk to others (for example, other workers, supervisors, customers, etc.) about *work-related* matterns while working on your job?

Responses

Never; Rarely; Sometimes; Often; Always; scored 1 to 5 respectively.

8.5   Perceived Intrinsic Job Characteristics

Source: Warr, Cook and Wall, 1979

The authors note the need for short, robust scales which are easily completed by blue-collar respondents of modest educational attainment. They set out to construct such a scale to measure individual perceptions of the presence or absence of job characteristics theoretically expected to give rise to intrinsic satisfaction. An overall index is created, rather than several component scores.

From a literature review, a pilot study and two investigations with samples of 200 and 390 blue-collar employees selected to be representative of male workers in British manufacturing industry, a ten-item scale was developed. This employs a five-point response dimension, recording the extent to which each characteristic is perceived to be present in the respondent's job. Scoring is from 1 to 5, totalled across items.

The sample of 390 employees yielded a mean score of 32.74 (s.d. 8.39) and an alpha coefficient of 0.86. A test–retest correlation of 0.69 was obtained from 60 respondents across six months. Principal components analysis with varimax rotation confirmed the independence of scale items from those to measure Work Involvement (7.5), Intrinsic Job Motivation (6.7), Self-rated Anxiety (5.15) and Higher-order Need Strength (7.8). However, there was a tendency for Perceived Intrinsic Job Characteristics items and those from the authors' scale of Overall Job Satisfaction (2.11) to straddle the same two factors. Thus it is not surprising to find that the two scales were intercorrelated 0.73. Other associated variables were skill level, Work Involvement (7.5) and Intrinsic Job Motivation (6.7), with correlations of 0.29, 0.28 and 0.36 respectively.

Cook and Wall (1980), in a further study of 260 British male blue-collar employees, recorded correlations with skill level of 0.30, with

Organizational Commitment (4.10) of 0.45, and with Interpersonal Trust at Work (9.12) of 0.27. With a sample of over 600 varied British employees Clegg and Wall (1981) found Perceived Intrinsic Job Characteristics scores to be positively associated with job level ($F=53.06$, $P<0.001$) and obtained an alpha coefficient of 0.86.

Items

1. The freedom to choose your own method of working
2. The amount of responsibility you are given
3. The recognition you get for good work
4. Being able to judge your work performance, right away, when actually doing the job
5. Your opportunity to use your abilities
6. The amount of variety in your job
7. Your chance of promotion
8. The attention paid to suggestions you make
9. The feeling of doing something which is not trivial, but really worthwhile
10. Doing a whole and complete piece of work

Responses

There's none of that in my job; There's just a little of that in my job; There's a moderate amount of that in my job; There's quite a lot of that in my job, There's a great deal of that in my job; scored 1 to 5 respectively.

8.6 Task, Job and Role Characteristics

Source: Cammann, Fichman, Jenkins and Klesh, 1979; Seashore, Lawler, Mirvis and Cammann, 1982

The Michigan Organizational Assessment Questionnaire contains a number of scales of work attitudes and perceptions; see also 2.9, 3.8, 3.9, 3.10, 4.13, 6.2, 6.6, 9.5 and 9.11. Module 3, entitled Task, Job and Role Characteristics, contains 46 items to measure aspects of jobs and roles as perceived by job-holders. These aspects, along with alpha coefficients of internal reliability as found with a sample of more than 400 varied respondents, are described below. They fall into four categories:
1. Nine sub-scales are designed to tap Task Characteristics, namely: Freedom (three items, alpha 0.75); Variety (three items, alpha 0.81); Task Feedback (two items, alpha 0.54); Task Completeness (two items, alpha 0.58); Task Impact (two items, alpha 0.71); Task Significance (two items, alpha 0.45); Training Adequacy (three items, alpha 0.59); Required Skill (three items, alpha 0.71); and Pace Control (three items, alpha 0.83).
2. Three sub-scales view the job more broadly in terms of the Role Characteristics of Role Conflict (two items, alpha 0.58), Role Clarity

(three items, alpha 0.53) and Role Overload (three items, alpha 0.65).
3. Four sub-scales are concerned with Psychological States assumed to result, at least in part, from the particular mix of job, task and role experiences. These are designed to measure Challenge (four items, alpha 0.81), Meaningfulness (two items, alpha 0.50), Responsibility (two items, alpha 0.41) and Knowledge of Results (two items, alpha 0.31).
4. Two sub-scales, of Uncertainty (three items) and Interdependency (two items), are under development and no reliability values are yet published.

The source publication includes a matrix of correlations between each of the sub-scales. Within Task Characteristics the median inter-correlation is 0.23 (range −0.06 to 0.59), within Role Characteristics it is −0.13 (range −0.19 to 0.32), and within Psychological States it is 0.33 (range 0.16 to 0.51).All items except number 8 have a seven-point response dimension (see below), and seven items are reverse-scored. Sub-scale scores are probably calculated in terms of means, although this is not specified in the source publication.

The instrument can be seen to cover features tapped by several other scales in this chapter, and not surprisingly there is some overlap of items. The Questionnaire is however notable for its attempt to bring together a very wide range of perceptions and attitudes within a single instrument. Arguably, this has sometimes resulted in excessively short sub-scales, and the authors recognize that not all of the alpha coefficients cited above are fully acceptable.

Factor analysis of the nine Task Characteristics sub-scales showed that items from the Freedom and Pace Control indices loaded on the same factor, that Task Feedback, Task Impact and Task Significance shared a factor, and that Training Adequacy and Variety were factorially distinct. The items from the three sub-scales measuring Role Characteristics resolved into two factors, with Role Clarity items loading on one and the Role Conflict and Role Overload items on the other. All the Psychological States items tended to load on a common factor. It seems clear that not all the 16 a priori dimensions are supported by observed scale reliabilities and factor structure. The authors suggest that unless the Knowledge of Results scale can be made more reliable it should be dropped, and that in view of common factorial loadings and intercorrelations the remaining three Psychological States sub-scales could be merged as an overall indicator of Job Challenge. Otherwise, they are optimistic about the practical potential of the instrument.

Means and standard deviations are not given in the source publication, but correlations with several other sub-scales of the full Questionnaire are provided. For example, the associations with Overall Job Satisfaction (2.9) of eight Task Characteristics (omitting Training Adequacy) in the sequence given above were 0.25, 0.26, 0.37, 0.24, 0.31, 0.01, 0.22 and 0.26 respectively. Correlations between Overall Job Satisfaction and Role Conflict, Clarity and Overload were −0.04, 0.17 and −0.13 respectively (N>400 in each case).

Versions of the measure have been used by Moch (1980b), and Moch, Bartunek and Brass (1979). The first of these papers contains means and intercorrelations from 379 packaging employees.

Items

Items in each sub-scale are as follows: Freedom, 20, 30, 35; Variety, 12, 15, 18; Task Feedback, 5, 23; Task Completeness, 6, 28; Task Impact, 3, 19; Task Significance, 2, 24; Training Adequacy, 9, 14, 33; Required Skill, 7, 8, 16; Pace Control, 4, 13, 26; Role Conflict, 34, 37; Role Clarity, 11, 40, 46; Role Overload, 32, 38, 42; Challenge, 22, 31, 41, 43; Meaningfulness, 29, 36; Responsibility, 39, 44; Knowledge of Results, 17, 45; Uncertainty, 1, 10, 25; Interdependency, 21, 27.

1. I often have to deal with new problems on my job
2. A lot of people can be affected by how well I do my work
3. I can see the results of my own work
4. My job allows me to control my own work pace
5. Just doing the work required by my job gives me many chances to figure out how well I am doing
6. On my job, I produce a whole product or perform a complete service
7. It takes a long time to learn the skills required to do my job well
8. What is the level of education you feel is needed by a person in your job? (1) Some elementary school (grades 1–7). (2) Completed elementary school (8 grades). (3) Some high school (9–11 years). (4) Graduated from high school or G.E.D. (5) Some college or technical training beyond high school (1–3 years). (6) Graduated from college (B.A., B.S., or other bachelor's degree). (7) Some graduate school. (8) Graduate degree (Masters, PhD, MD, etc.).
9. I do not have enough training to do my job well (R)
10. On my job, I often have to handle surprising or unpredictable situations
11. On my job, most of my tasks are clearly defined
12. I get to do a number of different things on my job
13. I determine the speed at which I work
14. I have more than enough training skills to do my job well
15. My job requires that I do the same things over and over (R)
16. My job is so simple that virtually anybody could handle it with little or no initial training (R)
17. I usually know whether or not my work is satisfactory on this job
18. How much variety is there in your job? (1) Very little; I do pretty much the same things over and over, using the

same equipment and procedures almost all the time. (4) Moderate variety. (7) Very much; I do many things; using a variety of equipment and procedures.

19. How much does the work you do on your job make a visible impact on a product or service?
(1) None at all; it is hard to tell what impact my work makes on the product or service. (4) A moderate amount; the impact of my job is visible along with that of others. (7) A great amount; my work is clearly visible, it makes a noticeable difference in the final product or service.

20. How much freedom do you have on your job? That is, how much do you decide on your own what you do on your job?
(1) Very little; there are few decisions about my job which I can make by myself. (4) A moderate amount; I have responsibility for deciding some of the things I do, but not others. (7) Very much; there are many decisions about my job which I can make by myself.

21. How often does your job require that you meet or check with other people in this organization?
(1) Not at all; I never have to meet or check with others. (4) I sometimes need to meet or check with others. (7) Very often; I must constantly meet or check with others.

22. How much challenge is there on your job?
(1) There is very little challenge on my job; I don't get a chance to use any special skills and abilities and I never have jobs which require all my abilities to complete them successfully. (4) Moderate challenge. (7) There is a great deal of challenge on my job; I get a chance to use my special skills and abilities and often have jobs which require all my abilities to complete successfully.

23. As you do your job, can you tell how well you're performing?
(1) Not at all; I could work on my job indefinitely without ever finding out how well I am doing unless somebody tells me. (4) Moderately; sometimes by just doing the job I can find out how well I'm performing, sometimes I can't. (7) A great deal; I can almost always tell how well I'm performing just by doing my job.

24. In general, how significant and important is your job? That is, are the result of your work likely to significantly affect the lives or well-being of other people?
(1) Not very significant; the outcomes of my work are not likely to have important effects on other people. (4) Moderately significant. (7) Highly significant; the outcomes of my work can affect other people in very important ways.

25. How much uncertainty is there in your job?
(1) Very little; I almost always know what to expect and am never surprised by something happening unexpectedly on my job. (4) Moderate uncertainty. (7) A great deal; I almost never am sure what is going to happen, and unexpected things frequently happen.

26. How much control do you have in setting the pace of your work?
(1) Very little; pace is predetermined and I must work at a strict pace set by someone or something else. (4) Moderate control of work pace. (7) A great deal; I determine my own work pace.

27. How much do you have to cooperate directly with other people in this organization in order to do your job?
    (1) Very little; I can do almost all my work by myself. (4) A moderate amount; some of my work requires cooperating with others. (7) Very much; all my work requires cooperating with others.
28. How much does your job involve your producing an entire product or an entire service?
    (1) My job involves doing only a small part of the entire product or service; it is also worked on by others or by automatic equipment and I may not see or be aware of much of the work which is done on the product or service. (4) My job involves doing a moderate sized 'chunk' of work; while others are involved as well, my own contribution is significant. (7) My job involves producing the entire product or service from start to finish, the final outcome of the work is clearly the result of my work.
29. The work I do on my job is meaningful to me
30. It is basically my own responsibility to decide how my job gets done
31. To be successful on my job requires all my skill and ability
32. I have too much work to do to do everything well
33. I have all the skills I need in order to do my job
34. To satisfy some people on my job, I have to upset others
35. I have the freedom to decide what I do on my job
36. I feel that most of the things I do on my job are meaningless (R)
37. On my job, I can't satisfy everybody at the same time
38. The amount of work I am asked to do is fair (R)
39. I feel personally responsible for the work I do on my job
40. Most of the time I know what I have to do on my job
41. On my job, I seldom get a chance to use my special skills and abilities (R)
42. I never seem to have enough time to get everything done
43. My job is very challenging
44. I deserve credit or blame for how well my work gets done
45. I seldom know whether I'm doing my job well or poorly (R)
46. On my job, I know exactly what is expected of me

Responses

Items 1 to 7, 9 to 17, 29 to 46: Strongly disagree; Disagree; Slightly disagree; Neither agree nor disagree; Slightly agree; Agree; Strongly agree; scored 1 to 7 respectively.

Items 8, 18 to 28: responses specific to each item; see above. Note that for items 18 to 28 responses 2, 3, 5 and 6 are unlabelled.

8.7   Routinization

Source: Hage and Aiken, 1969

The authors set out to measure Routinization as an organizational variable through the perceptions of individual employees. They describe a five-item scale with origins in the work of Hall (1963). A four-point response dimension is used, and a mean score is taken.

Average scores from 16 different organizations are summarized in the source publication. For example, three mental hospitals yielded a mean value of 1.73, and the range across all the organizations was from 1.31 to 2.46. The internal reliability of the scale is said to be supported by a factor analysis, but no details are given. However, Dewar, Whetten and Boje (1980) report alpha coefficients of 0.82, 0.94 and 0.74 from three studies using items 2 to 5.

Pierce and Dunham (1978b) calculated total scores rather than means, recording an overall value of 14.2 (s.d. 3.1) and an alpha coefficient of 0.85 from a sample of 155 office personnel (47% female). Significant correlations were reported with Job Characteristics indices from the Job Diagnostic Survey (Hackman and Oldham, 1975) (8.2), the median of which was -0.45 (range -0.32 to -0.65). With the Job Characteristics Inventory (Sims, Szilagyi and Keller, 1976) (8.3) the median correlation was -0.40, with a range between -0.32 and -0.80. The strongest association was with perceived Variety in each case. Routinization was correlated 0.43 and 0.36 with Hage and Aiken's (1967) measures of Centralization (8.25) and Formalization (8.46) respectively.

Bacharach and Aiken (1976, 1977) have used a slightly amended version of the scale in a study of 860 Belgian city administrators, and another variant has been used by Jermier and Berkes (1979) with 158 police officers. Note that in the initial version, below, a "false" response to item 3 is ambiguous.

Items

1. Would you describe your work as being: very routine; somewhat routine; somewhat nonroutine; or very nonroutine? Scored 4 to 1 respectively.
2. People here do the same job in the same way every day
3. One thing people like around here is the variety of work (R)
4. Most jobs have something new happening every day (R)
5. There is something different to do every day (R)

Responses

Items 2 to 5: Definitely true; True; False; Definitely false; scored 4 to 1 respectively.

8.8 Autonomy

Source: Bacharach and Aiken, 1976

A four-item instrument was designed to measure the degree to which organizational members' freedom of action is constrained. A four-point response dimension is used, and a mean score is taken. The measure is primarily intended for comparisons between groups or organizations, with the organization (rather than the individual) as the unit of analysis.

The authors report data from a sample of 860 Belgian city administrators, obtaining means of 2.02 (s.d. 0.40) and 2.14 (s.d. 0.26) for middle- and lower-level staff respectively. Corresponding alpha coefficients of 0.66 and 0.65 were recorded. For the middle-level sample Autonomy was correlated 0.34 with reported influence in work decisions, and for the lower-level group this value was 0.49 (N=44 organizations in each case).

Items

1. People here are allowed to do almost as they please
2. How things are done here are left pretty much up to the person doing the work
3. A person can make his own decisions without consulting anyone else
4. Most people here make up their own rules

Responses

Definitely true; More true than false; More false than true; Definitely false; scored 4 to 1 respectively.

8.9 Autonomy

Source: Beehr, 1976

The author adapts four items from Quinn and Shepard (1974) to yield a measure of employees' work Autonomy. A four-point response dimension is used, and a mean score is taken.

In a study of 651 varied employees (49% female) the mean score was 2.97 (s.d. 0.76), and a Spearman-Brown internal reliability coefficient of 0.74 was recorded. Significant associations with several affective measures were obtained, but note that these may be partly attributable to the inclusion of "enough" (an evaluative qualifier) in two of the items.

Items

How true is this of your job?
1. I have a lot of say over what happens on my job

2. I have enough authority to do my best
3. My job allows me to make a lot of decisions on my own
4. I have enough freedom as to how I do my work

Responses

Very true; Somewhat true; A little true; Not at all true; scored 4 to 1 respectively.

8.10 to 8.14   Other Measures of Perceived Job Characteristics

8.10 London and Klimoski (1975a, b) have used a 33-item measure of Job Complexity with a sample of 153 female nurses. The perceived Complexity of a job is indexed through five-point ratings (minimum to maximum) of Responsibility, Amount of Work, Challenge, Tension, Fatigue, etc.

8.11 Perceived Job Attributes have been studied by O'Brien and Dowling (1980) in terms of Influence, Skill Utilization, Variety, Pressure, and Social Interaction. Their scale contains 26 items, and means and intercorrelations based upon data from 1383 Australian respondents are presented.

8.12 A 30-item scale has been devised by Herold and Greller (1977) to assess the extent to which different types of Performance Feedback are perceived to be present in a job. Respondents indicate the frequency of occurrence of events such as being told they are doing a poor job or being teased by colleagues about doing too well.

8.13 Subjective Job Characteristics have been tapped by Dickson (1976) in terms of Discretion, Variety, Unpredictability and Work Interdependence. Results from 147 managers are presented, and the source publication also contains the items in full.

8.14 Billings, Klimoski and Breaugh (1977) have measured perceived Job Characteristics in terms of six factors: Supervisory Relations, Job Importance, Supervisory Closeness, Task Variety, Task Interdependence, and Required Task Effort. The items are presented in full, together with data from 123 hospital kitchen staff.

8.15 to 8.54   Work Role and Job Context

We turn now to examine 40 measures with a somewhat broader focus. As described in the introduction to the chapter, this section covers features of Role Ambiguity, Conflict, Overload, Responsibility, Participation, and Work-related Expectancies: features which are relatively more concerned with job context than are the measures of job content in section one of the chapter. Fourteen measures are presented as major entries, with brief descriptions of a further 26.

8.15 and 8.16   Role Ambiguity and Role Conflict

Source: Rizzo, House and Lirtzman, 1970

Drawing from role theory and from the prescription in classical organization theory that formal positions in a structure should each have clear task requirements, the authors set out to operationalize two features of role incumbency—degree of ambiguity and of conflict. A role is viewed as a set of expectations about behaviour and the two central concepts are as follows:

Role Ambiguity is defined in terms of the predictability of the outcomes of one's behaviour, and the existence of environmental guidelines to provide knowledge that one is behaving appropriately.

Role Conflict is viewed in terms of the incompatibility of demands; this may be in the form of conflict between organizational demands and one's own values, problems of personal resource allocation, conflict between obligations to several other people, and conflict between excessively numerous or difficult tasks. Note that "role overload", the last of these features, is included within role conflict; this follows the thinking of Kahn, Wolfe, Quinn and Snoek (1964, p. 20).

An initial pool of 30 items was administered to 290 managerial and technical employees, and factor analysis and item analyses led to the establishment of a six-item Role Ambiguity scale (8.15) and an eight-item Role Conflict scale (8.16). Responses are on a seven-point dimension, and a mean (between 1 and 7) is calculated, such that a high score indicates high Ambiguity or high Conflict. The sample of respondents was divided into two very similar sub-samples (N=199 and 91), which yielded means of 3.79 (s.d. 1.08) and 4.03 (s.d. 1.15) for Role Ambiguity and 4.19 (s.d. 1.21) and 3.86 (s.d. 1.17) for Role Conflict; note that these are around the midpoint (4) of the response scale. Kuder-Richardson internal reliability coefficients were 0.78 and 0.81 for Ambiguity and 0.82 and 0.82 for Conflict, and the correlation between the scales was 0.25 and 0.01 for the two sub-samples. See also House and Rizzo (1972a, b).

The measures have been used quite widely, and a number of authors have provided descriptive statistics. For example, Szilagyi, Sims and Keller (1976) report data from seven different occupational groups.

Within a large medical centre, Role Ambiguity means ranged from 3.53 (s.d. 1.38) for 53 senior administrators to 2.78 (s.d. 0.91) for 240 service employees; Role Conflict scores showed less variation across job levels, being 3.89 (s.d. 1.00) and 3.95 (s.d. 1.03) for those two sub-samples respectively. Within a manufacturing firm, average Role Ambiguity was 2.85 (s.d. 1.03) for 93 managers and 2.37 (s.d. 0.77) for 33 foremen; corresponding values for Role Conflict were 3.84 (s.d. 0.54) and 4.13 (s.d. 0.35) respectively. Schuler, Aldag and Brief (1977) quote means for six separate groups. For example, 374 nurses yielded average Role Ambiguity and Role Conflict scores of 2.60 (s.d. 0.96) and 3.26 (s.d. 1.05) respectively. Corresponding mean values for 159 computer professionals were 3.44 and 4.09 in Bartol's (1979b) study. Morris and Koch (1979), with samples of 75 manual, 129 clerical, and 55 professional non-academic university employees (see also Morris and Snyder, 1979), report means for Role Ambiguity of 2.79 (s.d. 1.35), 3.04 (s.d. 1.28) and 3.24 (s.d. 1.41) respectively. Corresponding values for Role Conflict were 3.02 (s.d. 1.36), 3.52 (s.d. 1.44) and 3.87 (s.d. 1.37).

However, care must be taken in the interpretation of published means for these scales, since many authors have deviated from the original scoring procedures. For example, in studies of Role Ambiguity, Dessler and Valenzi (1977) and Valenzi and Dessler (1978) used a five-point response continuum, and Schriesheim and Von Glinow (1977) reversed the direction of scoring. Total scores (rather than means) are quoted by Evans (1974) and Schuler (1975), with Evans reversing the direction of scoring for both scales and Schuler doing this for Ambiguity. (Note incidentally that reversal of scoring for Ambiguity yields a measure of what may be termed Role Clarity; Odewahn and Petty (1980) use the scale in that way. See also entries 8.6, 8.17, 8.21 and 8.38.) Total scores on five-point continua are quoted for both scales by Keenan and McBain (1978, 1979).

The internal reliability of the two scales has been confirmed as acceptable. Szilagyi, Sims and Keller (1976) report Spearman-Brown internal reliability coefficients of 0.76 and 0.90 for Role Ambiguity and 0.90 and 0.94 for Role Conflict in samples of 953 hospital employees (80% female) and 192 manufacturing managers respectively. See also Keller, Szilagyi and Holland (1976), Sims and Szilagyi (1975a, b), Szilagyi and Sims (1974b), and Szilagyi and Keller (1976). Schuler, Aldag and Brief (1977) present alpha coefficients for six different samples. For Role Ambiguity these range from 0.63 to 0.87 (median 0.79) and for Role Conflict the range is from 0.56 to 0.82 (median 0.74). See also Brief and Aldag (1976). For Role Ambiguity, an alpha coefficient of 0.76 is reported by Valenzi and Dessler (1978) and a Kuder-

Richardson reliability coefficient of 0.89 by Schriesheim and Von Glinow (1977). Other reports of high internal reliability coefficients are by Ivancevich (1979b) (alpha 0.83 and 0.79), Morris and Koch (1979) (alpha 0.79 and 0.80), Morris, Steers and Koch (1979) (alpha 0.78 and 0.82), Quick (1979) (alpha 0.94 and 0.82), Schriesheim (1979) and Schriesheim, Kinicki and Schriesheim (1979) (alpha 0.75 and 0.77), and Schuler (1979) (alpha between 0.75 and 0.87).

Intercorrelations between the two scales have been reported by Schuler, Aldag and Brief (1977) to range from 0.18 to 0.50 (median 0.35) across six samples. However, these authors' factor analyses of individual items confirmed the two-factor structure suggested by Rizzo, House and Lirtzman (1970). The same factorial result was reported by Szilagyi, Sims and Keller (1976). Schuler (1975) reports intercorrelations between the scales of 0.46, 0.31 and 0.33 for three samples of manufacturing employees; with 162 nurses the association between the scales was 0.39 (Seybolt and Pavett, 1979); with 90 British managers the value was 0.22 (Keenan and McBain, 1979); and with 252 non-academic university employees it was 0.47 (Morris, Steers and Koch, 1979).

Test–retest reliability has been examined in a study of 148 scientists and engineers by Miles (1975). Over a four-month period, values were 0.65 and 0.71 for Ambiguity and Conflict respectively. Szilagyi (1977), with 295 health-care employees, reports correlations over six months of 0.66 and 0.67; and Schuler, Aldag and Brief (1977) recorded values of 0.40 and 0.44 across seven months in a sample of 671 public utility employees (see also Schuler, 1979).

Schuler, Aldag and Brief (1977) also report correlations for six separate samples between Role Ambiguity and Conflict and the five sub-scales of the Job Descriptive Index of Job Satisfaction (3.3). Median correlations between Ambiguity and Satisfaction with Work, Pay, Co-workers, Supervision and Promotion Prospects were, respectively, −0.40 (range −0.09 to −0.47), −0.16 (range 0.06 to −0.30), −0.24 (range 0.05 to −0.31), −0.41 (range −0.16 to −0.49), and −0.28 (range −0.12 to −0.38). For Conflict the corresponding values were −0.28 (range −0.20 to −0.36), −0.20 (range −0.06 to −0.32), −0.31 (range −0.10 to −0.38), −0.36 (range −0.29 to −0.43), and −0.24 (range 0.04 to −0.35). Other authors reporting similar associations with the Job Descriptive Index include Brief and Aldag (1976), Keller (1975), Schuler (1975, 1980), and Szilagyi, Sims and Keller (1976). Anxiety-stress (House and Rizzo, 1972b) (5.4) has been studied by Miles (1975), who reported average correlations (from two administrations of the questionnaires) of 0.21 and 0.31 with Role Ambiguity and Role Conflict respectively; respondents were 148 scientists and engineers. Comparable correlations of 0.20 and 0.41 were reported by Brief and Aldag (1976) in their research with 77 nursing aides and assistants. Correlations with Lyons' (1971) Tension Index (5.2) were 0.30 and 0.48, and with Propensity to Leave (4.12) they were 0.25 and 0.23, for Role Ambiguity and Role Conflict respectively.

Other uses of the measures or variants of them have been described by Bernadin (1979), Brief, Aldag and Van Sell (1977), Greene (1978, 1979), Hamner and Tosi (1974), Johnson and Stinson (1975),Keller and Szilagyi (1976), Kerr and Jermier (1978), Miles (1976a, b), Miles and Perreault (1976), Muczyk (1978), Parkington and Schneider (1979), Rogers and Molnar (1976), Rousseau (1978b), Schriesheim (1980), Schriesheim and Schriesheim (1980), Schuler (1977a, b, c), Szilagyi and Holland (1980), and White and Mitchell (1979).

Note that the meaning of correlations between Role Ambiguity and Conflict and other variables is sometimes open to question, in the sense that minimum scores are not necessarily maximally desirable. One might expect moderate Ambiguity or Conflict to be the most desirable, but this possibility has rarely been considered in empirical research to date.

Items

Role Ambiguity

1. I feel certain about how much authority I have
2. Clear, planned goals and objectives exist for my job
3. I know that I have divided my time properly
4. I know what my responsibilities are
5. I know exactly what is expected of me
6. Explanation is clear of what has to be done

Role Conflict

1. I have to do things that should be done differently
2. I receive an assignment without the manpower to complete it
3. I have to buck a rule or policy in order to carry out an assignment
4. I work with two or more groups who operate quite differently
5. I receive incompatible requests from two or more people
6. I do things that are apt to be accepted by one person and not accepted by others
7. I receive an assignment without adequate resources and materials to execute it
8. I work on unnecessary things

Responses

A seven-point dimension from Very false to Very true; intermediate labels are not cited. For Role Ambiguity scoring is from 7 to 1 respectively; for Role Conflict it is from 1 to 7 respectively.

8.17 Role Ambiguity

Source: Caplan, 1971

The author presents a four-item measure of Role Ambiguity, described as present when a person does not know what is expected of him or her for adequate performance of a role or task demand. Five response alternatives are provided and a mean score is taken, with a high score indicating low Ambiguity.

The average inter-item correlation from a sample of 100 engineers and scientists was 0.46. A three-item version was used by Caplan and Jones (1975) in a study of 122 male university students and faculty members. They recorded a mean of 2.20 (s.d. 0.66) and an estimated reliability coefficient (formula 6.18 of Nunnally, 1967) of 0.82. Role Ambiguity correlated 0.42 with State Anxiety (5.13).

Items

1. The extent to which your work objectives are defined
2. The extent to which you can predict what others will expect of you tomorrow
3. The extent to which you are clear on what others expect of you now
4. The extent to which you are certain about what your responsibilities will be six months from now

Responses

Very little; Little; Some; Great; Very great; scored 1 to 5 respectively. Note that this direction of scoring yields an index which might better be described as Role Clarity.

8.18 Subjective Quantitative Work Load

Source: Caplan, 1971

Drawing upon research by Kahn, Wolfe, Quinn and Snoek (1964) and others, this measure is intended partially to cover the notion of role overload. Quantitative Overload is said to occur when a person find is that the environment has demanded more work than can be performed in a given period of time. The scale title emphasizes that the measure is of "subjective" overload.

Nine items are used, with five alternative responses. Two items are reverse scored, and a mean value is taken, a high score indicating high Overload.

The measure was used by Caplan, Cobb and French (1975) with administrators, engineers and scientists in an aerospace organization. Mean scores were 3.7 (N=58), 3.4 (N=94) and 3.1 (N=48) respectively. Estimated internal reliability (formula 6.18 of Nunnally, 1967) was 0.87. A comparable reliability coefficient of 0.77 was reported by Caplan and Jones (1975) with 122 male university students and faculty members, using a three-item version of the scale. That measure was associated 0.29 with State Anxiety (5.13).

Items

1. The number of projects and/or assignments you have
2. The amount of time you spend in meetings
3. The amount of time you have (R)
4. The number of conflicting demands you have
5. The work load, the amount of things that need to be done
6. The time to think and contemplate (R)
7. The quantity of work you are expected to do
8. The extent to which you feel you never have any time
9. The number of phone calls and office visits you have during the day

Responses

Very little; Little; Some; Great; Very great; scored 1 to 5 respectively.

8.19 and 8.20   Responsibility for Things and for Persons

Source: Caplan, 1971

As part of a broad assessment of role stressors (see also 8.17, 8.18), the author develops suggestions from Kahn, Wolfe, Quinn and Snoek (1964) and others that having responsibility for people, resources or procedures might be a source of strain. Two scales are constructed to tap Responsibility for Things (8.19) and Responsibility for Persons (8.20). The scales have four and two items respectively. A five-point response dimension is used, and a mean score is taken.

Caplan, Cobb and French (1975) report overall means for 200 administrators, engineers and scientists of 3.07 for Responsibility for Things and 2.96 for Responsibility for People. Both scales yielded a coefficient alpha of 0.66 on this sample.

Items

Responsibility for Things

1. The responsibility you have for initiating assignments and projects
2. The responsibility you have for budgets and expenditures
3. The responsibility you have for carrying out assignments and projects
4. The responsibility you have for equipment and facilities

Responsibility for Persons

1. The responsibility you have for the work of others
2. The responsibility you have for the future careers of others

Responses

Very little; Little; Some; Great; Very great; scored 1 to 5 respectively.

8.21 to 8.23   Role Ambiguity, Role Overload and Nonparticipation

Source: Beehr, Walsh and Taber, 1976

In a study of perceived role stressors the authors describe the administration of three scales to 143 white-collar employees in a single company (45% female). Each scale has a seven-point response dimension, and a mean score is taken, with high values indicating high Ambiguity, Overload or Nonparticipation. Five items are reverse-scored.

Role Ambiguity (8.21) is described as not knowing exactly what behaviour is expected in one's job. A four-item scale yielded a mean of 2.95 (s.d. 1.25) and an internal reliability coefficient of 0.71. In all cases reliability was assessed by making a Spearman-Brown correction to median inter-item correlations. An extended use of the index is described by Walsh, Taber and Beehr (1980), where reverse-scoring yields a measure of Role Clarity.

Role Overload (8.22) is viewed as having too much work to do in the time available. A three-item scale yielded a mean of 3.45 (s.d. 1.33) and an internal reliability coefficient of 0.56. Three items were also used to tap Nonparticipation (8.23), described as not being consulted about work-related happenings. Sample statistics as above were 3.46, 1.27 and 0.62.

Intercorrelations between these three perceived role stressors averaged 0.19 (range 0.16 to 0.27). Associations with the authors' two-item measure of Overall Job Satisfaction were 0.51, 0.18 and 0.34 for Role Ambiguity, Role Overload and Nonparticipation respectively. With a two-item measure of Job-related Tension the corresponding correlations were 0.26, 0.32 and 0.06.

Items

Role Ambiguity

1. My supervisor makes sure his people have clear goals to achieve (R)
2. My supervisor makes it clear how I should do my work (R)
3. I don't know what performance standards are expected of me
4. It is clear what is expected of me on my job (R)

Role Overload

1. I am given enough time to do what is expected of me on my job (R)
2. It often seems like I have too much work for one person to do
3. The performance standards on my job are too high

Nonparticipation

1. I am usually not told about important things that are happening in this company
2. Meetings are frequently held to discuss work problems with my co-workers and me (R)
3. Decisions are usually made without consulting the people who have to live with them

Responses

Strongly disagree; Disagree; Slightly disagree; Neither agree nor disagree; Slightly agree; Agree; Strongly agree; scored 1 to 7 respectively.

8.24   Psychological Participation

Source: Vroom, 1960

Participation is viewed as influence in a process of joint decision-making by two or more parties, in which the decisions have future effects on those making them. Vroom sets out to measure "psychological" participation, the amount of influence which a person perceives himself or herself to possess. The scale contains four items, each with a five-point response dimension. A total score is calculated, ranging from 4 to 20.

In research with 108 supervisors and managers the median inter-item correlation was only 0.05 (range -0.07 to 0.26), which the author characterizes as "surprisingly low". "However, the issue of how homogeneous items should be before they are combined is really a complex one. Homogeneity is not an end in itself but is important only as far as it contributes to the reliability and validity of the resulting score" (Vroom, 1960, p. 25). Test–retest reliability over seven months for 77 respondents remaining in the same job was 0.63; for 14 who were transferred this value dropped to 0.44. The mean value for the sample of 108 was 12.7.

The first three items of the scale were used by Abdel-Halim and Rowland (1976) in research with 106 managers. Using a six-point response dimension, Psychological Participation was reported to be correlated 0.32 and 0.54 respectively with the Work and Supervision sub-scales of the Job Descriptive Index of Job Satisfaction (3.3). A similar result is reported by Hamner and Tosi (1974). Morris, Steers and Koch (1979) have used a six-item version of the scale with an alpha coefficient of 0.85 ($N=252$ non-academic university employees). With a five-item version White (1978, 1979) recorded an alpha value of 0.81 ($N=9$ companies).

Other adaptations of the original scale are described by James, Gent, Hater and Coray (1975), Ruh, White and Wood (1975) and Schuler (1977a).

Items and Responses

1. In general, how much say or influence do you feel you have on what goes on in your station?
A very great deal of influence; A great deal of influence; Quite a bit of influence; Some influence; Little or no influence; scored 5 to 1 respectively.

2. Do you feel you can influence the decisions of your immediate superior regarding things about which you are concerned?
I can influence him to a great extent; To a considerable extent; To some extent; To a very little extent; I cannot influence him at all; scored 5 to 1 respectively.

3. Does your immediate superior ask your opinion when a problem comes up that involves your work?
He always asks my opinion; Often asks; Sometimes asks; Seldom asks; He never asks my opinion; scored 5 to 1 respectively.

4. If you have a suggestion for improving the job or changing the setup in some way, how easy is it for you to get your ideas across to your immediate superior?
It is very difficult; Somewhat difficult; Not too easy; Fairly easy; It is very easy to get my ideas across; scored 1 to 5 respectively.

8.25 Centralization

Source: Aiken and Hage, 1966; Hage and Aiken, 1967

The authors view Centralization as an organizational characteristic which is reflected in the locus of authority to make decisions affecting the organization. Two aspects are identified:
1. The degree of Hierarchy of Authority, defined as the extent to which members are assigned tasks and provided with the freedom to implement them without interruption from supervision.

2. The degree of Participation in Decision-making, the extent to which staff members participate in setting the goals and policies of the entire organization.

The author's measure of Centralization was based upon research by Hall (1963). It has a sub-scale to tap each of the two components, with five and four items in the two sub-scales respectively. The Hierarchy of Authority sub-scale employs a four-point response dimension, and the Participation in Decision-making sub-scale has a five-point dimension; a mean score is taken in each case.

The authors derive scores for organizational units (rather than for individuals), by first obtaining average scores for each organizational level and then taking a simple average across levels; note that this procedure gives greater weight to more senior staff, since they are typically less numerous but their average score enters into the total with a weight equal to that of subordinate staff.

Data are presented for 16 social welfare agencies (total N=314 professional employees). The range of organizations' scores for Hierarchy of Authority was from 1.50 to 2.10, and for Participation in Decision-Making the range was from 1.68 to 3.69. The two sub-scales were intercorrelated −0.55 (N=16 organizations), suggesting that the constructs are not independent. The relationships between the two indices of Centralization and the author's scales of Organizational Alienation (4.1) were reported as follows: Hierarchy of Authority with Alienation from Work and Alienation from Expressive Relations, 0.49 and 0.45 respectively; Participation in Decision-making with these two scores, −0.59 and −0.17 respectively. Dewar, Whetten and Boje (1980) present data from four separate studies, three of which were conducted by Aiken and Hage themselves. Median alpha coefficients were 0.86 and 0.92 for Hierarchy of Authority and Participation respectively.

Allen and LaFollette (1977) used the Hierarchy of Authority sub-scale with 86 managers in a single company, taking individuals as the unit of analysis. They observed a correlation with Alienation from Work (4.1) of 0.37 but an insignificant association with Alienation from Expressive relations (4.1). Pierce and Dunham (1978b), with a sample of 155 insurance clerical staff (47% female), also used the Hierarchy of Authority sub-scale only, reporting an alpha coefficient of 0.94 and a mean (total) score of 9.0 (s.d. 4.1). This sub-scale correlated negatively (median −0.40, range −0.32 to −0.69) with perceived Job Characteristics measures from the Job Diagnostic Survey (8.2). A modification of the Hierarchy of Authority sub-scale was employed with 833 varied employees by Dewar and Werbel (1979); and a version of the Participation sub-scale was used with 158 police officers by Jermier and Berkes

(1979), with 398 office employees by Pierce, Dunham and Blackburn (1979), and with 408 social workers by Glisson and Martin (1980).

Items

Hierarchy of Authority

1. There can be little action taken here until a supervisor approves a decision
2. A person who wants to make his own decisions would be quickly discouraged here
3. Even small matters have to be referred to someone higher up for a final answer
4. I have to ask my boss before I do almost anything
5. Any decision I make has to have my boss's approval

Participation in Decision-making

1. How frequently do you usually participate in the decision to hire new staff?
2. How frequently do you usually participate in decisions on the promotion of any of the professional staff?
3. How frequently do you participate in decisions on the adoption of new policies?
4. How frequently do you participate in the decisions on the adoption of new programs?

Responses

Hierarchy of Authority: a dimension from Definitely false to Definitely true; scored 1 to 4 respectively. Intermediate labels are not cited.
Participation in Decision-making: Never; Seldom; Sometimes; Often; Always; scored 1 to 5 respectively.

8.26   Work-related Expectancies

Source: Sims, Szilagyi and McKemey, 1976

This is a measure of the perceived outcomes of working hard. From the perspective of expectancy theory (see 6.12), two Work-related Expectancies are defined. The first (Expectancy 1, or E1) is an estimate of the probability that putting effort into one's job will yield good performance; and the second (E2) is the perceived probability that good performance will lead to rewards. Note that valence (perceived value) of outcomes is not assessed directly for each respondent but is assumed in the content of items. The measure is thus concerned entirely with perceptions.

The scale was developed from items used by House and Dessler (1974); see also Dessler and Valenzi (1977). It contains 26 items, nine tapping E1 and 17 covering E2, and items from the two sub-scales are interspersed in presentation. Responses are on a seven-point dimension from definitely true to definitely not true, which is probably scored from 7 to 1 and summed or averaged.

The source publication describes an investigation with 973 hospital employees (80% female) in five different occupational categories. Factor analysis yielded two principal factors, clearly corresponding to E1 and E2 (details of factor rotation are not given, but a complete set of loadings is published). Separate analyses for the five occupational groups revealed very high factor congruence between them, coefficients averaging 0.95 for E1 and 0.98 for E2. Spearman-Brown internal reliability coefficients for the two sub-scales were 0.87 and 0.94 respectively. Keller and Szilagyi (1976) used a sample of 192 professional, managerial and supervisory employees of a manufacturing company, reporting comparable Spearman-Brown coefficients of 0.82 and 0.85. Neither publication contains means or standard deviations.

With the hospital sample, Sims, Szilagyi and McKemey (1976) recorded a number of correlates of E2 (performance–reward expectancy). For example, correlations with leader's Positive Reward Behaviour (Sims and Szilagyi, 1975b) (9.7) and the Feedback sub-scale of the Job Characteristics Inventory (8.3) were 0.55 and 0.37 respectively; however, with leader's Punitive Reward Behavior the correlation was only 0.14. Similar analyses of data from the manufacturing sample (N = 192) yielded associations between E2 and leader's Positive and Punitive Leader Behavior of 0.61 and 0.15 respectively (Keller and Szilagyi, 1976). Correlatons with E1 (effort–performance expectancy) were mainly below 0.10 in both studies. Note that the association between E2 and leader's Positive Reward Behavior is partly due to overlapping item content. Related analyses are described by Sims and Szilagyi (1975a, b), Szilagyi and Keller (1976), and Keller and Szilagyi (1978). A variant of the E2 measure has been used by Schuler (1980).

Items

E1: Effort–Performance Expectancy

3. Doing things as well as I am capable results in completing my job on time
6. Working as hard as I can leads to high quality work
7. Doing things as well as I am capable leads to a high quantity of work
8. Working as hard as I can leads to completing my work on time
9. Getting my job done on time leads to the experience of accomplishment
14. Working as hard as I can leads to a high quantity of work
24. Putting forth as much energy as possible results in completing my work on time

25. Putting forth as much energy as possible leads to my producing high quality work
26. Putting forth as much energy as possible leads to my producing a high quantity of work

E2: Performance–Reward Expectancy

1. High quality work increases my chances for promotion
2. Handling a high quantity of work increases my chances for promotion
4. Producing high quality work is rewarded with higher pay here
5. Producing a high quality of work is rewarded with higher pay here
10. Getting the job done on time increases my chances for promotion
11. Getting work done on time is rewarded with high pay here
12. The people I work with respect me more when I get my job done on time
13. Completing my job in time leads to more influence with supervisors
15. The higher the quality of work the more recognition I receive from my supervisor
16. Supervisors in this organization listen to those who do the most effective work
17. My supervisor gives me more recognition when I produce a high quantity of work
18. Producing a high quantity of work leads to job security here
19. Completing my work in a timely manner leads to recognition
20. When I finish my job in time, I feel that my job is more secure
21. The people I work with respect me more when my work is of high quality
22. Producing high quality work leads to job security
23. Management gives me recognition when I produce high quality work

Responses

A seven-point continuum from Definitely not true to Definitely true; scored 1 to 7 respectively. Intermediate labels are not cited.

8.27 Task–Goal Attributes

Source: Steers, 1973

The author points out that task performance appears to be enhanced by the setting of clear goals, but that there is a need for more adequate measurement of Task–Goal Attributes. He identifies five aspects, and refines an initial scale through item analyses to 16 items, as follows: Participation in Goal Setting (four items), Feedback on Goal Effort (three items), Peer Competition (two items), Goal Specificity (three items), and Goal Difficulty (four items). A seven-point response dimension is used and four items are reverse-scored. A mean value is calculated for each sub-scale.

In a study of 133 female supervisors (Steers, 1975a, 1976), alpha coefficients were 0.72, 0.81, 0.69, 0.68 and 0.72 respectively, and correlations with Hackman and Lawler's (1971) three-item measure of General Job Satisfaction (entry 2.6) were 0.21, 0.26, 0.12, 0.35 and 0.21. Comparable correlations with Lodahl and Kejner's measure of Job Involvement (6.1) were 0.26, 0.11, 0.16, 0.33 and 0.27. Associations between perceived Task–Goal Attributes and rated work performance and effort were typically insignificant (median 0.08, range −0.06 to 0.20).

Items

Participation in Goal-Setting

1. I am allowed a high degree of influence in the determination of my work objectives
7. I really have little voice in the formulation of my work objectives (R)
11. The setting of my work goals is pretty much under my own control
16. My supervisor usually asks for my opinions and thoughts when determining my work objectives

Feedback on Goal Effort

3. I receive a considerable amount of feedback concerning my quantity of output on the job
8. I am provided with a great deal of feedback and guidance on the quality of my work
12. My boss seldom lets me know how well I am doing on my work toward my work objectives (R)

Peer Competition

4. Most of my co-workers and peers try to out-perform each other on their assigned work goals
13. There is a very competitive atmosphere among my peers and myself with regard to attaining our respective work goals; we all want to do better in attaining our goals than anyone else

Goal Specificity

5. My work objectives are very clear and specific; I know exactly what my job is
9. I think my work objectives are ambiguous and unclear (R)
14. I understand fully which of my work objectives are more important than others; I have a clear sense of priorities on these goals

Goal Difficulty

2. I should not have too much difficulty in reaching my work objectives; they appear to be fairly easy (R)
6. My work objectives will require a great deal of effort from me to complete them
10. It will take a high degree of skill and know-how on my part to attain fully my work objectives
15. My work objectives are quite difficult to attain

Responses

Strongly disagree; Moderately disagree; Slightly disagree; Neither agree nor disagree; Slightly agree; Moderately agree; Strongly agree; scored 1 to 7 respectively.

8.28 Critical Psychological States

Source: Hackman and Oldham, 1975

The authors' Job Characteristics Model (Hackman and Oldham, 1975, 1976, 1980) assumes that three critical psychological states mediate between the characteristics of jobs and employees' reactions to them. These are identified and defined as follows:

Experienced Meaningfulness of the Work: the degree to which the employee experiences the job as one which is generally meaningful, valuable, and worthwhile.

Experienced Responsibility for Work Outcomes: the degree to which the employee feels personally accountable and responsible for the results of the work he or she does.

Knowledge of Results: the degree to which the employee knows and understands, on a continuous basis, how effectively he or she is performing the job.

The Job Diagnostic Survey (see also 2.6, 3.6, 6.3, 7.7, 8.2) contains three sub-scales to measure these experienced states. The items are split between two sections of the questionnaire, (the last two items in each sub-scale below comprising a separate section) with the same seven-point response continuum for all items. A mean score between 1 and 7 is derived for each sub-scale, and five items are reverse scored.

The source publication describes results from 658 employees (41% female) working on 62 jobs in seven organizations. A summary of applications of the Job Diagnostic Survey to 6930 employees (46% female) working on 876 jobs in 56 organizations has subsequently been reported by Oldham, Hackman and Stepina (1978). Table 11 contains data from both these publications; the calculation of internal reliability coefficients is described in entry 8.2.

The three sub-scales are themselves positively intercorrelated. Co-efficients from the two publications cited above are as follows: Mean-ingfulness and Responsibility, 0.64, 0.58; Meaningfulness and Knowledge of Results, 0.33, 0.40; Responsibility and Knowledge of Results, 0.32, 0.34. Oldham, Hackman and Stepina (1978) report significant positive associations between job level and the first two Critical Psychological States, but a non-significant association with Knowledge of Results.

Table 11. Critical Psychological States. Data from: 1 Hackman and Oldham (1975); and 2 Oldham, Hackman and Stepina (1978). (N=658 and 6930 respectively)

	Mean and standard deviation	Internal reliability coefficient	Motivating Potential Score (8.2)	General Job Satisfaction (2.6)	Correlation with: Internal Work Motivation (6.3)	Growth Satisfaction (3.6)
Experienced Meaningfulness of the work	1 5.12 (1.10)	0.74	0.57	0.66	0.63	0.68
	2 5.10 (1.14)	0.71	0.52	0.66	0.57	0.65
Experienced Responsibility for Work Outcomes	1 5.48 (0.91)	0.72	0.53	0.48	0.66	0.54
	2 5.40 (0.96)	0.67	0.47	0.49	0.59	0.51
Knowledge of Results	1 5.18 (1.09)	0.76	0.43	0.34	0.25	0.36
	2 5.04 (1.14)	0.71	0.43	0.42	0.23	0.39

Wall, Clegg and Jackson (1978) employed the measure of Critical Psychological States with 47 British shop-floor employees, recording for example associations with the General Health Questionnaire (Goldberg, 1972) (5.21) of 0.39, 0.23 and 0.22 respectively. General significant correlations with perceived Job Characteristics (8.2) are described by Arnold and House (1980) (N=89 varied employees), and mean values before and after an organizational change are reported by Bhagat and Chassie (1980). In a study of 138 Canadian office employees (69% female), Kiggundu (1980) recorded mean values of 5.27 (s.d. 1.10), 5.74 (s.d. 0.89) and 5.32 (s.d. 1.02) for the three indices in the sequence given above.

Items

Experienced Meaningfulness of the Work

1. The work I do on this job is very meaningful to me
2. Most of the things I have to do on this job seem useless or trivial (R)
3. Most people on this job find the work very meaningful
4. Most people on this job feel that the work is useless or trivial (R)

Experienced Responsibility for Work Outcomes

1. It's hard, on this job, for me to care very much about whether or not the work gets done right (R)
2. I feel a very high degree of personal responsibility for the work I do on this job
3. I feel I should personally take the credit or blame for the results of my work on this job
4. Whether or not this job gets done right is clearly my responsibility
5. Most people on this job feel a great deal of personal responsibility for the work they do
6. Most people on this job feel that whether or not the job gets done right is clearly their own responsibility

Knowledge of Results

1. I usually know whether or not my work is satisfactory on this job
2. I often have trouble figuring out whether I'm doing well or poorly on this job (R)
3. Most people on this job have a pretty good idea of how well they are performing their work
4. Most people on this job have trouble figuring out whether they are doing a good or a bad job (R)

Responses

Disagree strongly; Disagree; Disagree slightly; Neutral; Agree slightly; Agree; Agree strongly; scored 1 to 7 respectively.

8.29 to 8.54   Other Measures of Work Role and Job Context

8.29 A six-item index of Job Demands, in terms of rapid pace and excessive workload, has been used by Karasek (1979). This is partly based upon items used by Quinn and Shepard (1974).

8.30 Dewar and Werbel (1979) describe a four-item measure of Technological Routineness, containing items like: I do about the same job in the same way most of the time.

8.31 The same authors present in full a measure of perceived Surveillance and Enforcement. This contains five items of the kind: I feel that I am constantly being watched to see that I obey all rules pertaining to my job.

8.32 Howard, Cunningham and Rechnitzer (1977) have identified five Job Tension Factors: Ambiguity, Being Locked-in, Stagnation, Isolation and Contentment. Perception of the extent to which these are present in one's job is tapped through a 25-item measure.

8.33 Substitutes for Leadership have been examined by Kerr and Jermier (1978). These are job features which are considered likely to moderate the success of particular leadership styles. Thirteen sub-scales are presented, for example Organizational Formalization, Task-provided Feedback, and Spatial Distance between Superior and Subordinates.

8.34 Work Experience during early job tenure have been measured through 13 sub-scales by Buchanan (1974). Examples are Role Clarity, Reality Shock, First-Year Job Challenge, and Organizational Dependability.

8.35 Reinharth and Wahba (1975) have developed a 39-item measure of Work-related Expectancies, tapping both Expectancy 1 and Expectancy 2 (see p. 115, 6.12, 8.26). Items are in the form of conditional statements, for instance: If I don't apply myself, I may get fired.

8.36 Fineman (1975b) has developed and validated a 25-item measure of managers' perceived Achievement Climate. Respondents describe their job in terms of the relative appropriateness of 25 job characteristics or their opposites, each pair containing an achievement-related and another feature. An alpha coefficient of 0.88 is reported, and the scale is intended to tap one possible moderating variable between need for achievement and effective performance.

8.37 Beehr (1976) has adapted from Quinn and Shepard (1974) a four-item measure of Role Ambiguity, examining associations with Job and Life Dissatisfaction, low Self-esteem and Depressed Mood. Other aspects of the study are described by Gupta and Beehr (1979).

8.38 Lyons (1971) has presented in full a four-item measure of Role Clarity, with questions of the kind: Do you feel that you are always as clear as you would like to be about what you have to do on this job? Role Clarity scores correlated −0.59 with the author's Tension Index (5.2) and −0.27 with Propensity to Leave (4.12).

8.39 Role Clarity is tapped in a similar fashion by Berkowitz (1980) through a five-item scale. Correlations with attitudinal and behavioural measures are cited, and the items are set out in full. An illustrative question is: How clear are you about the limits of responsibility in your present job?

8.40 The same publication presents in full a 15-item Role Strain measure. This is shown to be factorially independent of Role Clarity (8.39), and contains items to measure both ambiguity and conflict.

8.41 Holahan and Gilbert (1979a, b) briefly describe their Role Conflict Scales. Four life roles are identified, those of worker, spouse, parent and self (as a self-actualizing person). The instrument comprises six sub-scales designed to measure the degree of conflict experienced between each pair of roles, that is between Worker and Spouse (three items), Worker and Parent (four items), Worker and Self (four items), Spouse and Parent (three items), Spouse and Self (four items), and Parent and Self (three items).

8.42 and 8.43 Sutton and Rousseau (1979) describe a four-item measure of perceived Participative Decision-Making, and a three-item index of Autonomy. An example from 8.42 is: In this organization, when a superior is trying to make a decision about a new idea, how likely is he or she to ask a subordinate for advice? An item from the second is: To what extent are you free to control your own pace of work?

8.44 Driscoll (1978) has developed a measure of Perceived Participation for use in a study of 109 university faculty members. Respondents indicate their amount of input to each of five organizational decisions.

8.45 Dittrich and Carrell (1979) have described a 31-item Organizational Fairness Questionnaire to measure employee perceptions of equity or inequity. Five features are assessed: Pay Rules, Pay Administration, Work Pace, Pay Level and Rules Administration.

8.46 Aiken and Hage (1966) and Hage and Aiken (1969) describe a measure of Formalization. This has two components: a five-item Index of Codification, which reflects the degree to which employees must consult organizational rules in fulfilling their responsibilities; and a two-item Index of Rule Observation, reflecting the degree to which employees are checked for rule violations. The Index of Codification has been used by Allen and LaFollette (1977) and Sutton and Rousseau (1979), and an amended version by Pierce and Dunham (1978b) and Pierce, Dunham and Blackburn (1979). A review of four applications of the measure is provided by Dewar, Whetten and Boje (1980).

8.47 A six-item measure of Rule Observance has been developed by Bacharach and Aiken (1976). Items are given in full and are of the kind: I always stick to the letter of the rules.

8.48 Perceptions of Organizational Communication have been tapped by Roberts and O'Reilly (1974, 1979) through sub-scales of Trust, Accuracy, Overload, etc. Roberts and O'Reilly (1974) present illustrative items and indicate that a revision of the questionnaire is available on request.

8.49 French and Raven's (1959) typology of Social Power Bases (Reward, Coercive, Legitimate, Referent and Expert Power) has been operationalized by Spekman (1979) through items like: He can make things difficult for me if I fail to follow his advice. Spekman found that the five a priori dimensions were moderately intercorrelated and suggests that four independent Bases of Power derived through factor analysis might instead be measured (Expert, Coercive, Non-coercive 1 and 2). Items are given in full.

8.50 Self-perceived Power has been tapped by Dieterly and Schneider (1974) in terms of five seven-item sub-scales. These refer to one's own power, rather than that of others, including items like: My position gives me a great deal of authority. In a study of 120 students, the sub-scales (Referent, Expert, Legitimate, Coercive and Reward Power; see 8.49) were moderately intercorrelated (median 0.36, range 0.24 to 0.56). A modified version of the measure (four items in each sub-scale) has been used by McPhail and Gavin (1979).

8.51 Arvey and Dewhirst (1976) describe a 15-item measure of Perceived Goal-Setting Attributes, developed to tap the extent to which employees perceive their superiors as managing according to the principles of Management by Objectives. Factor analyses of responses yielded four interpretable factors: Goal Clarity and Planning, Subordinate Freedom, Feedback and Evaluation, and Participation in Goal-Setting. Other reports have been provided by Arvey, Dewhirst and Boling (1976), Arvey, Dewhirst and Brown (1978), and Zultowski, Arvey and Dewhirst (1978).

8.52 An index of perceived Task–Goal Attributes has been described by Ivancevich and McMahon (1976). This contains 28 items loaded on six orthogonal factors: Goal Challenge, Goal Clarity, Goal Feedback, Goal Participation, Goal Program Commitment, and Personal Goal Commitment. An illustrative item from Goal Clarity is: The goals for my job are easy to understand. Descriptive statistics and associations with performance measures are reported in the source publication, and a development of the scale has been used by Quick (1979).

8.53 A measure of the Quality of Union–Management Relationships developed by the Office of Labor–Management Relations of the U.S. Civil Service Commission (Ingrassia, 1974; U.S. Civil Service Commission, 1974) is described and evaluated by Biasatti and Martin (1979). It comprises 11 descriptive items of the form: Both labor and management fully accept the importance of the institution of collective bargaining.

8.54 A four-item index of Boundary Spanning Activities is described by Keller and Holland (1975a, b). The focal construct is described as "the interpersonal transfer of information across organizational boundaries" (Keller, Szilagyi and Holland, 1976), and items are of the kind: During the last month, indicate the frequency with which you have sought information or advice from members of other organizations. The scale has also been used by Dailey (1979).

8.55 to 8.80   Organizational Climate

The final section of the chapter contains outline descriptions of 26 measures of Organizational Climate and their uses during our search period. As noted in the introduction to the chapter, the focus of Climate measures is broader than that of the instruments described earlier. However the line of distinction is a blurred and uncertain one, and some of the measures presented here could perhaps have appeared in the previous section, and vice versa. In all cases however the information gathered is intended to be primarily of a descriptive rather than an evaluative kind.

8.55 The Profile of Organizational Characteristics (Likert, 1967) was designed in the light of the author's four-fold classification of management systems. Each of its 51 items has a 20-point response continuum worded to reflect the four systems, namely Exploitive Authoritative (system 1), Benevolent Authoritative (system 2), Consultative (system 3) and Participative (system 4). The items are in eight main categories, designed to measure perceptions of Leadership Processes, Motivational Forces, Communication Processes, Interaction-Influence, Decision-making Processes, Goal-Setting, Control Processes, and Performance Goals and Training. The instrument is designed principally for use with managers and supervisors. An earlier version is described by Likert (1961), and several shorter forms exist. Studies using the Profile include those by Beehr (1977), Bennett (1977b), Butterfield and Farris (1974), Hollman (1976), Peterson (1975) and Renwick (1975a).

8.56 Litwin and Stringer's (1968) 50-item Organization Climate Questionnaire (Form B) is designed to measure nine characteristics reflecting the degree of organizational emphasis on Structure, Responsibility, Reward, Risk, Warmth, Support, Standards, Conflict, and Identity. Recent uses include those by Downey, Sheridan and Slocum (1975), Muchinsky (1976), Sims and LaFollette (1975), Sims, Szilagyi and Keller (1976), Szilagyi and Keller (1976), and Waters, Roach and Batlis (1974).

8.57 House and Rizzo (1972a) have developed the Organization Description Questionnaire, also referred to as the Organization Practices Questionnaire. Its theoretical base lies within the organic-mechanistic distinction drawn by Burns and Stalker (1961), Lawrence and Lorsch (1967) and Woodward (1965), and in McGregor's (1960) Theory X–Theory Y perspective. As originally described the instrument consists of 19 scales constructed from 82 items.

The scales have the following labels: Conflict and Inconsistency, Decision Timeliness, Emphasis on Analytic Method, Emphasis on Personal Development, Formalization, Goal Consensus and Clarity, Communication Adequacy, Information Distortion and Suppression, Job Pressure, Adequacy of Planning, Smoothness of Horizontal Communication, Selection on Ability and Performance, Tolerance of Error, Top Management Receptiveness, Upward Information Requirements, Violations in Chain of Command, Work Flow Coordination, Adaptability, and Adequacy of Authority. Uses of the instrument or of selected scales include those by Greene (1978), Hunt, Osborn and Schuler (1978), Schuler (1977c), Sims, Szilagyi and Keller (1976), Sims, Szilagyi and McKemey (1976), and Waters, Roach and Batlis (1974).

8.58 The Survey of Organizations (Taylor and Bowers, 1972) includes 22 items designed to measure Organizational Climate. Smallest space analysis revealed five principal clusters subsuming 13 items. These are labelled Technological Readiness, Human Resources Primacy, Communication Flow, Motivational Conditions, and Decision-Making Practices. A subsequent study yielded four main indices corresponding to the last four above, and two "tentative indices" of Technological

Readiness and Lower Level Influence. Applications include those by Bowers and Hausser (1977), Drexler (1977), Franklin (1975a, b), and Koch (1979).

8.59 Payne and Pheysey (1971) describe the Business Organization Climate Index. Three hundred items from Stern's (1967) Organizational Climate Index were reduced through content analysis and examination of empirical findings to 192 items which comprise the measure. These are distributed across 24 scales, labelled as follows: Leader's Psychological Distance, Questioning Authority, Egalitarianism, Management Concern for Employee Involvement, Openmindedness, Emotional Control, Physical Caution, Practical Orientation, Future Orientation, Scientific and Technical Orientation, Intellectual Orientation, Job Challenge, Task Orientation, Industriousness, Altruism, Sociability, Interpersonal Aggression, Homogeneity, Rules Orientation, Administrative Efficiency, Conventionality, Readiness to Innovate, Variety in Physical Environment, and Orientation to Wider Community.

Payne and Mansfield (1973) describe a 157-item revision of this measure covering 20 of the original scales. Example items are provided in both publications, as are scale means and reliabilities. Recent uses include those by Payne and Mansfield (1978) and Pheysey (1977).

8.60 Jones and James (1979) describe a 145-item Psychological Climate Questionnaire (see also James and Jones, 1973, 1974, 1976; Jones, James and Hornick, 1973). This has a very broad focus, covering perceptions of jobs and work roles (as described earlier in this chapter), as well as organizational properties, aspects of leadership style and trust (as considered in Chapter 9).

Developed and worded for use with navy personnel its 35 scales fall into four sets. The first group is concerned with perceived job and role characteristics, namely Role Ambiguity, Role Conflict, Job Autonomy, Job Variety, Job Importance, Job Feedback, Job Challenge, Job Pressure, Efficiency of Job Design, Job Standards, and Opportunities to Deal with Others. The second set of scales reflects leadership style: Support, Goal Emphasis, Work Facilitation, Interaction Facilitation, Planning and Co-ordination, Upward Interaction, Confidence and Trust-Up, and Confidence and Trust-Down.

The third set of scales is focussed on the work group, covering Co-operation, Friendliness and Warmth, Reputation for Effectiveness, and Workgroup Esprit de Corps. The final scales are concerned with the sub-system or organization as a whole, with measures of the following: Openness of Expression, Organizational Communication-Down,

Interdepartmental Cooperation, Conflict of Organizational Goals and Objectives, Ambiguity of Organizational Structure, Consistent Applications of Organizational Policies, Organizational Esprit de Corps, Professional Esprit de Corps, Planning and Effectiveness, Fairness and Objectiveness of the Reward Process, Opportunities for Growth and Advancement, and Awareness of Employee Needs and Problems.

Scale definitions and multivariate analyses are presented in the source publication. Other uses of some or all of the items include those by Butler and Jones (1979), James and Jones (1980), James, Hartman, Stebbins and Jones (1977), Jones, James and Bruni (1975), and Jones, James, Bruni and Sells (1977).

8.61 A 64-item Organizational Climate Description Questionnaire is introduced by Halpin and Croft (1963) and Halpin (1966). It contains eight scales, namely Disengagement, Hindrance, Esprit, Intimacy, Aloofness, Production Emphasis, Trust, and Consideration. The instrument was developed for educational organizations and the item content reflects this; the first four scales refer to teachers' behaviour and experience, the last four to the principal's behaviour. Earlier research with the questionnaire is reviewed by Lake and Miles (1973), and more recent uses include those by Lyon and Ivancevich (1974), Wallace, Ivancevich and Lyon (1975), and Waters, Roach and Batlis (1974).

8.62 Hoiberg and Berry (1978) describe the 138-item Navy Environment Scale which itself was developed from Insel and Moos's (1974) Work Environment Scale. It consists of ten sub-scales to measure Involvement, Peer Cohesion, Staff Support, Personal Growth or Autonomy, Task Orientation, Work Pressure, Clarity, Control, Innovation, and Physical Comfort. The source publication contains means and standard deviations for large samples of seven different occupational groups within the navy.

8.63 Lawler, Hall and Oldham (1974) describe a 15-item Organizational Climate questionnaire. Each item is in the form of a seven-point semantic differential scale, and factor analysis suggested a five-dimensional solution. The five scales are labelled as Competent, Responsible, Practical, Risk-Oriented, and Impulsive. A three-factor solution apparently based on the same data is described by Hall and Mansfield (1975).

8.64 The development of a Perceived Work Environment measure is described by Newman (1975, 1977). This has 60 items in 11 scales, as follows: Supervisory Style, Task Characteristics, Performance–Reward Relationships, Co-worker Relations, Employee Work Motivation, Equipment/People-Equipment Arrangement, Employee Competence,

Decision-Making Policy, Work Space Adequacy, Pressure to Produce, and Job Responsibility/Importance. A shorter version covers nine scales with 38 items.

8.65 Pritchard and Karasick (1973) provide the first published source for an Organizational Climate measure developed by Pritchard and Campbell. Eleven dimensions are described: Autonomy, Conflict versus Cooperation, Social Relations, Structure, Level of Rewards, Performance–Reward Dependency, Motivation to Achieve, Status Polarization, Flexibility and Innovation, Decision Centralization, and Supportiveness. Sheridan and Vredenburgh (1978b) make use of ten of the scales.

8.66 Downey, Hellriegel and Slocum (1975) report the use of a six-dimensional measure of Organizational Climate originally described by Downey, Hellriegel, Phelps and Slocum (1974). Based on factor analysis, its scales are Decision-Making, Warmth, Risk, Openness, Rewards, and Structure.

8.67 Dunham (1975, 1976, 1977b) introduces the Perceived Environmental Characteristics Scales, which yield seven measures derived through factor analyses. These are: Organizational Climate, described as the favourableness of the organizational atmosphere as a whole; Work Group Climate, defined as above except that its referent is the work group; Company Support, described as the assistance provided by the company for job performance and career development; Interpersonal Leadership, which refers to the favourableness of leaders' interpersonal relations; Task-oriented Leadership, which is defined as the overall favourableness of task-oriented apects of leadership; a Work Assignment Scale, tapping the overall favourableness of the present work assignment; and a Career Description Scale, to measure the overall favourableness of the career situation.

The items and factor loadings are given in full in Appendix B of Dunham (1975), and scale intercorrelations and alpha reliability co-efficients (the latter between 0.76 and 0.93) are described by Dunham (1977b). Given the clearly evaluative nature of this instrument, as evident both in the scale descriptions and items, its classification by the author as a measure of climate seems questionable. In practice, all the scales were found to be strongly correlated with measures of Job Satisfaction (Dunham, 1977b).

8.68 Dieterly and Schneider (1974) offer a measure of Perceived Organizational Climate, which has 28 items equally divided across scales of Individual Autonomy, Position Structure, Reward Orientation, and

Consideration. Items are given in full as are scale reliabilities and intercorrelations obtained in a laboratory study of 120 undergraduate students.

8.69 Perceived Organizational Structure is measured by Duncan (1971b) through scales of Hierarchy of Authority, Rules and Procedures, and Division of Labor. Sathe (1978) and Ford (1979) have used a modified version of this instrument.

8.70 Duncan's (1971a, b; 1972) Perceived Environmental Uncertainty Questionnaire is designed to measure three dimensions of uncertainty: the level of available information relevant to decision-making; knowledge of the organizational effects of decisions; and the ability to predict the effects of a given factor on the success or failure of a work group or organization. From a list of 25 factors, respondents identify up to 12 they consider most important to decision-making. They then indicate, with respect to each chosen factor, the level of information, knowledge of effects, and predictability they perceive to exist. Five items are of a more general kind, each requiring a single response. The instrument or a variant of it has been used by Downey, Hellriegel and Slocum (1975, 1977), Kopp and Litschert (1980), Spekman (1979) and Tung (1979).

8.71 Leifer and Huber (1977) describe a seven-item Perceived Environmental Uncertainty scale with supportive factor analytic data. Items are of the kind: How often do you know what to expect in your dealings with other people or organizations?

8.72 The same authors use a 22-item measure of Organicness, partially derived from Duncan (1971a). This is based upon the organic–mechanistic distinction (see also 8.57) and is operationalized through six scales: Hierarchy of Authority, Impersonality in Decision-Making, Participation in Work Decisions, Formalization, Division of Labor, and Participation in Strategic Decisions.

8.73 The Management System Questionnaire described by Keller, Slocum and Susman (1974) and Keller (1978) is also designed to tap the organic-mechanistic dimension. It is intended for use with senior managers, and four indices are recommended: Impersonal Hierarchy, Group Decision-Making, Rules for Decision-Making, and a composite score called Organic Management System. The items are presented in full.

8.74 Meadows (1980a, b) has described a nine-item Organicity interview schedule to tap the Sharing of Tasks, Supportiveness of Communication, and Members' Contributions to Decisions.

8.75 A ten-item measure of Preferred Organizational Structure reflecting the organic-mechanistic dimension is described by Bourgeois, McAllister and Mitchell (1978). Some validity evidence is presented from three experimental studies, and items are given in full.

8.76 A Scale of Support for Innovation was developed by Siegel and Kaemmerer (1978) to measure characteristics of organizations that foster or inhibit creativity. In its final version the instrument has three intercorrelated dimensions: Support for Creativity (24 items), Tolerance of Differences (32 items), and Personal Commitment (8 items).

8.77 A six-item Control System Responsiveness Scale is introduced by Kopelman (1976) and Kopelman and Thompson (1976), to measure perceptions of the relationship between organizational rewards (e.g. salary or promotion) and performance. The items were selected on the basis of factor analysis and are given in full.

8.78 Gavin and Maynard (1975) describe a measure of Perceptions of Corporate Social Responsibility. Factor analysis revealed two dimensions: Concern for the Environment (eight items) and Equal Work Opportunity (four items, relating to race, sex, religion and ethnic origin).

8.79 A measure of Racial Awareness was developed by Bass, Cascio, McPherson and Tragash (1976). The construct refers to "the recognition of issues, forces and behaviors that impede the full utilization of black employees in a predominantly white organization" (page 357). In its final form the instrument contains 20 items equally distributed across five dimensions. These are labelled: System Biased, Policy Implementation Limited, Black Employees Competent, Need Inclusion, and New Self-Esteem.

8.80 Zohar (1980) has constructed and validated a 40-item Safety Climate measure, which reflects employees' perceptions about the relative importance of safe conduct in their occupational behaviour. Eight factors are covered: Perceived Importance of Safety Programmes, Perceived Management Attitudes towards Safety, Perceived Effects of Safe Conduct on Promotion, Perceived Level of Risk at Workplace, Perceived Effects of Required Work Pace on Safety, Perceived Status of Safety Officer, Perceived Effects of Safe Conduct on Social Status, and Perceived Status of Safety Committee.

9 Leadership Style and Perceptions of Others

The scales considered in this chapter are all directed towards obtaining descriptions of salient individuals or groups within organizations. Following the central historical interest in the topic by organizational and occupational psychologists, by far the most common focus is on individuals in supervisory, managerial or other leadership positions. Here the Leader Behavior Description Questionnaire (Form XII, Stogdill, 1963) (9.1), the Supervisory Behavior Description Questionnaire (Fleishman, 1953a, 1957a) (9.2), the Leader Opinion Questionnaire (Fleishman, 1953b, 1957b) (9.3), and the Least Preferred Co-worker scale (Fiedler, 1967) (9.4) stand out as being the most frequently used in recent empirical research. This has led to the accumulation of a large amount of information about their psychometric properties and correlates.

The other scales accorded major entries in this chapter (9.5 to 9.12) have been used less frequently, and as a result they lack comprehensive supportive evidence. Some are alternatives to the more established scales named above, whereas others cover such potentially important constructs as Peer Leadership, Group Atmosphere, Leader Reward Behaviour, Conflict Resolution Styles, and Group Functioning.

The final section of the chapter follows the procedure adopted throughout the book. We set out briefly a further 20 measures which cover topics within the present field. Their content is summarized and references are provided.

9.1 Leader Behavior Description Questionnaire Form XII

Source: Stogdill, 1963

The Leader Behavior Description Questionnaire Form XII (LBDQ XII) was designed to obtain descriptions of individuals' leadership behaviour from the people whom they supervise. It is intended for use with any leader in any type of organization, provided the followers have the opportunity to observe his or her behaviour as a leader of their own group. Form XII rather than earlier versions of the LBDQ is the focus here since this has been most frequently used during our search period. It evolved from work initiated in the 1940's (e.g. Hemphill, 1949), which also gave rise to the Supervisory Behavior Description Questionnaire (SBDQ, Fleishman, 1953a, 1957a) (9.2) and the Leader Opinion Questionnaire (LOQ, Fleishman, 1953b, 1957b) (9.3).

The LBDQ XII was developed to cover 12 aspects of leadership behaviour, which are defined as follows: (1) *Representation*—speaks and acts as the representative of the group; (2) *Demand Reconciliation*—reconciles conflicting demands and reduces disorder in the system; (3) *Tolerance of Uncertainty*—is able to tolerate uncertainty and postponement without anxiety or upset; (4) *Persuasiveness*—uses persuasion and argument effectively; (5) *Initiating Structure*—clearly defines his or her own role, and lets followers know what is expected of them; (6) *Tolerance of Freedom*—allows followers scope for initiative, decision and action; (7) *Role Assumption*—actively exercises the leadership role rather than surrendering leadership to others; (8) *Consideration*—has regard for the comfort, well-being and contribution of his or her followers; (9) *Produc-*

tion Emphasis—applies pressure for output; (10) *Predictive Accuracy*—shows foresight and the ability to predict outcomes; (11) *Integration*—maintains a close knit group and resolves inter-member conflicts; (12) *Superior Orientation*—maintains good relations with supervisors, has influence with them and is striving for advancement.

The instrument comprises 100 items, 20 of which are reverse-scored, each with a five-point response dimension running from Always to Never, scored 5 to 1 respectively and summed within each sub-scale. The first, second, tenth and eleventh sub-scales consist of five items, the remainder of ten. The items from each sub-scale are systematically distributed throughout the instrument.

Means and standard deviations abstracted from the source document are presented in tabular form below, together with cited Kuder-Richardson internal reliabilities values (IR).

	235 Army Officers			185 Administrative Officers			55 Corporation Presidents		
Sub-scale	Mean	s.d	IR	Mean	s.d	IR	Mean	s.d.	IR
(1) Representation	20.0	3.0	0.82	19.9	2.8	0.85	20.5	1.8	0.54
(2) Demand Reconciliation	–	–	–	–	–	–	20.6	2.7	0.59
(3) Tolerance of Uncertainty	36.2	4.7	0.58	35.6	4.6	0.66	35.9	5.4	0.79
(4) Persuasiveness	38.3	6.2	0.84	37.9	5.9	0.85	40.1	4.2	0.69
(5) Initiating Structure	38.6	5.7	0.79	39.7	4.5	0.75	38.5	5.0	0.77
(6) Tolerance of Freedom	35.9	6.5	0.81	36.3	5.3	0.79	38.9	4.9	0.84
(7) Role Assumption	42.7	6.1	0.85	42.7	5.3	0.84	42.7	3.5	0.57
(8) Consideration	37.1	5.6	0.76	36.9	6.5	0.87	41.5	4.0	0.78
(9) Production Emphasis	36.3	5.1	0.70	35.8	5.7	0.79	38.9	4.4	0.71
(10) Predictive Accuracy	18.1	2.1	0.76	17.8	2.1	0.82	20.1	1.8	0.84
(11) Integration	19.5	2.6	0.73	19.1	2.7	0.79	–	–	–
(12) Superior Orientation	39.9	4.9	0.64	39.1	5.1	0.75	43.2	3.1	0.66

Across the nine samples originally described, the internal reliability of the 12 sub-scales is generally acceptable, though it is characteristically lower or less stable for Representation, Demand Reconciliation, Tolerance of Uncertainty and Superior Orientation. No analyses of the relationships among the scales, nor multivariate analyses to explore scale independence, are described in the source publication.

A feature of recent investigations with the LBDQ XII is that rarely has the complete instrument been used. All investigators have administered sub-scales 5 (Initiating Structure) and 8 (Consideration), and occasional use has been made of sub-scales 6, 7, 9 and 11. The description which follows reflects this bias by being concerned mainly with sub-scales 5 and 8.

Greene, Nebeker and Boni (1976), Ilgen and Fujii (1976), Mitchell, Larson and Greene (1977) and Rush, Thomas and Lord (1977) have provided descriptive statistics from student subjects in simulated studies (the last-named using the full measure), but recent information on means and standard deviations from full-time employees is relatively scarce. An exception is the study by Valenzi and Dessler (1978), who from a sample of some 250 varied respondents in two manufacturing firms report figures which convert to a mean for perceived Consideration of 35.6 (s.d. 7.8) and for Initiating Structure of 39.7 (s.d. 7.6). The correlation between the two sub-scales was 0.58, and both were associated negatively (-0.46 and -0.32 respectively) with Role Ambiguity (Rizzo, House and Lirtzman, 1970) (8.15). In a sub-analysis of the same data Dessler and Valenzi (1977) present figures for 25 supervisors and 47 assemblers which yield means for Consideration of 31.2 (s.d. 9.1) and 37.2 (s.d. 6.2) respectively, and for Initiating Structure of 38.1 (s.d. 6.4) and 40.4 (s.d. 8.8).

Wexley and Nemeroff (1975) obtained responses to four sub-scales of the LBDQ XII from samples of 37 and 43 hospital employees (in nursing, administration, supplies and maintenance), whose immediate first-line supervisors had previously undertaken training in order to improve their consideration and integrating skills, with 34 employees forming a control group. For Consideration the means across these three groups respectively were: 34.12 (s.d. 7.57), 35.38 (s.d. 5.10) and 30.53 (s.d. 7.43); for Integration 16.70 (s.d. 4.36), 15.68 (s.d. 4.20) and 14.21 (s.d. 5.21); for Production Emphasis 29.58 (s.d. 7.00), 27.73 (s.d. 5.28) and 27.94 (s.d. 6.64); and for Initiating Structure 37.09 (s.d. 6.51), 36.32 (s.d. 5.54) and 34.35 (s.d. 6.78).

A larger proportion of published studies include details of reliability or factor structure, and the following are typical. Schriesheim and Stogdill (1975), with a sample of 230 hourly paid university employees, report Kuder-Richardson internal reliability coefficients of 0.90 and 0.78 for the Consideration and Initiating Structure sub-scales respectively. A factor analysis with varimax rotation gave four primary factors, the first two of which corresponded to the constructs in question. A comparison with parallel factor analyses of responses to an earlier version of the LBDQ and to the Supervisory Behavior Description Questionnaire (9.2) were interpreted as showing that the LBDQ XII gave the most clearly interpretable structure. Greene (1975) administered the same two LBDQ sub-scales on three occasions (approximately a month apart) to the immediate subordinates of each of 103 managers from a variety of organizations. Correlations among the Consideration scores obtained on the three measurement occasions ranged from 0.68 to 0.78 and for Initiating Structure from 0.58 to 0.73.

Szilagyi and Keller (1976), with a sample of 192 male managerial engineering and supervisory employees in a manufacturing organization, obtained a Spearman-Brown internal reliability coefficient of 0.89 for Consideration and 0.87 for Initiating Structure. The sub-scales were correlated one to another (0.31) and with their counterparts from the SBDQ (9.2); for Consideration the latter correlation was 0.86 and for Initiating Structure it was 0.50. Johns (1978a) reports alpha coefficients of internal reliability of 0.86 and 0.75 respectively for Consideration and Initiating Structure with a sample of 232 shop-floor French Canadian employees. Using the same index of reliability Valenzi and Dessler (1978) report coefficients of 0.86 and 0.87 for the two sub-scales, and Sheridan and Vredenburgh (1978a, b) with a sample of 372 nurses record 0.82 for both. The sub-scales intercorrelated 0.42 in this latter study, but 0.59 with a sub-set of 209 respondents (Sheridan and Vredenburgh, 1979). Alpha coefficients between 0.80 and 0.90 are reported by Schriesheim, Kinicki and Schriesheim (1979) in research with 230 blue-collar and 409 white-collar employees.

Numerous correlates of perceived Consideration and Initiating Structure have been reported. For example, Evans (1974), Schriesheim, Kinicki, and Schriesheim (1979) and Valenzi and Dessler (1978) showed significant relationships with Role Ambiguity and Role Conflict (Rizzo, House and Lirtzman, 1970) (8.15, 8.16); and Aldag and Brief (1975) reported a correlation of -0.30 between rated leader Consideration and Blood's measure of non-Protestant Work Ethic (7.4). By far the most widely associated variable, however, has been Job Satisfaction, with rated Consideration typically showing a stronger positive relationship than Initiating Structure. For example, correlations with total JDI Satisfaction scores (3.3) in research with 308 managerial and clerical employees were 0.68 and 0.18 for the two sub-scales respectively (Schriesheim, Kinicki and Schriesheim, 1979). Further information on the correlates of the sub-scales can be obtained from the substantial published reviews of research in this area, which are referenced in the penultimate paragraph of this entry. Earlier experimental validation is described by Stogdill (1969).

Other studies using the LBDQ XII (or its earlier version, the LBDQ) but which generally provide less detail of its characteristics or involve modifications are those by Aldag and Brief (1977), Bartol and Wortman (1975), Bons and Fiedler (1976), Downey, Sheridan and Slocum (1975), Durand and Nord (1976), Gilmore, Beehr and Richter

(1979), Greene (1979), Greene and Schriesheim (1980), Hammer and Dachler (1975), Herman, Dunham and Hulin (1975), Herold (1974), Hunt, Osborn and Larson (1975), Kavanagh (1975), Larson, Hunt and Osborn (1976), Mitchell, Larson and Greene (1977), Mobley, Hand, Baker and Meglino (1979), Moore and Rickel (1980), Oldham (1976), Osborn and Hunt (1975), Osborn and Vicars (1976), Petty and Pryor (1974), Pfeffer and Salancik (1975), Schriesheim (1980), Schriesheim and Murphy (1976), Schriesheim and Schriesheim (1980), Schriesheim and Von Glinow (1977), Schriesheim, House and Kerr (1976), Schuler (1976), Sgro, Worchel, Pence and Orban (1980), Stinson and Johnson (1975), Stinson and Tracy (1974), Weed and Mitchell (1980), Weed, Mitchell and Moffit (1976), and Yunker and Hunt (1976).

Any assessment of the LBDQ XII should distinguish between an evaluation of the instrument as a 12-dimensional measure, and an evaluation of its sub-scales of Consideration and Initiating Structure. With respect to the full version there exists a scarcity of information in the recent literature. Researchers have not used many of the sub-scales and hence information on means, standard deviations, correlates, reliability and the underlying structure of the instrument as a whole has not accumulated.

In contrast the sub-scales of Consideration and Initiating Structure have been widely deployed. Some normative information is available, and there is extensive evidence documenting good reliability across a wide range of samples. Correlational field studies and laboratory and field experimental research have provided useful validational evidence. Two problems should however be raised. The first concerns the theoretical independence of these two sub-scales. In practice they have often been found to be positively intercorrelated. Factor analytic studies have nevertheless tended to support the separate identity of these two dimensions (e.g. Schriesheim and Stogdill, 1975). Readers wishing to pursue this and other issues reflecting on the LBDQ XII are referred to existing review papers, which consider the measure in greater detail than is possible here. An authoritative assessment is provided by Korman (1966), and this was updated by Kerr and Schriesheim (1974) and Schriesheim and Kerr (1974, 1977). Also of interest are papers by Bish and Schriesheim (1974), Schriesheim (1979), Schriesheim, House and Kerr (1976), Kerr, Schriesheim, Murphy and Stogdill (1974), and the book by Stogdill (1974).

The second problem concerns the positive relationship between leaders' Consideration and subordinates' Satisfaction with Work or with Supervision, which is characteristically shown in the literature. It should not go unnoticed that some of the items which form the Consideration sub-scale appear in a very similar form in measures of Satisfaction. Findings in this respect may therefore be somewhat tautologous (Warr and Wall, 1975). This point has been extended and demonstrated empirically by Schriesheim, Kinicki and Schriesheim (1979) who showed that social desirability factors substantially influence correlations with reported Consideration but that Initiating Structure appears to be relatively unaffected by this bias.

Items

Items comprising the 12 sub-scales are as follows: Representation 1, 11, 21, 31, 41; Demand Reconciliation 51, 61, 71, 81, 91; Tolerance of Uncertainty 2, 12, 22, 32, 42, 52, 62, 72, 82, 92; Persuasiveness 3, 13, 23, 33, 43, 53, 63, 73, 83, 93; Initiating Structure 4, 14, 24, 34, 44, 54, 64, 74, 84, 94; Tolerance of Freedom 5, 15, 25, 35, 45, 55, 65, 75, 85, 95; Role Assumption 6, 16, 26, 36, 46, 56, 66, 76, 86, 96; Consideration, 7, 17, 27, 37, 47, 57, 67, 77, 87, 97; Production Emphasis 8, 18, 28, 38, 48, 58, 68, 78, 88, 98; Predictive Accuracy 9, 29, 49, 59, 89; Integration 19, 39, 69, 79, 99; Superior Orientation 10, 20, 30, 40, 50, 60, 70, 80, 90, 100.

1. Acts as the spokesperson of the group
2. Waits patiently for the results of a decision
3. Makes pep talks to stimulate the group
4. Lets group members know what is expected of them
5. Allows the members complete freedom in their work
6. Is hesitant about taking initiative in the group (R)
7. Is friendly and approachable
8. Encourages overtime work
9. Makes accurate decisions
10. Gets along well with the people above him or her
11. Publicizes the activities of the group
12. Becomes anxious when he or she cannot find out what is coming next (R)
13. His or her arguments are convincing
14. Encourages the use of uniform procedures
15. Permits the members to use their own judgment in solving problems
16. Fails to take necessary action (R)
17. Does little things to make it pleasant to be a member of the group
18. Stresses being ahead of competing groups
19. Keeps the group working together as a team
20. Keeps the group in good standing with higher authority
21. Speaks as the representative of the group
22. Accepts defeat in stride
23. Argues persuasively for his or her point of view
24. Tries out his or her ideas in the group
25. Encourages initiative in the group members
26. Lets other persons take away his or her leadership in the group (R)
27. Puts suggestions made by the group into operation
28. Needles members for greater effort

29. Seems able to predict what is coming next
30. Is working hard for a promotion
31. Speaks for the group when visitors are present
32. Accepts delays without becoming upset
33. Is a very persuasive talker
34. Makes his or her attitudes clear to the group
35. Lets the members do their work the way they think best
36. Lets some members take advantage of him or her (R)
37. Treats all group members as his or her equals
38. Keeps the work moving at a rapid pace
39. Settles conflicts when they occur in the group
40. His or her superiors act favourably on most of his or her suggestions
41. Represents the group at outside meetings
42. Becomes anxious when waiting for new developments (R)
43. Is very skillful in an argument
44. Decides what shall be done and how it will be done
45. Assigns a task, then lets the members handle it
46. Is the leader of the group in name only (R)
47. Give advance notice of changes
48. Pushes for increased production
49. Things usually turn out as he or she predicts
50. Enjoys the privileges of his or her position
51. Handles complex problems efficiently
52. Is able to tolerate postponement and uncertainty
53. Is not a very convincing talker (R)
54. Assigns group members to particular tasks
55. Turns the members loose on a job, and lets them go to it
56. Backs down when he or she ought to stand firm (R)
57. Keeps to himself or herself (R)
58. Asks the members to work harder
59. Is accurate is predicting the trend of events
60. Gets his or her superiors to act for the welfare of the group members
61. Gets swamped by details (R)
62. Can wait just so long, then blows up (R)
63. Speaks from a strong inner conviction
64. Makes sure that his or her part in the group is understood by the group members
65. Is reluctant to allow the members any freedom of action (R)
66. Lets some members have authority that he or she should keep (R)
67. Looks out for the personal welfare of group members
68. Permits the members to take it easy in their work (R)
69. Sees to it that the work of the group is co-ordinated
70. His or her word carries weight with superiors
71. Gets things all tangled up (R)
72. Remains calm when uncertain about coming events
73. Is an inspiring talker
74. Schedules the work to be done
75. Allows the group a high degree of initiative
76. Takes full charge when emergencies arise

77. Is willing to make changes
78. Drives hard when there is a job to be done
79. Helps group members settle their differences
80. Gets what he or she asks for from his or her superiors
81. Can reduce a madhouse to system and order
82. Is able to delay action until the proper time occurs
83. Persuades others that his or her ideas are to their advantage
84. Maintains definite standards of performance
85. Trusts members to exercise good judgement
86. Overcomes attempts made to challenge his or her leadership
87. Refuses to explain his or her action (R)
88. Urges the group to beat its previous record
89. Anticipates problems and plans for them
90. Is working his or her way to the top
91. Gets confused when too many demands are made of him or her (R)
92. Worries about the outcomes of any new procedures (R)
93. Can inspire enthusiasm for a project
94. Asks that group members follow standard rules and regulations
95. Permits the group to set its own pace
96. Is easily recognized as the leader of the group
97. Acts without consulting the group (R)
98. Keeps the group working up to capacity
99. Maintains a closely knit group
100. Maintains cordial relations with superiors

Responses

Always; Often; Occasionally; Seldom; Never; scored 5 to 1 respectively.

9.2   Supervisory Behavior Description Questionnaire

Source: Fleishman, 1953a, 1957a

The Supervisory Behavior Description Questionnaire (SBDQ) shares its history with the LBDQ XII. Both are developments from earlier work on the measurement of leadership as described in the introduction to entry 9.1. Like the LBDQ XII, the scale is designed to measure individuals' leadership behaviour through descriptions from those who they supervise. However, the instrument is more focussed than the LBDQ XII, being designed to measure only the dimensions of leaders' Consideration and Initiating Structure. As previously measured these dimensions were found to be moderately intercorrelated, and, to use Fleishman's (1953a) words, "some reorganization of the items into relatively more independent categories of leader behavior, therefore, seemed necessary" (p. 2).

The instrument consists of 48 items, 28 of which tap Consideration and 20 Initiating Structure, and respondents record their descriptions of their supervisors' behaviour. The initial sample of respondents was a group of foremen, so that items are worded in terms of foremen's perceptions of their supervisors; minor changes in wording are necessary for other groups. Twelve of the Consideration items and two of the Initiating Structure items are reverse-scored, and a total is computed for each sub-scale. Each item has five response alternatives, scored 4 to 0, but three different sets of verbal anchors are used. Items from the two sub-scales are interspersed in presentation.

In order to obtain independent sub-scales, 136 items were first administered to a pre-test sample of 100 foremen and examined in terms of the Wherry-Gaylord rationale (Wherry and Gaylord, 1943; Wherry, Campbell and Perloff, 1951). Forty-eight items were retained and form the SBDQ. This was then administered to a sample of 122 foremen and 394 non-supervisory employees. For the sample of foremen the means for Consideration and Initiating Structure were 82.3 (s.d. 15.5) and 51.5 (s.d. 8.8) respectively, and the Spearman-Brown internal reliabilities were 0.92 and 0.68. The correlation between the sub-scales was −0.02. For the sample of non-supervisory employees no means are reported in the source publication, but the Spearman-Brown internal reliability coefficients for Consideration and Initiating Structure were 0.98 and 0.78 respectively, with a correlation between the sub-scales of −0.33. Test–retest correlations from a sample of 18 subordinates describing the same foreman on two occasions 11 months apart yielded a value of 0.87 for Consideration and 0.75 for Initiating Structure. Further test–retest data and inter-rater agreement statistics are given in Fleishman (1957a).

Only a small minority of reports of SBDQ usage during our search period presents means and standard deviations, and those which do are usually based on small selected samples (e.g. Matsui, Ohtsuka and Kikuchi, 1978; Miles and Petty, 1977; Petty and Lee, 1975) or employ modifications to the original instrument (e.g. Matsui, Ohtsuka and Kikuchi, 1978; Weiss, 1978). Readers requiring detailed descriptive statistics are therefore referred to earlier publications, most notably that of Fleishman (1972).

Rather more evidence has emerged with respect to reliability and factor structure. Downey, Sheridan and Slocum (1976), with samples of 68 managers and 68 machine operators who completed the measure on two occasions a year apart, obtained alpha coefficients for the Consideration sub-scale ranging from 0.78 to 0.81, and for Initiating Structure from 0.89 to 0.93. Test–retest reliability for Consideration was 0.77 for the managers and 0.68 for the machine operators; for

Initiating Structure it was 0.63 in both cases. The average correlation between the two sub-scales was 0.01 for the machine operators and 0.47 for the managers. Szilagyi and Sims (1974a) describe a factor analysis of responses from 1161 mainly female employees in a medical centre. This yielded two factors corresponding to Consideration and Initiating Structure, very similar to those originally reported by Fleishman (1953a) and subsequently by Tscheulin (1973). Factor congruency indices (phi-coefficients) for Consideration were 0.91 and 0.95 in relation to the two previous studies respectively, and for Initiating Structure 0.80 and 0.93. Spearman-Brown internal reliability coefficients were 0.93 for Consideration and 0.89 for Initiating Structure. (See also Szilagyi and Sims, 1974b; Sims, Szilagyi and McKemey, 1976.) Rather less clear-cut results were obtained by Schriesheim and Stogdill (1975) in a factor analytic study of 230 hourly paid university employees (see also Schriesheim, House and Kerr, 1976). Whilst obtaining Kuder-Richardson internal reliabilities of 0.81 and 0.68 for Consideration and Initiating Structure respectively, neither varimax rotation nor a hierarchical factor analysis (Wherry, 1959) provided the expected two-factor solution.

Recent evidence on the correlates of leaders' Consideration and Initiating Structure is compatible with earlier findings, as reviewed for example by Kerr and Schriesheim (1974) and Schriesheim, House and Kerr (1976). The two sub-scales are generally observed to be weakly associated with each other, whereas the corresponding LBDQ XII sub-scales (9.1) are more often found to be moderately positively inter-correlated. Consideration as measured by the SBDQ is strongly and positively related to Job Satisfaction, particularly where the latter is specific to supervisors, whereas Initiating Structure shows a weak and sometimes negative association.

Two investigations serve to illustrate these latter generalizations. Petty and Lee (1975) describe a study of four groups of non-academic university employees (N=50, 54, 50 and 10). In all cases perceived Consideration was positively correlated with measures of Satisfaction with Work (median 0.51, range 0.29 to 0.61) and Satisfaction with Supervision (median 0.79, range 0.73 to 0.81) (both Satisfaction indices come from the Job Descriptive Index (3.3)), but leaders' Initiating Structure was not generally associated with these Satisfaction scores. Szilagyi and Sims (1974b) used the same measures with 53 administrative, 240 professional, 117 technical and 231 service employees in a medical centre. The median correlation of leaders' Consideration with Satisfaction with Work was 0.37 (range 0.32 to 0.42), and with Satisfaction with Supervision it was 0.78 (range 0.75 to 0.83). However, in the case of Initiating Structure there were substantial differences between the sub-samples, correlations with the two measures of Satisfaction ranging between −0.33 and 0.38 (median −0.10) across the employee groups.

Other studies reporting the use of the SBDQ or a modification of it include those by Arvey and Neel (1974), Badin (1974), Beatty (1974), Greller (1978), Nystrom (1978), Petty and Miles (1976), Schriesheim and Von Glinow (1977), Sims and Szilagyi (1975a), Szilagyi and Keller (1976), and Weiss (1977).

Readers requiring additional information are advised to consult the theoretical and empirical reviews offered by Korman (1966), Fleishman (1973), Kerr and Schriesheim (1974), Schriesheim and Kerr (1974, 1977), Schriesheim, House and Kerr (1976), Kerr, Schriesheim, Murphy and Stogdill (1974), and Schriesheim and Stogdill (1975). Finally, as was the case for the LBDQ, it should be noted that the Consideration sub-scale includes items which appear in similar form in measures of Satisfaction. Relationships between these two variables may therefore be somewhat tautologous.

Items

Note that items from the two sub-scales are interspersed in presentation.

Consideration

1. He refuses to give in when people disagree with him (R)
2. He does personal favours for the foremen under him
3. He expresses appreciation when one of us does a good job
4. He is easy to understand
5. He demands more than we can do (R)
6. He helps his foremen with their personal problems
7. He criticizes his foremen in front of others (R)
8. He stands up for his foremen even though it makes him unpopular
9. He insists that everything be done his way (R)
10. He sees that a foreman is rewarded for a job well done
11. He rejects suggestions for changes (R)
12. He changes the duties of people under him without first talking it over with them (R)
13. He treats people under him without considering their feelings (R)
14. He tries to keep the foremen under him in good standing with those in higher authority
15. He resists changes in ways of doing things (R)
16. He "rides" the foreman who makes a mistake (R)
17. He refuses to explain his actions (R)
18. He acts without consulting his foremen first (R)
19. He stresses the importance of high morale among those under him
20. He backs up his foreman in their actions
21. He is slow to accept new ideas (R)

22. He treats all his foremen as his equal
23. He criticizes a specific act rather than a particular individual
24. He is willing to make changes
25. He makes those under him feel at ease when talking with him
26. He is friendly and can be easily approached
27. He puts suggestions that are made by foremen under him into operation
28. He gets the approval of his foremen on important matters before going ahead

Initiating Structure

29. He encourages overtime work
30. He tries out his new ideas
31. He rules with an iron hand
32. He criticizes poor work
33. He talks about how much should be done
34. He encourages slow-working foremen to greater effort
35. He waits for his foremen to push new ideas before he does (R)
36. He assigns people under him to particular tasks
37. He asks for sacrifices from his foremen for the good of the entire department
38. He insists that his foremen follow standard ways of doing things in every detail
39. He sees to it that people under him are working up to their limits
40. He offers new approaches to problems
41. He insists that he be informed on decisions made by foremen under him
42. He lets others do their work the way they think best (R)
43. He stresses being ahead of competing work groups
44. He "needles" foremen under him for greater effort
45. He decides in detail what shall be done and how it shall be done
46. He emphasizes the meeting of deadlines
47. He asks foremen who have slow groups to get more out of their groups
48. He emphasizes the quantity of work

Responses

Items 1, 3, 4, 8, 9, 10, 11, 13, 14, 15, 20, 21, 22, 23, 24, 25, 26, 27, 28, 31, 32, 35, 36, 37, 38, 39, 41, 42 and 45 use the response alternatives: Always; Often; Occasionally; Seldom; Never. Items 2, 5, 6, 7, 12, 16, 17, 18, 30, 34, 40 and 47 use the responses: Often; Fairly often; Occasionally; Once in a while; Very seldom. Items 19, 29, 33, 43, 44, 46, and 48 use the responses: A great deal; Fairly much; To some degree; Comparatively little; Not at all. In all three cases the verbal anchors are assigned weights of 4, 3, 2, 1 or 0 respectively.

9.3   Leadership Opinion Questionnaire

Source: Fleishman, 1953b, 1957b

The Leadership Opinion Questionnaire (LOQ) is a measure of leaders' opinions about desirable leadership behaviour. It is a vehicle for asking the respondent how he or she *should* behave as a supervisor, and is focussed on the constructs of Consideration and Initiating Structure. As the use of these two terms suggests, the LOQ derives from the same research programme as the Leader Behavior Description Questionnaire (LBDQ) (Stogdill, 1963) (9.1) and the Supervisory Behavior Description Questionnaire (SBDQ) (Fleishman, 1953a 1957a) (9.2). It is more similar to the SBDQ, being identically restricted to two dimensions of leadership and having all but six of its items in direct parallel. It differs from both these other instruments in its focus on the self rather than perceptions of another, and on expressed opinions rather than descriptions of behaviour.

The instrument contains 40 items, equally divided between sub-scales of Consideration and Initiating Structure. Ten of the Consideration items and two of the Initiating Structure items are reverse-scored, and a total is computed for each sub-scale. Each item has five response alternatives, scored 4 to 0, but three different sets of verbal anchors are used. Items from the two sub-scales are interspersed in presentation. Eighteen of the 20 items measuring Consideration and 16 of the items for Initiating Structure are directly parallel to those in the SBDQ.

The 40 items comprising the LOQ were selected from 110 administered in a pretest with 100 foremen. Two criteria for selection were used: the response distributions for the items as revealed by the pretest; and factor loadings of parallel items obtained in the development of the SBDQ (note that direct factor loadings were not used). Administrations of the LOQ to samples of foremen and other employees yielded data on means, standard deviations, scale reliability and sub-scale intercorrelations, of which an illustrative selection is summarized below; internal reliability (I.R.) is there assessed by Spearman-Brown correlations. Further information is provided in the source publication, and in the subsequently produced manuals (Fleishman, 1960, 1963, 1969).

	Consideration			Initiating Structure			Sub-scale inter-correlation
	Mean	s.d.	I.R.	Mean	s.d.	I.R.	
122 Foremen	53.9	7.2	0.70	53.3	7.8	0.79	−0.01
46 Foremen	54.7	7.7		54.4	5.6		−0.07
394 Workers*	57.0	5.5	0.89	44.2	3.9	0.88	0.04

*Scale modified to measure "how an ideal foreman should lead".

Lefkowitz (1974), with 312 police personnel, obtained means of 56.13 (s.d. 9.18) and 47.15 (s.d. 8.37) for Consideration and Initiating Structure respectively. Palmer (1974), in a study of 90 middle managers, obtained a correlation of −0.11 between the two sub-scales, but found no relationship between either measure and performance ratings obtained from the respondents' immediate subordinates (first-line managers). Kuehl, Di Marco and Wims (1975), using half of the LOQ items with a sample of 245 first-line male supervisors, obtained a correlation of −0.35 between the two sub-scales. Other investigations using the LOQ during our search period include Di Marco, Kuehl and Wims (1975), Nystrom (1978) and Oldham (1976).

Useful accounts of earlier evidence are provided by Buros (1965), Kerr and Schriesheim (1974), Kerr, Schriesheim, Murphy and Stogdill (1974), Korman (1966), and Weissenberg and Kavanagh (1972). These suggest that the LOQ successfully provides essentially independent indices of expressed Consideration and Initiating Structure each with reasonable reliability coefficients, but that the sub-scales typically yield less strong relationships with external criteria than parallel sub-scales from the SBDQ or LBDQ. Socially desirable responding on the LOQ may be one factor responsible for this difference.

Items

Note that items from the two sub-scales are interspersed in presentation.

For each item, choose the alternative which most nearly expresses your opinion on how frequently you *should* do what is described by that item. Always indicate what you, as a supervisor or manager, sincerely believe to be the desirable way to act.

Consideration

1. Refuse to compromise a point (R)
2. Do personal favors for people in the work group
3. Speak in a manner not to be questioned (R)
4. Ask for more than members of the work group can get done (R)
5. Help people in the work group with their personal problems
6. Stand up for those in the work group under you, even though it makes you unpopular with others
7. Insist that everything be done your way (R)
8. Reject suggestions for change (R)
9. Change the duties of people in the work group without first talking it over with them (R)
10. Resist changes in ways of doing things (R)
11. Refuse to explain your actions (R)
12. Act without consulting the work group (R)
13. Back up what people under you do

14. Be slow to accept new ideas (R)
15. Treat all people in the work group as your equal
16. Criticize a specific act rather than a particular member of the work group
17. Be willing to make changes
18. Put suggestions made by people in the work group into operation
19. Get the approval of the work group on important matters before going ahead
20. Give in to others in discussions with your work group

Initiating Structure

21. Encourage overtime work
22. Try out your own ideas in the work group
23. Rule with an iron hand
24. Criticize poor work
25. Talk about how much should be done
26. Encourage slow-working people in the work group to work harder
27. Wait for people in the work group to push new ideas (R)
28. Assign people in the work group to particular tasks
29. Ask for sacrifices from the men under you for the good of your entire section
30. Ask that people under you follow to the letter those standard routines handed down to you
31. Offer new approaches to problems
32. Put the section's welfare above the welfare of any member in it
33. Insist that you be informed on decisions made by people in the work group under you
34. Let others do their work the way they think best (R)
35. Stress being ahead of competing work groups
36. "Needle" people in the work group for greater effort
37. Emphasize meeting of deadlines
38. Decide in detail what shall be done and how it shall be done by the work group
39. Meet with the group at regularly scheduled times
40. See to it that people in the work group are working up to capacity

Responses

Items 1, 3, 6, 7, 8, 13, 14, 15, 16, 17, 18, 19, 23, 24, 27, 28, 30, 32, 33, 34, 38, 39, and 40 use the response alternatives: Always; Often; Occasionally; Seldom; Never. Items 2, 4, 5, 9, 11, 12, 20, 21, 22, 26, 29, and 31 have the alternatives: Often; Fairly often; Occasionally; Once in a while; Very seldom. Items 10, 25, 35, 36 and 37 use responses: A great deal; Fairly much; To some degree; Comparatively little; Not at all. In all three cases the verbal anchors are assigned weights of 4, 3, 2, 1 or 0 respectively.

9.4   Least Preferred Co-worker

Source: Fiedler, 1967

Fiedler's (1967) contingency model remains one of the most influential approaches to the study of leadership, and the Least Preferred Co-worker (LPC) scale provides the means to measure its central construct, that of leadership style or motivation. The ideas behind the LPC approach evolved from Fiedler's (1953, 1954, 1958) earlier work on person perception, where he was interested in the impact of personality dispositions upon perceptual styles.

A difficulty in providing a description of the Least Preferred Co-worker Scale arises from the fact that definitions of its focal construct have changed over the years, being repeatedly adjusted to reflect available empirical evidence. Paradoxically, the meaning of the construct has followed its measurement, rather than the measure being introduced to operationalize the construct. Fiedler and Chemers (1974) and others have pointed out that the meaning of LPC responses has proved difficult to interpret, and much discussion in the literature is devoted to the question of what the scale really measures. In view of this uncertainty we will use the account offered in the source publication, but draw attention to the fact that this is only one of several variations.

Fiedler (1967) describes the high LPC leader as one who "tells us in effect that the person with whom he is least able to work on a common task might still be reasonably nice, intelligent, competent, etc.. The low-LPC leader . . . says in effect that the person with whom he cannot work is uncooperative, unintelligent and incompetent, etc". (p. 44). This characteristic reflects an "implicit personality theory" in which "high-LPC leaders are concerned with having good interpersonal relations and gaining prominence and self-esteem through these interpersonal relations" and "low-LPC leaders are concerned with achieving success on assigned tasks even at the risk of having poor interpersonal relations" (p. 45). Fiedler concludes that the LPC score is a motivational index (see also Fiedler, 1972).

As Fiedler (1967) and Fox (1976) point out, there is no standard LPC instrument comprising a fixed number of specified items with a uniform response mode. More important to the measure is its basic rationale, and minor variations in procedure are usually seen as relatively inconsequential. The LPC scale given in the source publication consists of 16 items in the form of semantic differential response dimensions (Osgood, 1952), and this version has been the most frequently used.

The instructions ask the respondent to choose "the person with whom you had most difficulty in getting a job done", and then to describe that person through a series of items each consisting of paired adjectival antonyms separated by an eight-interval scale. One adjective is clearly favourable, the other unfavourable (e.g. Cooperative–Uncooperative; Intelligent–Unintelligent). The favourable end of each item carries a value of 8 and the unfavourable pole a value of 1. The positive and negative verbal anchors appear in varying order, with reverse-scoring as appropriate, and the LPC score is obtained by summing item scores.

Information on scale properties is given in only general terms in the source publication, and the absence of a standard LPC instrument has resulted in a variety of subsequent practices with respect to the number and choice of items and, to a lesser extent, in the response format. Scale scores across many studies are therefore not directly comparable. Fiedler (1967) reports that "the means for various samples, expressed as mean item scores, range from 3.19 to 4.13. This would be 63.8 to 82.6 on a 20-item scale" (p. 44). Internal reliability coefficients (of various types) are described as "uniformally high, ranging from 0.85 to 0.95", and test–retest correlations are indicated to range from 0.31 to 0.70.

Posthuma (1970) presents further normative data. Across 2014 real and role playing leaders he reports a mean for items of 3.17 (s.d. 1.05). Noting the diversity of practice with respect to scale length, and the predominance of use of the shorter versions, he recommends that "future research should be confined to the 16-item scale" (p. 10). For this version the mean was 62.40 (s.d. 16.80). Given the theoretically required identification of high- and low-LPC leaders, the corresponding cut-off points, selected to be one standard deviation above and below the mean respectively, were 79.20 and 45.60.

Bons and Fieldler (1976) with a sample of 115 infantry squad leaders report a mean for 16 items of 62. Larson and Rowland (1974) observed means for a 17-item version of 67.7 with 24 managers, 64.0 for male civil engineers, and 62.4, 71.2 and 59.3 respectively for three groups of university students (N=30, 49 and 44). Greene, Nebeker and Boni (1976) with 60 male students recorded a mean of 62.1, and Sashkin, Taylor and Tripathi (1974) means of 62.1 and 61.2 for office managers. Other reports of LPC use are of limited value for present purposes since they employ scale modifications or lack necessary detail. These include Bennett (1977a), Chapman (1975), Csoka (1974), Duffy, Shiflett and Downey (1977), Greene and Nebeker (1977), Hewett, O'Brien and Hornick (1974), Konar-Goldband, Rice and Monkarsh (1979), and Vecchio (1977).

Rather more information is available about reliability. In Fox's (1976) investigation 114 tax inspectors completed the 16-item instrument, with standard instructions, on two occasions four weeks apart. Test-retest correlations for the items ranged from 0.45 to 0.73 with a median of 0.57, and for the scale as a whole the value was 0.75. For 61 students using a 24-item version, the range of item test–retest correlations over a nine-week period ran from 0.37 to 0.76 with a median of 0.58; for the overall scale the correlation was 0.68. Bons and Fiedler (1976) with 153 infantry squad leaders obtained a correlation of 0.54 between scores on the 16-item LPC scale administered on two occasions six to nine months apart.

Stinson and Tracy (1974), using an unspecified version, report test–retest correlations of 0.49 between scores obtained from 30 students on occasions eight weeks apart, 0.23 over the same period for a group of 104 students, 0.73 with a sample of 24 industrial supervisors using a three-week interval, and 0.80 with 42 students over a three-week period. Using a test–retest interval of eight weeks they obtained similar co-efficients of 0.81 for a group of 13 supervisors, and 0.46 for 47 students. Schneier (1978) with 207 students recorded a test–retest correlation of 0.79 over a nine-week period, and Helmich (1975) with a 12-item LPC scale obtained a split-half internal reliability coefficient of 0.89 with a sample of 108 corporate presidents.

Empirical findings bearing on construct validity do not yield a clearly interpretable pattern. The relationship of LPC scores to indices of performance does not correspond uniformly to the differential predictions of Fiedler's contingency model (e.g. Hovey, 1974; Saha, 1979; Utecht and Heier, 1976; Vecchio, 1977, 1979). Nevertheless, training programmes based upon the model have been found to enhance leader performance (Csoka and Bons, 1978; Fiedler and Maher, 1979a, b).

Studies attempting to identify the meaning of the construct tapped by LPC scales through its association with known measures have yielded inconsistent results. Thus the proposal that the LPC scales are indirect measures of cognitive complexity is not clearly confirmed in the literature (Csoka, 1975; Evans and Dermer, 1974; Larson and Rowland, 1974; Rice and Chemers, 1975). Similarly the interpretation of LPC offered earlier, of high scorers being relationship-oriented and low scorers task-oriented, has not been consistently supported in studies using other measures of these constructs. Whilst Kuehl, Di Marco and Wims (1975) found that LPC scores correlated 0.35 and −0.38 with the leadership opinion dimensions of Consideration and Initiating Structure (from the LOQ, Fleishman, 1957b; 9.3), the findings of Stinson and Tracy (1974) fail to confirm the generality of such an association. In short, recent findings reflecting on the construct validity of LPC scales parallel earlier results in being somewhat contradictory, having fuelled rather than resolved controversy over the usefulness of the measure. Contrasting perspectives on the evidence are provided in reviews by Ashour, (1973a, b), Fiedler (1971), Graen, Alvarez, Orris and Martella (1970), Graen, Orris and Alvarez (1971), McMahon (1972), Rice (1978a, b; 1979), Schriesheim and Kerr (1977), and Schriesheim, Bannister and Money (1979).

Instructions and Items

Think of the person *with whom you can work least well*. He or she may be someone you work ·with now, or may be someone you knew in the past. He or she does not have to be the person you like least well, but should be the person with whom you had the most difficulty in getting a job done. Describe this person as he or she appears to you.

	8	7	6	5	4	3	2	1	
1. Pleasant	:_	:_	:_	:_	:_	:_	:_	:_	Unpleasant
2. Friendly	:_	:_	:_	:_	:_	:_	:_	:_	Unfriendly
3. Rejecting	:_	:_	:_	:_	:_	:_	:_	:_	Accepting (R)
4. Helpful	:_	:_	:_	:_	:_	:_	:_	:_	Frustrating
5. Unenthusiastic	:_	:_	:_	:_	:_	:_	:_	:_	Enthusiastic (R)
6. Tense	:_	:_	:_	:_	:_	:_	:_	:_	Relaxed (R)
7. Distant	:_	:_	:_	:_	:_	:_	:_	:_	Close (R)
8. Cold	:_	:_	:_	:_	:_	:_	:_	:_	Warm (R)
9. Cooperative	:_	:_	:_	:_	:_	:_	:_	:_	Uncooperative
10. Supportive	:_	:_	:_	:_	:_	:_	:_	:_	Hostile
11. Boring	:_	:_	:_	:_	:_	:_	:_	:_	Interesting (R)
12. Quarrelsome	:_	:_	:_	:_	:_	:_	:_	:_	Harmonious (R)
13. Self-Assured	:_	:_	:_	:_	:_	:_	:_	:_	Hesitant
14. Efficient	:_	:_	:_	:_	:_	:_	:_	:_	Inefficient
15. Gloomy	:_	:_	:_	:_	:_	:_	:_	:_	Cheerful (R)
16. Open	:_	:_	:_	:_	:_	:_	:_	:_	Guarded

9.5   Supervision

Source: Cammann, Fichman, Jenkins and Kesh, 1979; Seashore, Lawler, Mirvis and Cammann, 1982

The Michigan Organizational Assessment Questionnaire contains a number of scales to measure work attitudes and perceptions; see also 2.9, 3.8, 3.9, 3.10, 4.13, 6.2, 6.6, 8.6, and 9.11. Module 5 of the questionnaire, entitled Supervision, comprises 30 items to measure ten aspects of leadership which involve subordinates, as perceived by those subordinates. The ten aspects, with alpha coefficients of internal reliability as found on a sample of more than 400 employees, are as follows: Production Orientation (three items, 0.86); Control of Work (five items, 0.87);

Work Facilitation–Goal Setting (three items, 0.82); Work Facilitation–Problem Solving (two items, 0.83); Work Facilitation–Subordinate Relations (seven items, 0.93), Bias (two items, 0.77); Consideration (three items, 0.89); Participation (two items, 0.76); Decision Centralization (two items, 0.81); and Competence (one item). Responses are on a seven-point dimension, and mean values across items constitute the sub-scale scores.

Factor analysis revealed a clear identity for the Production Orientation and Bias sub-scales, where items loaded uniquely into separate factors, but items from the other sub-scales tended to load on a large general factor or more than one mixed factor. Intercorrelations presented in the source publication make it clear that there is considerable overlap between the sub-scales. For example, the three forms of Work Facilitation intercorrelate 0.65, 0.76, and 0.73; and they are themselves associated with Control of Work 0.75, 0.71 and 0.79 in the sequence given above. Another illustration of overlap is the recorded correlation of 0.69 between Consideration and Participation. For this reason the authors expect that, in addition to its use in full, "short forms of this module (e.g. sampling items from the Work Facilitation scales) will be used in many situations".

Items

Production Orientation

7. My supervisor demands that people give their best effort
26. My supervisor insists that subordinates work hard
11. My supervisor demands that subordinates do high quality work

Control of Work

9. My supervisor keeps informed about the work which is being done
2. My supervisor plans out work in advance
8. My supervisor handles the administrative parts of his or her job extremely well
24. My supervisor maintains high standards of performance
27. My supervisor knows the technical parts of his or her job extremely well

Work Facilitation–Goal Setting

6. My supervisor makes sure subordinates have clear goals to achieve
13. My supervisor makes sure subordinates know what has to be done
10. My supervisor makes it clear how I should do my job

Work Facilitation–Problem Solving

12. My supervisor helps me solve work-related problems
15. My supervisor helps me discover problems before they get too bad

Work Facilitation–Subordinate Relations

16. My supervisor keeps informed about the way subordinates think and feel about things
3. My supervisor keeps subordinates informed
17. My supervisor helps subordinates develop their skills
20. My supervisor has the respect of subordinates
23. My supervisor deals with subordinates well
4. My supervisor is always fair with subordinates
28. My supervisor tends to play favorites (R)

Bias

21. My supervisor is biased on the basis of race (R)
30. My supervisor is biased on the basis of sex (R)

Consideration

25. My supervisor helps subordinates with their personal problems
14. My supervisor is concerned about me as a person
18. My supervisor feels each subordinate is important as an individual

Participation

1. My supervisor encourages subordinates to participate in important decisions
5. My supervisor encourages people to speak up when they disagree with a decision

Decision Centralization

19. My supervisor makes most decisions without asking subordinates for their opinions
22. My supervisor makes important decisions without involving subordinates

Competence

29. My supervisor is competent

Responses

Strongly disagree; Disagree; Slightly disagree; Neither agree nor disagree; Slightly agree; Agree; Strongly agree; scored 1 to 7 respectively.

9.6   Supervisory and Peer Leadership

Source: Taylor and Bowers, 1972

This instrument covers four aspects of leadership, namely Support, Goal Emphasis, Work Facilitation and Interaction Facilitation. It is designed to obtain descriptions of the respondent's superior (Supervisory Leadership) and his peers (Peer Leadership), yielding eight indices. It forms part of the Survey of Organizations questionnaire

(Taylor and Bowers, 1972) (see 9.10 for more details, and 2.5 for another component), and the theoretical background to its four-fold focus is set out by Bowers and Seashore (1966).

The Supervisory Leadership measure comprises 13 items of which 3, 3, 4 and 3 respectively make up the four sub-scales. The Peer Leadership measure consists of 11 items, with the four sub-scales made up of 3, 2, 3 and 3 items respectively. In all cases sub-scale scores are calculated by taking the average item response on a five-point continuum; individual averages are then combined to yield a mean work-group score.

No means or standard deviations are presented in the source publication, but internal reliability data are cited for 325 work groups in an oil refinery. For Supervisory Support, Supervisory Goal Emphasis, Supervisory Work Facilitation, and Supervisory Interaction Facilitation the alpha coefficients (N=325 groups) were 0.94, 0.85, 0.88, and 0.89 respectively. For the same four dimensions of Peer Leadership the corresponding coefficients were 0.87, 0.70, 0.89 and 0.90 respectively. For seven samples totalling 1048 respondents, the Spearman-Brown reliability coefficients for Supervisory Support ranged from 0.90 to 0.93, for Supervisory Goal Emphasis from 0.85 to 0.91, for Supervisory Work Facilitation from 0.81 to 0.88, and for Supervisory Interaction Facilitation from 0.83 to 0.91. The respective ranges for the internal reliabilities of parallel scales measuring Peer Leadership were 0.83 to 0.92, 0.84 to 0.90, 0.89 to 0.93, and 0.78 to 0.95. Cluster analysis generally supported the a priori classification of the dimensions of leadership, but the scales were found to be highly intercorrelated (0.72 to 0.81 among the Managerial Leadership scales and 0.56 to 0.71 among the Peer Leadership scales) suggesting considerable overlap. Studies by Franklin (1975a, b) and Bowers and Hausser (1977) describe alternative analyses of the material which provides the basis for the source publication.

Other applications of the measure include those by Koch (1978, 1979) and Yunker and Hunt (1976). See also Schriesheim and Kerr (1977) for a more general review, and Butler and Jones (1979), James and Jones (1974, 1976), Jones, James and Bruni (1975), and Jones, James, Bruni and Sells (1979) for further empirical evidence on selected items included in the Psychological Climate Questionnaire (8.60).

Items

Supervisory Leadership

Support

1. How friendly and easy to approach is your supervisor?

2. When you talk with your supervisor, to what extent does he pay attention to what you're saying?
3. To what extent is your supervisor willing to listen to your problems?

Goal Emphasis

4. How much does your supervisor encourage people to give their best effort?
5. To what extent does your supervisor maintain high standards of performance?
6. To what extent does your supervisor set an example by working hard himself?

Work Facilitation

7. To what extent does your supervisor encourage subordinates to take action without waiting for detailed review and approval from him?
8. To what extent does your supervisor show you how to improve your performance?
9. To what extent does your supervisor provide the help you need so that you can schedule work ahead of time?
10. To what extent does your supervisor offer new ideas for solving job-related problems?

Interaction Facilitation

11. To what extent does your supervisor encourage the persons who work for him to work as a team?
12. To what extent does your supervisor encourage people who work for him to exchange opinions and ideas?
13. How often does your supervisor hold group meetings where the people who work for him can really discuss things together?

Peer Leadership

Support

1. How friendly or easy to approach are the persons in your work group?
2. When you talk with persons in your work group to what extent do they pay attention to what you're saying?
3. To what extent are persons in your work group willing to listen to your problems?

Goal Emphasis

4. How much do persons in your work group encourage each other to give their best effort?
5. To what extent do persons in your work group maintain high standards of performance?

Work Facilitation

6. To what extent do persons in your work group help you find ways to do a better job?
7. To what extent do persons in your work group provide the help you need so that you can plan, organize and schedule work ahead of time?

8. To what extent do persons in your work group offer each other new ideas for solving job-related problems?

Interaction Facilitation

9. How much do persons in your work group encourage each other to work as a team?
10. How much do persons in your work group emphasize a team goal?
11. To what extent do persons in your work group exchange opinions and ideas?

Responses

To a very little extent; To a little extent; To some extent; To a great extent; To a very great extent; scored 1 to 5 respectively. However, responses to item 13 of Supervisory Leadership are: Never; Once or twice per year; Three to six times per year; About once a month; More often than once per month; scored 1 to 5 respectively.

9.7   Leader Reward Behavior

Source: Sims and Szilagyi, 1975b

This instrument contains two sub-scales, of Positive Reward Behavior and Punitive Reward Behavior. These are designed to measure the extent to which a subordinate perceives that positive or negative rewards received through his supervisor reflect his job performance. Whereas the above reference is to the first published source, the instrument was previously developed by W. E. Scott, H. J. Reitz and R. D. Johnson, and was initially documented in a doctoral dissertation by Johnson (1973).

The Positive Reward Behavior sub-scale consists of 16 items and the Punitive Reward Behavior sub-scale of six items. Each item is in the form of a hypothetical statement: Your supervisor would do X if you did Y. Within each sub-scale items are worded in the same direction, such that agreement is indicative of a higher instance of the focal behaviour. Items from the two sub-scales are intermingled in use. Each item has seven reponse alternatives, but the source publication provides no details of these. In a subsequent use of the instrument (Keller and Szilagyi, 1978) it is indicated that the response dimension runs from Very false to Very true. Sub-scale scores are obtained by summing across items.

The source publication is based on 1161 paramedical and support personnel in a university medical centre, of which some 630 appear to have formed the basis for the main analyses. No means or standard deviations are reported, but the Spearman-Brown internal reliability coefficients were 0.93 for Positive Reward Behavior and 0.70 for Punitive Reward Behavior. A factor analysis (type and rotation unspecified) showed that all items loaded appropriately on two factors, which together explained 47% of the total variance.

For sub-samples of 53 administrative, 243 professional, 116 technical and 216 service personnel, the Positive Reward Behavior sub-scale was found to correlate positively with all five sub-scales of the Job Descriptive Index of Satisfaction (3.3), from 0.18 to 0.83 with a median of 0.42. Correlations were predictably higher with the Satisfaction with Supervisor sub-scale, ranging from 0.68 to 0.83, with a median of 0.75. For the professional, technical and service employees, perceptions of Positive Reward Behavior were positively associated (0.36, 0.30 and 0.13 respectively) with rated performance. The Punitive Reward Behavior Scale was generally independent of the Satisfaction sub-scales, and negatively but weakly correlated with rated performance for administrative (-0.34) and service personnel (-0.15).

Keller and Szilagyi (1976), with a sample of 192 managerial, engineering and supervisory manufacturing employees, report a mean for Positive Reward Behavior of 85.54 (s.d. 17.89) and for Punitive Reward Behavior of 24.00 (s.d. 4.62). The latter scale comprised only five items in this instance. A factor analysis is reported to have confirmed the two-component structure of the instrument, with congruency coefficients with original factor loadings of 0.95 for Positive Reward Behavior and 0.91 for Punitive Reward Behavior. Spearman-Brown internal reliabilities were 0.92 and 0.88 respectively, with an intercorrelation of 0.12. The sub-scales correlated with Job Satisfaction indices in much the same manner as reported in the original study. Szilagyi and Keller (1976) report further results from the same investigation. Of particular interest here is the finding that perceived Positive Reward Behavior correlated 0.66 with leaders' Consideration as measured by the LBDQ XII (9.1) and 0.81 as measured by the SBDQ (9.2). Rated Punitive Reward Behavior correlated 0.33 and 0.49 with leaders' Initiating Structure as measured by the LBDQ XII and SBDQ respectively.

In a follow-up study of the same subjects, of whom 132 were obtained, Keller and Szilagyi (1978) found cross-lagged correlation results compatible with the interpretation of Positive Reward Behavior being a cause rather than effect of Overall Job Satisfaction, Work Satisfaction and Promotion Satisfaction (all from the Job Descriptive Index, 3.3). Sims, Szilagyi and McKemey (1976) describe other analyses of data from the source publication. Positive Reward Behavior was found to be related (0.55) to a measure of the belief that performance leads to reward (Expectancy II) (8.26). Data from previous studies are further analyzed by Sims and Szilagyi (1979), and Szilagyi (1980) reports several means from an additional investigation, using a five-point response continuum; the latter author reports coefficients alpha of 0.91 and 0.92 for Positive and Punitive Reward Behavior respectively.

Items

Positive Reward Behavior

 1. Your supervisor would personally pay you a compliment if you did outstanding work
 3. Your supervisor would lend a sympathetic ear if you had a complaint
 4. Your supervisor would be very much aware of it if there was a temporary change in the quality of your work
 6. Your supervisor would see that you will eventually go as far as you would like to go in this organization, if your work is consistently above average
 8. Your supervisor would recommend that you be promoted if your work was better than others who were otherwise equally qualified
 9. Your supervisor would help you get a transfer if you asked for one
10. Your supervisor would tell his/her boss if your work was outstanding
13. Your supervisor would show a great deal of interest if you suggested a new and better way of doing things
14. Your supervisor would give you special recognition if your work performance was especially good
15. Your supervisor would do all he/she could to help you if you were having problems in your work
16. Your supervisor's recommendation for a pay increase for you would be consistent with his/her evaluation of your performance
18. Your supervisor would encourage you to do better if your performance was acceptable but well below what you were capable of
19. Your supervisor would recommend additional training or schooling if it would help your job performance
20. Your supervisor's evaluation of your performance would be in agreement with your own evaluation of your performance
21. Your supervisor would increase your job responsibilities if you were performing well in your job
22. Your supervisor would always give you feedback on how your work affects the total service of the organization

Punitive Reward Behavior

 2. You would receive a reprimand from your supervisor if you were late in coming to work
 5. Your supervisor would recommend that you should be dismissed if you were absent for several days without notifying the organization or without a reasonable excuse
 7. Your supervisor would get on to you if your work was not as good as the work of others in your department
11. Your supervisor would give you a reprimand (written or verbally) if your work was consistently below acceptable standards

12. Your supervisor would recommend that you get no pay increase if your work was below standard

17. Your supervisor would recommend that you not be promoted to a higher level job if your performance was only average

Responses

A seven-point continuum runs from Very false to Very true, scored from 1 to 7 respectively. Intermediate labels are not cited.

9.8   Conflict Resolution Strategies

Source: Howat and London, 1980

Studies of conflict in organizations have primarily examined union–management relationships. This instrument has a rather more specific focus, providing measures of how conflicts are handled within named superior–subordinate or other dyads. Following the work of Blake and Mouton (1964), five strategies are identified, for each of which there is a sub-scale: Confrontation, Withdrawal, Forcing, Smoothing and Compromise.

The present instrument is the most recent of three closely related operationalizations of the same five-facet approach to the measurement of conflict resolution. It is selected as the source here since the earlier versions do not meet the requirements of being generally applicable scales. Renwick's (1975a, b) instruments relied on single-item measures of each of the five strategies. London and Howat (1978) and Zammuto, London and Rowland (1979) used Renwick's basic format but obtained responses for each of the five strategies for four areas of disagreement. Whilst correlations between the same conflict resolution strategies across the different areas of disagreement were high and justified the use of a single index as a scale, the areas of disagreement were either sample-specific (London and Howat, 1978) or unspecified (Zammuto, London and Rowland, 1979).

The instrument described by Howat and London (1980) is composed of 25 items, five for each of the strategies covered. Individuals' perceptions of their superior's or their subordinate's behaviour are obtained on a five-point dimension running from Describes behaviour which never occurs to Describes very typical behaviour which usually occurs. Sub-scale scores are obtained by averaging item scores.

In an investigation of 226 managers (113 superior–subordinate dyads) (Howat and London, 1980) and a follow-up study one year later involving 122 from this original sample (61 dyads) (London and Howat, 1980: London, personal communication), the results shown in the following table were obtained.

| | Study 1: 113 dyads | | | | | | Study 2: 61 dyads | | | | | | |
| | Superior rated by subordinate | | Subordinate rated by superior | | Internal Reliability (n=226) | Superior rated by subordinate | | Subordinate rated by superior | | Internal Reliability (n=122) | Test–retest correlation |
	Mean	s.d.	Mean	s.d.	Alpha	Mean	s.d.	Mean	s.d.	Alpha	r
Confrontation	3.77	0.91	4.09	0.60	0.86	3.80	0.84	3.95	0.65	0.84	0.68
Withdrawal	2.50	0.73	2.28	0.65	0.71	2.28	0.76	2.21	0.54	0.66	0.49
Forcing	2.59	0.88	2.07	0.84	0.88	2.41	0.82	1.97	0.59	0.84	0.55
Smoothing	3.99	0.68	3.51	0.70	0.79	3.49	0.67	3.38	0.66	0.73	0.55
Compromise	–	–	–	–	0.80	3.58	0.75	3.65	0.52	0.64	0.49

Note: Means and standard deviations cited for Study 2 are from the second administration. Descriptive statistics for Compromise in Study 1 are not cited in the source publication.

In study 1 the Confrontation, Smoothing and Compromise sub-scales were positively intercorrelated for both superiors and subordinates (median $r=0.43$) as were Forcing and Withdrawal (median $r=0.23$). In study 2 the respective statistics were 0.17 and 0.12.

Items

When conflict occurs between you and *your subordinate (superior)*, to what extent does *your subordinate (superior)* use each of the following behaviors to resolve the conflict? Remember you are rating how *your subordinate (superior)* behaves when resolving conflict, not how you behave or what you think is desirable.

Confrontation

1. Brings the problem clearly into the open and carries it out to resolution
6. Confronts the issue openly
11. Does not drop the issue until it is resolved
16. Faces the conflict directly
21. Clearly expresses a point of view

Withdrawal

2. Refrains from argument
7. Tries not to get involved
12. Gives in easily
17. Withdraws from the situation
22. Ignores the conflict

Forcing

3. Forces acceptance of his/her point of view
8. Insists on one solution
13. Demands to get his/her way
18. Will not take no for an answer
23. Imposes his/her solution

Smoothing

4. Emphasizes common interests
9. Stresses that our differences are less important than our common goals
14. Plays down our differences
19. Tries to smooth over our differences
24. Acts as though our common goals are of prime importance

Compromise

5. Tries to find a compromise
10. Searches for an intermediate position
15. Is willing to give and take
20. Gives in a little to get a little
25. Takes both sides of the issue into account

Responses

Describes behavior which never occurs; Describes untypical behavior which seldom occurs; Describes behavior which sometimes occurs; Describes behavior which occurs frequently; Describes very typical behavior which usually occurs; scored 1 to 5 respectively.

9.9 Group Atmosphere

Source: Fiedler, 1967

Group Atmosphere is the most heavily weighted of three constructs comprising Fiedler's (1967) notion of "situation favourability", the others being Task Structure and Position Power. Situation favourability and leadership style (as measured by the Least Preferred Co-worker (LPC) scale, (9.4) are in turn central elements of the author's contingency model of leadership effectiveness. The Group Atmosphere scale is designed to measure the leader's perception of the climate of his or her work group with respect to leader-member affective relations. It indicates the extent to which the leader feels accepted by his or her subordinates and sees the group as relatively tension-free; note that, unlike other measures in this chapter, the scale is not completed by subordinates.

The Group Atmosphere scale uses the same semantic differential format as LPC scales, being composed of ten items each with an eight-interval response dimension anchored by pairs of adjectives. The positive and negative poles are scored 8 and 1 respectively, and the scale score is the sum or the mean. As presented, the scale is vulnerable to response bias, since all items run in the same direction; this is in contrast to the LPC instrument (9.4) where the polarity varies.

The source publication provides little detail on the development of the measure, nor does it contain means and standard deviations. A split-half reliability coefficient (type and source unspecified) of up to 0.90 is cited, along with test–retest correlations of between 0.73 and 0.83. More specific early normative data are presented by Posthuma (1970). Bons and Fiedler (1976), with a sample of 115 infantry squad leaders, report means of 62.83 and 62.59, and a test–retest correlation of 0.29 between scores obtained on two occasions six to nine months apart. Nebeker (1975) recorded a mean of 62.98 (s.d. 8.04) with a sample of 43 aircraft maintenance supervisors. Bartol (1974) in a laboratory study with 100 male and female students obtained means running from 52.82 to 67.00 and an alpha reliability coefficient of 0.86. Factor analysis with items from several other measures showed that Group Atmosphere items loaded discretely onto a single factor. Hunt, Osborn and Larson (1975) in a study involving mental care nurses (N=94 groups) found that Group Atmosphere scores correlated 0.52 with total Job Satisfaction (from the Job Descriptive Index, 3.3), 0.22 with a measure of rated performance, and −0.11 with expressed Anxiety (the Anxiety Differential, Alexander and Husek, 1962; 5.17). With four samples of military cadets Rice, Bender and Vitters (1980) reported coefficients alpha between 0.89 and 0.93; in their laboratory study the correlations between leaders' ratings and average group member ratings were 0.56 and 0.15 for structured and unstructured tasks respectively (N=72 groups). Other uses include those by Konar-Goldband, Rice and Monkarsh (1979) and Utecht and Heier (1976).

Instructions and Items

Describe the atmosphere of your group by checking the following items.

1. Friendly – Unfriendly
2. Accepting – Rejecting
3. Satisfying – Frustrating
4. Enthusiastic – Unenthusiastic
5. Productive – Non-productive
6. Warm – Cold
7. Cooperative – Uncooperative
8. Supportive – Hostile
9. Interesting – Boring
10. Successful–Unsuccessful

Format and Responses

As entry 9.4

9.10   Group Processes

Source: Taylor and Bowers, 1972

This scale is part of the Survey of Organizations questionnaire, a machine-scored standardized instrument developed at the Institute for Social Research at the University of Michigan. The instrument itself is designed to operationalize the constructs central to the "meta-theory of organizational functioning" as described by Likert (1961, 1967) and Bowers (1972). It is intended to provide a standard set of measures usable without modification across differing samples. Procedures for the administration of the questionnaire are described in detail in the source publication, but scale development only in general terms. It is stated (p. 2) that scales are made up of "only the most valid, reliable and efficient single items" as shown by earlier Michigan studies, but no further information is offered. The questionnaire is also represented in this volume by entries 2.5 and 9.6.

A formal definition of Group Process is not given in the source publication though the concept is described in terms of levels of co-operation, competence and task motivation of group members; the construct appears to have much in common with group morale. The scale measuring these characteristics comprises seven items, each with five response alternatives, scored from 1 to 5. Scores are calculated by averaging items for each individual, and then averaging group member scores for each work group.

A hierarchical cluster analysis based on data from 754 work groups supported the use of the seven items as a single index with an alpha coefficient of 0.96. The test–retest correlation (time interval unspecified) based on 284 work groups was found to be 0.38. No information is provided on the factorial independence of this scale from others included in the total questionnaire, nor on means or standards deviations. However, up-to-date group norms have been calculated by the Institute for Social Research.

Franklin (1975a, b) and Bowers and Hausser (1977) have described alternative analyses of data which form the basis for the source publication, and other studies using the Group Process scale are by Koch (1978, 1979).

Items

1. To what extent does your work group plan together and coordinate its efforts?
2. To what extent does your work group make good decisions and solve problems well?
3. To what extent do persons in your work group know what their jobs are and know how to do them well?
4. To what extent is information about important events and situations shared within your work group?
5. To what extent does your work group really want to meet its objectives successfully?
6. To what extent is your work group able to respond to unusual work demands placed upon it?
7. To what extent do you have confidence and trust in the persons in your work group?

Responses

To a very little extent; To a little extent; To some extent; To a great extent; To a very great extent; scored 1 to 5 respectively.

9.11   Work Group Functioning

Source: Cammann, Fichman, Jenkins and Klesh, 1979; Seashore, Lawler, Mirvis and Cammann, 1982

The Michigan Organizational Assessment Questionnaire contains a number of scales for measuring work attitudes and perceptions; see also 2.9, 3.8, 3.9, 3.10, 4.13, 6.2, 6.6, 8.6 and 9.5. Module 4 is focussed on Work Group Functioning and consists of 14 items which are grouped into five sub-scales. The sub-scales, along with alpha coefficients of internal reliability as obtained with a sample of more than 400 respondents, are as follows: Group Homogeneity (two items, 0.62); Group Goal Clarity (two items, 0.61); Group Cohesiveness (two items, 0.64); Open Group Process (four items, 0.72); and Internal Fragmentation (four items, 0.79). Responses are on a seven-point dimension, and mean values across items constitute the sub-scale scores. One item is reverse-scored.

Sub-scale intercorrelations show that the Group Homogeneity sub-scale is unrelated to the others (median $r=0.07$), which are themselves strongly interrelated (median $r=0.42$). Factor analysis confirms the clear identity of this one sub-scale and the existence of overlap among the others. Correlations with the authors' measure of Overall Job Satisfaction (2.9) are reported as 0.13, 0.37, 0.48, 0.43 and -0.37 for the five sub-scales as sequenced above.

Items

Group Homogeneity

4. Members of my work group vary widely in their skills and abilities
8. My work group contains members with widely varying backgrounds

Group Goal Clarity

2. My work group knows exactly what things it has to get done
6. Each member of my work group has a clear idea of the group's goals

Group Cohesiveness

1. I feel I am really part of my work group
11. I look forward to being with the members of my work group each day

Open Group Process

9. We tell each other the way we are feeling
5. My co-workers are afraid to express their real views (R)
13. In my work group everyone's opinion gets listened to
7. If we have a decision to make, everyone is involved in making it

Internal Fragmentation

12. There are feelings among members of my work group which tend to pull the group apart
10. Some of the people I work with have no respect for others
14. There is constant bickering in my work group
 3. People who offer new ideas in my work group are likely to get "clobbered"

Responses

Strongly disagree; Disagree; Slightly disagree; Neither agree nor disagree; Slightly agree; Agree; Strongly agree; scored 1 to 7 respectively.

9.12   Interpersonal Trust at Work

Source: Cook and Wall, 1980

The authors define trust in terms of "the extent to which one is willing to ascribe good intentions to and have confidence in the words and actions of other people" (p. 39). A distinction is made between faith in the intentions of others and confidence in the ability of others, and a 12-item instrument is developed to measure these two aspects of trust with respect to both peers and superiors. It comprises four three-item sub-scales which may be treated separately or combined into a single score. Responses are obtained on a seven-point agree–disagree dimension with scale and sub-scale scores being the sum of item scores. Two items are reverse-scored.

The measure was constructed using samples of 390 and 260 blue-collar British employees, selected according to a predetermined sampling frame designed to match British demographic characteristics. The mean scores for the scale as a whole in the two samples were 60.48 (s.d. 12.33) and 63.04 (s.d. 10.23) respectively, the corresponding alpha coefficients were 0.85 and 0.80, and the test–retest correlation over a six month interval with a sample of 63 was 0.60. Sub-scale statistics from the two studies were as follows: Faith in Peers, mean 17.28 (s.d. 3.27) and 17.77 (s.d. 2.90), alpha 0.77 and 0.71, and test–retest correlation 0.51; Faith in Management, mean 13.68 (s.d. 4.62) and 14.48 (s.d. 4.10), alpha 0.78 and 0.69, and test–retest correlation 0.60; Confidence in Peers, mean 15.87 (s.d. 3.83) and 16.74 (s.d. 3.69), alpha 0.74 and 0.77, and test–retest correlation 0.32; Confidence in Management, mean 13.74 (s.d. 4.69) and 14.05 (s.d. 14.14), alpha 0.79 and 0.74, and test–retest correlation 0.43. Principal components analysis with vari-max rotation showed that the Trust scale resolved as the two a priori factors, one reflecting Trust in Management, the other Trust in Peers.

Correlational analysis showed Trust to be unrelated to age, skill level, degree of company unionization, or length of service; and associated 0.58 with Overall Job Satisfaction (2.11), 0.30 with Intrinsic Job Motivation (6.7), 0.28 with Work Involvement (7.5) and −0.30 with Self-Rated Anxiety (5.15). Clegg and Wall (1981) describe another use of this Trust Scale.

Items

Faith in Peers

3. If I got into difficulties at work I know my workmates would try and help me out
5. I can trust the people I work with to lend me a hand if I need it
8. Most of my workmates can be relied upon to do as they say they will do

Faith in Management

1. Management at my firm is sincere in its attempt to meet the workers' point of view
7. I feel quite confident that the firm will always try to treat me fairly
12. Our management would be quite prepared to gain advantage by deceiving the workers (R)

Confidence in Peers

9. I have full confidence in the skills of my workmates
10. Most of my fellow workers would get on with the job even if supervisors were not around
11. I can rely on other workers not to make my job more difficult by careless work

Confidence in Management

2. Our firm has a poor future unless it can attract better managers (R)
4. Management can be trusted to make sensible decisions for the firm's future
6. Management at work seems to do an efficient job

Responses

No, I strongly disagree; No, I disagree quite a lot; No, I disagree just a little; I'm not sure; Yes, I agree just a little; Yes, I agree quite a lot; Yes, I strongly agree; scored 1 to 7 respectively.

9.13 to 9.32   Other Measures of Leadership Style and Perceptions of Others

9.13 Barnowe (1975) presents a measure of Leadership Facets, which is based to a large extent on the work of Bowers and Seashore (1966). It comprises five sub-scales: Task Emphasis (two items, alpha 0.91),

Supportiveness (four items, alpha 0.77), Technical Skill and Assistance (four items, alpha 0.82), Participation (three items, alpha 0.57), and Closeness of Supervision (one item). The first four are combined to form a single index of Leader Assistance (alpha 0.93).

9.14 and 9.15 Beehr (1976) introduces a three-item measure of Supervisor Support (9.14) based on items from the LBDQ (9.1), and a five-item index of Group Cohesiveness derived in part from the earlier work of Seashore (1954). Items are given in full.

9.16 Heller, Drenth, Koopman and Rus (1977) and Drenth, Koopman, Rus, Odar, Heller and Brown (1979) described an Influence–Power Continuum; designed to measure power-sharing style with respect to decision-making in hierarchical groups of two or more people. It comprises a list of 12 decisions, each of which is rated on a response continuum running from No information to Complete control, where answers reflect supervisors' perceptions of the amount of influence accorded to subordinates. The latter paper reports data from the Netherlands, United Kingdom and Yugoslavia.

9.17 Kirchoff (1975) has developed a Management Style Questionnaire, the purpose of which is to measure use of Management by Objectives within organizations. It comprises 47 items, 11 of which contribute to the score. The remaining items are intended "to disguise the otherwise obvious intent of the instrument" (p. 353). The items are presented in full, along with descriptive statistics, and evidence of reliability and construct validity.

9.18 Lawshe and Nagle (1953) describe a 22-item Attitude toward the Supervisor Scale. The items are presented by Nagle (1953) and Shaw and Wright (1967). Despite being labelled "attitude" the scale focusses on perceived behaviour. A more recent use is by Di Marco (1974), and useful evaluative comment is offered by Guion and Robins (1964).

9.19 Rousseau (1978b) presents a six-item index of Coordination, which is defined in terms of the extent to which an individual receives materials, resources and support from others upon whom he or she depends. The items are given in full.

9.20 A Personal Contact Questionnaire is presented by Schwartz and Jacobson (1977), as a means of quantifying the communication relationship between a respondent and named contacts. The measure is described in only general terms, further information being obtainable in the doctoral thesis of Schwartz (1968).

9.21 Conflict Management Style is the focus of a measure introduced by Taylor (1971), based on the theoretical work of Blake and Mouton

(1964). Consisting of 15 proverbs it is designed to yield five indices of conflict resolution mode with respect both to their perceived prevalence and to their desirability. The five indices are labelled Confronting Resolution, Smoothing Resolution, Compromise, Force, and Withdrawal (cf. 9.8). This instrument was used by Sashkin, Taylor and Tripathi (1974).

9.22 to 9.24 Weiss (1977, 1978) offers measures of perceived Supervisor Reward Power (9.22), Supervisor Success (9.23), and Supervisor Competence (as developed by Comrey, Pfiffner and High, 1954) (9.24). The first scale yields ratings of the importance of one's supervisor in respect of ten outcomes (e.g. getting a raise in salary). Perceived Supervisor Success contains four items of the kind: How highly do his/her bosses think of your superior? And the third instrument (9.24) obtains five ratings of the quality of a superior's decisions.

9.25 Within a wide-ranging Profile Questionnaire, Bass, Valenzi, Farrow and Solomon (1975) introduce five measures of perceived Management Style. These are Directive (nine items, alpha 0.69), Negotiative (ten items, alpha 0.58), Consultative (seven items, alpha 0.88), Participative (six items, alpha 0.81) and Delegative (four items, alpha 0.67). The perceived styles had a median intercorrelation of 0.26 (range 0.02 to 0.84). Other data have been described by Bass and Mitchell (1976), Shapira (1976) and Solomon (1976).

9.26 Schriesheim (1978b) has developed three five-item sub-scales to measure Leaders' Role Clarification, Work Assignment and Specification of Procedures. Descriptive statistics and relationships with evaluative and perceptual responses are described by Jermier and Berkes (1979).

9.27 Yukl and Kanuk (1979) describe their Leadership Behavior Scales. Nine aspects of perceived leadership behaviour are tapped: Consideration, Positive Reinforcement, Decision Participation, Production Emphasis, Work Facilitation, Direction, Planning–Coordination, Team Building, and Autonomy–Delegation. Details of scale development are presented by Yukl and Nemeroff (1979), who indicate that the measure is currently being broadened to cover 18 dimensions.

9.28 Aran, Morgan and Esbeck (1971) describe an 18-item Perceived Team Collaboration measure, designed to measure the level of mutual influence between team members, communication and conflict resolution, and support for innovation. A subsequent use is by Dailey (1979).

9.29 Dailey (1979) also mentions the use of 19-item measure of Team Cohesiveness, which factor analysis revealed to be composed of two

dimensions labelled Team Attractiveness, and Involvement and Satisfaction with the Team. Kuder-Richardson internal reliabilities for both
sub-scales are cited as 0.98, with a value of 0.99 for the composite index.

9.30 White and Mitchell (1979) introduce an eight-item Social Cues
Index designed to measure individuals' perceptions of their co-workers'
reactions to jobs. Illustrative items are: My co-workers think this job is
important and My co-workers are able to figure out how well they are
performing on this job.

9.31 A 21-item Social Support scale is offered by Caplan (1971) and
subsequently used by Caplan, Cobb and French (1975). Items are
given in full in the former publication, and the latter article offers
descriptive statistics and reliability coefficients for groups of administrators, engineers and scientists.

9.32 Zemelman, Di Marco and Norton (1979) describe the use of
Friedlander's (1971) Organizational Structure Questionnaire. This
comprises three eight-item scales, derived through factor analysis and
designed to measure perceived work group functioning in terms of
Bureaucratic, Collaborative and Coordinative dimensions.

References

ABDEL-HALIM, A. A. (1978). Employee affective responses to organizational stress: Moderating effects of job characteristics. *Personnel Psychology*, **31**, 561–579.

ABDEL-HALIM, A. A. (1979a). Individual and interpersonal moderators of employee reactions to job characteristics: A re-examination. *Personnel Psychology*, **32**, 121–137.

ABDEL-HALIM, A. A. (1979b). Interaction effects of power equalization and subordinate personality on job satisfaction and performance. *Human Relations*, **32**, 489–502.

ABDEL-HALIM, A. A. (1980a). Power equalization and work effectiveness: An empirical investigation. *Journal of Occupational Behaviour*, **1**, 223–237.

ABDEL-HALIM, A. A. (1980b). Effects of higher-order need strength on the job performance-job satisfaction relationship. *Personnel Psychology*, **33**, 335–347.

ABDEL-HALIM, A. A. and ROWLAND, K. M. (1976). Some personality determinants of the effects of participation: A further investigation. *Personnel Psychology*, **29**, 41–55.

ADAM, E. E. (1975). Behavior modification in quality control. *Academy of Management Journal*, **18**, 662–679.

ADAMS, E. F. (1978). A multivariate study of subordinate perceptions of the attitudes towards minority and majority managers. *Journal of Applied Psychology*, **63**, 277–288.

ADAMS, E. F., LAKER, D. R., and HULIN, C. L. (1977). An investigation of the influence of job level and functional speciality on job attitudes and perceptions. *Journal of Applied Psychology*, **62**, 335–343.

ADLER, S. (1980). Self-esteem and causal attributions for job satisfaction and dissatisfaction. *Journal of Applied Psychology*, **65**, 327–332.

ADORNO, T. W., FRENKEL-BRUNSWIK, E., LEVINSON, D. J. and SANFORD, R. N. (1950). *The Authoritarian Personality*. Harper, New York.

AIKEN, M. and HAGE, J. (1966). Organizational alienation: A comparative analysis. *American Sociological Review*, **31**, 497–507.

ALDAG, R. J. and BRIEF, A. P. (1975). Some correlates of work values. *Journal of Applied Psychology*, **60**, 757–760.

ALDAG, R. J. and BRIEF, A. P. (1977). Relationships between leader behavior variability indices and subordinate responses. *Personnel Psychology*, **30**, 419–426.

ALDAG, R. J. and BRIEF, A. P. (1978). Examination of alternative models of job satisfaction. *Human Relations*, **31**, 91–98.

ALDAG, R. J. and BRIEF, A. P. (1979). Examination of a measure of higher-order need strength. *Human Relations*, **32**, 705–718.

ALDERFER, C. P. (1969). An empirical test of a new theory of human needs. *Organizational Behavior and Human Performance*, **4**, 142–175.

ALDERFER, C. P. (1972). *Existence, Relatedness, and Growth: Human Needs in Organizational Settings*. The Free Press, New York.

ALDERFER, C. P. and GUZZO, R. A. (1979). Life experiences and adults' enduring strength of desires in organizations. *Administrative Science Quarterly*, **24**, 347–361.

ALEXANDER, S. and HUSEK, T. R. (1962). The Anxiety Differential: Initial steps in the development of a measure of situational anxiety. *Educational and Psychological Measurement*, **22**, 325–348.

ALLEN, B. H. and LaFOLLETTE, W. R. (1977). Perceived organizational structure and alienation among management trainees. *Academy of Management Journal*, **20**, 334–341.

ALUTTO, J. A. and ACITO, F. (1974). Decisional participation and sources of job satisfaction: A study of manufacturing personnel. *Academy of Management Journal*, **17**, 160–167.

ALUTTO, J. A. and VREDENBURGH, D. J. (1977). Characteristics of decisional participation by nurses. *Academy of Management Journal*, **20**, 341–347.

ALUTTO, J. A., HREBENIAK, L. G. and ALONSO, R. C. (1973). On operationalizing the concept of commitment. *Social Forces*, **51**, 448–454.

ANASTASI, A. (1976). *Psychological Testing* (4th edition). Macmillan, New York.

ANDERSON, J. C. (1979). Local union participation: A re-examination. *Industrial Relations*, **18**, 18–31.

ARAN, J. D., MORGAN, C. P. and ESBECK, E. S. (1971). Relation of collaborative interpersonal relationsips to individual satisfactions and organizational performance. *Administrative Science Quarterly*, **16**, 289–296.

ARMENAKIS, A. and SMITH, L. (1978). A practical alternative to comparison group designs in OD evaluations: The abbreviated time series design. *Academy of Management Journal*, **21**, 499–507.

ARMENAKIS, A. A., FEILD, H. S., HOLLEY, W. H., BEDEIAN, A. G. and LEDBETTER, B. (1977). Human resource considerations in textile work redesign. *Human Relations*, **30**, 1147–1156.

ARNOLD, H. J. and HOUSE, R. J. (1980). Methodological and substantive extensions to the Job Characteristics Model of motivation. *Organizational Behavior and Human Performance*, **25**, 161–183.

ARVEY, R. D. and DEWHIRST, H. D. (1976). Goal-setting attributes, personality variables, and job satisfaction. *Journal of Vocational Behavior*, **9**, 179–189.

ARVEY, R. D. and DEWHIRST, H. D. (1979). Relationships between diversity of interests, age, job satisfaction and job performance. *Journal of Occupational Psychology*, **52**, 17–23.

ARVEY, R. D. and MUSSIO, S. J. (1973). A test of expectancy theory in a field setting using female clerical employees. *Journal of Vocational Behavior*, **3**, 421–432.

ARVEY, R. D. and NEEL, C. W. (1974). Testing expectancy theory predictions using behaviorally anchored based measures of motivational effort for engineers. *Journal of Vocational Behavior*, **4**, 299–310.

ARVEY, R. D, DEWHIRST, H. D., and BOLING, J. C. (1976). Relationships between goal clarity, participation in goal setting, and personality characteristics on job satisfaction in a scientific organization. *Journal of Applied Psychology*, **61**, 103–105.

ARVEY, R. D., DEWHIRST, H. D., and BROWN, E. M. (1978). A longitudinal study of the impact of changes in goal-setting on employee satisfaction. *Personnel Psychology*, **31**, 595–608.

ASHOUR, A. S. (1973a). The contingency model of leadership effectiveness: An evaluation. *Organizational Behavior and Human Performance*, **9**, 339–355.

ASHOUR, A. S. (1973b). Further discussion of Fiedler's contingency model of leadership effectiveness. *Organizational Behavior and Human Performance*, **9**, 369–376.

ATKINSON, J. W. (1958). *Motives in Fantasy, Action and Society*. Van Nostrand, New York.

BACHARACH, S. B. and AIKEN, M. (1976). Structural and process constraints on influence in organizations: A level-specific analysis. *Administrative Science Quarterly*, **21**, 623–642.

BACHARACH, S. B. and AIKEN, M. (1977). Communication in administrative bureaucracies. *Academy of Management Journal*, **20**, 365–377.

BADIN, I. J. (1974). Some moderator influences on relationships between Consideration, Initiating Structure, and organizational criteria. *Journal of Applied Psychology*, **59**, 380–382.

BAIRD, L. S. (1976). Relationship of performance to satisfaction in stimulating and nonstimulating jobs. *Journal of Applied Psychology*, **61**, 721–727.

BAIRD, L. S. (1977). Self and superior ratings of performance: As related to self-esteem and satisfaction with supervision. *Academy of Management Journal*, **20**, 291–300.

BAKER, S. H. and HANSEN, R. A. (1975). Job design and worker satisfaction: A challenge to assumptions. *Journal of Occupational Psychology*, **48**, 79–91.

BANKS, M. H., CLEGG, C. W., JACKSON, P. R., KEMP, N. J., STAFFORD, E. M. and WALL, T. D. (1980). The use of the General Health Questionnaire as an indicator of mental health in occupational studies. *Journal of Occupational Psychology*, **53**, 187–194.

BARNOWE, J. T. (1975). Leadership and performance outcomes in research organizations: The supervisor of scientists as a source of assistance. *Organizational Behavior and Human Performance*, **14**, 264–280.

BARTH, R. T. (1976). An empirical examination of several job attraction and job satisfaction measures. *International Review of Applied Psychology*, **25**, 53–68.

BARTOL, K. M. (1974). Male versus female leaders: The effect of leader need for dominance on follower satisfaction. *Academy of Management Journal*, **17**, 225–233.

BARTOL, K. M. (1979a). Individual versus organizational predictors of job satisfaction and turnover among professionals. *Journal of Vocational Behavior*, **15**, 55–67.

BARTOL, K. M. (1979b). Professionalism as a predictor of organizational commitment, role stress and turnover: A multidimensional approach. *Academy of Management Journal*, **22**, 815–821.

BARTOL, K. M. and MANHARDT, P. J. (1979). Sex differences in job outcome preferences: Trends among newly hired college graduates. *Journal of Applied Psychology*, **64**, 477–482.

BARTOL, K. M. and WORTMAN, M. S. (1975). Male versus female leaders: Effects on perceived leader behavior and satisfaction in a hospital. *Personnel Psychology*, **28**, 533–547.

BASS, B. M. and MITCHELL, C. W. (1976). Influences on the felt need for collective bargaining by business and science professionals. *Journal of Applied Psychology*, **61**, 770–773.

BASS, B. M., CASCIO, W. F., McPHERSON, J. W. and TRAGASH, H. J. (1976). PROSPER: Training and research for increasing management awareness of affirmative action in race relations. *Academy of Management Journal*, **19**, 353–369.

BASS, B. M., VALENZI, E. R., FARROW, D. L. and SOLOMON, R. J. (1975). Management styles associated with organizational, task, personal, and interpersonal contingencies. *Journal of Applied Psychology*, **60**, 720–729.

BASSETT, G. A. (1979). A study of the effects of task goal and schedule choice on work performance. *Organizational Behavior and Human Performance*, **24**, 202–227.

BEATTY, R. W. (1974). Supervisory behavior related to job success of hard-core unemployed over a two-year period. *Journal of Applied Psychology*, **59**, 38–42.

BEEHR, T. A. (1976). Perceived situational moderators of the relationship between subjective role ambiguity and role strain. *Journal of Applied Psychology*, **61**, 35–40.

BEEHR, T. A. (1977). Hierarchical cluster analysis of the Profile of Organizational Characteristics. *Journal of Applied Psychology*, **62**, 120–123.

BEEHR, T. A., WALSH, J. T. and TABER, T. D. (1976). Relationship of stress to individually and organizationally valued states: Higher order needs as a moderator. *Journal of Applied Psychology*, **61**, 41–47.

BENNETT, M. (1977a). Testing management theories cross-culturally. *Journal of Applied Psychology*, **62**, 578–581.

BENNETT, M. (1977b). Response characteristics of bilingual managers to organizational questionnaires. *Personnel Psychology*, **30**, 29–36.

BERGER, C. J. and SCHWAB, D. P. (1980). Pay incentives and pay satisfaction. *Industrial Relations*, **19**, 206–211.

BERKOWITZ, E. N. (1980). Role theory, attitudinal constructs, and actual performance: A measurement issue. *Journal of Applied Psychology*, **65**, 240–245.

BERNARDIN, H. J. (1979). The predictability of discrepancy measures of role constructs. *Personnel Psychology*, **32**, 139–153.

BHAGAT, R. S. and CHASSIE, M. B. (1978). The role of self-esteem and locus of control in the differential prediction of performance, program satisfaction, and life satisfaction in an educational organization. *Journal of Vocational Behavior*, **13**, 317–326.

BHAGAT, R. S. and CHASSIE, M. B. (1980). Effects of changes in job characteristics on some theory-specific attitudinal outcomes: Results from a naturally occurring quasi-experiment. *Human Relations*, **33**, 297–313.

BIASATTI, L. L. and MARTIN, J. E. (1979). A measure of the quality of unit-management relationships. *Journal of Applied Psychology*, **64**, 387–390.

BIGONESS, W. J. (1978). Correlates of faculty attitudes toward collective bargaining. *Journal of Applied Psychology*, **63**, 228–233.

BILLINGS, R. S., KLIMOSKI, R. J. and BREAUGH, J. A. (1977). The impact of a change in technology on job characteristics: A quasi-experiment. *Administrative Science Quarterly*, **22**, 318–339.

BISH, J. and SCHRIESHEIM, C. (1974). An exploratory dimensional analysis of Form XII of the Ohio State leadership scales. *Academy of Management Proceedings*, thirty-fourth annual meeting.

BLAKE, R. R. and MOUTON, J. S. (1964). *The Managerial Grid.* Gulf, Houston.

BLAUNER, R. (1964). *Alienation and Freedom.* University of Chicago Press, Chicago.

BLOOD, M. R. (1969). Work values and job satisfaction. *Journal of Applied Psychology*, **53**, 456–459.

BLOOD, M. R. (1971). The validity of importance. *Journal of Applied Psychology*, **55**, 487–488.

BLOOD, M. R. and HULIN, C. L. (1967). Alienation, environmental characteristics and worker responses. *Journal of Applied Psychology*, **51**, 284–290.

BLUMBERG, M. (1980). Job switching in autonomous work groups: An exploratory study in a Pennsylvania coal mine. *Academy of Management Journal*, **23**, 287–306.

BONS, P. M. and FIEDLER, F. E. (1976). Changes in organizational leadership and the behavior of relationship- and task-motivated leaders. *Administrative Science Quarterly*, **21**, 453–473.

BORGATTA, E. F. (1967). The Work Components Study: A set of measures for work motivation. *Journal of Psychological Studies*, **15**, 1–11.

BORGATTA, E. F., FORD, R. N. and BOHRNSTEDT, G. W. (1968). The Work Components Study (WCS): A revised set of measures for work motivation. *Multivariate Behavioral Research*, **3**, 403–414.

BOURGEOIS, L. J., McALLISTER, D. W. and MITCHELL, T. R. (1978). The effects of different organizational environments upon decisions about organizational structure. *Academy of Management Journal*, **21**, 508–514.

BOWERS, D. G. (1972). *System 4: The Ideas of Rensis Likert.* Basic Books, New York.

BOWERS, D. G. and HAUSSER, D. L. (1977). Work group types and intervention effects in organizational development. *Administrative Science Quarterly*, **22**, 76–94.

BOWERS, D. G. and SEASHORE, S. E. (1966). Predicting organizational effectiveness with a four factor theory of leadership. *Administrative Science Quarterly*, **11**, 238–263.

BRADBURN, N. M. (1969). *The Structure of Psychological Well-being.* Aldine, Chicago.

BRAYFIELD, A. H. and ROTHE, H. F. (1951). An index of job satisfaction. *Journal of Applied Psychology*, **35**, 307–311.

BRAYFIELD, A. H., WELLS, R. V. and STRATE, M. W. (1957). Interrelationships among measures of job satisfaction and general satisfaction. *Journal of Applied Psychology*, **41**, 201–205.

BRIEF, A. P. and ALDAG, R. J. (1975). Employee reactions to job characteristics: A constructive replication. *Journal of Applied Psychology*, **60**, 182–186.

BRIEF, A. P. and ALDAG, R. J. (1976). Correlates of role indices. *Journal of Applied Psychology*, **61**, 468–472.

BRIEF, A. P. and ALDAG, R. J. (1978). The job characteristics inventory: An examination. *Academy of Management Journal*, **21**, 659–670.

BRIEF, A. P., ALDAG, R. J. and VAN SELL, M. (1977). Moderators of the relationships between self and superior evaluations of job performance. *Journal of Occupational Psychology*, **50**, 129–134.

BRIEF, A. P., WALLACE, J. J. and ALDAG, R. J. (1975). Linear versus nonlinear models of the formation of affective reactions: The case of job enlargement. *Proceedings of the 7th Annual Convention of the National American Institute for Decision Sciences.*

BROUSSEAU, K. R. (1978). Personality and job experience. *Organizational Behavior and Human Performance*, **22**, 235–252.

BUCHANAN, B. (1974). Building organizational commitment: The socialization of managers in work organizations. *Administrative Science Quarterly*, **19**, 533–546.

BUCHHOLZ, R. A. (1976). Measurement of beliefs. *Human Relations*, **29**, 1177–1188.

BUCHHOLZ, R. A. (1977). The belief structure of managers relative to work concepts measured by a factor analytic model. *Personnel Psychology*, **30**, 567–587.

BUCHHOLZ, R. A. (1978). An empirical study of contemporary beliefs about work in American society. *Journal of Applied Psychology*, **63**, 219–227.

BULLOCK, R. P. (1952). *Social Factors Related to Job Satisfaction: A Technique for the Measurement of Job Satisfaction.* Bureau of Business Research, Ohio State University, Columbus, Ohio.

BURKE, R. J., WEIR, T. and DU WORS, R. E. (1979). Type A behavior of administrators and wives' reports of marital satisfaction and well-being. *Journal of Applied Psychology*, **64**, 57–65.

BURKE, R. J., WEIR, T. and DU WORS, R. E. (1980a). Work demands on administrators and spouse well-being. *Human Relations*, **33**, 253–278.

BURKE, R. J., WEIR, T. and DU WORS, R. E. (1980b). Perceived type A behavior of husbands and wives' satisfaction and well-being. *Journal of Occupational Behaviour*, **1**, 139–150.

BURNS, T and STALKER, C. M. (1961). *The Management of Innovation.* Tavistock, London.

BUROS, O. K. (1965). *The Sixth Mental Measurements Year Book.* Gryphon Press, Highland Park, New Jersey.

BUTLER, M. C. and JONES A. P. (1979). Perceived leader behavior, individual characteristics and injury occurrence in hazardous work environments. *Journal of Applied Psychology*, **64**, 299–304.

BUTTERFIELD, D. A. and FARRIS, G. F. (1974). The Likert organizational profile: Methodological analysis and test of System 4 theory in Brazil. *Journal of Applied Psychology*, **59**, 15–23.

CAMMANN, C., FICHMAN, M., JENKINS, D. and KLESH, J. (1979). The Michigan Organizational Assessment Questionnaire. Unpublished Manuscript, University of Michigan, Ann Arbor, Michigan.

CAMPBELL, J. P. (1976). Psychometric theory. In M. D. Dunnette (ed.), *Handbook of Industrial and Organizational Psychology.* Rand McNally, Chicago.

CAMPBELL, J. P., DUNNETTE, M. D., LAWLER, E. E. and WEICK, K. E. (1970). *Managerial Behavior, Performance and Effectiveness.* McGraw-Hill, New York.

CAPLAN, R. D. (1971). *Organizational Stress and Individual Strain: A Social-Psychological Study of Risk Factors in Coronary Heart Disease among Administrators, Engineers, and Scientists.* Institute for Social Research, University of Michigan, University Microfilms No. 72-14822, Ann Arbor, Michigan.

CAPLAN, R. D. and JONES, K. W. (1975). Effects of work load, role ambiguity and type-A personality on anxiety, depression and heart rate. *Journal of Applied Psychology*, **60**, 713–719.

CAPLAN, R. D., COBB, S. and FRENCH, J. R. P. (1975). Relationships of cessation of smoking with job stress, personality and social support. *Journal of Applied Psychology*, **60**, 211–219.

CAPLAN, R. D. COBB, S., FRENCH, J. R. P., VAN HARRISON, R. and PINNEAU, S. R. (1975). *Job Demands and Worker Health.* National Institute for Occupational Safety and Health, Washington, D.C.

CARRELL, M. R. and ELBERT, N. F. (1974). Some personal and organizational determinants of job satisfaction of postal clerks. *Academy of Management Journal*, **17**, 368–373.

CASHMAN, J., DANSEREAU, F., GRAEN, G. and HAGA, W. J. (1976). Organizational understructure and leadership: A longitudinal investigation of the managerial role-making process. *Organizational Behavior and Human Performance*, **15**, 278–296.

CHAMPOUX, J. E. (1978). A serendipitous field experiment in job design. *Journal of Vocational Behavior*, **12**, 364–370.

CHAPMAN, J. B. (1975). Comparison of male and female leadership styles. *Academy of Management Journal*, **18**, 645–650.

CHERRINGTON, D. J. and ENGLAND, J. L. (1980). The desire for an enriched job as a moderator of the enrichment–satisfaction relationship. *Organizational Behavior and Human Performance*, **25**, 139–159.

CHERRINGTON, D. J., CONDIE, S. J. and ENGLAND, J. L. (1979). Age and work values. *Academy of Management Journal*, **22**, 617–623.

CLEGG, C. W. and WALL, T. D. (1981). Note on some new scales for measuring aspects of psychological well-being. *Journal of Occupational Psychology*, **52**, 221–225.

COHEN, S. L. and LEAVENGOOD, S. (1978). The utility of the WAMS: Shouldn't it relate to discriminatory behavior? *Academy of Management Journal*, **21**, 742–748.

COMREY, A. L., PFIFFER, J. M. and HIGH, W. S. (1954). Factors influencing organizational effectiveness. Technical Report, University of Southern California.

COOK, J. and WALL, T. D. (1980). New work attitude measures of trust, organizational commitment and personal need non-fulfilment. *Journal of Occupational Psychology*, **53**, 39–52.

COOPERSMITH, S. (1967). *The Antecedents of Self-Esteem.* Freeman, San Francisco.

CORNELIUS, E. T. and LYNESS, K. S. (1980). A comparison of holistic and decomposed strategies in job analyses by job incumbents. *Journal of Applied Psychology*, **65**, 155–163.

CRONBACH, L. J. (1951). Coefficient alpha and the internal structure of tests. *Psychometrika*, **16**, 297–334.

CROSS, D. (1973). The Worker Opinion Survey: A measure of shop-floor satisfactions. *Occupational Psychology*, **47**, 193–208.

CROWNE, D. P. and MARLOWE, D. (1960). A new scale of social desirability independent of psychopathology. *Journal of Consulting and Clinical Psychology*, **24**, 349–354.

CROWNE, D. P. and MARLOWE, D. (1964). *The Approval Motive*. Wiley, New York.

CSOKA, L. S. (1974). A relationship between leader intelligence and leader rated effectiveness. *Journal of Applied Psychology*, **59**, 43–47.

CSOKA, L. S. (1975). Relationship between organizational climate and the situational favorableness dimension of Fiedler's contingency model. *Journal of Applied Psychology*, **60**, 273–277.

CSOKA, L. S. and BONS, P. M. (1978). Manipulating the situation to fit the leader's style: Two validation studies of LEADER MATCH. *Journal of Applied Psychology*, **63**, 295–300.

CULHA, M. (1977). A classification and careers counselling battery for use in personnel work. *International Review of Applied Psychology*, **26**, 71–76.

CUMMINGS, T. G. and BIGELOW, J. (1976). Satisfaction, job involvement and intrinsic motivation: An extension of Lawler and Hall's factor analysis. *Journal of Applied Psychology*, **61**, 523–525.

CUMMINGS, T. G. and MANRING, S. L. (1977). The relationship between worker alienation and work-related behavior. *Journal of Vocational Behavior*, **10**, 167–179.

DAILEY, R. C. (1979). Group, task, and personality correlates of boundary-spanning activities. *Human Relations*, **32**, 273–285.

DALTON, D. R. (1979). Orientation to work and grievance behavior. Doctoral Dissertation, University of California at Irvine.

DALTON, D. R. and TODOR, W. D. (1979). Manifest needs of stewards: Propensity to file a grievance. *Journal of Applied Psychology*, **64**, 654–659.

DANSEREAU, F., CASHMAN, J. and GRAEN, G. (1974). Expectancy as a moderator of the relationship between job attitudes and turnover. *Journal of Applied Psychology*, **59**, 228–229.

DANSEREAU, F., GRAEN, G. and HAGA, W. J. (1975). A vertical dyad linkage approach to leadership within formal organizations. *Organizational Behavior and Human Performance*, **13**, 46–78.

DAWIS, R. V., PINTO, P. R., WEITZEL, W. and NEZZER, M. (1974). Describing organizations as reinforcer systems: A new use for job satisfaction and employee attitude surveys. *Journal of Vocational Behavior*, **4**, 55–66.

DESMOND, R. E. and WEISS, D. J. (1975). Worker estimation of ability requirements of their jobs. *Journal of Vocational Behavior*, **7**, 13–27.

DESSLER, G. and VALENZI, E. R. (1977). Initiation of structure and subordinate satisfaction: A path analysis test of path–goal theory. *Academy of Management Journal*, **20**, 251–259.

DEWAR, R. and WERBEL, J. (1979). Universalistic and contingency predictions of employee satisfaction and conflict. *Administrative Science Quarterly*, **24**, 426–448.

DEWAR, R. D., WHETTEN, D. A. and BOJE, D. (1980). An examination of the reliability and validity of the Aiken and Hage scales of centralization, formalization, and task routineness. *Administrative Science Quarterly*, **25**, 120–128.

DICKSON, J. W. (1976). The relation of individual search activity to subjective job characteristics. *Human Relations*, **29**, 911–928.

DICKSON, J. W. and BUCHHOLZ, R. A. (1977). Managerial beliefs about work in Scotland and the USA. *Journal of Management Studies*, **14**, 80–101.

DICKSON, J. W. and BUCHHOLZ, R. A. (1979). Differences in beliefs about work between managers and blue-collar workers. *Journal of Management Studies*, **16**, 235–251.

DIETERLY, D. L. and SCHNEIDER, B. (1974). The effect of organizational environment on perceived power and climate: A laboratory study. *Organizational Behavior and Human Performance*, **11**, 316–337.

DIETRICH, M. C. (1977). Work values evolution in a baccalaureate student nurse population. *Journal of Vocational Behavior*, **10**, 25–34.

DI MARCO, N. J. (1974). Supervisor–subordinate life-style and interpersonal need compatibilities as determinants of subordinate's attitudes toward the supervisor. *Academy of Management Journal*, **17**, 575–578.

DI MARCO, N. J. (1975). Life style, work-group structure, compatability, and job satisfaction. *Academy of Management Journal*, **18**, 313–322.

DI MARCO, N. J., KUEHL, C. R. and WIMS, E. W. (1975). Leadership style and interpersonal need orientation as moderators of changes in leadership dimension scores. *Personnel Psychology*, **28**, 207–213.

DIPBOYE, R. L., ZULTOWSKI, W. H., DEWHIRST, H. D. and ARVEY, R. D. (1978). Self-esteem as a moderator of the relationship between scientific interests and the job satisfaction of physicists and engineers. *Journal of Applied Psychology*, **63**, 289–294.

DIPBOYE, R. L., ZULTOWSKI, W. H., DEWHIRST, H. D. and ARVEY, R. D. (1979). Self-esteem as a moderator of performance–satisfaction relationships. *Journal of Vocational Behavior*, **15**, 193–206.

DITTRICH, J. E. and CARRELL, M. R. (1979). Organizational equity perceptions, employee job satisfaction, and departmental absence and turnover rates. *Organizational Behavior and Human Performance*, **24**, 29–40.

DORNSTEIN, M. (1977). Organizational conflict and role stress among chief executives in state business enterprises. *Journal of Occupational Psychology*, **50**, 253–263.

DOSSETT, D., LATHAM, G. and MITCHELL, T. R. (1979). Effects of assigned versus participatively set goals, knowledge of results, and individual differences on employee behavior when goal difficulty is held constant. *Journal of Applied Psychology*, **64**, 291–298.

DOWNEY, H. K., HELLRIEGEL, D. and SLOCUM, J. W. (1975). Congruence between individual needs, organizational climate, job satisfaction and performance. *Academy of Management Journal*, **18**, 149–155.

DOWNEY, H. K., HELLRIEGEL, D. and SLOCUM, J. W. (1977). Individual characteristics as sources of perceived uncertainty variability. *Human Relations*, **30**, 161–174.

DOWNEY, H. K. SHERIDAN, J. E. and SLOCUM, J. W. (1975). Analysis of relationships among leader behavior, subordinate job performance and satisfaction: A path–goal approach. *Academy of Management Journal*, **18**, 253–262.

DOWNEY, H. K., SHERIDAN, J. E. and SLOCUM, J. W. (1976). The path–goal theory of leadership: A longitudinal analysis. *Organizational Behavior and Human Performance*, **16**, 156–176.

DOWNEY, H. K., HELLRIEGEL, D., PHELPS, M. and SLOCUM, J. W. (1974).

Organizational climate and job satisfaction: A comparative analysis. *Journal of Business Research*, **2**, 233–248.

DRENTH, P. J. D., KOOPMAN, P. L., RUS, V., ODAR, M., HELLER, F. and BROWN, A. (1979). Participative decision making: A comparative study. *Industrial Relations*, **18**, 295–309.

DREXLER, J. A. (1977). Organizational climate: Its homogeneity within organizations. *Journal of Applied Psychology*, **62**, 38–42.

DRISCOLL, J. W. (1978). Trust and participation in organizational decision-making as predictors of satisfaction. *Academy of Management Journal*, **21**, 44–56.

DUBIN, R. (1956). Industrial workers' worlds: A study of the "Central Life Interests" of industrial workers. *Social Problems*, **3**, 131–142.

DUBIN, R. (ed.). (1976). *Handbook of Work, Organization and Society*. Rand McNally, Chicago.

DUBIN, R. and CHAMPOUX, J. E. (1975). Workers' central life interests and personality characteristics. *Journal of Vocational Behavior*, **6**, 165–174.

DUBIN, R. and CHAMPOUX, J. E. (1977). Central life interests and job satisfaction. *Organizational Behavior and Human Performance*, **18**, 366–377.

DUBIN, R., CHAMPOUX, J. E. and PORTER, L. W. (1975). Central life interests and organizational commitment of blue-collar and clerical workers. *Administrative Science Quarterly*, **20**, 411–421.

DUBIN, R., PORTER, L. W., STONE, E. F. and CHAMPOUX, J. E. (1974). Implications of differential job perceptions. *Industrial Relations*, **13**, 265–271.

DUFFY, P. J., SHIFLETT, S. and DOWNEY, R. G. (1977). Locus of control: Dimensionality and predictability using Likert scales. *Journal of Applied Psychology*, **62**, 214–219.

DUNCAN, R. G. (1971a). Multiple decision-making structures in adapting to environmental uncertainty: The impact of organizational effectiveness. Working Paper, Northwestern University, Graduate School of Management.

DUNCAN, R. G. (1971b). The effects of perceived environmental uncertainty on organizational decision unit structure: A cybernetic model. Doctoral Dissertation, Yale University.

DUNCAN, R. G. (1972). Characteristics of organizational environments and perceived environmental uncertainty. *Administrative Science Quarterly*, **17**, 313–327.

DUNHAM, R. B. (1975). Affective responses to task characteristics: The role of organizational function. Doctoral Dissertation, University of Illinois, Urbana, Illinois.

DUNHAM, R. B. (1976). The measurement and dimensionality of job characteristics. *Journal of Applied Psychology*, **61**, 404–409.

DUNHAM, R. B. (1977a). Relationships of perceived job design characteristics to job ability requirements and job value. *Journal of Applied Psychology*, **62**, 760–763.

DUNHAM, R. B. (1977b). Reactions to job characteristics: Moderating effects of the organization. *Academy of Management Journal*, **20**, 42–65.

DUNHAM, R. B. and HERMAN, J. B. (1975). Development of a female Faces Scale for measuring job satisfaction. *Journal of Applied Psychology*, **60**, 629–631.

DUNHAM, R. B., ALDAG, R. J. and BRIEF, A. P. (1977). Dimensionality of task design as measured by the Job Diagnostic Survey. *Academy of Management Journal*, **20**, 209–223.

DUNHAM, R. B., SMITH, F. J. and BLACKBURN, R. S. (1977). Validation of the Index of Organizational Reactions with the JDI, the MSQ and Faces scales. *Academy of Management Journal*, **20**, 420–432.

DUNNE, E. J., STAHL, M. J. and MELHART, L. J. (1978). Influence sources of project and functional managers in matrix organizations. *Academy of Management Journal*, **21**, 135–140.

DUNNETTE, M. D. (1966). Fads, fashions and folderol in psychology. *American Psychologist*, **21**, 343–352.

DURAND, D. E. and NORD, W. R. (1976). Perceived leader behavior as a function of personality characteristics of supervisors and subordinates. *Academy of Management Journal*, **19**, 427–438.

DYER, L. and THERIAULT, R. D. (1976). The determinants of pay satisfaction. *Journal of Applied Psychology*, **61**, 596–604.

DYER, L., SCHWAB, D. P. and THERIAULT, R. D. (1976). Managerial perceptions regarding salary increase criteria. *Personnel Psychology*, **29**, 233–242.

EDEN, D. (1975). Organizational membership vs. self-employment: Another blow to the American dream. *Organizational Behavior and Human Performance*, **13**, 79–94.

EDEN, D. and JACOBSON, D. (1976). Propensity to retire among older executives. *Journal of Vocational Behavior*, **8**, 145–154.

ELIZUR, D. and TZINER, A. (1977). Vocational needs, job rewards, and satisfaction: A canonical analysis. *Journal of Vocational Behavior*, **10**, 205–211.

ENDERLEIN, T. E. (1975). Causal patterns related to post high school employment satisfaction. *Journal of Vocational Behavior*, **7**, 67–80.

EREZ, M. (1979). Expectancy theory prediction of willingness to be retrained. *Journal of Occupational Psychology*, **52**, 35–40.

EVANS, M. G. (1969). Conceptual and operational problems in the measurement of various aspects of job satisfaction. *Journal of Applied Psychology*, **53**, 93–101.

EVANS, M. G. (1974). Extensions of a path–goal theory of motivation. *Journal of Applied Psychology*, **59**, 172–178.

EVANS, M. G. and DERMER, J. (1974). What does the Least Preferred Co-Worker scale really measure?: A cognitive interpretation. *Journal of Applied Psychology*, **59**, 202–206.

EVANS, M. G., KIGGUNDU, M. N. and HOUSE, R. J. (1979). A partial test and extension of the Job Characteristics Model of motivation. *Organizational Behavior and Human Performance*, **24**, 354–381.

EYDE, L. D. (1962). Work values and background factors as predictors of women's desire to work. Research Monograph No. 10, Bureau of Business Research, Ohio State University.

FANNIN, P. C. (1979). The relation between ego-identity status and sex-role attitude, work-role salience, atypicality of major, and self-esteem in college women. *Journal of Vocational Behavior*, **14**, 12–22.

FARR, J. L. (1976a). Incentive schedules, productivity, and satisfaction in work groups: A laboratory study. *Organizational Behavior and Human Performance*, **17**, 159–170.

FARR, J. L. (1976b). Task characteristics, reward contingency, and intrinsic motivation. *Organizational Behavior and Human Performance*, **16**, 294–307.

FARR, J. L., VANCE, R. J. and McINTYRE, R. M. (1977). Further examinations of the relationship between reward contingency and intrinsic motivation. *Organizational Behavior and Human Performance*, **20**, 31–53.

FEILD, H. S. and RIDENHOUR, C. B. (1975). Presentation of positive and negative policy changes: What effects on members' satisfaction with their organization? *Personnel Psychology*, **28**, 525–532.

FELDMAN, D. C. (1976). A contingency theory of socialization. *Administrative Science Quarterly*, **21**, 433–452.

FELDMAN, D. C. (1977). The role of initiation activities in socialization. *Human Relations*, **11**, 977–990.

FELDMAN, D. C. and ARNOLD, H. J. (1978). Position choice: Comparing the importance of organizational and job factors. *Journal of Applied Psychology*, **63**, 706–710.

FIEDLER, F. E. (1953). Quantitative studies in the role of therapists' feelings towards their patients. In O. H. Mowrer (ed.), *Psychotherapy: Theory and Research*. Ronald Press, New York.

FIEDLER, F. E. (1954). Assumed similarity measures as predictors of team effectiveness. *Journal of Abnormal and Social Psychology*, **49**, 381–388.

FIEDLER, F. E. (1958). *Leader Attitudes and Group Effectiveness*: University of Illinois Press, Urbana, Illinois.

FIEDLER, F. E. (1967). *A Theory of Leadership Effectiveness*. McGraw-Hill, New York.

FIEDLER, F. E. (1971). Validation and extension of the contingency model of leadership effectiveness: A review of empirical findings. *Psychological Bulletin*, **76**, 128–148.

FIEDLER, F. E. (1972). Personality, motivational system, and the behavior of high- and low-LPC persons. *Human Relations*, **25**, 391–412.

FIEDLER, F. E. and CHEMERS, M. M. (1974). *Leadership and Effective Management*. Scott Foresman, Glenview, Illinois.

FIEDLER, F. E. and MAHAR, L. (1979a). The effectiveness of contingency model training: A review of the validation of LEADER MATCH. *Personnel Psychology*, **32**, 45–62.

FIEDLER, F. E. and MAHAR, L. (1979b). A field experiment validating contingency model leadership training. *Journal of Applied Psychology*, **64**, 247–254.

FILLEY, A. C. and ALDAG, R. J. (1978). Characteristics and measurement of an organizational typology. *Academy of Management Journal*, **21**, 578–591.

FINEMAN, S. (1975a). The Work Preference Questionnaire: A measure of managerial need for achievement. *Journal of Occupational Psychology*, **48**, 11–32.

FINEMAN, S. (1975b). The influence of perceived job climate on the relationship between managerial achievement motivation and performance. *Journal of Occupational Psychology*, **48**, 113–124.

FINEMAN, S. (1975c). Reply to Nelson's letter to the Editor on the Work Preference Questionnaire. *Journal of Occupational Psychology*, **48**, 196–197.

FINEMAN, S. (1979). A psychosocial model of stress and its application to managerial unemployment. *Human Relations*, **32**, 323–345.

FISHER, C. D. (1978). The effects of personal control, competence and extrinsic reward systems on intrinsic motivation. *Organizational Behavior and Human Performance*, **21**, 273–288.

FLANAGAN, M. F. and ROBINSON, B. (1978). The secrecy game revisited. *American Psychologist*, **33**, 775–776.

FLEISHMAN, E. A. (1953a). The description of supervisory behavior. *Journal of Applied Psychology*, **37**, 1–6.

FLEISHMAN, E. A. (1953b). The measurement of leadership attitudes in industry. *Journal of Applied Psychology*, **37**, 153–158.

FLESIHMAN, E. A. (1957a). A leader behavior description for industry. In R. M. Stogdill and A. E. Coons (eds.), *Leader Behavior: Its Description and Measurement*. Bureau of Business Research, Ohio State University, Columbus, Ohio.

FLEISHMAN, E. A. (1957b). The Leadership Opinion Questionnaire. In R. M. Stogdill and A. E. Coons (eds.). *Leader Behavior: Its Description and Measurement*. Bureau of Business Research, Ohio State University, Columbus, Ohio.

FLEISHMAN, E. A. (1960). *Manual for the Leadership Opinion Questionnaire*. Science Research Associates Inc., 259 East Erie Street, Chicago, Illinois.

FLEISHMAN, E. A. (1963). *Recent Results on the Validity of the Leadership Opinion Questionnaire: Manual Supplement*. Science Research Associates, Inc., 259 East Erie Street, Chicago, Illinois.

FLEISHMAN, E. A. (1969). *Manual for the Leadership Opinion Questionnaire (1969 Revision)*. Science Research Associates Inc., 259 East Erie Street, Chicago, Illinois.

FLEISHMAN, E. A. (1972). *Manual for the Supervisory Description Questionnaire*. Science Research Associates Inc., 259 East Erie Street, Chicago, Illinois.

FLEISHMAN, E. A. (1973). Twenty years of Consideration and Structure. In E. A. Fleishman and J. G. Hunt (eds.), *Current Developments in the Study of Leadership*. Southern Illinois University Press, Carbondale, Illinois.

FORBES, J. B. and BARRETT, G. V. (1978). Individual abilities and task demands in relation to performance and satisfaction on two repetitive monitoring tasks. *Journal of Applied Psychology*, **63**, 188–196.

FORD, J. D. (1979). Institutional versus questionnaire measures of organizational structure: A re-examination. *Academy of Management Journal*, **22**, 601–610.

FORD, R. N., BORGATTA, E. F. and BOHRNSTEDT, G. W. (1969). Use of the Work Components Study with new college-level employees. *Journal of Applied Psychology*, **53**, 367–376.

FOTTLER, M. D. and SCHALLER, F. W. (1975). Overtime acceptance among blue-collar workers. *Industrial Relations*, **14**, 327–336.

FOX, W. M. (1976). Reliabilities, means, and standard deviations for LPC scales: Instrument refinement. *Academy of Management Journal*, **19**, 450–461.

FRANKLIN, J. L. (1975a). Down the organization: Influence processes across levels of hierarchy. *Administrative Science Quarterly*, **20**, 153–164.

FRANKLIN, J. L. (1975b). Relations among four social psychological aspects of organizations. *Administrative Science Quarterly*, **20**, 422–433.

FRANKLIN, J. L. (1975c). Power and commitment: An empirical assessment. *Human Relations*, **28**, 737–753.

FRIEDLANDER, F. (1963). Underlying sources of job satisfaction. *Journal of Applied Psychology*, **47**, 246–250.

FRIEDLANDER, F. (1965). Comparative work value systems. *Personnel Psychology*, **18**, 1–20.

FRIEDLANDER, F. (1971). Congruence in organization development. *Proceedings of the 31st Annual Meeting of the Academy of Management*, 153–161.

FRENCH, J. and RAVEN, B. (1959). The bases of social power. In D. Cartwright (ed.), *Studies in Social Power*. Institute for Social Research, Ann Arbor, Michigan.

FROST, P. J. and JAMAL, M. (1979). Shift work, attitudes, and reported behavior: Some associations between individual characteristics and hours of work and leisure. *Journal of Applied Psychology*, **64**, 77–81.

FUTRELL, C. M. (1978). Effects of pay disclosure on satisfaction for sales managers: A longitudinal study. *Academy of Management Journal*, **21**, 140–144.

GANSTER, D. C. (1980). Individual differences and task design: A laboratory experiment. *Organizational Behavior and Human Performance*, **26**, 131–148.

GARLAND, H. and PRICE, K. H. (1977). Attitudes towards women in management and attributions for their success and failure in managerial positions. *Journal of Applied Psychology*, **62**, 29–33.

GARRISON, K. R. and MUCHINSKY, P. M. (1977). Attitudinal and biographical predictors of incidental absenteeism. *Journal of Vocational Behavior*, **10**, 221–230.

GAVIN, J. F. and AXELROD, W. L. (1977). Managerial stress and strain in a mining organization. *Journal of Vocational Behavior*, **11**, 66–74.

GAVIN, J. F. and KELLEY, R. E. (1978). The psychological climate and reported well-being of underground miners: An exploratory study. *Human Relations*, **31**, 567–581.

GAVIN, J. F. and MAYNARD, W. S. (1975). Perceptions of corporate social responsibility. *Personnel Psychology*, **28**, 377–387.

GAY, E. G., WEISS, D. J., HENDEL, D. D., DAWIS, R. V. and LOFQUIST, L. H. (1971). *Manual for the Minnesota Importance Questionnaire*. Industrial Relations Center, University of Minnesota.

GECHMAN, A. S. and WIENER, Y. (1975). Job involvement and satisfaction as related to mental health and personal time devoted to work. *Journal of Applied Psychology*, **60**, 521–523.

GETMAN, J., GOLDBERG, J. and HERMAN, J. (1976). *Union Representation Elections: Law and Reality*. Russell Sage, New York.

GHISELLI, E. E. (1971). *Explorations in Managerial Talent*. Goodyear, Pacific Palisades, California.

GILES, W. F. (1977a). Volunteering for job enrichment: A test of expectancy theory predictions. *Personnel Psychology*, **30**, 427–435.

GILES, W. F. (1977b). Volunteering for job enrichment: Reaction to job characteristics or to change? *Journal of Vocational Behavior*, **11**, 232–238.

GILLET, B. and SCHWAB, D. P. (1975). Convergent and discriminant validities of corresponding Job Descriptive Index and Minnesota Satisfaction Questionnaire scales. *Journal of Applied Psychology*, **60**, 313–317.

GILMORE, D. C., BEEHR, T. A. and RICHTER, D. J. (1979). Effects of leader behaviors on subordinate performance and satisfaction: A laboratory experiment with student employees. *Journal of Applied Psychology*, **64**, 166–172.

GLICK, W., MIRVIS, P. and HARDER, D. (1977). Union satisfaction and participation. *Industrial Relations*, **16**, 145–151.

GLISSON, C. A. and MARTIN, P. Y. (1980). Productivity and efficiency in human service organizations as related to structure, size, and age. *Academy of Management Journal*, **23**, 21–37.

GOLDBERG, D. P. (1972). *The Detection of Psychiatric Illness by Questionnaire.* Oxford University Press, Oxford.

GOLEMBIEWSKI, R. T., and YEAGER, S. (1978). Testing the applicability of the JDI to various demographic groupings. *Academy of Management Journal*, **21**, 514–519.

GOLEMBIEWSKI, R. T., YEAGER, S. and HILLES, R. (1975). Factor analysis of some flexitime effects: Attitudinal and behavioral consequences of a structural intervention. *Academy of Management Journal*, **18**, 500–509.

GOODALE, J. G. (1969). A canonical regression analysis of work values and biographical information of civil service employees. Unpublished Manuscript, Bowling Green State University.

GORDON, L. V. (1970). Measurement of bureaucratic orientation. *Personnel Psychology*, **23**, 1–11.

GORDON, L. V. (1973). *Work Environment Preference Schedule.* The Psychological Corporation, New York.

GORDON, M. E. and ARVEY, R. D. (1975). The relationship between education and satisfaction with job content. *Academy of Management Journal*, **18**, 888–892.

GOULD, S. (1979a). Characteristics of career planners in upwardly mobile occupations. *Academy of Management Journal*, **22**, 539–550.

GOULD, S. (1979b). Age, job complexity, satisfaction and performance. *Journal of Vocational Behavior*, **14**, 209–223.

GOULD, S. and HAWKINS, B. L. (1978). Organizational career stage as a moderator of the satisfaction-performance relationship. *Academy of Management Journal*, **21**, 434–450.

GRAEN, G. (1969). Instrumentality theory of work motivation: Some experimental results and suggested modifications. *Journal of Applied Psychology Monograph*, **53**, 1–25.

GRAEN, G. and DAWES, R. V. (1971). A measure of work attitudes for high school age youth. *Journal of Vocational Behavior*, **1**, 343–353.

GRAEN, G. and GINSBURGH, S. (1977). Job resignation as a function of role orientation and leader acceptance: A longitudinal investigation of organizational assimilation. *Organizational Behavior and Human Performance*, **19**, 1–17.

GRAEN, G., DANSEREAU, F. and MINAMI, T. (1972). Dysfunctional leadership styles. *Organizational Behavior and Human Performance*, **7**, 216–236.

GRAEN, G., ORRIS, J. B. and ALVAREZ, K. M. (1971). Contingency model of leadership effectiveness: Some methodological issues. *Journal of Applied Psychology*, **55**, 205–210.

GRAEN, G., ORRIS, J. B. and JOHNSON, T. W. (1973). Role assimilation processes in a complex organization. *Journal of Vocational Behavior*, **3**, 395–420.

GRAEN, G., ALVAREZ, K. M., ORRIS, J. B. and MARTELLA, J. A. (1970). Contingency model of leadership effectiveness: Antecedent and evidential results. *Psychological Bulletin*, **74**, 285–296.

GRAEN, G., CASHMAN, J. F., GINSBURG, S. and SCHIEMAN, W. (1977). Effects of linking-pin quality on the quality of working life of lower participants. *Administrative Science Quarterly*, **22**, 491–504.

GREEN, S. B., ARMENAKIS, A. A., MARBERT, L. D. and BEDEIAN, A. G. (1979). An evaluation of the response format and scale structure of the Job Diagnostic Survey. *Human Relations*, **32**, 181–188.

GREENBERG, J. (1977). The Protestant Work Ethic and reactions to negative performance evaluations on a laboratory task. *Journal of Applied Psychology*, **62**, 682–690.

GREENBERG, J. (1978). Protestant Ethic endorsement and attitudes towards commuting to work among mass transit riders. *Journal of Applied Psychology*, **63**, 755–758.

GREENE, C. N. (1975). The reciprocal nature of influence between leader and subordinate. *Journal of Applied Psychology*, **60**, 187–193.

GREENE, C. N. (1978). Identification modes of professionals: Relationship with formalization, role strain, and alienation. *Academy of Management Journal*, **21**, 486–492.

GREENE, C. N. (1979). Questions of causation in the path–goal theory of leadership. *Academy of Management Journal*, **22**, 22–41.

GREENE, C. N. and SCHRIESHEIM, C. A. (1980). Leader–group interactions: A longitudinal investigation. *Journal of Applied Psychology*, **65**, 50–59.

GREENE, S. G. and NEBEKER, D. M. (1977). The effects of situational factors and leadership style on leader behavior. *Organizational Behavior and Human Performance*, **19**, 368–377.

GREENE, S. G., NEBEKER, D. M. and BONI, M. A. (1976). Personality and situational effects on leader behavior. *Academy of Management Journal*, **19**, 184–194.

GREENHAUS, J. H. and SIMON, W. E. (1976). Self-esteem, career salience, and the choice of an ideal occupation. *Journal of Vocational Behavior*, **8**, 51–58.

GREENHAUS, J. H. and SIMON, W. E. (1977). Career salience, work values, and vocational indecision. *Journal of Vocational Behavior*, **10**, 104–110.

GRELLER, M. M. (1978). The nature of subordinate participation in the appraisal interview. *Academy of Management Journal*, **21**, 646–658.

GROSS, N., MASON, W. and MCEACHERN, A. (1958). *Explorations in Role Analysis*. Wiley, New York.

GUILFORD, J. P. (1954). *Psychometric Methods* (2nd edition). McGraw-Hill, New York.

GUILFORD, J. P. and FRUCHTER, B. (1973). *Fundamental Statistics in Psychology and Education* (5th edition). McGraw-Hill, New York.

GUION, R. M. (1973). A note on organizational climate. *Organizational Behavior and Human Performance*, **9**, 120–125.

GUION, R. M. and ROBINS, J. E. (1964). A note on the Nagle attitude scale. *Journal of Applied Psychology*, **48**, 29–30.

GUPTA, N. and BEEHR, T. A. (1979). Job stress and employee behaviors. *Organizational Behavior and Human Performance*, **23**, 373–387.

GURIN, G., VEROFF, J. and FELD, S. (1960). *Americans View their Mental Health*. Basic Books, New York.

HACKMAN, J. R. (1973). Scoring key for the Yale Job Inventory. Yale University, Department of Administrative Sciences, New Haven.

HACKMAN, J. R. and LAWLER, E. E. (1971). Employee reactions to job characteristics. *Journal of Applied Psychology*, **55**, 259–286.

HACKMAN, J. R. and OLDHAM, G. R. (1974). The Job Diagnostic Survey: An instrument for the diagnosis of jobs and the evaluation of job redesign projects. Yale University, Department of Administrative Sciences, Technical Report 4.

HACKMAN, J. R. and OLDHAM, G. R. (1975). Development of the Job Diagnostic Survey. *Journal of Applied Psychology*, **60**, 159–170.

HACKMAN, J. R. and OLDHAM, G. R. (1976). Motivation through the design of work: Test of a theory. *Organizational Behavior and Human Performance*, **16**, 250–279.

HACKMAN, J. R. and OLDHAM, G. R. (1980). *Work Redesign*. Addison-Wesley, Reading, Massachusetts.

HACKMAN, J. R., PEARCE, J. L. and WOLFE, J. C. (1978). Effects of changes in job characteristics on work attitudes and behaviors: A naturally occurring quasi-experiment. *Organizational Behavior and Human Performance*, **21**, 289–304.

HAGE, J. and AIKEN, M. (1967). Relationship of centralization to other structural properties. *Administrative Science Quarterly*, **12**, 72–92.

HAGE, J. and AIKEN, M. (1969). Routine technology, social structure, and organization goals. *Administrative Science Quarterly*, **14**, 366–376.

HALL, D. T. and FOSTER, L. W. (1977). A psychological success cycle and goal setting: Goals, performance and attitudes. *Academy of Management Journal*, **20**, 282–290.

HALL, D. T. and MANSFIELD, R. (1975). Relationships of age and seniority with career variables of engineers and scientists. *Journal of Applied Psychology*, **60**, 201–210.

HALL, D. T., SCHNEIDER, B. and NYGREN, H. T. (1970). Personal factors in organizational identification. *Administrative Science Quarterly*, **15**, 176–190.

HALL, D. T., GOODALE, J. G., RABINOWITZ, S. and MORGAN, M. A. (1978). Effects of top-down departmental and job change upon perceived employee behavior and attitudes: A natural field experiment. *Journal of Applied Psychology*, **63**, 62–72.

HALL, J. and DONNELL, S. M. (1979). Managerial achievement: The personal side of behavioral theory. *Human Relations*, **32**, 77–101.

HALL, R. (1963). The concept of bureaucracy: An empirical assessment. *American Journal of Sociology*, **69**, 32–40.

HALL, R. (1968). Professionalization and bureaucratization. *American Sociological Review*, **33**, 92–104.

HALPIN, A. W. (1966). *Theory and Research in Administration*. Macmillan, New York.

HALPIN, A. W. and CROFT, D. B. (1963). *The Organizational Climate of Schools*. University of Chicago Press, Chicago.

HAMMER, T. H. (1978). Relationships between local union characteristics and worker behavior and attitudes. *Academy of Management Journal*, **21**, 560–577.

HAMMER, T. H. and DACHLER, H. P. (1975). A test of some assumptions underlying the path–goal model of supervision: Some suggested modifications. *Organizational Behavior and Human Performance*, **14**, 60–75.

HAMMER, T. H. and STERN, R. N. (1980). Employee ownership: Implications for the organizational distribution of power. *Academy of Management Journal*, **23**, 78–100.

HAMNER, W. C. and SMITH, F. J. (1978). Work attitudes as predictors of unionization activity. *Journal of Applied Psychology*, **63**, 415–421.

HAMNER, W. C. and TOSI, H. L. (1974). Relationship of role conflict and role ambiguity to job involvement measures. *Journal of Applied Psychology*, **59**, 497–499.

HANSER, L. M. and MUCHINSKY, P. M. (1978). Work as an information environment. *Organizational Behavior and Human Performance*, **21**, 47–60.

HELLER, F. A., DRENTH, P. J. D., KOOPMAN, P. and RUS, V. (1977). A longitudinal study in participative decision-making. *Human Relations*, **30**, 567–587.

HELMICH, D. L. (1975). Corporate succession: An examination. *Academy of Management Journal*, **18**, 429–441.

HELMICH, R. and STAPP, J. (1974). Short forms of the Texas Social Behavior Inventory, an objective measure of self-esteem. *Bulletin of the Psychonomic Society*, **4**, 473–475.

HEMPHILL, J. K. (1949). Situational factors in leadership. Monograph No. 32. Ohio State University, Bureau of Educational Research, Columbus, Ohio.

HEPWORTH, S. J. (1980). Moderating factors of the psychological impact of unemployment. *Journal of Occupational Psychology*, **53**, 139–145.

HERMAN, J. B., DUNHAM, R. B. and HULIN, C. L. (1975). Organizational structure, demographic characteristics and employee responses. *Organizational Behavior and Human Performance*, **13**, 206–232.

HEROLD, D. M. (1974). Interaction of subordinate and leader characteristics in moderating the consideration–satisfaction relationship. *Journal of Applied Psychology*, **59**, 649–651.

HEROLD, D. M. and GRELLER, M. M. (1977). Feedback: The definition of a construct. *Academy of Management Journal*, **20**, 142–147.

HERRIOT, P. and ECOB, R. (1979). Occupational choice and expectancy-value theory: Some modifications. *Journal of Occupational Psychology*, **52**, 311–324.

HERZBERG, F., MAUSNER, B., and SNYDERMAN, B. (1959). *The Motivation to Work*. Wiley, New York.

HEWETT, T. T., O'BRIEN, G. E. and HORNICK, J. (1974). The effects of work organization, leadership style, and member compatibility upon the productivity of small groups working on a manipulative task. *Organizational Behavior and Human Performance*, **11**, 283–301.

HILL, W. A. and RUHE, J. A. (1974). Attitudes and behaviors of black and white supervisors in problem-solving groups. *Academy of Management Journal*, **17**, 563–569.

HOIBERG, A. and BERRY, N. W. (1978). Expectations and perceptions of navy life. *Organizational Behavior and Human Performance*, **21**, 130–145.

HOLAHAN, C. K. and GILBERT, L. A. (1979a). Interrole conflict for working women: Careers versus jobs. *Journal of Applied Psychology*, **64**, 86–90.

HOLAHAN, C. K. and GILBERT, L. A. (1979b). Conflict between major life roles: Women and men in dual career couples. *Human Relations*, **32**, 451–467.

HOLLAND, J. L. (1956). *The Vocational Preference Inventory*. Consulting Psychologists Press, Palo Alto, California.

HOLLMAN, R. W. (1976). Supportive organizational climate and managerial assessment of MBO effectiveness. *Academy of Management Journal*, **19**, 560–576.

HOLLON, C. J. and CHESSER, R. J. (1976). The relationship of personal influence dissonance to job tension, satisfaction and involvement. *Academy of Management Journal*, **19**, 308–314.

HOM, P. W. (1979). Effects of job peripherality and personal characteristics on the job satisfaction of part-time workers. *Academy of Management Journal*, **22**, 551–565.

HOM, P. W. (1980). Expectancy predictions of reenlistment in the national guard. *Journal of Vocational Behavior*, **16**, 235–248.

HOM, P. W., KATERBERG, R. and HULIN, C. L. (1979). Comparative examination of three approaches to the prediction of turnover. *Journal of Applied Psychology*, **64**, 280–290.

HOPPOCK, R. (1935). *Job Satisfaction*. Harper and Brothers, New York. Reprint Edition by Arno Press, New York, 1977.

HOUSE, R. J. (1970). A path–goal theory of leader effectiveness. *Administrative Science Quarterly*, **16**, 321–338.

HOUSE, R. J. and DESSLER, G. (1974). The path–goal theory of leadership: Some post hoc and a priori tests. In J. G. Hunt and L. T. Larson (eds.), *Contingency Approaches to Leadership*. Southern Illinois University Press, Carbondale, Illinois.

HOUSE, R. J. and RIZZO, J. R. (1972a). Toward the measurement of organizational practices: Scale development and validation. *Journal of Applied Psychology*, **56**, 388–396.

HOUSE, R. J. and RIZZO, J. R. (1972b). Role conflict and ambiguity as critical variables in a model of organizational behavior. *Organizational Behavior and Human Performance*, **7**, 467–505.

HOVEY, D. E. (1974). The low-powered leader confronts a messy problem: A test of Fiedler's theory. *Academy of Management Journal*, **17**, 358–362.

HOWARD, J. H., CUNNINGHAM, D. A. and RECHNITZER, P. A. (1977). Work patterns associated with type A behavior: A managerial population. *Human Relations*, **30**, 825–836.

HOWAT, G. and LONDON, M. (1980). Attributions of conflict management strategies in supervisor–subordinate dyads. *Journal of Applied Psychology*, **65**, 172–175.

HOWELL, P., STRAUSS, J. and SORENSEN, P. F. (1975). Research note: Cultural and situational determinants of job satisfaction among management in Liberia. *Journal of Management Studies*, **12**, 225–227.

HREBENIAK, L. G. (1974). Effects of job level and participation on employee attitudes and perceptions of influence. *Academy of Management Journal*, **17**, 649–662.

HREBENIAK, L. G. and ALUTTO, J. A. (1972). Personal and role-related factors in the development of organizational commitment. *Administrative Science Quarterly*, **17**, 555–573.

HULIN, C. L. and BLOOD, M. R. (1968). Job enlargement, individual differences, and worker responses. *Psychological Bulletin*, **69**, 41–55.

HUNT, J. G., OSBORN, R. N. and LARSON, L. L. (1975). Upper-level technical orientation and first level leadership within a noncontingency and contingency framework. *Academy of Management Journal*, **18**, 476–488.

HUNT, J. G., OSBORN, R. N. and SCHULER, R. S. (1978). Relations of discretionary and nondiscretionary leadership to performance and satisfaction in a complex organisation. *Human Relations*, **31**, 507–523.

HUNT, J. W. and SAUL, P. N. (1975). The relationship of age, tenure and job satisfaction in males and females. *Academy of Management Journal*, **18**, 690–702.

HUNT, S., SINGER, K. and COBB, S. (1967). Components of depression: Identified from a self-rating inventory for survey use. *Archives of General Psychiatry*, **16**, 441–447.

ILGEN, D. R. and FUJII, D. S. (1976). An investigation of the validity of leader behavior descriptions obtained from subordinates. *Journal of Applied Psychology*, **61**, 642–651.

ILGEN, D. R. and HOLLENBACK, J. H. (1977). The role of job satisfaction in absence behavior. *Organizational Behavior and Human Performance*, **19**, 148–161.

INDIK, B., SEASHORE, S. E. and SLESINGER, J. (1964). Demographic correlates of psychological strain. *Journal of Abnormal and Social Psychology*, **69**, 26–38.

INGRASSIA, A. F. (1974). Coefficients of success in Federal LMR programs. *Civil Service Journal*, **15**, 6–10.

INKSON, J. H. K. (1978). Self-esteem as a moderator of the relationship between job performance and job satisfaction. *Journal of Applied Psychology*, **63**, 243–247.

INSEL, P. M. and MOOS, R. H. (1974). The Work Environment Scale. Stanford University, Social Ecology Laboratory, Department of Psychiatry, Palo Alto, California.

IVANCEVICH, J. M. (1974). Effects of the shorter workweek on selected satisfaction and performance measures. *Journal of Applied Psychology*, **59**, 717–721.

IVANCEVICH, J. M. (1976a). Expectancy theory predictions and behaviorally anchored scales of motivation: An empirical test with engineers. *Journal of Vocational Behavior*, **8**, 59–75.

IVANCEVICH, J. M. (1976b). Predicting job performance by use of ability tests and studying job satisfaction as a moderating variable. *Journal of Vocational Behavior*, **9**, 87–97.

IVANCEVICH, J. M. (1976c). Effects of goal setting on performance and job satisfaction. *Journal of Applied Psychology*, **61**, 605–612.

IVANCEVICH, J. M. (1977). Different goal setting treatments and their effects on performance and job satisfaction. *Academy of Management Journal*, **20**, 406–419.

IVANCEVICH, J. M. (1978). The performance to satisfaction relationship: A causal analysis of stimulating and non-stimulating jobs. *Organizational Behavior and Human Performance*, **22**, 350–365.

IVANCEVICH, J. M. (1979a). High and low task stimulation jobs: A causal analysis of performance–satisfaction relationships. *Academy of Management Journal*, **22**, 206–222.

IVANCEVICH, J. M. (1979b). An analysis of participation in decision making among engineers. *Academy of Management Journal*, **22**, 253–269.

IVANCEVICH, J. M. (1980). A longitudinal study of behavioral expectation scales: Attitudes and performance. *Journal of Applied Psychology*, **65**, 139–146.

IVANCEVICH, J. M. and DONNELLY, J. H. (1974). A study of role clarity and need for clarity for three occupational groups. *Academy of Management Journal*, **17**, 28–36.

IVANCEVICH, J. M. and DONNELLY, J. H. (1975). Relation of organizational structure to job satisfaction, anxiety-stress and performance. *Administrative Science Quarterly*, **20**, 272–280.

IVANCEVICH, J. M. and LYON, H. L. (1977). The shortened workweek: A field experiment. *Journal of Applied Psychology*, **62**, 34–37.

IVANCEVICH, J. M. and MCMAHON, J. T. (1976). Group development, trainer style and carry-over job satisfaction and performance. *Academy of Management Journal*, **19**, 395–412.

JACKSON, D. N. (1967). *Personality Research Form Manual*. Academic Press, New York.

JACOBS, R. and SOLOMON, T. (1977). Strategies for enhancing the prediction of job performance from job satisfaction. *Journal of Applied Psychology*, **62**, 417–421.

JACOBSON, D. and ERAN, M. (1980). Expectancy theory components and non-expectancy moderators as predictors of physicians' preference for retirement. *Journal of Occupational Psychology*, **53**, 11–26.

JACOBY, J. and TERBORG, J. R. (1975a). Managerial Philosophies Scale. Teleometrics International, Conroe, Texas.

JACOBY, J. and TERBORG, J. R. (1975b). Development and validation of Theory X and Y scales for assessing McGregor's managerial philosophies. Teleometrics International, Conroe, Texas.

JAMAL, M. and MITCHELL, V. F. (1980). Work, non-work and mental health: A model and a test. *Industrial Relations*, **19**, 88–93.

JAMES, L. R. and JONES, A. P. (1973). Organizational climate: Construct, global concept or tautology? Texas Christian University, Institute of Behavioral Research, Fort Worth.

JAMES, L. R. and JONES, A. P. (1974). Organizational climate: A review of theory and research. *Psychological Bulletin*, **81**, 1096–1112.

JAMES, L. R. and JONES, A. P. (1976). Organizational structure: A review of structural dimensions and their conceptual relationships with individual attitudes and behavior. *Organizational Behavior and Human Performance*, **16**, 74–113.

JAMES, L. R. and JONES, A. P. (1980). Perceived job characteristics and job satisfaction: An examination of reciprocal causation. *Personnel Psychology*, **33**, 97–135.

JAMES, L. R., GENT, M. J., HATER, J. J. and CORAY, K. E. (1979). Correlates of psychological influence: An illustration of the psychological climate approach to work environment perceptions. *Personnel Psychology*, **32**, 563–588.

JAMES, L. R., HARTMAN, E. A., STEBBINS, M. W. and JONES, A. P. (1977). An examination of the relationship between psychological climate and a VIE model for work motivation. *Personnel Psychology*, **30**, 229–254.

JAUCH, L. R., GLUECK, W. F. and OSBORN, R. N. (1978). Organizational loyalty, professional commitment and academic research productivity. *Academy of Management Journal*, **21**, 84–92.

JERMIER, J. M. and BERKES, L. J. (1979). Leader behavior in a police command bureaucracy: A closer look at the quasi-military model. *Administrative Science Quarterly*, **24**, 1–23.

JOHNS, G. (1978a). Task moderators of the relationship between leadership style and subordinate responses. *Academy of Management Journal*, **21**, 319–325.

JOHNS, G. (1978b). Attitudinal and non attitudinal predictors of two forms of absence from work. *Organizational Behavior and Human Performance*, **22**, 431–444.

JOHNSON, R. D. (1973). An investigation of the interaction effects of ability and motivational variables on task performance. Unpublished Doctoral Dissertation, Indiana University.

JOHNSON, T. W. and STINSON, J. E. (1975). Role ambiguity, role conflict and satisfaction: Moderating effects of individual differences. *Journal of Applied Psychology*, **60**, 329–333.

JONES, A. P. and JAMES, L. R. (1979). Psychological climate: Dimensions and relationships of individual and aggregated work environment perceptions. *Organizational Behavior and Human Performance*, **23**, 201–250.

JONES, A. P., JAMES, L. R. and BRUNI, J. R. (1975). Perceived leadership behavior and employee confidence in the leader as moderated by job involvement. *Journal of Applied Psychology*, **60**, 146–149.

JONES, A. P., JAMES, L. R. and HORNICK, C. W. (1973). Organizational climate related to shipboard functioning: A preliminary study. Texas Christian University, Institute of Behavioral Research, Fort Worth.

JONES, A. P., JAMES, L. R., BRUNI, J. R. and SELLS, S. B. (1977). Black–white differences in work envi;onment perceptions and job satisfaction and its correlates. *Personnel Psychology*, **30**, 5–16.

KAHN, R. L., WOLFE, D. M., QUINN, R. P., SNOEK, J. D. and ROSENTHAL, R. (1964). *Organizational Stress: Studies in Role Conflict and Ambiguity*. Wiley, New York.

KANUNGO, R. N. (1979). The concepts of alienation and involvement revisited. *Psychological Bulletin*, **86**, 119–138.

KANUNGO, R. N., MISRA, S. B. and DAYAL, I. (1975). Relationship of job involvement to perceived importance and satisfaction of employee needs. *International Review of Applied Psychology*, **24**, 49–59.

KARASEK, R. A. (1979). Job demands, job decision latitude, and mental strain: Implications for job redesign. *Administrative Science Quarterly*, **24**, 285–308.

KATERBERG, R., HOM, P. W. and HULIN, C. I. (1979). Effects of job complexity on the reactions of part-time employees. *Organizational Behavior and Human Performance*, **24**, 317–322.

KATERBERG, R., SMITH, F. J. and HOY, S. (1977). Language, time, and person effects on attitude scale translations. *Journal of Applied Psychology*, **62**, 385–391.

KATZ, R. (1978a). Job longevity as a situational factor in job satisfaction. *Administrative Science Quarterly*, **23**, 204–223.

KATZ, R. (1978b). The influence of job longevity on employee reactions to task characteristics. *Human Relations*, **31**, 703–725.

KATZ, R. and VAN MAANEN, J. (1977). The loci of work satisfaction: Job, interaction, and policy. *Human Relations*, **30**, 469–486.

KATZELL, R. A., EWEN, R. and KORMAN, A. K. (1974). Job attitudes of black and white workers: Male blue-collar workers in six companies. *Journal of Vocational Behavior*, **4**, 365–376.

KAVANAGH, M. J. (1975). Expected supervisory behavior, interpersonal trust and environmental preferences. *Organizational Behavior and Human Performance*, **13**, 17–30.

KAVANAGH, M. J. and HALPERN, M. (1977). The impact of job level and sex differences on the relationship between life and job satisfaction. *Academy of Management Journal*, **20**, 66–73.

KAZANAS, H. C. (1978). Relationship of job satisfaction and productivity to work values of vocational education graduates. *Journal of Vocational Behavior*, **12**, 155–164.

KAZANAS, H. C., HANNAH, L. D. and GREGOR, T. G. (1975). An instrument to measure the meaning and the value associated with work. *Journal of Industrial Teacher Education*, **12**, 68–73.

KEENAN, A. (1979). Initial graduate recruitment interviews: Candidate characteristics and interview outcomes. *Personnel Review*, **8**, 1, 14–19.

KEENAN, A. and MCBAIN, G. D. M. (1978). The job-related consequences of different types of role stress. *Personnel Review*, **7**, 3, 41–44.

KEENAN, A. and MCBAIN, G. D. M. (1979). Effects of type A behaviour, intolerance of ambiguity, and locus of control on the relationship between role stress and work-related outcomes. *Journal of Occupational Psychology*, **52**, 277–285.

KELLER, R. T. (1975). Role conflict and ambiguity: Correlates with job satisfaction and values. *Personnel Psychology*, **28**, 57–64.

KELLER, R. T. (1978). Dimensions of management system and performance in continuous-process organizations. *Human Relations*, **31**, 59–75.

KELLER, R. T. and HOLLAND, W. E. (1975a). Boundary spanning activity and research and development management: A comparative study. *IEEE Transactions on Engineering Management*, **22**, 130–133.

KELLER, R. T. and HOLLAND, W. E. (1975b). Boundary spanning roles in research and development organizations: An empirical investigation. *Academy of Management Journal*, **18**, 388–393.

KELLER, R. T. and HOLLAND, W. E. (1978). Individual characteristics of innovativeness and communication in research and development organizations. *Journal of Applied Psychology*, **63**, 759–762.

KELLER, R. T. and SZILAGYI, A. D. (1976). Employee reactions to leader reward behavior. *Academy of Management Journal*, **19**, 619–627.

KELLER, R. T. and SZILAGYI, A. D. (1978). A longitudinal study of leader behavior, subordinate expectancies, and satisfaction. *Personnel Psychology*, **31**, 119–129.

KELLER, R. T., SLOCUM, J. W. and SUSMAN, G. I. (1974). Uncertainty and type of management system in continuous process organizations. *Academy of Management Journal*, **17**, 56–68.

KELLER, R. T., SZILAGYI, A. D. and HOLLAND, W. E. (1976). Boundary spanning activity and employee reactions: An empirical study. *Human Relations*, **29**, 699–710.

KERR, S. and JERMIER, J. M. (1978). Substitutes for leadership: Their meaning and measurement. *Organizational Behavior and Human Performance*, **22**, 375–403.

KERR, S. and SCHRIESHEIM, C. A. (1974). Consideration, Initiating Structure and organizational criteria: An update of Korman's 1966 review. *Personnel Psychology*, **27**, 555–568.

KERR, S., SCHREISHEIM, C. A., MURPHY, C. J. and STOGDILL, R. M. (1974). Toward a contingency theory of leadership based upon the Consideration and Initiating Structure literature. *Organizational Behavior and Human Performance*, **12**, 62–82.

KESSELMAN, G. A., HAGEN, E. L. and WHERRY, R. J. (1974). A factor analytic test of the Porter-Lawler expectancy model of work motivation. *Personnel Psychology*, **27**, 569–579.

KESSELMAN, G. A., WOOD, M. T. and HAGEN, E. L. (1974). Relationships between performance and satisfaction under contingent and non-contingent reward systems. *Journal of Applied Psychology*, **59**, 374–376.

KIDRON, A. (1978). Work values and organizational commitment. *Academy of Management Journal*, **21**, 239–247.

KIGGUNDU, M. N. (1980). An empirical test of the theory of job design using multiple job ratings. *Human Relations*, **33**, 339–351.

KIM, J. S. (1980). Relationships of personality to perceptual and behavioral responses in stimulating and non-stimulating tasks. *Academy of Management Journal*, **23**, 307–319.

KIM, J. S. and HAMNER, W. C. (1976). Effect of performance feedback and goal setting on productivity and satisfaction in an organizational setting. *Journal of Applied Psychology*, **61**, 48–57.

KIM, J. S. and SCHULER, R. S. (1979). The nature of the task as a moderator of the relationship between extrinsic feedback and employee responses. *Academy of Management Journal*, **22**, 157–162.

KING, D. C. (1960). A multiplant factor analysis of employees' attitudes toward their company. *Journal of Applied Psychology*, **44**, 241–243.

KIRCHOFF, B. A. (1975). A diagnostic tool for management by objectives. *Personnel Psychology*, **28**, 351–364.

KLEIN, K. L. and WIENER, Y. (1977). Interest congruency as a moderator of the relationships between job tenure and job satisfaction and mental health. *Journal of Vocational Behavior*, **10**, 92–98.

KOCH, J. L. (1977). Status inconsistency and the technician's work adjustment. *Journal of Occupational Psychology*, **50**, 121–128.

KOCH, J. L. (1978). Managerial succession in a factory and changes in supervisory leadership patterns: A field study. *Human Relations*, **31**, 49–58.

KOCH, J. L. (1979). Effects of goal specificity and performance feedback to work groups on peer leadership, performance and attitudes. *Human Relations*, **32**, 819–840.

KOCH, J. L. and STEERS, R. M. (1978). Job attachment, satisfaction and turnover among public sector employees. *Journal of Vocational Behavior*, **12**, 119–128.

KONAR-GOLDBAND, E., RICE, R. W. and MONKARSH, W. (1979). Time-phased interrelationships of group atmosphere, group performance and leader style. *Journal of Applied Psychology*, **64**, 401–409.

KOPELMAN, R. E. (1976). Organizational control system responsiveness, expectancy theory constructs, and work motivation: Some intercorrelations and causal connections. *Personnel Psychology*, **29**, 205–220.

KOPELMAN, R. E. (1979). A causal correlation test of the Porter and Lawler framework. *Human Relations*, **32**, 545–556.

KOPELMAN, R. E. and THOMPSON, P. H. (1976). Boundary conditions for expectancy theory predictions of work motivation and job performance. *Academy of Management Journal*, **19**, 237–258.

KOPP, D. G. and LITSCHERT, R. J. (1980). A buffering response in light of variation in core technology, perceived environmental uncertainty, and size. *Academy of Management Journal*, **23**, 252–266.

KORMAN, A. K. (1966). Consideration, Initiating Structure and organizational criteria: A review. *Personnel Psychology*, **19**, 349–361.

KORNHAUSER, A. (1965). *Mental Health of the Industrial Worker*. Wiley, New York.

KUEHL, C. R., DI MARCO, N. and WIMS, E. W. (1975). Leadership orientation as a function of interpersonal need structure. *Journal of Applied Psychology*, **60**, 143–145.

KUNIN, T. (1955). The construction of a new type of attitude measure. *Personnel Psychology*, **8**, 65–78.

LAFOLLETTE, W. R. and SIMS, H. P. (1975). Is satisfaction redundant with organizational climate? *Organizational Behavior and Human Performance*, **13**, 257–278.

LAKE, D. G. and MILES, M. B. (1973). Organizational Climate Description Questionnaire. In D. G. Lake, M. B. Miles and R. B. Earle (eds.), *Measuring Human Behavior*. Teachers College Press, New York.

LAKE, D. G., MILES, M. B. and EARLE, A. B. (1973). *Measuring Human Behavior*. Teachers College Press, New York.

LARSON, L. L. and ROWLAND, K. M. (1974). Leadership style and cognitive complexity. *Academy of Management Journal*, **17**, 37–45.

LARSON, L. L., HUNT, J. G. and OSBORN, R. N. (1976). The great hi-hi leader behavior myth: A lesson from Occam's razor. *Academy of Management Journal*, **19**, 628–641.

LA ROCCO, J. M., PUGH, W. M. and GUNDERSON, E. K. E. (1977). Identifying determinants of retention decisions. *Personnel Psychology*, **30**, 199–215.

LATHAM, G. P. and YUKL, G. A. (1976). Effects of assigned and participative goal setting on performance and job satisfaction. *Journal of Applied Psychology*, **61**, 166–171.

LAWLER, E. E. (1969). Job design and employee motivation. *Personnel Psychology*, **22**, 426–435.

LAWLER, E. E. and HALL, D. T. (1970). Relationship of job characteristics to job involvement, satisfaction and intrinsic motivation. *Journal of Applied Psychology*, **54**, 305–312.

LAWLER, E. E. and SUTTLE, J. L. (1973). Expectancy theory and job behavior. *Organizational Behavior and Human Performance*, **9**, 482–503.

LAWLER, E. E., HALL, D. T. and OLDHAM, G. R. (1974). Organizational climate: Relationship to organizational structure, process and performance. *Organizational Behavior and Human Performance*, **11**, 139–155.

LAWRENCE, P. R. and LORSCH, J. W. (1967). *Organization and Environment*. Harvard University Press, Boston.

LAWSHE, C. H. and NAGLE, B. F. (1953). Productivity and attitude toward supervisor. *Journal of Applied Psychology*, **37**, 159–162.

LEE, A. (1972). An obituary for "alienation". *Social Problems*, **20**, 121–126.

LEFKOWITZ, J. (1974). Job attitudes of police: Overall description and demographic correlates. *Journal of Vocational Behavior*, **5**, 221–230.

LEFKOWITZ, J. and BRIGANDO, L. (1980). The redundancy of work alienation and job satisfaction: Some evidence of convergent and discriminant validity. *Journal of Vocational Behavior*, **16**, 115–131.

LEIFER, R. P. and HUBER, G. P. (1977). Relations among perceived environmental uncertainty, organizational structure and boundary-spanning behavior. *Administrative Science Quarterly*, **22**, 235–247.

LEON, F. R. (1979). Number of outcomes and accuracy of prediction in expectancy research. *Organizational Behavior and Human Performance*, **23**, 251–267.

LIED, T. R. and PRITCHARD, R. D. (1976). Relationships between personality variables and components of the expectancy-valence model. *Journal of Applied Psychology*, **61**, 463–467.

LIKERT, R. L. (1961). *New Patterns of Management*. McGraw-Hill, New York.

LIKERT, R. L. (1967). *The Human Organization*. McGraw-Hill, New York.

LISCHERON, J. A. and WALL, T. D. (1975a). Attitudes towards participation among local authority employees. *Human Relations*, **28**, 499–517.

LISCHERON, J. A. and WALL, T. D. (1975b). Employee participation: A experimental field study. *Human Relations*, **28**, 863–884.

LITWIN, G. H. and STRINGER, R. A. (1968). *Motivation and Organizational Climate*. Harvard University, Graduate School of Business Administration, Boston.

LOCKE, E. A. (1976). The nature and causes of job satisfaction. In M. D. Dunnette (ed.), *Handbook of Industrial and Organizational Psychology*. Rand McNally, Chicago.

LODAHL, T. and KEJNER, M. (1965). The definition and measurement of job involvement. *Journal of Applied Psychology*, **49**, 24–33.

LOFQUIST, L. H. and DAWIS, R. V. (1969). *Adjustment to Work: A Psychological View of Man's Problems in a Work-Oriented Society*. Appleton-Century-Crofts, New York.

LOFQUIST, L. H. and DAWIS, R. V. (1978). Values as second order needs in the theory of work adjustment. *Journal of Vocational Behavior*, **12**, 12–19.

LONDON, M. and HOWAT, G. (1978). The relationship between employee commitment and conflict resolution behavior. *Journal of Vocational Behavior*, **13**, 1–14.

LONDON, M. and HOWAT, G. (1980). Attributions of conflict management and perceptions of interpersonal relations: A longitudinal study. Working Paper, American Telephone and Telegraph Company.

LONDON, M. and KLIMOSKI, R. J. (1975a). Self-esteem and job complexity as moderators of performance and satisfaction. *Journal of Vocational Behavior*, **6**, 293–304.

LONDON, M. and KLIMOSKI, R. J. (1975b). A study of perceived job complexity. *Personnel Psychology*, **28**, 45–56.

LOPEZ, E. M. and GREENHAUS, J. H. (1978). Self-esteem, race and job satisfaction. *Journal of Vocational Behavior*, **13**, 75–83.

LORD, F. M. and NOVICK, M. R. (1968). *Statistical Theories of Mental Test Scores*. Addison-Wesley, Reading, Massachusetts.

LYON, H. L. and IVANCEVICH, J. M. (1974). An exploratory investigation of organizational climate and job satisfaction in a hospital. *Academy of Management Journal*, **17**, 635–648.

LYONS, T. F. (1971). Role clarity, need for clarity, satisfaction, tension, and withdrawal. *Organizational Behavior and Human Performance*, **6**, 99–110.

MACEACHRON, A. E. (1977). Two interactive perspectives on the relationship between job level and job satisfaction. *Organizational Behavior and Human Performance*, **19**, 226–246.

MACKINNON, N. J. (1978). Role strain: An assessment of a measure and its invariance of factor structure across studies. *Journal of Applied Psychology*, **63**, 321–328.

MAHONEY, T. A. and WEITZEL, W. (1978). Secrecy and managerial communication. *Industrial Relations*, **17**, 245–251.

MANHARDT, P. J. (1972). Job orientation of male and female college graduates in business. *Personnel Psychology*, **25**, 361–368.

MARGERISON, C. and GLUBE, R. (1979). Leadership decision-making: An empirical test of the Vroom and Yetton model. *Journal of Management Studies*, **16**, 45–55.

MARTIN, T. N. (1979). A contextual model of employee turnover intentions. *Academy of Management Journal*, **22**, 313–324.

MASLOW, A. H. (1943). A theory of human motivation. *Psychological Review*, **50**, 370–396.

MASLOW, A. H. (1954). *Motivation and Personality*. Harper, New York.

MATSUI, T., OHTSUKA, Y. and KIKUCHI, A. (1978). Consideration and Structure behavior as reflections of supervisory interpersonal values. *Journal of Applied Psychology*, **63**, 259–262.

MCCLELLAND, D. C., ATKINSON, J. W., CLARK, R. A. and LOWELL, E. L. (1953). *The Achievement Motive*. Appleton-Century-Crofts, New York.

MCDONALD, B. W. and GUNDERSON, E. K. E. (1974). Correlates of job satisfaction in naval environments. *Journal of Applied Psychology*, **59**, 371–373.

MCFILLEN, J. M. (1978). Supervisory power as an influence in supervisor-subordinate relations. *Academy of Management Journal*, **21**, 419–433.

MCFILLEN, J. M. and NEW, J. R. (1979). Situational determinants of supervisor attributions and behavior. *Academy of Management Journal*, **22**, 793–809.

MCGEHEE, W. and TULLAR, W. L. (1979). Single-question measures of overall job satisfaction: A comment on Quinn, Staines, and McCullough. *Journal of Vocational Behavior*, **14**, 112–117.

MCGREGOR, D. (1960). *The Human Side of Enterprise*. McGraw-Hill, New York.

MCKELVEY, B. and SEKARAN, U. (1977). Toward a career-based theory of job involvement: A study of scientists and engineers. *Administrative Science Quarterly*, **22**, 281–305.

McMahon, J. T. (1972). The contingency model: Logic and method revisited. *Personnel Psychology*, **25**, 697–710.

McNichols, C. W., Stahl, M. J. and Manley, T. R. (1978). A validation of Hoppock's job satisfaction measure. *Academy of Management Journal*, **21**, 737–742.

McPhail, S. M. and Gavin, J. F. (1979). Some suggestions for modifying the incremental influence of organizational members. *Journal of Vocational Behavior*, **15**, 12–24.

Meadows, I. S. G. (1980a). Organic structure and innovation in small work groups. *Human Relations*, **33**, 369–382.

Meadows, I. S. G. (1980b). Organic structure, satisfaction, and personality. *Human Relations*, 33, 383–392.

Merrens, M. R. and Garrett, J. B. (1975). The Protestant Ethic scale as a predictor of repetitive work performance. *Journal of Applied Psychology*, **60**, 125–127.

Mikes, P. S. and Hulin, C. L. (1968). Use of importance as a weighting component of job satisfaction. *Journal of Applied Psychology*, **52**, 394–398.

Miles, R. H. (1975). An empirical test of causal inference between role perceptions of conflict and ambiguity and various personal outcomes. *Journal of Applied Psychology*, **60**, 334–339.

Miles, R. H. (1976a). A comparison of the relative impacts of role perceptions of ambiguity and conflict by role. *Academy of Management Journal*, **19**, 25–35.

Miles, R. H. (1976b). Role requirements as sources of organizational stress. *Journal of Applied Psychology*, **61**, 172–179.

Miles, R. H. and Perreault, W. D. (1976). Organizational role conflict: Its antecedents and consequences. *Organizational Behavior and Human Performance*, **17**, 19–44.

Miles, R. H. and Petty, M. M. (1975). Relationships between role clarity, need for clarity, and job tension and satisfaction for supervisory and nonsupervisory roles. *Academy of Management Journal*, **18**, 877–883.

Miles, R. H. and Petty, M. M. (1977). Leader effectiveness in small bureaucracies, *Academy of Management Journal*, **20**, 238–250.

Miller, G. A. (1967). Professionals in bureaucracy: Alienation among industrial scientists and engineers. *American Sociological Review*, **32**, 755–768.

Miller, G. A. and Wager, L. W. (1971). Adult socialization, organizational structure, and role orientations. *Administrative Science Quarterly*, **16**, 151–163.

Miller, H. E., Katerberg, R. and Hulin, C. L. (1979). Evaluation of the Mobley, Horner and Hollingsworth model of employee turnover. *Journal of Applied Psychology*, **64**, 509–517.

Milutinovich, J. S. (1977). Black–white differences in job satisfaction, group cohesiveness, and leadership style. *Human Relations*, **30**, 1079–1087.

Milutinovich, J. S. and Tsaklanganos, A. A. (1976). The impact of perceived community prosperity on job satisfaction of black and white workers. *Academy of Management Journal*, **19**, 49–65.

Mirels, H. L. and Garrett, J. B. (1971). The Protestant Ethic as a personality variable. *Journal of Consulting and Clinical Psychology*, **36**, 40–44.

Mirvis, P. H. and Lawler, E. E. (1977). Measuring the financial impact of employee attitudes. *Journal of Applied Psychology*, **62**, 1–8.

MISKEL, C. (1974). Intrinsic, extrinsic, and risk propensity factors in the work attitudes of teachers, educational administrators and business managers. *Journal of Applied Psychology*, **59**, 339–343.

MISKEL, C. and HELLER, L. E. (1973). The Educational Works Component Study: An adapted set of measures for work motivation. *Journal of Experimental Education*, **42**, 45–50.

MITCHELL, T. R. (1974). Expectancy models of job satisfaction, occupational preference and effort: A theoretical, methodological and empirical appraisal. *Psychological Bulletin*, **81**, 1053–1077.

MITCHELL, T. R., LARSON, J. R. and GREENE, S. G. (1977). Leader behavior, situational moderators, and group performance: An attributional analysis. *Organizational Behavior and Human Performance*, **18**, 254–268.

MITCHELL, T. R., SMYSER, C. M. and WEED, S. E. (1975). Locus of control: Supervision and work satisfaction. *Academy of Management Journal*, **18**, 623–631.

MITCHELL, V. F. and MOUDGILL, P. (1976). Measurement of Maslow's need hierarchy. *Organizational Behavior and Human Performance*, **16**, 334–349.

MOBLEY, W. H., HORNER, S. O. and HOLLINGSWORTH, A. T. (1978). An evaluation of precursors of hospital employee turnover. *Journal of Applied Psychology*, **63**, 408–414.

MOBLEY, W. H., HAND, H. H., BAKER, R. L. and MEGLINO, B. M. (1979). Conceptual and empirical analysis of military recruit training attrition. *Journal of Applied Psychology*, **64**, 10–18.

MOCH, M. K. (1980a). Racial differences in job satisfaction: Testing four common explanations. *Journal of Applied Psychology*, **65**, 299–306.

MOCH, M. K. (1980b). Job involvement, internal motivation and employees' integration into networks of work relationships. *Organizational Behavior and Human Performance*, **25**, 15–31.

MOCH, M. K., BARTUNEK, J. and BRASS, D. J. (1979). Structure, task characteristics, and experienced role stress in organizations employing complex technology. *Organizational Behavior and Human Performance*, **24**, 258–268.

MOORE, L. M. and RICKEL, A. U. (1980). Characteristics of women in traditional and non-traditional managerial roles. *Personnel Psychology*, **33**, 317–333.

MORRIS, J. H. and KOCH, J. L. (1979). Impacts of role perceptions on organizational commitment, job involvement, and psychosomatic illness among three vocational groupings. *Journal of Vocational Behavior*, **14**, 88–101.

MORRIS, J. H. and SNYDER, R. A. (1979). A second look at need for achievement and need for autonomy as moderators of role perception–role outcome relationships. *Journal of Applied Psychology*, **64**, 173–178.

MORRIS, J. H., STEERS, R. M. and KOCH, J. L. (1979). Influence of organizational structure on role conflict and ambiguity for three occupational groupings. *Academy of Management Journal*, **22**, 58–71.

MORSE, N. (1953). *Satisfactions in the White Collar Job*. University of Michigan Press, Ann Arbor, Michigan.

MOSHER, D. L. (1966). The development and multitrait-multimethod matrix analysis of three measures of three aspects of guilt. *Journal of Consulting and Clinical Psychology*, **30**, 25–29.

MOTOWIDLO, S. J. and BORMAN, W. C. (1977). Behaviorally anchored scales for measuring morale in military units. *Journal of Applied Psychology*, **62**, 177–184.

MOTOWIDLO, S. J. and BORMAN, W. C. (1978). Relationships between military morale, motivation, satisfaction, and unit effectiveness. *Journal of Applied Psychology*, **63**, 47–52.

MOUNT, M. K. and MUCHINSKY, P. M. (1978). Person–environment congruence and employee job satisfaction: A test of Holland's theory. *Journal of Vocational Behavior*, **13**, 84–100.

MOWDAY, R. T. (1979). Leader characteristics, self-confidence, and methods of upward influence in organizational decision situations. *Academy of Management Journal*, **22**, 709–725.

MOWDAY, R. T., PORTER, L. W. and DUBIN, R. (1974). Unit performance, situational factors, and employee attitudes in spatially separated work units. *Organizational Behavior and Human Performance*, **12**, 231–248.

MOWDAY, R. T., STEERS, R. M. and PORTER, L. W. (1979). The measurement of organizational commitment. *Journal of Vocational Behavior*, **14**, 224–247.

MOWDAY, R. T., STONE, E. F. and PORTER, L. W. (1979). The interaction of personality and job scope in predicting turnover. *Journal of Vocational Behavior*, **15**, 78–89.

MUCHINSKY, P. M. (1976). An assessment of the Litwin and Stringer Organization Climate Questionnaire: An empirical and theoretical extension of the Sims and LaFollette study. *Personal Psychology*, **29**, 371–392.

MUCHINSKY, P. M. and HARRIS, S. L. (1977). The effect of applicant sex and scholastic standing on the evaluation of job applicant resumés in sextyped occupations. *Journal of Vocational Behavior*, **11**, 95–108.

MUCZYK, J. P. (1978). A controlled field experiment measuring the impact of MBO on performance data. *Journal of Management Studies*, **15**, 318–329.

MURPHY, G. C. and FRASER, B. J. (1978). Intuitive-theoretical scales of content and context satisfaction. *Personnel Psychology*, **31**, 485–494.

MURRAY, H. A. (1938). *Explorations in Personality*. Oxford University Press, New York.

NAGLE, B. F. (1953). Productivity, employee attitude and supervisor sensitivity. Unpublished Doctoral Dissertation, Purdue University.

NEBEKER, D. M. (1975). Situational favorability and environmental uncertainty: An integrative approach. *Administrative Science Quarterly*, **20**, 281–294.

NELSON, D. M. (1975). Fineman on the Work Preference Questionnaire. *Journal of Occupational Psychology*, **48**, 195–196.

NEUGARTEN, D. L., HAVIGHURST, R. J. and TOBIN, S. S. (1961). The measurement of life satisfaction. *Journal of Gerontology*, **16**, 134–143.

NEWMAN, J. E. (1974). Predicting absenteeism and turnover: A field comparison of Fishbein's model and traditional job attitude measures. *Journal of Applied Psychology*, **59**, 610–615.

NEWMAN, J. E. (1975). Understanding the organizational structure–job attitude relationship through perceptions of the work environment. *Organizational Behavior and Human Performance*, **14**, 371–397.

NEWMAN, J. E. (1977). Development of a measure of perceived work environment. *Academy of Management Journal*, **20**, 520–534.

NICHOLSON, N., BROWN, C. A. and CHADWICK-JONES, J. K. (1976). Absence from work and job satisfaction. *Journal of Applied Psychology*, **61**, 728–737.

NICHOLSON, N., WALL, T. D. and LISCHERON, J. (1977). The predictability of absence and propensity to leave from employees' job satisfaction and attitudes toward influence in decision-making. *Human Relations*, **30**, 499–514.

NORD, W. R. (1977). Job satisfaction reconsidered. *American Psychologist*, **32**, 1026–1035.

NOVICK, M. R. and LEWIS, C. (1967). Coefficient alpha and the reliability of composite measurements. *Psychometrika*, **32**, 1–13.

NUNNALLY, J. C. (1967). *Psychometric Theory*. McGraw-Hill, New York.

NYSTROM, P. C. (1978). Managers and the hi-hi leader myth. *Academy of Management Journal*, **21**, 325–331.

O'BRIEN, G. E. and DOWLING, P. (1980). The effects of congruency between perceived and desired job attributes upon job satisfaction. *Journal of Occupational Psychology*, **53**, 121–130.

ODEWAHN, C. A. and PETTY, M. M. (1980). A comparison of levels of job satisfaction, role stress, and personal competence between union members and non-members. *Academy of Management Journal*, **23**, 150–155.

OLDHAM, G. R. (1976). Job characteristics and internal motivation: The moderating effect of interpersonal and individual variables. *Human Relations*, **29**, 559–569.

OLDHAM, G. R. and BRASS, D. J. (1979). Employee reactions to an open-plan office: A naturally occurring field experiment. *Administrative Science Quarterly*, **24**, 267–284.

OLDHAM, G. R. and MILLER, H. E. (1979). The effect of significant others' job complexity on employee reactions to work. *Human Relations*, **32**, 247–260.

OLDHAM, G. R., HACKMAN, J. R. and PEARCE, J. L. (1976). Conditions under which employees respond positively to enriched work. *Journal of Applied Psychology*, **61**, 395–403.

OLDHAM, G. R., HACKMAN, J. R. and STEPINA, L. P. (1978). Norms for the Job Diagnostic Survey. Yale University School of Organization and Management, New Haven.

ORCUTT, M. A. and WALSH, W. B. (1979). Traditionality and congruence of career aspirations for college women. *Journal of Vocational Behavior*, **14**, 1–11.

O'REILLY, C. A. (1977). Personality-job fit: Implications for individual attitudes and performance. *Organizational Behavior and Human Performance*, **18**, 36–46.

O'REILLY, C. A. (1978). The intentional distortion of information in organizational communications: A laboratory and field investigation. *Human Relations*, **31**, 173–193.

O'REILLY, C. A. and CALDWELL, D. F. (1979). Informational influence as a determinant of perceived task characteristics and job satisfaction. *Journal of Applied Psychology*, **64**, 157–165.

O'REILLY, C. A. and ROBERTS, K. H. (1975). Individual differences in personality, position in the organization, and job satisfaction. *Organizational Behavior and Human Performance*, **14**, 144–150.

O'REILLY, C. A. and ROBERTS, K. H. (1978). Supervisor influence and subordinate mobility aspirations as moderators of Consideration and Initiating Structure. *Journal of Applied Psychology*, **63**, 96–102.

O'REILLY, C. A., BRETTON, G. E. and ROBERTS, K. H. (1974). Professional employees' preference for upward mobility: An extension. *Journal of Vocational Behavior*, **5**, 139–145.

O'REILLY, C. A., PARLETTE, G. N. and BLOOM, J. R. (1980). Perceptual measures of task characteristics: The biasing effects of differing frames of reference and job attitudes. *Academy of Management Journal*, **23**, 118–131.

ORGAN, D. W. and GREENE, C. N. (1974a) Role ambiguity, locus of control, and work satisfaction. *Journal of Applied Psychology*, **59**, 101–102.

ORGAN, D. W. and GREENE, C. N. (1974b). The perceived purposefulness of job behavior: Antecedents and consequences. *Academy of Management Journal*, **17**, 69–78.

ORPEN, C. (1974a). Discrimination, work attitudes, and job satisfaction: A comparative study of whites and coloureds in South Africa. *International Review of Applied Psychology*, **23**, 33–44.

ORPEN, C. (1974b). Social desirability as a moderator of the relationship between job satisfaction and personal adjustment. *Personnel Psychology*, **27**, 103–108.

ORPEN, C. (1978a). Work and nonwork satisfaction: A causal-correlational analysis. *Journal of Applied Psychology*, **63**, 530–532.

ORPEN, C. (1978b). Relationship between job satisfaction and job performance among western and tribal black employees. *Journal of Applied Psychology*, **63**, 263–265.

ORPEN, C. (1979a). The reactions of western and tribal black workers to job characteristics. *International Review of Applied Psychology*, **28**, 117–125.

ORPEN, C. (1979b). The effects of job enrichment on employee satisfaction, motivation, involvement, and performance: A field experiment. *Human Relations*, **32**, 189–217.

ORPEN, C. and NKOHANDE, J. (1977). Self-esteem, internal control and expectancy beliefs of white and black managers in South Africa. *Journal of Management Studies*, **14**, 192–199.

OSBORN, R. N. and HUNT, J. G. (1975). Relations between leadership, size, and subordinate satisfaction in a voluntary organization. *Journal of Applied Psychology*, **60**, 730–735.

OSBORN, R. N. and VICARS, W. M. (1976). Sex stereotypes: An artifact in leader behavior and subordinate satisfaction analysis. *Academy of Management Journal*, **19**, 439–449.

OSGOOD, C. E. (1952). The nature and measurement of meaning. *Psychological Bulletin*, **49**, 251–262.

OUCHI, W. G. and JOHNSON, J. B. (1978). Types of organizational control and their relationship to emotional well-being. *Administrative Science Quarterly*, **23**, 293–317.

PALMER, W. J. (1974). Management effectiveness as a function of personality traits of the manager. *Personnel Psychology*, **27**, 283–295.

PARKER, D. F. and DYER, L. (1976). Expectancy theory as a within-person behavioral choice model: An empirical test of some conceptual and methodological refinements. *Organizational Behavior and Human Performance*, **17**, 97–117.

PARKINGTON, J. J. and SCHNEIDER, B. (1979). Some correlates of experienced job stress: A boundary role study. *Academy of Management Journal*, **22**, 270–281.

PARRY, G. and WARR, P. B. (1980). The measurement of mothers' work attitudes. *Journal of Occupational Psychology*, **53**, 245–252.

PATCHEN, M. (1970). *Participation, Achievement, and Involvement on the Job*. Prentice-Hall, Englewood Cliffs, New Jersey.

PATCHEN, M., PELZ, D. and ALLEN, C. (1965). *Some Questionnaire Measures of Employee Motivation and Morale*. Institute for Social Research, Ann Arbor, Michigan.

PAYNE, R. L. and MANSFIELD, R. M. (1973). Relationships of perceptions of organizational climate to organizational structure, context and hierarchical position. *Administrative Science Quarterly*, **18**, 515–526.

PAYNE, R. L. and MANSFIELD, R. M. (1978). Correlates of individual perceptions of organizational climate. *Journal of Occupational Psychology*, **51**, 209–218.

PAYNE, R. L. and PHEYSEY, D. C. (1971). G. G. Stern's Organizational Climate Index: A reconceptualization and application to business organizations. *Organizational Behavior and Human Performance*, **6**, 77–98.

PAYNE, R. L., FINEMAN, S. and WALL, T. D. (1976). Organizational climate and job satisfaction: A conceptual synthesis. *Organizational Behavior and Human Performance*, **16**, 45–62.

PENLEY, L. E. and HAWKINS, B. L. (1980). Organizational communication, performance, and job satisfaction as a function of ethnicity and sex. *Journal of Vocational Behavior*, **16**, 368–384.

PERONE, M., DEWAARD, R. J. and BARON, A. (1979). Satisfaction with real and simulated jobs in relation to personality variables and drug use. *Journal of Applied Psychology*, **64**, 660–668.

PETERS, L. H., O'CONNOR, E. J. and RUDOLF, C. J. (1980). The behavioral and affective consequences of performance-relevant situational variables. *Organizational Behavior and Human Performance*, **25**, 79–96.

PETERS, L. H., TERBORG, J. R. and TAYNOR, J. (1974). Women as Managers Scale (WAMS): A measure of attitudes towards women in management positions. *JSAS Catalog of Selected Documents in Psychology*, **4**, No. 585.

PETERSON, R. B. (1975). The interaction of technological process and perceived organizational climate in Norwegian firms. *Academy of Management Journal*, **18**, 288–299.

PETTY, M. M. and LEE, G. K. (1975). Moderating effects of sex of supervisor and subordinate on relationships between supervisory behavior and subordinate satisfaction. *Journal of Applied Psychology*, **60**, 624–628.

PETTY, M. M. and MILES, R. H. (1976). Leader sex-role stereotyping in a female-dominated work culture. *Personnel Psychology*, **29**, 393–404.

PETTY, M. M. and PRYOR, N. M. (1974). A note on the predictive validity of Initiating Structure and Consideration in ROTC training. *Journal of Applied Psychology*, **59**, 383–385.

PFEFFER, J. and SALANCIK, G. R. (1975). Determinants of supervisory behavior: A role set analysis. *Human Relations*, **28**, 139–154.

PHEYSEY, D. C. (1977). Managers' occupational histories, organizational environments and climates for management development. *Journal of Management Studies*, **14**, 58–79.

PHILLIPS, J. S. and LORD, R. G. (1980). Determinants of intrinsic motivation. Locus of control and competence information as components of Deci' cognitive evaluation theory. *Journal of Applied Psychology*, **65**, 211–218.

PIERCE, J. L. and DUNHAM, R. B. (1978a). The measurement of perceived job characteristics: The Job Diagnostic Survey versus the Job Characteristics Inventory. *Academy of Management Journal*, **21**, 123–128.

PIERCE, J. L. and DUNHAM, R. B. (1978b). An empirical demonstration of the convergence of common macro- and micro-organization measures. *Academy of Management Journal*, **21**, 410–418.

PIERCE, J. L., DUNHAM, R. B. and BLACKBURN, R. S. (1979). Social system structure, job design, and growth need strength: A test of a congruency model. *Academy of Management Journal*, **22**, 223–240.

PINDER, C. C. (1977). Multiple predictors of post-transfer satisfaction: The role of urban factors. *Personnel Psychology*, **30**, 543–556.

PINTO, P. R. and DAVIS, T. C. (1974). The moderating effect of need type on the prediction of overall job satisfaction. *Journal of Vocational Behavior*, **4** 339–348.

PORTER, L. W. (1961). A study of perceived need satisfactions in bottom and middle management jobs. *Journal of Applied Psychology*, **45**, 1–10.

PORTER, L. W. (1962). Job attitudes in management: I. Perceived deficiencies in need fulfilment as a function of job level. *Journal of Applied Psychology* **46**, 375–384.

PORTER, L. W. and LAWLER, E. E. (1968). *Managerial Attitudes and Performance* Irwin Dorsey, Homewood, Illinois.

PORTER, L. W. and SMITH, F. J. (1970). The etiology of organizational commitment. Unpublished paper, University of California at Irvine.

PORTER, L. W., CRAMPON, W. J. and SMITH, F. J. (1976). Organizational commitment and managerial turnover: A longitudinal study. *Organizational Behavior and Human Performance*, **15**, 87–98.

PORTER, L. W., STEERS, R. M., MOWDAY, R. T. and BOULIAN, P. V. (1974). Organizational commitment, job satisfaction, and turnover among psychiatric technicians. *Journal of Applied Psychology*, **59**, 603–609.

POSTHUMA, A. B. (1970). Normative data on the Least Preferred Co-worker Scale and the Group Atmosphere Questionnaire. Technical Report 70–8. University of Washington, Organizational Research, Seattle.

PRITCHARD, R. D. and KARASICK, B. (1973). The effects of organizational climate on managerial job performance and job satisfaction. *Organizational Behavior and Human Performance*, **9**, 126–146.

PRITCHARD, R. D. and PETERS, L. H. (1974). Job duties and job interests as predictors of intrinsic and extrinsic satisfaction. *Organizational Behavior and Human Performance*, **12**, 315–330.

PRYOR, R. G. L. (1980). Some types of stability in the study of students' work values. *Journal of Vocational Behavior*, **16**, 146–157.

QUICK, J. C. (1979). Dyadic goal setting and role stress: A field study. *Academy of Management Journal*, **22**, 241–252.

QUINN, R. P. and GONZALES, T. A. (1979). A consumer's guide to job satisfaction measures. In T. Abrahamson, C. K. Tittle, and L. Cohen (eds.) *Handbook of Vocational Education Evaluation*. Sage Publications, London.

QUINN, R. P. and MANGIONE, T. (1973). Evaluating weighted models of measuring job satisfaction: A Cinderella story. *Organizational Behavior and Human Performance*, **10**, 1–23.

QUINN, R. P. and SHEPARD, L. J. (1974). *The 1972–73 Quality of Employment Survey.* Institute for Social Research, University of Michigan, Ann Arbor, Michigan.

QUINN, R. P. and STAINES, G. L. (1979). *The 1977 Quality of Employment Survey.* Institute for Social Research, University of Michigan, Ann Arbor, Michigan.

QUINN, R. P., STAINES, G. L. and McCULLOUGH, M. R. (1974). *Job Satisfaction: Is there a Trend?* US Department of Labor, Washington, DC.

QUINN, R. P., SEASHORE, S. E., KAHN, R. L., MANGIONE, T., CAMPBELL, D., STAINES, G. and McCULLOUGH, M. (1971). *Survey of Working Conditions.* US Goverment Printing Office (Document 2916–0001), Washington, DC.

RABINOWITZ, S. and HALL, D. T. (1977). Organizational research on job involvement. *Psychological Bulletin*, **84**, 265–288.

RABINOWITZ, S., HALL, D. T. and GOODALE, J. G. (1977). Job scope and individual differences as predictors of job involvement: Independent or interactive? *Academy of Management Journal*, **20**, 273–281.

REGOLI, R. M. and POOLE, E. D. (1980). Police professionalism and role conflict: A comparison of rural and urban departments. *Human Relations*, **33**, 241–252.

REIF, W. E., NEWSTROM, J. W. and ST LOUIS, R. D. (1976). Sex as a discriminating variable in organizational reward decisions. *Academy of Management Journal*, **19**, 469–476.

REINHARTH, L. and WAHBA, M. A. (1975). Expectancy theory as a predictor of work motivation, effort expenditure and job performance. *Academy of Management Journal*, **18**, 520–537.

REINHARTH, L. and WAHBA, M. A. (1976). A test of alternative models of expectancy theory. *Human Relations*, **29**, 257–272.

RENWICK, P. A. (1975a). Perception and management of supervisor–subordinate conflict. *Organizational Behavior and Human Performance*, **13**, 444–455.

RENWICK, P. A. (1975b). Impact of topic and source of disagreement on conflict management. *Organizational Behavior and Human Performance*, **14**, 416–425.

RICE, R. W. (1978a). Psychometric properties of the Esteem for Least Preferred Co-worker (LPC) scale. *Academy of Management Review*, **3**, 106–118.

RICE, R. W. (1978b). Construct validity of the Least Preferred Co-worker score. *Psychological Bulletin*, **85**, 1199–1237.

RICE, R. W. (1979). Reliability and validity of the LPC scales: A reply. *Academy of Management Review*, **4**, 291–294.

RICE, R. W. and CHEMERS, M. M. (1975). Personality and situational determinants of leader behavior. *Journal of Applied Psychology*, **60**, 20–27.

RICE, R. W., BENDER, L. R. and VITTERS, A. G. (1980). Leader sex, follower attitudes toward women, and leadership effectiveness: A laboratory experiment. *Organizational Behavior and Human Performance*, **25**, 46–78.

RICHARDSON, M. A. (1974). The dimensions of career and work orientation in college women. *Journal of Vocational Behavior*, **5**, 161–172.

RIM, Y. (1977). Significance of work and personality. *Journal of Occupational Psychology*, **50**, 135–138.

RIZZO, J., HOUSE, R. J. and LIRTZMAN, S. I. (1970). Role conflict and ambiguity in complex organizations. *Administrative Science Quarterly*, **15**, 150–163.

ROBERTS, K. H. and O'REILLY, C. A. (1974). Measuring organizational communication. *Journal of Applied Psychology*, **59**, 321–326.

ROBERTS, K. H. and O'REILLY, C. A. (1979). Some correlates of communication roles in organizations. *Academy of Management Journal*, **22**, 42–57.

ROBEY, D. (1974). Task design, work values, and worker response: An experimental test. *Organizational Behavior and Human Performance*, **12**, 264–273.

ROBEY, D. (1978). Industrial moderators of the task design – job attitude relationship: A note on measurement. *Journal of Management Studies*, **15**, 68–76.

ROBEY, D. (1979). User attitudes and management information system use. *Academy of Management Journal*, **22**, 527–538.

ROBEY, D. and BAKR, M. M. (1978). Task redesign: Individual moderating and novelty effects. *Human Relations*, **31**, 689–701.

ROGERS, D. L. and MOLNAR, J. (1976). Organizational antecedents of role conflict and ambiguity in top-level administrators. *Administrative Science Quarterly*, **21**, 598–610.

ROKEACH, M. (1960). *The Open and Closed Mind*. Basic Books, New York.

RONAN, W. W., COBB, J. M., GARRETT, T. L., LAZARRI, J. D., MOSSER, D. R. and RACINE, A. E. (1974). Occupational level and mental health: A note. *Journal of Vocational Behavior*, **5**, 157–160.

RONEN, S. (1977). A comparison of job facet satisfaction between paid and unpaid industrial workers. *Journal of Applied Psychology*, **62**, 582–588.

RONEN, S. (1978a). Personal values: A basis for work motivational set and work attitude. *Organizational Behavior and Human Performance*, **21**, 80–107.

RONEN, S. (1978b). Job satisfaction and the neglected variable of job seniority. *Human Relations*, **31**, 297–308.

ROSENBERG, M. (1965). *Society and the Adolescent Self-Image*. Princeton University Press, Princeton.

ROTONDI, T. (1975). Organizational identification: Issues and implications. *Organizational Behavior and Human Performance*, **13**, 95–109.

ROUSSEAU, D. M. (1977). Technological differences in job characteristics, employee satisfaction, and motivation: A synthesis of job design research and sociotechnical systems theory. *Organizational Behavior and Human Performance*, **19**, 18–42.

ROUSSEAU, D. M. (1978a). Measures of technology as predictors of employee attitude. *Journal of Applied Psychology*, **63**, 213–218.

ROUSSEAU, D. M. (1978b). Characteristics of departments, positions, and individuals: Contexts for attitudes and behavior. *Administrative Science Quarterly*, **23**, 521–540.

ROUSSEAU, D. M. (1978c). Relationship of work to nonwork. *Journal of Applied Psychology*, **63**, 513–517.

RUH, R. A., WHITE, J. K. and WOOD, R. R. (1975). Job involvement, values, personal background, participation in decision-making, and job attitudes. *Academy of Management Journal*, **18**, 300–312.

Rush, M. C., Thomas, J. C. and Lord, R. G. (1977). Implicit leadership theory: A potential threat to the internal validity of leader behavior questionnaires. *Organizational Behavior and Human Performance*, **20**, 93–110.

Saal, F. E. (1978). Job involvement: A multivariate approach. *Journal of Applied Psychology*, **63**, 53–61.

Saha, S. K. (1979). Contingency theories of leadership: A study. *Human Relations*, **32**, 313–322.

Salancik, G. R. (1977). Commitment and the control of organizational behavior and belief. In B. M. Staw and G. R. Salancik (eds.), *New Directions in Organizational Behavior*. St. Clair Press, Chicago.

Salancik, G. R. and Pfeffer, J. (1977). An examination of need-satisfaction models of job attitudes. *Administrative Science Quarterly*, **22**, 427–456.

Saleh, S. D. and Hosek, J. (1976). Job involvement: Concepts and measurements. *Academy of Management Journal*, **19**, 213–224.

Saleh, S. D. and Pasricha, V. (1975). Job orientation and work behavior. *Academy of Management Journal*, **18**, 638–645.

Sashkin, M., Taylor, F. C. and Tripathi, R. C. (1974). An analysis of situational moderating effects on the relationships between Least Preferred Co-worker and other psychological measures. *Journal of Applied Psychology*, **59**, 731–740.

Sathe, V. (1978). Institutional versus questionnaire measures of organizational structure. *Academy of Management Journal*, **21**, 227–238.

Sauser, W. I. and York, C. M. (1978). Sex differences in job satisfaction: A re-examination. *Personnel Psychology*, **31**, 537–547.

Schmitt, N. and Mellon, P. M. (1980). Life and job satisfaction: Is the job central? *Journal of Vocational Behavior*, **16**, 51–58.

Schmitt, N. and White, J. K. (1978). Relationships between job motivation variables and interest measures. *Journal of Vocational Behavior*, **12**, 333–341.

Schmitt, N., Coyle, B. W., Rauschenberger, J. and White, J. K. (1979). Comparison of early retirees and non-retirees. *Personnel Psychology*, **32**, 327–340.

Schmitt, N., Coyle, B. W., White, J. K. and Rauschenberger, J. (1978). Background, needs, job perceptions, and job satisfaction: A causal model. *Personnel Psychology*, **31**, 889–901.

Schmitt, N., White, J. K., Coyle, B. W. and Rauschenberger, J. (1979). Retirement and life satisfaction. *Academy of Management Journal*, **22**, 282–291.

Schneider, B. and Dachler, H. P. (1978). A note on the stability of the Job Descriptive Index. *Journal of Applied Psychology*, **63**, 650–653.

Schneier, C. E. (1978). The contingency model of leadership: An extension to emergent leadership and leader's sex. *Organizational Behavior and Human Performance*, **21**, 220–239.

Schriesheim, C. A. (1978a). Job satisfaction, attitudes toward unions, and voting in a union representation election. *Journal of Applied Psychology*, **63**, 548–552.

Schriesheim, C. A. (1978b). Development, validation and application of new leadership behavior and expectancy research instruments. Unpublished Doctoral Dissertation, Ohio State University.

SCHRIESHEIM, C. A. (1979). The similarity of individual-directed and group-directed leader behavior descriptions. *Academy of Management Journal*, **22**, 345–355.

SCHRIESHEIM, C. A. and KERR, S. (1974). Psychometric properties of the Ohio State leadership scales. *Psychological Bulletin*, **81**, 756–765.

SCHRIESHEIM, C. A. and KERR, S. (1977). Theories and measures of leadership: A critical appraisal of current and future directions. In J. G. Hunt and L. L. Larson (eds.), *Leadership: The Cutting Edge*. Illinois University Press, Carbondale, Illinois.

SCHRIESHEIM, C. A. and MURPHY, C. J. (1976). Relationships between leader behavior and subordinate satisfaction and performance: A test of some situational moderators. *Journal of Applied Psychology*, **61**, 634–641.

SCHRIESHEIM, C. A. and STOGDILL, R. M. (1975). Differences across three versions of the Ohio State leadership scales. *Personnel Psychology*, **28**, 189–206.

SCHRIESHEIM, C. A. and VON GLINOW, M. A. (1977). The path–goal theory of leadership: A theoretical and empirical analysis. *Academy of Management Journal*, **20**, 398–405.

SCHRIESHEIM, C. A., BANNISTER, B. D. and MONEY, W. H. (1979). Psychometric properties of the LPC scale: An extension of Rice's review. *Academy of Management Review*, **4**, 287–290.

SCHRIESHEIM, C. A., HOUSE, R. J. and KERR, S. (1976). Leader initiating structure: A reconciliation of discrepant research results and some empirical tests. *Organizational Behavior and Human Performance*, **15**, 297–321.

SCHRIESHEIM, C. A., KINICKI, A. J. and SCHRIESHEIM, J. F. (1979). The effect of leniency on leader behavior descriptions. *Organizational Behavior and Human Performance*, **23**, 1–29.

SCHRIESHEIM, J. F. (1980). The social context of leader-subordinate relations: An investigation of the effects of group cohesiveness. *Journal of Applied Psychology*, **65**, 183–194.

SCHRIESHEIM, J. F. and SCHRIESHEIM, C. A. (1980). A test of the path–goal theory of leadership and some suggested directions for future research. *Personnel Psychology*, **33**, 349–370.

SCHULER, R. S. (1975). Role perceptions, satisfaction, and performance: A partial reconciliation. *Journal of Applied Psychology*, **60**, 683–687.

SCHULER, R. S. (1976). Participation with supervisor and subordinate authoritarianism: A path–goal theory reconciliation. *Administrative Science Quarterly*, **21**, 320–325.

SCHULER, R. S. (1977a). Role perceptions, satisfaction and performance moderated by organizational level and participation in decision making. *Academy of Management Journal*, **20**, 159–165.

SCHULER, R. S. (1977b). The effects of role perceptions on employee satisfaction and performance moderated by employee ability. *Organizational Behavior and Human Performance*, **18**, 98–107.

SCHULER, R. S. (1977c). Role conflict and ambiguity as a function of the task–structure–technology interaction. *Organizational Behavior and Human Performance*, **20**, 66–74.

SCHULER, R. S. (1979). A role perception transactional process model for organizational communication-outcome relationships. *Organizational Behavior and Human Performance*, **23**, 268–291.

CHULER, R. S. (1980). A role and expectancy perception model of participation in decision making. *Academy of Management Journal*, **23**, 331–340.

CHULER, R. S., ALDAG, R. J. and BRIEF, A. P. (1977). Role conflict and ambiguity: A scale analysis. *Organizational Behavior and Human Performance*, **20**, 111–128.

CHULTZ, R. L. and SLEVIN, D. P. (1975). Implementation and organizational validity. In R. L. Schultz and D. P. Slevin (eds.), *Implementing Operations Research and Management Science*. Elsevier, New York.

CHWAB, D. P. (1980). Construct validity in organizational behavior. In B. M. Staw and L. L. Cummings (eds.), *Research in Organizational Behavior*, vol. 2. JAI Press, Greenwich, Connecticut.

CHWAB, D. P. and HENEMAN, H. G. (1977). Age and satisfaction with dimensions of work. *Journal of Vocational Behavior*, **10**, 212–220.

CHWAB, D. P. and WALLACE, M. J. (1974). Correlates of employee satisfaction with pay. *Industrial Relations*, **13**, 78–89.

CHWARTZ, D. F. (1968). Liaison communication roles in formal organization. Doctoral Dissertation, Michigan State University.

CHWARTZ, D. F. and JACOBSON, E. (1977). Organizational communication network analysis: The liaison communication role. *Organizational Behavior and Human Performance*, **18**, 158–174.

COTT, W. E. (1967). The development of semantic differential scales as measures of "morale". *Personnel Psychology*, **20**, 179–198.

COTT, W. E. and ERSKINE, J. A. (1980). The effects of variations in task design and monetary reinforcers on task behavior. *Organizational Behavior and Human Performance*, **25**, 311–335.

COTT, W. E. and ROWLAND, K. M. (1970). The generality and significance of semantic differential scales as measures of "morale". *Organizational Behavior and Human Performance*, **5**, 576–591.

EASHORE, S. E. (1954). *Group Cohesiveness in the Industrial Work Group*. University of Michigan Press, Ann Arbor, Michigan.

EASHORE, S. E., LAWLER, E. E., MIRVIS, P. and CAMMANN, C. (eds.) (1982). *Observing and Measuring Organizational Change: A Guide to Field Practice*. Wiley, New York.

EEMAN, M. (1959). On the meaning of alienation. *American Sociological Review*, **24**, 783–791.

EEMAN, M. (1967). On the personal consequences of alienation in work. *American Sociological Review*, **32**, 273–285.

EYBOLT, J. W. (1976). Work satisfaction as a function of the person–environment interaction. *Organizational Behavior and Human Performance*, **17**, 66–75.

EYBOLT, J. W. and GRUENFELD, L. (1976). The discriminant validity of work alienation and work satisfaction measures. *Journal of Occupational Psychology*, **49**, 193–202.

EYBOLT, J. W. and PAVETT, C. M. (1979). The prediction of effort and performance among hospital professionals: Moderating effects of feedback on expectancy theory formulations. *Journal of Occupational Psychology*, **52**, 91–105.

GRO, J. A., WORCHEL, P., PENCE, E. C. and ORBAN, J. A. (1980). Perceived leader behavior as a function of the leader's interpersonal trust orientation. *Academy of Management Journal*, **23**, 161–165.

SHAPIRA, Z. (1976). A facet analysis of leadership styles. *Journal of Applie Psychology*, **61**, 136–139.

SHAW, M. E. and WRIGHT, J. M. (eds.), (1967). *Scales for the Measurement Attitudes*. McGraw-Hill, New York.

SHEPARD, J. M. (1972). Alienation as a process: Work as a case in point. *T Sociological Quarterly*, **13**, 161–173.

SHEPPARD, H. L. and HERRICK, N. Q. (1972). *Where Have All the Robots Gone* The Free Press, New York.

SHERIDAN, J. E. and SLOCUM, J. W. (1975). The direction of the caus relationship between job satisfaction and work performance. *Organiza tional Behavior and Human Performance*, **14**, 159–172.

SHERIDAN, J. E. and VREDENBURGH, D. J. (1978a). Usefulness of leadershi behavior and social power variables in predicting job tension, perfo mance, and turnover of nursing employees. *Journal of Applied Psycholog* **63**, 89–95.

SHERIDAN, J. E. and VREDENBURGH, D. J. (1978b). Predicting leadershi behavior in a hospital organization. *Academy of Management Journal*, **2** 679–689.

SHERIDAN, J. E. and VREDENBURGH, D. J. (1979). Structural model of leade ship influence in a hospital organization. *Academy of Management Journa* **22**, 6–21.

SHIFLET, S. and COHEN, S. L. (1980). Number and specificity of performanc outcomes in the prediction of attitudes and behavioral intention *Personnel Psychology*, **33**, 137–150.

SIEGEL, S. and KAEMMERER, W. F. (1978). Measuring the perceived suppo for innovation in organizations. *Journal of Applied Psychology*, **63**, 553–562

SIMS, H. P. and LaFOLLETTE, W. (1975). An assessment of the Litwin an Stringer Organization Climate Questionnaire. *Personnel Psychology*, **2** 19–38.

SIMS, H. P. and SZILAGYI, A. D. (1975a). Leader structure and subordinat satisfaction for two hospital administrative levels: A path analys approach. *Journal of Applied Psychology*, **60**, 194–197.

SIMS, H. P. and SZILAGYI, A. D. (1975b). Leader reward behavior and subo dinate satisfaction and performance. *Organizational Behavior and Huma Performance*, **14**, 426–438.

SIMS, H. P. and SZILAGYI, A. D. (1979). Time lags in leader reward researc *Journal of Applied Psychology*, **64**, 66–71.

SIMS, H. P., SZILAGYI, A. D. and KELLER, R. T. (1976). The measureme of job characteristics. *Academy of Management Journal*, **19**, 195–212.

SIMS, H. P., SZILAGYI, A. D. and McKEMEY, D. R. (1976). Antecedents work-related expectancies. *Academy of Management Journal*, **19**, 547–559.

SMITH, F. J. (1962). Problems and trends in the operational use of employe attitude measurements. Paper presented to the Annual Meeting of th American Psychological Association.

SMITH, F. J. (1976). Index of Organizational Reactions (IOR). *JSAS Catalog Selected Documents in Psychology*, **6**, (1), 54, No. 1265.

SMITH, F. J. (1977). Work attitudes as predictors of attendance on a specifi day. *Journal of Applied Psychology*, **62**, 16–19.

SMITH, F. J., ROBERTS, K. H. and HULIN, C. L. (1976). Ten-year job satisfac tion trends in a stable organization. *Academy of Management Journal*, **19**, 462–469.

SMITH, P. C., KENDALL, L. M. and HULIN, C. L. (1969). *The Measurement of Satisfaction in Work and Retirement*. Rand-McNally, Chicago.

SMITH, P. C., SMITH, O. W. and ROLLO, J. (1974). Factor structure for blacks and whites of the Job Descriptive Index and its discrimination of job satisfaction. *Journal of Applied Psychology*, **59**, 99–100.

SOLOMON, R. J. (1976). An examination of the relationship between a survey feedback OD technique and the work environment. *Personnel Psychology*, **29**, 583–594.

SOUTH, J. C. and WHERRY, R. J. (1975). The relationship of need achievement and job perception to personal, job and company variables in a sample of industrial workers. Unpublished Manuscript.

SPECTOR, P. E. (1975). Relationships of organizational frustration with reported behavioral reactions of employees. *Journal of Applied Psychology*, **60**, 635–637.

SPEKMAN, R. E. (1979). Influence and information: An exploratory investigation of the boundary role person's basis of power. *Academy of Management Journal*, **22**, 104–117.

SPIELBERGER, C. D. (1972). Anxiety as an emotional state. In C. D. Spielberger (ed.), *Anxiety: Current Trends in Theory and Practice*. Academic Press, New York.

SPIELBERGER, C. D., GORSUCH, R. L. and LUSHENE, R. (1968). *Self-Evaluation Questionnaire*. Consulting Psychologists Press, Palo Alto, California.

SPIELBERGER, C. D., GORSUCH, R. L. and LUSHENE, R. (1970). *Manual for the State-Trait Anxiety Inventory*. Consulting Psychologists Press, Palo Alto, California.

SROLE, L. (1956). Social integration and certain corollaries: An exploratory study. *American Sociological Review*, **21**, 709–716.

STAHL, M. J., MANLEY, T. R. and McNICHOLS, C. W. (1978). Operationalizing the Moskos institution–occupation model: An application of Gouldner's cosmopolitan–local research. *Journal of Applied Psychology*, **63**, 422–427.

STAW, B. M. and OLDHAM, G. R. (1978). Reconsidering our dependent variables: A critique and empirical study. *Academy of Management Journal*, **21**, 539–559.

STEERS, R. M. (1973). Task goals, individual need strength, and supervisory performance. Unpublished Doctoral Dissertation, University of California at Irvine.

STEERS, R. M. (1975a). Task–goal attributes, n achievement, and supervisory performance. *Organizational Behavior and Human Performance*, **13**, 392–403.

STEERS, R. M. (1975b). Effects of need for achievement on the job performance – job attitude relationship. *Journal of Applied Psychology*, **60**, 678–682.

STEERS, R. M. (1976). Factors affecting job attitudes in a goal setting environment. *Academy of Management Journal*, **19**, 6–16.

STEERS, R. M. (1977). Antecedents and outcomes of organizational commitment. *Administrative Science Quarterly*, **22**, 46–56.

STEERS, R. M. and BRAUNSTEIN, D. N. (1976). A behaviorally-based measure of manifest needs in work settings. *Journal of Vocational Behavior*, **9**, 251–266.

STEERS, R. M. and SPENCER, D. G. (1977). The role of achievement motivation in job design. *Journal of Applied Psychology*, **62**, 472–479.

STERN, G. G. (1967). People in context: The measurement of environmental interaction in school and society, vol 1. Unpublished Report, University of Syracuse.

STEVENS, G. E. and DE NISI, A. S. (1980). Women as managers: Attitudes and attributions for performance by men and women. *Academy of Management Journal*, **23**, 355–361.

STINSON, J. E. and JOHNSON, T. W. (1975). The path–goal theory of leadership: A partial test and suggested refinement. *Academy of Management Journal*, **18**, 242–252.

STINSON, J. E. and JOHNSON, T. W. (1977). Tasks, individual differences, and job satisfaction. *Industrial Relations*, **16**, 315–322.

STINSON, J. E. and TRACY, L. (1974). Some disturbing characteristics of the LPC score. *Personnel Psychology*, **27**, 477–485.

STOGDILL, R. M. (1963). Manual for the Leader Behavior Description Questionnaire-Form XII: An experimental revision. Bureau of Business Research, Ohio State University, Columbus, Ohio.

STOGDILL, R. M. (1965). *Job Satisfaction and Job Expectations Manual*. Ohio State University, Columbus, Ohio.

STOGDILL, R. M. (1969). Validity of leader behavior descriptions. *Personnel Psychology*, **20**, 153–158.

STOGDILL, R. M. (1974). *Handbook of Leadership: A Survey of Theory and Research*. The Free Press, New York.

STONE, E. F. (1974). The moderating effect of work-related values on the job scope–job satisfaction relationship. Unpublished Doctoral Dissertation, University of California at Irvine.

STONE, E. F. (1975). Job scope, job satisfaction, and the protestant ethic: A study of enlisted men in the US navy. *Journal of Vocational Behavior*, **7**, 215–234.

STONE, E. F. (1976). The moderating effect of work-related values on the job scope – job satisfaction relationship. *Organizational Behavior and Human Performance*, **15**, 147–167.

STONE, E. F. (1979). Field independence and perceptions of task characteristics: A laboratory investigation. *Journal of Applied Psychology*, **64**, 305–310.

STONE, E. F. and PORTER, L. W. (1975). Job characteristics and job attitudes: A multivariate study. *Journal of Applied Psychology*, **60**, 57–64.

STONE, E. F., GANSTER, D. C., WOODMAN, R. W. and FUSILIER, M. R. (1979). Relationships between growth need strength and selected individual difference measures employed in job redesign research. *Journal of Vocational Behavior*, **14** 329–340.

STONE, E. F., MOWDAY, R. T. and PORTER, L. W. (1977). Higher-order need strengths as moderators of the job scope–job satisfaction relationship. *Journal of Applied Psychology*, **62**, 466–471.

STRONG, E. K. (1951). *Vocational Interest Inventory*. Stanford University Press, Stanford.

STULMAN, D. A. and DAWIS, R. V. (1976). Experimental validation of two MIQ scales. *Journal of Vocational Behavior*, **9**, 161–167.

SUPER, D. E. (1970). *Work Values Inventory*. Houghton Mifflin, Boston.

SUTTON, R. I. and ROUSSEAU, D. M. (1979). Structure, technology, and dependence on a parent organization: Organizational and environmental correlates of individual responses. *Journal of Applied Psychology*, **64**, 675–687.

SZILAGYI, A. D. (1977). An empirical test of causal inference between role perceptions, satisfaction with work, performance and organizational level. *Personnel Psychology*, **30**, 375–388.

SZILAGYI, A. D. (1980). Reward behavior by male and female leaders: A causal inference analysis. *Journal of Vocational Behavior*, **16**, 59–72.

SZILAGYI, A. D. and HOLLAND, W. E. (1980). Changes in social density: Relationships with functional interaction and perceptions of job characteristics, role stress, and work satisfaction. *Journal of Applied Psychology*, **65**, 28–33.

SZILAGYI, A. D. and KELLER, R. T. (1976). A comparative investigation of the Supervisory Behavior Description Questionnaire (SBDQ) and the revised Leader Behavior Description Questionnaire (LBDQ-Form XII). *Academy of Management Journal*, **19**, 642–649.

SZILAGYI, A. D. and SIMS, H. P. (1974a). Cross-sample stability of the Supervisory Behavior Description Questionnaire. *Journal of Applied Psychology*, **59**, 767–770.

SZILAGYI, A. D. and SIMS, H. P. (1974b). An exploration of the path–goal theory of leadership in a health care environment. *Academy of Management Journal*, **17**, 622–634.

SZILAGYI, A. D., SIMS, H. P. and KELLER, R. T. (1976). Role dynamics, locus of control, and employee attitudes and behavior. *Academy of Management Journal*, **19**, 259–276.

SZURA, J. P. and VERMILLION, M. E. (1975). Effects of defensiveness and self-actualization on a Herzberg replication. *Journal of Vocational Behavior*, **7**, 181–187.

TAGUIRI, R. (1968). The concept of organizational climate. In R. Taguiri and G. H. Litwin (eds.), *Organizational Climate*. Harvard University Press, Boston.

TAVEGGIA, T. C. and HEDLEY, R. A. (1976). Job specialization, work values, and worker dissatisfaction. *Journal of Vocational Behavior*, **9**, 293–309.

TAVEGGIA, T. C. and ZIEMBA, T. (1978). Linkages to work: A study of the "central life interests" and "work attachments" of male and female workers. *Journal of Vocational Behavior*, **12**, 305–320.

TAYLOR, F. C. (1971). Associations among personal and organizational characteristics in forty branch offices of a securities brokerage firm. Unpublished Doctoral Dissertation, University of Michigan.

TAYLOR, J. A. A. (1953). A personality scale of manifest anxiety. *Journal of Abnormal and Social Psychology*, **48**, 285–298.

TAYLOR, J. C. and BOWERS, D. G. (1972). *Survey of Organizations: A Machine Scored Standardized Questionnaire Instrument*. Institute for Social Research, University of Michigan, Ann Arbor, Michigan.

TAYLOR, R. N. and THOMPSON, M. (1976). Work value systems of young workers. *Academy of Management Journal*, **19**, 522–536.

TERBORG, J. R. and ILGEN, D. R. (1975). A theoretical approach to sex discrimination in traditionally masculine occupations. *Organizational Behavior and Human Performance*, **13**, 352–376.

TERBORG, J. R., PETERS, L. H. and ILGEN, D. R. (1974). The description and validation of a questionnaire on attitudes towards women as managers. Unpublished Paper, Purdue University.

TERBORG, J. R., PETERS, L. H., ILGEN, D. R. and SMITH, F. (1977). Organizational and personal correlates of attitudes towards women as managers. *Academy of Management Journal*, **20**, 89–100.

THAMHAIN, H. J. and GEMMILL, G. R. (1974). Influence styles of project managers: Some project performance correlates. *Academy of Management Journal*, **17**, 216–224.

THOMAS, H. B. (1974). The effects of social position, race and sex on work values of ninth-grade students. *Journal of Vocational Behavior*, **4**, 357–364.

THOMPSON, J. D. (1967). *Organizations in Action*. McGraw-Hill, New York.

TOSI, H. L. (1971). Organization stress as a moderator of the relationship between influence and role response. *Academy of Management Journal*, **14**, 7–20.

TSCHEULIN, D. (1973). Leader behavior measurement in German industry. *Journal of Applied Psychology*, **57**, 28–31.

TUNG, R. L. (1979). Dimensions of organizational environments: An exploratory study of their impact on organization structure. *Academy of Management Journal*, **22**, 672–693.

TURNER, A. N. and LAWRENCE, P. R. (1965). *Individual Jobs and the Worker*. Harvard University Press, Boston.

TURNEY, J. R. (1974). Activity outcome expectancies and intrinsic activity values as predictors of several motivation indexes for technical-professionals. *Organizational Behavior and Human Performance*, **11**, 65–82.

UMSTOT, D. D., BELL, C. H. and MITCHELL, T. R. (1976). Effects of job enrichment and task goals on satisfaction and productivity: Implications for job design. *Journal of Applied Psychology*, **61**, 379–394.

UPHOFF, W. H. and DUNNETTE, M. D. (1956). *Understanding the Union Member*. University of Minnesota, Industrial Relations Center, Minneapolis.

U.S. CIVIL SERVICE COMMISSION (1974). *Elements of Success in Federal Labor-Management Relations*. Office of Labor-Management Relations, Washington, DC.

UTECHT, R. E. and HEIER, W. D. (1976). The contingency model and successful military leadership. *Academy of Management Journal*, **19**, 606–618.

VALENZI, E. R. and DESSLER, G. (1978). Relationships of leader behavior, subordinate role ambiguity and subordinate job satisfaction. *Academy of Management Journal*, **21**, 671–678.

VAN MAANEN, J. (1975). Police socialization: A longitudinal examination of job attitudes in an urban police department. *Administrative Science Quarterly*, **20**, 207–228.

VAN MAANEN, J. and KATZ, R. (1974). Work satisfaction in the public sector. National Training and Development Service, Washington, D.C.

VAN MAANEN, J. and KATZ, R. (1976). Individuals and their careers: Some temporal considerations for work satisfaction. *Personnel Psychology*, **29**, 601–616.

VECCHIO, R. P. (1977). An empirical examination of the validity of Fiedler's model of leadership effectiveness. *Organizational Behavior and Human Performance*, **19**, 180–206.

VECCHIO, R. P. (1979). A dyadic interpretation of the contingency model of leadership effectiveness. *Academy of Management Journal*, **22**, 590–600.

VREDENBURGH, D. J. and SHERIDAN, J. E. (1979). Individual and occupational determinants of life satisfaction and alienation. *Human Relations*, **32**, 1023–1038.

VROOM, V. H. (1960). *Some Personality Determinants of the Effects of Participation.* Prentice-Hall, Englewood Cliffs.

VROOM, V. H. (1964). *Work and Motivation.* Wiley, New York.

WAHBA, M. A. and BRIDWELL, L. G. (1976). Maslow reconsidered: A review of research on the need hierarchy theory. *Organizational Behavior and Human Performance*, **15**, 212–240.

WALL, T. D. and CLEGG, C. W. (1980). A longitudinal field study of group work redesign. *Journal of Occupational Behaviour*, **2**, 31–49.

WALL, T. D. and LISCHERON, J. A. (1977). *Worker Participation: A Critique of the Literature and Some Fresh Evidence.* McGraw-Hill, London.

WALL, T. D. and PAYNE, R. L. (1973). Are deficiency scores deficient? *Journal of Applied Psychology*, **58**, 322–326.

WALL, T. D., CLEGG, C. W. and JACKSON, P. R. (1978). An evaluation of the Job Characteristics Model. *Journal of Occupational Psychology*, **51**, 183–196.

WALLACE, M. J., IVANCEVICH, J. M. and LYON, H. L. (1975). Measurement modifications for assessing organizational climate in hospitals. *Academy of Management Journal*, **18**, 82–97.

WALSH, J. T., TABER, T. D. and BEEHR, T. A. (1980). An integrated model of perceived job characteristics. *Organizational Behavior and Human Performance*, **25**, 252–267.

WANOUS, J. P. (1974a). A causal-correlational analysis of the job satisfaction and performance relationship. *Journal of Applied Psychology*, **59**, 139–144.

WANOUS, J. P. (1974b). Individual differences and reactions to job characteristics. *Journal of Applied Psychology*, **59**, 616–622.

WANOUS, J. P. (1976). Organizational entry: From naïve expectations to realistic beliefs. *Journal of Applied Psychology*, **61**, 22–29.

WANOUS, J. P. and LAWLER, E. E. (1972). Measurement and meaning of job satisfaction. *Journal of Applied Psychology*, **56**, 95–105.

WARR, P. B. (1978a). Attitudes, actions and motives. In P. B. Warr (ed.), *Psychology at Work*, 2nd edition. Penguin, Harmondsworth.

WARR, P. B. (1978b). A study of psychological well-being. *British Journal of Psychology*, **69**, 111–121.

WARR, P. B. and ROUTLEDGE, T. (1969). An opinion scale for the study of managers' job satisfaction. *Occupational Psychology*, **43**, 95–109.

WARR, P. B. and WALL, T. D. (1975). *Work and Well-being.* Penguin, Harmondsworth.

WARR, P. B., COOK, J. and WALL, T. D. (1979). Scales for the measurement of some work attitudes and aspects of psychological well-being. *Journal of Occupational Psychology*, **52**, 129–148.

WATERS, L. K., ROACH, D. and BATLIS, N. (1974). Organizational climate dimensions and job related attitudes. *Personnel Psychology*, **27**, 465–476.

WATERS, L. K., ROACH, D. and WATERS, C. W. (1976). Estimates of future tenure, satisfaction, and biographical variables as predictors of termination. *Personnel Psychology*, **29**, 57–60.

WEAVER, C. N. (1980). Job satisfaction in the United States in the 1970's. *Journal of Applied Psychology*, **65**, 364–367.

WEBER, M. (1946). *Essays in Sociology*. Translated and edited by H. H. Gerth and C. W. Mills. Oxford University Press, New York. Originally published separately between 1906 and 1921.

WEBER, M. (1958). *The Protestant Ethic and the Spirit of Capitalism*. Translated by T. Parsons. Scribner, New York. Originally published in two parts in 1904 and 1905.

WEED, S. E. and MITCHELL, T. R. (1980). The role of environmental and behavioural uncertainty as a mediator of situation–performance relationships. *Academy of Management Journal*, **23**, 38–60.

WEED, S. E., MITCHELL, T. R. and MOFFITT, W. (1976). Leadership style, subordinate personality and task type as predictors of performance and satisfaction with supervision. *Journal of Applied Psychology*, **61**, 58–66.

WEISS, D. J., DAWIS, R. V., ENGLAND, G. W. and LOFQUIST, L. H. (1967). *Manual for the Minnesota Satisfaction Questionnaire*. Industrial Relations Center, University of Minnesota.

WEISS, H. M. (1977). Subordinate imitation of supervisor behavior: The role of modeling in organizational socialization. *Organizational Behavior and Human Performance*, **19**, 89–105.

WEISS, H. M. (1978). Social learning of work values in organizations. *Journal of Applied Psychology*, **63**, 711–718.

WEISS, H. M. and KNIGHT, P. A. (1980). The utility of humility: Self-esteem, information search, and problem-solving efficiency. *Organizational Behavior and Human Performance*, **25**, 216–223.

WEISS, H. M. and SHAW, J. B. (1979). Social influences on judgments about tasks. *Organizational Behavior and Human Performance*, **24**, 126–140.

WEISSENBERG, P. and KAVANAGH, M. J. (1972). The independence of Initiating Structure and Consideration: A review of the evidence. *Personnel Psychology*, **25**, 119–130.

WEITZ, J. (1952). A neglected concept in the study of job satisfaction. *Personnel Psychology*, **5**, 201–205.

WEITZEL, W., HARPAZ, I. and WEINER, N. (1977). Predicting pay satisfaction from nonpay work variables. *Industrial Relations*, **16**, 323–334.

WEITZEL, W., PINTO, P. R., DAWIS, R. V. and JURY, P. A. (1973). The impact of the organization on the structure of job satisfaction: Some factor analytic findings. *Personnel Psychology*, **26**, 545–557.

WEXLEY, K. N. and NEMEROFF, W. F. (1975). Effectiveness of positive reinforcement and goal setting as methods of management development. *Journal of Applied Psychology*, **60**, 446–450.

WEXLEY, K. N., McLAUGHLIN, J. L. and STERNS, H. L. (1975). A study of perceived need fulfilment and life satisfaction before and after retirement. *Journal of Vocational Behavior*, **7**, 81–87.

WEXLEY, K. N., ALEXANDER, R. A., GREENAWALT, J. P. and COUCH, M. A. (1980). Attitudinal congruence and similarity as related to interpersonal evaluations in manager–subordinate dyads. *Academy of Management Journal*, **23**, 320–330.

WHERRY, R. J. (1959). Hierarchical factor solutions without rotation. *Psychometrika*, **24**, 45–51.

WHERRY, R. J. and GAYLORD, R. H. (1943). The concept of test and item reliability in relation to factor pattern. *Psychometrika*, **8**, 247–264.

WHERRY, R. J. and SOUTH, J. C. (1977). A worker motivation scale. *Personnel Psychology*, **30**, 613–636.

WHERRY, R. J. and WATERS, L. K. (1968). Motivative constructs: A factor analysis of feelings. *Educational and Psychological Measurement*, **28**, 1035–1046.

WHERRY, R. J., CAMPBELL, J. T. and PERLOFF, R. (1951). An empirical verification of the Wherry-Gaylord iterative factor analysis procedure. *Psychometrika*, **16**, 67–74.

WHITE, J. K. (1978). Generalizability of individual difference moderators of the participation in decision making–employee response relationship. *Academy of Management Journal*, **21**, 36–43.

WHITE, J. K. (1979). The Scanlon Plan: Causes and correlates of success. *Academy of Management Journal*, **22**, 292–312.

WHITE, S. E. and MITCHELL, T. R. (1979). Job enrichment versus social cues: A comparison and competitive test. *Journal of Applied Psychology*, **64**, 1–9.

WHITE, S. E., MITCHELL, T. R. and BELL, C. H. (1977). Goal setting, evaluation apprehension, and social cues as determinants of job performance and job satisfaction in a simulated organization. *Journal of Applied Psychology*, **62**, 665–673.

WIENER, Y. and GECHMAN, A. S. (1977). Commitment: A behavioral approach to job involvement. *Journal of Vocational Behavior*, **10**, 47–52.

WIENER, Y. and KLEIN, K. L. (1978). The relationship between vocational interests and job satisfaction: Reconciliation of divergent results. *Journal of Vocational Behavior*, **13**, 298–304.

WIENER, Y. and VARDI, Y. (1980). Relationships between job, organization, and career commitment and work outcomes: An integrative approach. *Organizational Behavior and Human Performance*, **26**, 81–96.

WIGGINS, J. D. (1976). The relation of job satisfaction to vocational preferences among teachers of the educable mentally retarded. *Journal of Vocational Behavior*, **8**, 13–18.

WIJTING, J. P. (1969). A canonical regression of background factors and work values among underprivileged workers. Unpublished Manuscript, Bowling Green State University.

WIJTING, J. P., ARNOLD, C. R. and CONRAD, K. A. (1978). Generational differences in work values between parents and children and between boys and girls across grade levels 6, 9, 10 and 12. *Journal of Vocational Behavior*, **12**, 245–260.

WILCOVE, G. L. (1978). The ERG model: Expansion and application to navy personnel. *Journal of Vocational Behavior*, **13**, 305–316.

WIMPERIS, B. R. and FARR, J. L. (1979). The effects of task content and reward contingency upon task performance and satisfaction. *Journal of Applied Social Psychology*, **9**, 229–249.

WOLLACK, S. (1968). The work values of occupational groups: A multiple discriminant analysis. Unpublished Manuscript, Bowling Green State University.

WOLLACK, S., GOODALE, J. G., WIJTING, J. P. and SMITH, P. C. (1971). Development of the Survey of Work Values. *Journal of Applied Psychology*, **55**, 331–338.

WOOD, D. A. (1974). Effect of worker orientation differences on job attitude correlates. *Journal of Applied Psychology*, **59**, 54–60.

WOODWARD, J. (1965). *Industrial Organization: Theory and Practice*. Oxford University Press, London.

YUKL, G. A. and KANUK, L. (1979). Leadership behavior and effectiveness of beauty salon managers. *Personnel Psychology*, **32**, 663–675.

YUKL, G. A. and LATHAM, G. P. (1978). Interrelationships among employee participation, individual differences, goal difficulty, goal acceptance, goal instrumentality, and performance. *Personnel Psychology*, **31**, 305–323.

YUKL, G. A. and NEMEROFF, W. (1979). Identification and measurement of specific categories of leadership behavior: A progress report. In J. G. Hunt and L. L. Larson (eds.), *Crosscurrents in Leadership*. Southern Illinois University Press, Carbondale, Illinois.

YUNKER, G. W. and HUNT, J. G. (1976). An empirical comparison of the Michigan four-factor and Ohio State LBDQ leadership scales. *Organizational Behavior and Human Performance*, **17**, 45–65.

ZAMMUTO, R. F., LONDON, M. and ROWLAND, K. M. (1979). The effects of sex differences on commitment and conflict resolution. *Journal of Applied Psychology*, **64**, 227–231.

ZEDECK, S. (1971). Problems with the use of "moderator" variables. *Psychological Bulletin*, **76**, 295–310.

ZELLER, R. A. and CARMINES, E. G. (1980). *Measurement in the Social Sciences*. Cambridge University Press, Cambridge.

ZEMELMAN, D., DI MARCO, N. and NORTON, S. D. (1979). Life style–work group structure–task congruence and job satisfaction and performance: A three dimensional contingency model. *Journal of Management Studies*, **16**, 317–333.

ZOHAR, D. (1980). Safety climate in industrial organizations: Theoretical and applied implications. *Journal of Applied Psychology*, **65**, 96–102.

ZULTOWSKI, W. H., ARVEY, R. D. and DEWHIRST, H. D. (1978). Moderating effects of organizational climate on relationships between goal-setting attributes and employee satisfaction. *Journal of Vocational Behavior*, **12**, 217–227.

ZUNG, W. W. K. (1965). A self-rating depression scale. *Archives of General Psychiatry*, **12**, 63–70.

Index of Scales and Sub-scales

References are given alphabetically according to the scale or sub-scale title. This is followed by information on authorship, entry number and page number(s). Numbers in bold characters refer to the primary page reference.

Please note that, because they are listed according to their actual titles, measures of the same construct do not necessarily group together in the index. For example, whilst some measures of Alienation appear under that term, others come under *Work Alienation*. Similarly measures of Job Satisfaction appear at different points in the index, reflecting several variations of the terms used by different authors, such as *Job Satisfaction*, *Overall Job Satisfaction*, *Overall Satisfaction* and *Specific Satisfaction*. However, those concerned to trace classes of instruments, rather than particular scales, will be greatly helped by the fact that the measures of the same construct are grouped together in the text.